Finding Voice to Give God Praise

# Finding Voice to Give God Praise

## Essays in the Many Languages of the Liturgy

*Editor*

Kathleen Hughes, R.S.C.J.

*A Liturgical Press Book*

 THE LITURGICAL PRESS
Collegeville, Minnesota

1    2    3    4    5    6    7    8    9

**Library of Congress Cataloging-in-Publication Data**

Finding voice to give God praise : essays in the many languages of the
    liturgy  /  editor, Kathleen Hughes.
        p.    cm.
    Festschrift honoring Gilbert Ostdiek.
    Includes bibliographical references.
    ISBN 0-8146-2496-0 (alk. paper)
        1. Catholic Church—Liturgy.    I. Hughes, Kathleen, 1942–    .
    II. Ostdiek, Gilbert.
    BX1970.F53    1998
    264'.02—dc21                                                         98-5541
                                                                          CIP

*To Gilbert Ostdiek, O.F.M., who has spent his life
helping others find their own voice
for the praise of God*

# Contents

Introduction xi
*Kathleen Hughes, R.S.C.J.*

Art and the Reign of God 1
*James Devereux, S.J.*

Seminary Chapel Buildings and Spiritual Formation 4
*James F. White*

Contributions to Religious Art and Architecture:
Looking Through a Rear View Mirror 14
*Richard S. Vosko*

The Christmas Octave Feasts of St. Stephen, St. John,
and the Holy Innocents 23
*Marchita B. Mauck*

Secular Music in the Liturgy:
Are There Any Rules? 36
*Virgil C. Funk*

Why Catholics Must Sing 59
*Frank C. Quinn, O.P.*

Psalmody as "Word of Christ" 73
*Margaret Daly-Denton*

Ritual Language and Liturgy 87
*Anscar J. Chupungco, O.S.B.*

Brother Sun, Sister Death:
Gender, the Other, and the Liturgy 100
*Gail Ramshaw*

Some Musings on the Poetry of Prayer 105
*Kathleen Hughes, R.S.C.J.*

The Language of Ministry in
Contemporary Roman Catholicism    118
  *John F. Baldovin, S.J.*

*Lex Orandi:*
Memorial in the Eucharistic Prayers of the Roman Missal    128
  *Patrick McGoldrick*

Observant Participation:
Ethics, "Hard Words," and Liturgical Inculturation    139
  *Anthony J. Gittins, C.S.Sp.*

Ritual Moment and Pastoral Process:
Rethinking Pastoral Theology    151
  *Herbert Anderson*

Ethics and Ritual: Lessons from Freud    163
  *Lawrence A. Hoffman*

Announcing God's Reign:
Liturgy, Life, and Justice    177
  *Mark R. Francis, C.S.V.*

Liturgy and Spirituality:
Making Some Sense of a Whirlwind    190
  *Richard N. Fragomeni*

St. Francis of Assisi's *Canticle of Creatures*
as an Exercise of the Moral Imagination    202
  *Thomas A. Nairn, O.F.M.*

From the *Rubricae Generales* and *Ritus Servandus* of 1570
to the *Institutio Generalis* of 1969    214
  *Frederick R. McManus*

The Revised Sacramentary:
Revisiting the Eucharistic Renewal of Vatican II    243
  *James M. Schellman*

From Maintenance to Mission:
The Rite of Christian Initiation of Children and Their Families    260
  *Jeanette Lucinio, S.P.*

Musical Mystagogy:
A Mystagogy of the Moment    276
  *Edward Foley, Capuchin*

The Quest for Liturgy Both Catholic and Contemporary   288
   *Donald W. Trautman*

The Very Nature of the Liturgy   299
   *Gabe Huck*

Gilbert W. Ostdiek, O.F.M.:
Franciscan, Scholar, Educator, Liturgist   311
   *Zachary Hayes, O.F.M.*

Major Works of Gilbert W. Ostdiek, O.F.M.   315

Contributors   319

# Introduction

This collection of essays honors a remarkable man, Gilbert Ostdiek, O.F.M., on the occasion of his sixty-fifth birthday. A child of the Great Plains and a son of Francis, Gil was educated in Rome during the heady days of the Second Vatican Council. He returned to the United States in time to participate in the shaping and founding of the Catholic Theological Union at Chicago in the late sixties and has subsequently spent his academic life preparing women and men for ministry in the Church envisioned by that council.

Gil's scholarly interests are many. Certainly the major contribution he has made in the last decade has been his work with the International Commission on English in the Liturgy [ICEL]. He has served as Vice Chairperson of the Advisory Committee of ICEL, Chairperson of the Translations and Revisions Subcommittee, and member of the Roman Missal Editorial Committee. Work for ICEL is arduous; it is also anonymous. The name Gilbert Ostdiek will appear nowhere in the revised *Sacramentary*, but his hand will be everywhere evident in the grace of its translations.

Gil's interest in liturgical art and architecture led to the establishment of the Institute for Liturgical Consultants [ILC] at the Catholic Theological Union. This institute is a first of its kind in the United States, an opportunity for trained architects and liturgists to work together to learn the skills of building and renovation of sacred space. Gil has been founder and co-director of this program since its inception.

Besides language and architecture, Gil's interests include ritual studies, catechesis, and spirituality. Indeed, the titles of his publications reflect a broad pastoral concern for the continuing work of liturgical renewal in our day. He has written about the sacramental mission of the Church, liturgy-based catechesis, crafting prayer texts, liturgical presidency, ritual process and the human journey, ritual and symbol, priesthood, concelebration, reconciliation, the role of Sunday, human situations in need of ritual, marriage, and the ordination of women— to name a few of his preoccupations.

But above all, Gil has been absorbed with the renewal of hearts which the liturgical reform has yet to achieve. It has led him to an extraordinary generosity with his time and talent, speaking with a broad range of individuals and groups, leading workshops, giving seminars, helping students and colleagues alike to understand the many languages of prayer so that those with whom he worked could more easily find their own voice to give God praise.

It is said that we can know a person by the company he or she keeps. The authors who have contributed to this collection are Gil's colleagues and friends from the Catholic Theological Union, the International Commission on English in the Liturgy, the North American Academy of Liturgy (which he has served as president), and the Institute for Liturgical Consultants. They are a remarkable assortment of pastors, scholars, teachers, and writers who have known and admired Gil and who share his preoccupation with *the many languages* of our prayer.

One of the contributors, Anscar Chupungco, O.S.B., aptly summarizes these *many languages* of liturgy as "the entire system of signs and symbols, words and speech or song, moments of silence, gestures and postures, sacred images or icons, and the material elements such as water, bread, wine, and oil with which the Church celebrates the saving mystery of Christ." This collection of essays addresses these many liturgical languages, the languages of space and time, of music and icon, of spoken prayer and the silence which surrounds it. The collection also addresses how we prepare to do liturgy well—catechesis and mystagogical reflection, and how we live its demands in everyday life—spirituality and justice.

Here is an overview of the riches that await you.

We begin with a homiletic reflection entitled *Art and the Reign of God*, perhaps a way of setting the tone, perhaps a way of inviting the reader to start paying attention more acutely, to watch, to wonder, to become attuned to the variety of ways that Godself is revealed when we gather for prayer. The author, James Devereux, contends that the arts give us new languages to express the things that matter most to us: who we are, how we live, what we long for. Art can mediate grace, another kind of grace than sanctifying: grace of line, grace of melody, grace of words that are set in patterns to reveal the longing of the human heart. Devereux proposes that genuine religious art is impossible unless the People of God care about the beauty of God's house.

James White would concur. In *Seminary Chapel Buildings and Spiritual Formation* he discusses the formative power of sacred space and the way that buildings convey messages about the nature of the God whom we worship and our relationships one to another in the assembly. In addition, space communicates about the meaning and practice of Christian worship. White focuses on seminary chapels because they form both the seminarian and, in turn, the communities the seminarian will serve. As he says, "No one calculates the cost of teaching students wrong. Chapel renovation may be a bargain."

The building and renovation of liturgical space has been the lifework of Richard Vosko as both designer and consultant. In *Contributions to Religious Art and Architecture: Looking Through a Rear View Mirror*, Vosko offers a glimpse of the evolution of religious art and architecture in North America. His wide-angled rear view mirror captures the prophetic vision and hard work of pre-conciliar pioneers and prophets through two full generations of organizations, centers, academic programs, publications, conferences, and people passionately discussing issues of environment and art which are alive today.

Another designer and consultant, Marchita Mauck, contributes to our conversation on the many languages of the liturgy not—perhaps as expected—by exploring the arts, but by looking at one aspect of the language of time. *The Christmas Octave Feasts of St. Stephen, St. John, and the Holy Innocents* have often puzzled liturgical commentators. *Comites Christi*, we called them, supplying a theological rationale for an historical anomaly. Where did they come from and why are they grouped after the celebration of the Nativity in the Roman Calendar? Mauck reviews early evidence and proposes the historical origin and evolution of the calendar for the octave of the Nativity.

Next, a number of contributors address the languages of music and song. Virgil Funk looks at the question of *Secular Music in the Liturgy: Are There Any Rules?* Indeed there are, but such rules differ depending on what national/linguistic group one inhabits. Funk examines three different approaches to the question of "appropriate" music for worship, suggesting that one's starting point about the nature and function of music in liturgy affects one's attitude toward the use of secular music. He calls for a greater exchange among nations in order to express the multifaceted mystery that is Church and, therefore, worship.

Frank Quinn's *Why Catholics Must Sing* takes its cue from Gilbert Ostdiek's reflections about the major advances and changes in the singing patterns of the post-Vatican II liturgy. Quinn tells us that Catholics now *must* sing because liturgy is inherently musical, not only in aesthetic terms, but in terms of how ritual celebrations are actually accomplished by a group of people. Moreover, because of the fundamentally dialogical character of liturgical celebrations, liturgy is accomplished best when the assembly and its ministers sing together and in dialogue.

Such would delight the heart of Margaret Daly-Denton, particularly if the assembly and its ministers paid more attention to the psalms. In *Psalmody as "Word of Christ"* the author contends that as psalmody has been eclipsed by the singing of hymnody something valuable has been lost, namely, the breadth, the biblical richness, the capacity of an unexpected antiphon to challenge and stretch us beyond our presuppositions. This essay is in two parts, the first historical: The Psalter has been, from the beginning of the Church, the basis of Christian liturgical song. Daly-Denton examines Jewish conceptions of "authorship" by David and the early Church's delight in the psalms as "word of Christ," the "new David." The psalms thus served as both model and quarry for the composition of new prayers. In a second section the author addresses the potential revival and flourishing of the psalms in the revised Sacramentary, and the renewal of appreciation for the psalms which the second generation Sacramentary may occasion because of the provision of a companion Antiphonary.

From music we shift to the verbal language of the liturgy. Anscar Chupuncgo's essay on *Ritual Language and Liturgy* reflects on the nature, purpose, and function of ritual language in the liturgy. He provides a synthesis of the contributions of Christine Mohrmann (philological), Gail Ramshaw (metaphorical), and Gianfranco Venturi (semiological), offers some "disputable assumptions" regarding ritual language, and suggests how such assumptions affect the current debate. Chupuncgo makes a case for understanding liturgical language as of a literary rather than sacral nature. Moreover, it is not made up of dogmatic statements because words are plurivalent. It is not systematic theology nor is it colloquial speech. At the same time, ritual language is supple enough to incorporate some of the language patterns of popular religion.

In *Brother Sun, Sister Death: Gender, the Other, and the Liturgy*, Gail Ramshaw continues a discussion about the nature of liturgical language. She uses the categories of the French feminist, Helene Cixous, of *closed* writing (the I striving for self-definition and always partial) and *open* writing (about the other and tending to inclusion). In conversation with the very "gendered" Canticle of St. Francis, Ramshaw notes that the liturgy is the ultimate gathering of openness to the other, the celebration not of the I but of the whole body, and thus in liturgy gendered speech can only be metaphor opening us to the other.

Kathleen Hughes explores *The Poetry of Prayer*, a reflection on liturgy as a speech act where speaker (minister), hearer (assembly), and word spoken (the many languages, but especially the verbal language of the liturgy) are in a dynamic interplay. It is her contention that the liturgical reform has attended far more to the words we use and the skills of the minister than to the hearers, yet the role of the hearer is equally critical to the success of the speech act. As participants in liturgy, "hearers" must bring to bear "all the attention we can muster, all the stillness and composure, all the knowledge of our present situation, all the vulnerability and need, all the dyings and the risings below the surface of our lives in that place where we meet the Divine Poet."

Two more essays reflect on word: John Baldovin looks at *The Language of Ministry in Contemporary Roman Catholicism,* and Patrick McGoldrick examines *Lex Orandi: Memorial in the Eucharistic Prayers of the Roman Missal.* Does it matter how we talk about ministry? John Baldovin proposes that language does not simply describe reality but in some measure creates and sustains it. His essay analyzes the language that contemporary Roman Catholics use about ministry, especially in official liturgical texts, and proposes that new language and terminology will develop for ministerial tasks and persons as more rites are performed by lay persons. The aim of Patrick McGoldrick's essay is to consider memorial as the concept is expressed in the Eucharistic Prayers of the Roman Missal, particularly Eucharistic Prayer IV where it is most fully developed. When we celebrate the memorial of our redemption we are not concerned with something that is simply past: the mystery we commemorate is also of the present and the future, the whole mystery of Christ, a mystery that in the glorified humanity of the risen Lord transcends all limits of time.

Sublime realities . . . but sometimes the way the liturgy is celebrated does not invite the community's active participation in the memorial. That is obviously the case being explored in Anthony Gittins' *Observant Participation: Ethics, 'Hard Words' and Liturgical Inculturation.* The author raises serious issues and questions about the meaning and methods of liturgical inculturation following a personal —and shocking—account of a funeral he witnessed in the Pacific Islands. Speaking out about the unspeakable, saying the 'hard word' aloud, is, in Gittins' view, not only legitimate but urgent: the good of people, the credibility of theological training, and the hope of the inculturation of the Gospel and the liturgy depend upon it.

In *Ritual Moment and Pastoral Process: Rethinking Pastoral Theology,* Herbert Anderson invites us to reflect on the relationship between ritual and process, between liturgy and the human/religious experience that supports and sustains it. Worship needs pastoral care, he contends, because of the stories it hears, and pastoral care needs worship as a reminder that our story has significance in God's story.

Freud would have had a hay day with such language, but Lawrence Hoffman takes a second look at Freud's ritual theory in *Ethics and*

*Ritual: Lessons from Freud.* The author looks at Sigmund Freud's conclusion that ritual is like an obsessional neurosis and proposes that
Freud based his theory not on scientific but on ethical grounds. Hoffman's essay gives new impetus to the nagging questions about what
difference liturgy makes in the way we live our lives.

That topic is taken up explicitly by Mark Francis in *Announcing God's
Reign: Liturgy, Life, and Justice.* Francis asks whether liturgy is capable of
calling us to live just lives and if so, under what conditions. After exploring the intrinsic relationship of liturgy and justice as depicted in
Scripture and tradition, he looks at aspects of the present situation
which temper the rehearsal of God's reign in liturgy as in life, and finally
proposes some strategies and directions in this continuing quest.

Liturgy as a way of life is also the theme of Richard Fragomeni's
essay entitled *Liturgy and Spirituality: Making Some Sense of a Whirlwind.*
Fragomeni believes that the liturgical renewal, from the beginning,
was at its very heart about holiness of life. So, too, Christian spirituality. After beginning with a helpful series of definitions of spirituality,
and after exploring the nature of the liturgy as God's transforming
self-communication, Fragomeni joins the dialogue between liturgy
and spirituality. His conclusions: Christian spirituality is vital and passionate life in the Holy Spirit. Such life is true worship of God. The
liturgy affords us the way to render it.

One last author looks at the way we live out the Christian life. In
*St. Francis of Assisi's Canticle of Creatures as an Exercise of the Moral Imagi-
nation* Thomas Nairn explores the Canticle as an exercise of the moral
imagination. Believing, with David Tracy, that every classic encourages a pluralism of readings, Nairn explores the way a number of contemporary authors interpret the Canticle and then proposes his own
interpretation, one he believes more adequate to the medieval world
view and more emphatically a call to moral conversion and human
freedom.

The last series of essays all fit loosely under the rubric of "catechesis" and all offer new insights for preparing assemblies and their ministers to enter into the liturgy more fully. *From the Rubricae Generales
and Ritus Servandus of 1570 to the Institutio Generalis of 1969* is a fasci-
nating comparison by Frederick McManus of documents meant to introduce and assist in implementing liturgical reform. While the
documents of 1570 are preoccupied with rubrical directions and
norms, the 1969 instruction is admirably concerned with the meaning
and rationale of liturgical celebration. McManus' survey of the front
matter of the two missals, late medieval and modern, marks the latter
as a remarkable part of the liturgical reform mandated by Vatican II.
McManus concludes with some suggestions for future direction.

By commenting on the front matter of the revised *Sacramentary,* James Schellman picks up where Fred McManus leaves off. In *The Revised Sacramentary: Revisiting the Eucharistic Renewal of Vatican II* Schellman outlines the new Pastoral Introduction to the Order of Mass and makes comments selectively about some of the innovations to be found there. It is his contention that the Pastoral Introduction might serve as the basis for a renewed eucharistic catechesis so that we might more faithfully and effectively worship through, with, and in Christ to the glory of God.

Renewed catechesis is also on the mind of Jeanette Lucinio. Her essay, *From Maintenance to Mission: The Rite of Christian Initiation of Children and their Families,* takes a look at the implementation of the RCIA for children of catechetical age. By using quotations from a series of interviews with children and their families, she looks at typical patterns of implementation of this rite as well as some of the unique features of contemporary initiation of children which this rite and its accompanying process illustrate.

Another aspect of the formative process of liturgy is the mystagogical. Edward Foley argues that authentic mystagogy is less a question of when than of how in *Musical Mystagogy: A Mystagogy of the Moment.* It is not so much a post-ritual or post-experience manner of formation as it is a way of entering into the mystery that respects both personal experience as well as the "event" nature of worship. Drawing on the insights of George Steiner and Gordon Lathrop, Foley explores music in worship as a particular mode of the mystagogical.

After describing the development of second generation liturgical books and their formative influence on priest celebrants and the assembly, Bishop Donald Trautman looks at experience, culture, tradition, and Scripture as additional formative factors operative in Church and world which will shape future directions in parish liturgical life. In his essay, *The Quest for Liturgy Both Catholic and Contemporary,* he concludes with a strong plea for a living liturgy.

*The Very Nature of the Liturgy* is Gabe Huck's essay. A man himself "imbued" with the spirit of the liturgy, Huck takes apart paragraph fourteen of the *Constitution on the Sacred Liturgy.* "Full, conscious, and active participation" became the shorthand for this paragraph, indeed, the shorthand for the liturgical renewal. Huck explores the questions: what do these magnificent adjectives mean and what would we look like if the true Christian spirit, Christ's own spirit, week by week seeped into and transformed our spirits. He concludes with some concrete proposals to make the vision of this paragraph a reality.

A final essay is not about liturgy but about a liturgist, *Gilbert W. Ostdiek, O.F.M., Franciscan, Scholar, Educator, Liturgist.* Zachary Hayes,

Gil's colleague at Catholic Theological Union and his Franciscan brother, gives us a brief synopsis of Gil's life and ministry. It can only hint at the richness of a life given that others might find voice to sing God's praise.

Special thanks are due to Kurt Hartrich, O.F.M., and the Franciscan Province of the Sacred Heart, for their moral and financial support of this collection.

Zachary Hayes prompted me to think about putting this collection together. I am grateful to him for this inspiration and to John R. Page, Executive Secretary of the International Commission on English in the Liturgy, for obtaining Gil's curriculum vitae without alerting him to this work in progress. I am also indebted to my two student assistants from the Catholic Theological Union, Meriel Owen and Bryan Cones, for enabling me to complete the project because of their technical assistance and their unfailing grace.

It is not insignificant that this labor is completed on the Feast of the Triumph of the Cross. That is, after all, what we celebrate each time we gather to give God thanks and praise, that is the life we are invited to live and the witness we are asked to give to our world.

Kathleen Hughes, R.S.C.J.
September 14, 1997

# Art and the Reign of God

*James Devereux, S.J.*

In this essay I use as my subject the work of art that covers the back wall of the sanctuary of our church, an illustration of which appears on the next page.

Why is this mural in our sanctuary in the first place? Many Christians exclude paintings and statues from their churches on principle. After all, God forbade the Israelites to make for themselves graven images (Lev 26:1), and presumably the prohibition still stands. Still, visual representations of the Lord and his saints were found in the earliest places of Christian worship. A frequent figure on the walls of the catacombs in Rome is Christ, the Good Shepherd. And from the time of Constantine onward, Christian basilicas and chapels were rich with mosaics, paintings, and statues inspired by the stories of the Old and New Testaments. Even after the Reformation, when many Protestant churches were emptied of paintings and statues, they remained full of sacred music and the art of sacred eloquence.

It was natural that Christians, like human beings everywhere, should seek to embody their faith in music, architecture, painting, sculpture, dance. The arts give us new languages to express the things that matter most to us: who we are, how we live, what we long for. What philosopher has ever protested the obscenity of war so powerfully as Picasso in his painting, "Guernica"? Where will you learn more about the pain of growing old than in Shakespeare's *King Lear*? Has the virtue of forgiveness ever been expressed more movingly than in the final measures of *The Marriage of Figaro*?

If art is so powerful a means of sounding the depths of human experience it is no wonder that Christians have used it to express their life of faith. Religious art is an attempt to capture in shape or sound or color the moment of our encounter with God. All great art draws us into the mystery of the human person. Religious art searches the

*Mural by Ben Long. Located in St. Peter's Catholic Church, Charlotte, North Carolina. Photo by Chip Padgett Photography.*

depths of that mystery; it seeks out the point where finite intersects with infinite, where our human being encounters the Ground of All Being. It is a raid on the inarticulate, and one that is bound to fail—but never completely.

Consider the Agony in the Garden pictured in our fresco. Having drawn apart from his sleeping disciples, Jesus is isolated—alone. On the far left in the distance Judas guides a detachment of soldiers to the garden. All this is narrative. But look at the lines of Jesus' body. See how his arms plunge down toward the bare earth, locked together by the clasp of his hands. See how, at the same time, the lines of his torso reach up in anguish to the Father. The painting gives new power to the story of the gospel. If we allow its images to take hold of us, we begin to understand: "yes, it was something like that—not just that, but something like that." And we begin to suffer with the Lord.

There is a special relationship between art and the creed we profess. At the center of all Christian belief is the Incarnation—the mystery of the Word made flesh. And at the core of every work of art is spirit in material form. Melody, texture, line, color, movement all give physical expression to an intangible reality which ordinary language can hardly grasp. This is why Christianity is naturally open to the arts. In music, sculpture, painting, and the rest—just as in the creed—the Word is made flesh.

I do not mean to imply that art or its appreciation is necessary in order to be saved. Art is not grace; neither is it prayer. But it can mediate God's grace and our prayer. There is, after all, another kind of grace besides that which we call sanctifying: grace of line, grace of melody, grace of words that are set in patterns to reveal the longing of the human heart.

Art is precious, then, in Christian life, and where it is neglected by the community of believers, their own experience of God is impoverished. Is that our case? Yes and no. The twentieth century is not a great age of Christian art. Few among its painters, musicians, and poets deal with religious subjects. Our experience at St. Peter's is a happy exception, not only because the fresco succeeds, but because the parish had the daring to commission it in the first place.

The Church needs more such daring. Consider the words we use in our liturgy. They may be inspired by the Holy Spirit, but certainly not by the Muses. Thus far no one has written music to stand beside the Plain Chant of our Catholic past or the great Protestant hymns that we now happily borrow. Too often we permit our churches to be built in imitation of outworn styles or in contemporary fashions that are doomed to instant obsolescence. Indifferent surroundings do little to help us pray or to imagine what God might be like.

It is true that no great work of art, whether sacred or profane, was ever created without genius, and God does not send us a Michelangelo or a Mozart very often. But the emergence of great art does not depend simply on artists and composers. Shakespeare would never have written his plays without the audience at the Globe Theater. Genuine religious art is impossible unless the People of God care about the beauty of God's house. The townspeople of Chartres were as much responsible for their cathedral as were its architects and master glaziers.

Great religious art calls for a Christian people of deep faith. It also requires enlightened faith. Art can mislead as well as sustain our belief. Sentimental religious painting may comfort an individual soul, but it will misguide Christians as a body. It matters what we sing. The words and music of our hymns fashion our faith. And so we must insist that our poets find words and our composers melodies that are true to the Mystery that has been revealed to us.

It is said that when Michelangelo had completed his great statue of Moses, he was so overwhelmed by its reality that he commanded it: "Speak." Every work of genuine religious art—indeed, all great works of art—speaks to us of the divine. God can embody the divine presence in painting, in poetry, in all the forms of art. What we must do is what the disciples in the garden failed to do: we must watch and pray and listen and recognize the gift of God. May God give us all that grace.

# Seminary Chapel Buildings and Spiritual Formation

*James F. White*

Bishop J.A.T. Robinson once said while speaking of church architecture: "the building will always win."[1] That is a very strong statement but a profoundly accurate one. It is particularly relevant when dealing with seminary chapel buildings and the reason why they must be taken so seriously as a major player in the spiritual formation of seminarians. Indeed, I am quite willing to say that during a student's years in seminary *the seminary chapel building will probably teach more about spirituality than any single faculty member.*

The problem, all too often, is that the building teaches the wrong thing. We might get rid of a faculty member who was contravening the purpose of the seminary; usually we tolerate the building even though it may be teaching all the wrong things. But ought not worship spaces receive as much time and concern as tenure committees place on faculty evaluations?

Much of the power of the chapel building lies in the fact that students are exposed to it on a regular, if not daily, basis. It becomes the most familiar worship space for them. For students converted while in college or later, it is often the only familiar worship space. What is normal has a way of becoming normative in Christian worship. A good example of this is the propensity of seminary graduates to build the same type of building they knew in seminary when they become pastors. There are a number of replications of Perkins Chapel at Perkins School of Theology all over Texas. Usually the size was increased but all the problems inherent in that particular building were simply passed on to other congregations. Thus we have a disheartening example of liturgical traditioning. The building that formed the seminarians' imaginations gets transmitted to their flocks when they become pastors.

Of course, the chapel building can teach good things; my concern is that frequently they do not. And one might say that these buildings are usually no worse and frequently better than the buildings that graduates will go forth to minister in. But this is faint comfort. Our real concern is a positive one: that the chapel building will be a strong force for equipping one for ministry in the most competent way possible. I shall try to be positive but we need to confront the down side in order to understand the problems engendered by seminary chapels.

## I

The first problem is that such buildings give the wrong message about the nature of the God whom we worship. Many of the older buildings and some of the newer ones promote a strong sense of a God who is utterly remote and transcendent. The image they give is of a God who dwells somewhere out beyond the east window. There is a strong directional emphasis in the buildings and it is not directed to the community or even to the world beyond but somewhere up in the wild blue yonder. Thus the buildings suggest degrees of sacredness which increase the further one gets from the community as a whole.

The two cathedrals in Burlington, Vermont, both had successful fires in the 1970s. Both congregations built new cathedrals a few blocks apart but many ages separate in theology. The Episcopal cathedral is explicitly a two-volume structure with substantial dark space for God and clergy and another distinct volume for congregation and choir. The Roman Catholic cathedral, on the other hand, wraps congregational space around the altar-table so no one is more than eight rows removed from the liturgical action. Clearly God is in the midst of the community, not dissociated from them. A distinguished contemporary architect, Edward Sövik, likes to place the processional cross in the midst of congregational space. God, after all, is found in community, not on the east wall or isolated in a chancel.

Another problem is that so many seminary chapel buildings are overtly and explicitly hierarchical. Now I do not regard hierarchy as necessarily synonymous with evil, although when coupled with patriarchy that connection is hard to escape. Many buildings make distinctions between clergy and laity that are larger than life and certainly an exaggeration of what the liturgy requires. Protestants are certainly subject to this and we still wince at the recollection of the three ambo chairs—minister, visiting preacher, and song leader—that dominated so many churches for so long. The Roman Catholic equivalent of that is when the presider's chair becomes a throne. Clergy seating raises all kinds of theological issues about the nature of the Christian community. The more the presider sits, the more he or she is delegating leadership roles to others: readers, singers, preachers, etc.

So the location and design of clergy seating are important concerns about the nature of the community. This also applies to the ambo. J.A.T. Robinson once spoke about preaching "six feet above contradiction." Is the authority of the Word dependent upon being high and lifted up or does the Word come to dwell among us?

A sufficient amount of elevation is necessary to make the leaders of worship visible to all present. But excessive height is a sign of power and prestige that in some cases makes a clerical caste out of worship leaders. This demands careful calculation of sight lines in order to avoid discrimination against short members of the community. Excessive height up front demands a tilt of the head from all present. It is a contradiction of a servant ministry and basically is a "built ecclesiology" which we would hesitate to teach in the classroom but often flaunt heedlessly in the chapel. In Roman Catholic terms, the built environment all too often reflects the extreme clericalism of *Mediator Dei* (1947) rather than Vatican II's *Lumen Gentium*.

So seminary chapel buildings raise some fundamental theological questions about the nature of God and the Church. And buildings must be observed, analyzed, and reformed when necessary. Unfortunately, we are all too often untrained to observe what buildings do to us. We can worry about full, conscious, and active participation, but when do we worry also about partial, unconscious, and passive participation? Yet these forms of participation may be equally important in the theological effect of chapel buildings.

## II

There is also a problem that seminary chapel buildings can educate or miseducate so much about the meaning and practice of Christian worship. All too often in older buildings, and in some newer ones, the paradigm of the structure is that of a passive audience that watches and hears others do worship for them. I once taught with an architect who was frustrated by not getting much response from students in an auditorium. So he put them on the stage and all kinds of responses ensued spontaneously.

The image of a passive congregation is accentuated in longitudinal buildings in which the people are arranged on a horizontal axis receding from the ambo and altar-table. Most of the experiments of the Reformation period were central buildings with a vertical axis. And many churches today have returned to variations on this theme. One of the most popular today is various forms of a fan-shaped floor plan. Others include squares, octagons, and Greek crosses. In each case, the effort is to make the community see themselves at the center as participants, not as observers. Worship is largely a do-it-yourself affair, not delegated to others.

Decisions need to be made about the various liturgical spaces: gathering, congregational, movement, altar-table, baptismal, and choir. The ways that these are organized in relation to each other raise all kinds of liturgical issues. How can one locate a choir without deciding what is its function: singing *to* the congregation, singing *for* the congregation, or singing *with* the congregation?

The same care must be used in designing and locating the liturgical centers: altar-table, ambo, font, and presider's chair. Indeed, it would be a good liturgical exercise to discuss whether a seminary chapel should have a font. In a celibate community, this might seem extraordinary but even celibates need to be put in mind of their baptism. And then there are serious liturgical questions about where the font should be located. Just about every possibility has been explored in newer Catholic churches. Further questions rise as to the design of the font for the most preferable mode of baptism. These are only sample questions but ones that should not be avoided although they frequently are.

Questions of acoustics are also essential. Usually floors are carpeted with impunity, no one realizing how this will change the whole acoustical environment. On the other hand, there are church spaces too reverberant to make preaching audible. If it sounds to people that they are singing solo they soon stop. Singing reinforced by the voices of others encourages less inhibited participation. The demands for good hearing of the Word include suitable eye contact as well as full audibility. How sound behaves is an important part of the environment of worship.

A further problem with regard to worship is that most seminary chapels are highly inflexible with the consequences that students are exposed to only one possibility, however good that may be. This means that usually they have one option whereas we might wish to expose them to several perhaps equally good arrangements. One solution, of course, is to get them out of the seminary chapel and into as wide a variety of parish churches as possible. This takes considerable systematic planning and probably is easier to do in a metropolitan area where there are abundant choices. We could say a student who knows only one type of liturgical architecture knows none. By comparing a variety of buildings with different types of baptisteries or different arrangements of congregational space, students can analyze the relative values of each.

The usual seminary chapel, unless very flexible, gives few alternative options. It is rather like having a library with only one book. And even if that is the Bible, that is hardly enough. Ways must be found to broaden students' experience of liturgical space either by trying alternative liturgical arrangements if flexibility is possible, or by off-campus visits.

Ironically, there are some advantages to poor liturgical space. It is rather like the student who fumbles in homiletics class and gives clear examples of what not to do. This may teach more than the student who preaches moderately well. Students can quickly grasp what went wrong in a poorly-planned or delivered sermon.

The advantage of poor liturgical space is that it sometimes can be used to teach the possibilities of fighting back. Since students are not likely to find better-designed churches in the real world to which they graduate, this introduces a level of reality. The difficulty, of course, is that usually it takes a trained imagination to see how to handle a difficult building. In retrospect, I am grateful for the rigidity of Perkins Chapel because it forced us to use our imaginations and to consult people with training. I must admit I was often less than grateful at the time. But we made a movable altar-table, ambo, and font and found how things change in relationship to each other. Eventually we hired theater professionals to install a scrim and rid us of the chancel altogether. But as a temporary expedient, it was marvelous what a screen made of three doors could do.

Our best teaching experience was to hire an architect and lock students in the chapel for eight hours on a Saturday. By covering the windows with opaque plastics, we could control light. Building towers of scaffolding gave us a vertical dimension never experienced before. Bolts of cloth gave us a new spectrum of color. The chief lesson the students learned was how important a trained imagination is in reshaping space.

Usually bad liturgical space creates nothing but frustration. But it can be used to show that the building need not always win. At least bad space can help students become aware of the problems inherent in such surroundings. It is frustrating to see so little being done in many seminaries to remedy bad liturgical space. It is all the more discouraging to realize that in many instances remedies often would cost little more than the effort of moving or removing some furniture, improving the lighting, and working on good acoustics. At least we can rise to the challenge.

## III

A somewhat more subtle problem comes in teaching seminary students discrimination with regard to architecture and art. Basically it is the issue of teaching them to see. The old attitude of "I know what I like and I like what I know" is not sufficient for those who are going to be providing leadership for Christian communities. Many of them will eventually be responsible for church building programs. They need grounding which is more than simply a subjective matter of personal taste. And the best way to teach these things is by living and worshiping in quality buildings.

In 1980, I had a grant from the Association of Theological Schools which enabled me to do a study on the teaching of worship in North America seminaries. During that year, I visited forty-seven seminaries, always starting first with the chapel. There are some seminary chapel buildings of considerable excellence which should be better known. I am assuming that it is no longer financially possible or even desirable to try to replicate Sainte Chapelle. Historic buildings aside, there are some good examples of contemporary architecture that are strengthening the spiritual formation of those students fortunate enough to be in their presence. I shall give a few examples as to why I think they make contributions. Several are by architects of national reputation although this is by no means a guarantee of success. Edward Stone attempted a modern version of King's Chapel at one seminary but I do not regard that as a desirable ambition nor helpful result. Any formalistic approach is already highly jeopardized and the results dubious.

One of the better examples is Bishop Cannon Chapel at Candler School of Theology of Emory University in Atlanta. Designed by architect Paul Rudolph, it is a highly sophisticated building yet with rough, even primitive, appearing surfaces of raw concrete. Obviously no students are going to duplicate this building in their future parishes. But it can teach them some things. Designed in consultation with the worship faculty, it provides a high degree of flexibility which enables a variety of liturgical arrangements. It also functions well with a variety of different sizes of gatherings so that as the congregation grows more areas are utilized.

Similar consultation apparently did not take place in the building for the Hartford Seminary in Connecticut. There is a worship space but it seems to have been designed without any concern for the location of an altar-table or how it would relate to congregational space. The total building is another masterpiece of architect Richard Meier, best known for his art museums. But there seems little for students to learn from the worship space except what not to do.

A much more successful collaboration of a prestige architect and seminary worship faculty is in the chapel at Christian Theological Seminary in Indianapolis. The work of architect Edward Larrabee Barnes, the chapel was the culmination of an entire campus designed by the same architect. In this instance, a deliberate effort was to make the baptistery an important part of the building even when not in use. It is certainly one of the most interesting pools for immersion anywhere and reflects careful discussion of the form and location of this liturgical center. The location and design of altar-table, ambo, and cross are carefully studied.

A similar careful consultation resulted in the chapel at Trinity Lutheran Seminary in Columbus, Ohio. In this case, Frank Kacmarcik, who is probably the most influential form maker for Catholic churches, was the liturgical designer. The result is familiar to those who know the first edition of *Art and Environment in Catholic Worship* (1978). As might be expected, there is a prominent baptismal font which would have satisfied Luther's preference for immersion. The relation of ambo and altar-table again are standard Kacmarcik arrangements and designs, substantiated by considerable use.

Other seminaries may be more or less lucky. The Lutheran Seminary in Fort Wayne boasts an entire campus designed by Eero Saarinen. The chapel is an integral part of the whole scheme, all designed to look like a northern European village. The chapel interior is not particularly exciting but represents conventional arrangements of the early 1960s. Students at the Episcopal Theological Seminary of the Southwest in Austin, Texas, rejoice in a fresh open space which allows for considerable experimentation. And seminary students at St. John's University, Collegeville, Minnesota, surely must be familiar with the Abbey Church, Marcel Breuer's masterpiece. But obviously this is an abbey church, not a parish.

In some cases, the chief learning experience is not in the original building but in its remodeling. This has advantages in teaching students the difference between remodeling and remuddling. Two examples by the well-known architect Edward Sövik will suffice. Sövik is very theologically literate and probably the leading form maker in Protestant church architecture. The chapel at Methodist Theological School in Ohio was a conventional Georgian auditorium built in 1960 with stage and sloping floor. Sövik leveled the floor, gave the building a non-directional orientation, and enhanced the lighting. It is in line with his concept of "non-church" worship spaces and philosophy of building the best space available as *centrum*. It has full flexibility and can be used to teach students a variety of possible arrangements. The Kacmarcik buildings are predicated on "getting it right" and making everything immovable. The Sövik buildings reflect a quite different approach with the understanding that the nature of services and congregations will change.

Sövik has more recently redone another United Methodist seminary chapel, Garrett-Evangelical in Evanston, Illinois. In this case, it was a relatively high-quality Gothic revival building. His effort was to free it up, to make it less clerical, and to open the community's imagination to desirable arrangements.

In some cases, more draconian measures have seemed necessary. The old seminary buildings for Immaculate Conception Seminary when it was at Mahwah, New Jersey, included a conventional chapel of moderate-quality Gothic revival. Here the building was completely reoriented with the altar-table placed in the middle of one long side. The shock was drastic and the new liturgical focus always seemed a bit provisional with the vacated chancel so prominent. But the significance of what was being attempted could hardly have escaped even the most dim-witted seminarian. So the value in terms of spiritual formation may have been extremely high.

Other buildings may call for such heroic efforts but the cost of remedies is usually considered too high. Unfortunately, no one calculates the cost of teaching students wrong. Chapel renovation may be a bargain.

The examples cited show an effort to have students experience excellent sacred space. We can only hope that exposure to quality music will have the same effect. One would hope that students can also be exposed to good liturgical art in the context of the seminary chapel. If they do not see good liturgical art while in seminary, where are they going to see it? Again, our problem is in teaching them how to see. If we leave them to what they know in their homes we shall have more paintings on black velvet. But our job is to stretch their minds beyond their elastic limit so they never snap back into conventionality. Good liturgical art grows out of tradition, reflects the life of community, and has genuine religious power to probe beneath the obvious.

This means seminary chapel committees should have a budget, even a modest budget, to commission professional artists to produce textiles, paintings, sculptures, etc. to proclaim the gospel and to say this is no ordinary place. Maybe if our students took their shoes off at the door they would grasp the meaning of sacred space. But some good liturgical art can help them sense the transcendent and will be remembered long after any sermon they have heard.

It will be an important learning experience for all seminary students to have contact with living artists. Maybe it should be a requirement for preparation for future ministry. Seminary education is so verbal that any contact with a non-verbal art form is greatly to be desired as remedial education.


## IV

It might be of interest to do a case study to show an example of how seminary chapel buildings function in the process of spiritual formation. Yale Divinity School occupies twenty-one magnificent neo-Georgian buildings, mostly built in 1932. Unfortunately, maintenance has been deferred so long that the buildings at present give exegesis to the text "here we have no lasting city." The chapel is the focal point of the ensemble and poses many interesting problems.

First of all, it is useful to understand it historically. In the 1930s when it was built, a dominant factor shaping mainline Protestant church architecture was the Interdenominational Bureau of Church Architecture headed up by the highly-active Elbert M. Conover (1885–1952). His books, such as *Building the House of God*,[2] were widely distributed and his influence significant on anyone liturgically left of Episcopalians. One of his firmest points, other than that Gothic or Georgian were the only real options stylistically, was that churches should have a full, distinct, divided chancel with an altar-table at the most remote spot in the building and an ambo and lectern at the entrance to the chancel. Conover's inspiration was a highly romanticized version of fourteenth-century English village parish churches. With very few exceptions, American churches, Puritan or Anglican, did not have chancels before the 1840s.

Marquand Chapel at Yale is a very elegant example of what was fashionable in the 1930s. Its arrangement has nothing to do with any of the eighty-five church buildings built before 1830 still standing in Connecticut. It is a good example of the imagination of the 1930s; in other words, a good example of a bad thing from today's perspective.

The building consists of two volumes: chancel and nave. The chapel is very clerical or hierarchical. The chancel is elevated and the clergy and choir were meant to be near the original altar-table. The presence of both lectern and ambo make a statement about the unrelatedness of Scripture and sermon which may have been an adequate reflection in the day of topical preaching in which the chapel was built. This seems out of place in a time of much more exegetical preaching. There is no font.

In recent years, the chancel has been almost unused. But the image is very strong that this is holy space which God, apparently, has all to Godself. A statement could be made by bringing out the processional cross from behind the altar-table and placing it in the nave. Temporary lecterns and altar-table have been placed in recent years in the front of the nave by removing several rows of pews. Yet these liturgical centers are hard to see by short people who come early to find an unobstructed seat. All this looks very provisional.

The question before the community is "Is the chapel redeemable?" With prominent liberation theologians on the faculty, it seems an anomaly to focus the community's life on a building that is so explicitly hierarchical. With liturgists expected to be added to the faculty, it seems problematic to have a building contradicting much that they likely will be teaching.

Many would argue that the building contradicts what the faculty are teaching and the students (hopefully) reading. If we put it into words, the message of the building is that of a largely inert and passive congregation dominated by professional clergy and musicians. This ought to make us a bit uneasy. Yet the chapel says this day after day. And space often speaks louder than words.

The question is whether minor surgery or even major surgery will be sufficient. Or would a totally different worship space in another building help the community to be more true to its nature?

In every case, the seminary chapel building's role in theological education must be acknowledged, if not approved in specific examples. And then maybe something can be done so that the building does not win by fighting the community's values but by reinforcing them.

After all, seminaries are training students for future ministries, not for past ones. At least we can avoid the mistakes of the past and give some hopeful indications of future ministry. John Ruskin's phrase, often quoted by building communities, "when we build, let us think that we build forever," ought to have been retired long ago. No one today would even think of building Ruskinian neo-gothic. But we can in our seminary chapel buildings give the best possible guidance for ministries of the future on the basis of present knowledge.

---

[1] *Making the Building Serve the Liturgy,* ed. Gilbert Cope (London: A.R. Mowbray, 1962) 5.

[2] (New York: Methodist Book Concern, 1928).

# Contributions to Religious Art and Architecture: Looking Through a Rear View Mirror

*Richard S. Vosko*

In the 1960s Marshall McLuhan suggested the possibility that people generally interpret a totally new situation or product in terms of their past experiences.[1] Although this sounds like a normative way to process new information, it can lead to frustration and disappointment. For example, people who have relied only on the print medium for accessing news could have a difficult time using the internet today. Surfing the web is not comparable to turning the pages of a newspaper. Although the objective, reading the news, is the same, the two mediums are not. Ultimately, according to McLuhan, attitudes and value systems are being shaped and information is being downloaded not so much because of the message but the medium. Thus, McLuhan's well known axiom "the medium is the message" describes what is really going on even though most people are not aware of it.

McLuhan's theory also implies that people who were born in the agrarian or industrial periods often survive in the electronic age by using the perceptive tools they acquired in a previous age. This approach will not always be satisfying because it does not present the whole picture. What is going on today will always be tempered or skewed by the individual's preconceived notions. He describes the way some people respond to each new development or each new age as looking at life "through a rear view mirror."

One could say that keeping up with new developments in the global village by looking through the rear view mirror is similar to the experience many Catholics are having. A significant number of them are trying to assess and understand what is going on in the Church today through the lenses they wore in a pre-conciliar time period. The memory of the previous ecclesiology and liturgy is still so fresh in their minds it is coloring the current experience. For example, some perceive that the reform of the eucharistic liturgy must be nothing more than a new way for the priest to say Mass for them. What they are missing is the understanding that the Mass is a not a private act dispensed to them but something that belongs to the entire Church and that this is the principle that set the stage for the reform of the liturgy.[2]

Similarly, some perceive the new environmental settings for worship which were prompted by the liturgical reforms as merely new stylistic ways to design or decorate churches for worship. What is not being grasped here is the significant role the worship environment plays in helping to foster active, conscious participation in the rites of the Church.

Normally there is nothing wrong with looking at life through a rear view mirror. After all, one can assess what is going on today by looking to the past and learning from it. Some would even say that it is a good way to avoid making the mistakes that were made before. This approach to life becomes problematic when the past is so revered there is no tolerance for what is contemporary or, in McLuhan's terms, when everything going on today is compared to or interpreted in terms of the past. In this regard it could be said that such people look at life (or the Church for that matter) through a very narrow rear view mirror.

To look at the past in order to learn about and respect what happened before is to look carefully and discerningly through a wide angle rear view mirror where a bigger picture and a broader perspective is discovered.

Certainly the Church is going through a crucial post-conciliar period of transition. During this time risks will be taken and mistakes will be made. While some Catholics will maintain a courageous focus on advancing to the future, others will retreat to the familiarity of the past. Still others will just stand still. What can be extremely helpful when fear and uncertainty accompany a journey is to look back and see that others have been there before. By taking this kind of "rear view mirror" perspective one notices that a great deal can be learned from the pioneers. Taking their achievements to new horizons then becomes a very tangible possibility. Arnold Toynbee's comment, "what is past is prologue," is a compelling reason for the Church to learn how to balance traditions with visions.

Many Catholics think the liturgical renewal and its reforms began with the Second Vatican Council. They have forgotten that the intent of the *Constitution on the Sacred Liturgy* was to continue the liturgical movement that began long before John XXIII called the council. Thus, for many the reforms became an arena for resisting change rather than embracing the gradual transformation of the Church that began in the nineteenth century. For these people the rear view mirror perspective indicated that the way in which the Church worshiped was always the same and never changed. Their memories focused on only part of the story.

While many wonderful works are available to describe the liturgical movement and its contributors,[3] this chapter will serve to review briefly some of the players and organizations that have had particular impact on the environment for worship. Perhaps of all the changes that have occurred because of the council the ones made to church buildings have caused the most stress for Catholics. In a positive light, this tension indicates how important the environment for worship is in the lives of religious people.

This glance through the rear view mirror will reveal that a wonderful foundation has been established in the area of religious art and architecture. The vision, courage, and leadership of many ordinary people has afforded ample opportunity for the Church to prepare for and understand the conciliar reforms and why the transformation of worship spaces is essential. I will review only some of the pioneer movements that contributed particularly to the work of liturgical art and architecture.

In the late 1920s a young American architect, Everitt Harman, proposed a "Benedictine Oblates Guild of Architects, Artists and Craftsmen" to combine artistic excellence with monastic organization, discipline, and spirituality.[4]

The scheme quickly evolved into the organization of the Liturgical Arts Society, 1930, at Portsmouth Priory in Portsmouth, Rhode Island. Maurice Lavanoux would become the tireless editor of the Society's magazine, *Liturgical Arts,* until 1972 when the Society could no longer survive fiscally. Susan White writes "during the 40 years of the Society the American Church was dealing with questions of modernity. The Society energetically answered that churches should be designed as settings for the liturgy and not as manipulators of pious sentiment."[5] This concern is still important. To what extent should a worship space that is primarily designed to house the public liturgy be set aside to accommodate private devotions?

The Catholic College Art Association was started in 1937 by Sr. Esther Newport, S.P. to address the "appalling conditions" of art in churches. Eventually this organization became the Catholic Art Association. Inspired by the arts and crafts movement and guild systems in England at the turn of the century and the work of Eric Gill the group attracted people like preservationist and historian Tom Phelan, liturgical artists Ade de Bethune and Bill Schickel, and church architects Patrick Quinn and Graham Carey. Their publication was first called *The Christian Social Arts Quarterly,* then *The Catholic Art Quarterly,* and eventually, *Good Work.*[6]

In August, 1965, the Association held its 28th Annual convention! The theme of that meeting was "Work and Unwork: A Christian Reappraisal of Industrialism." The Association's perennial concern was with human productive activity and of its avowed objective in promoting work that is for the real advantage of people—both as producers and consumers. The United Society Called Shakers was chosen as the inspiration for that convention because of its unyielding practicality and clear-minded avoidance of both commercial and aesthetic motivations.[7]

For more than thirty years the Catholic Art Association prophetically connected societal issues with ecclesiastical ones as they related to the arts. Creators of worship environments today must continue to address the many factors that can affect their work. Environmental, demographic, and preservation issues are among the many concerns that cannot be overlooked when building or renovating a worship space.

Also in the 1930s, other organizations provided impetus in matters pertaining to church art and architecture. The North American Conference of Architecture and the Church Architectural Guild, developed under the leadership of the Methodist minister Elbert M. Conover, was made up of Protestant clergy and architects.[8]

That decade also saw the birth of the Liturgical Conference. Largely a Catholic movement, the Conference provided a visionary stimulus during the pre-conciliar decades. Its reputation as the publisher of the provocative journal, *Liturgy*, sometimes overshadows its role as the sponsor of the stimulating Liturgical Weeks and, in particular, the meeting on church architecture held in Cleveland in February, 1965.[9] At that conference the illustrious roster of speakers had plenty to offer about the environment for worship. Here are a few examples:

Kevin Seasoltz, O.S.B., spoke on devotional areas and remarked that the sanctuary and baptistery are not places for shrines and images for private devotion (including the tabernacle). The latter could be placed in special areas in the church set aside for the private devotion of the faithful.[10] Again, looking through a rear view mirror, many Catholics still understand their churches as places for private devotion and not public prayer.

Frank Kacmarcik, Obl.S.B., had this to say on the role of consultants: "The consultant should not try to please the pastors who are temporary custodians of the community property . . . the consultant's job is to contribute to the making of a good church . . . to be concerned about liturgical details and architectural standards . . . to be helpful in obtaining approval from the bishops."[11]

The renowned church architect Edward Anders Sövik, F.A.I.A., made comments on the role of worship spaces. He said our churches are first of all and above all houses of the people of God. It is only in a secondary sense that they can be described as houses of God. They are called this because the Christian community which comes together in them—the *ecclesia*—is (and it alone is) the temple of the living God.[12] Sövik's concerns are still relevant. Catholic churches prior to Vatican II looked more like temples built to honor the deity. During the reactionary post-conciliar period the churches began to appear like meeting halls. Today, the Catholic challenge is to create more sacramental spaces that are beautiful and functional at the same time.

During the conference, architect Patrick Quinn commented on bad church buildings, suggesting architects ought to admit that "we, as a body, have been responsible for most of the incredibly bad churches that have been built in the last thirty years in this county [from 1935–65]. We built them; we must take the blame."[13]

According to architect Lawrence D. Cook, F.A.I.A., the open-mindedness of the 1960s led to many alliances. The American Society for Church Architecture [ASCA] represented various conservative Protestants. Also during this time The Guild For Religious Architecture [GRA] was formed as an affiliate of the American Institute of Architects.

The Union of American Hebrew Congregations, with notable members like Percival Goodman, and the Department of Church Building of the National Council of Churches, with members like Edward Frey, joined together in friendly conversation to discuss the contributions of beauty, art, and architecture to the life of the interfaith community.[14]

This inter-faith vision is still relevant, especially in a country like the United States where there is such religious diversity. The conversation should continue now about how once again to incorporate the time-honored ingredients of color, light, scale, proportion, and materiality into our worship centers.

In 1967, the Interfaith Research Center on Religious Architecture was established and sponsored the first International Congress on Religion, Architecture and the Arts held in New York. Liturgical artist and consultant Robert E. Rambusch was the key organizer of these conferences which totaled four altogether.

Twenty years ago Rambusch wrote on how our society lacks sensitivity to the transcendent quality found in the ordinary. For too long we have separated the fine arts from the everyday artifacts as if beauty and usefulness were mutually exclusive.[15] Today many Catholics will observe that their churches do not look or feel like churches. Their concern is really about how to sense the sacred amidst the hustle and bustle that characterizes American life-styles.

The 1970s also greeted the founding of the North American Academy of Liturgy [NAAL] by the Jesuit, John Gallen.[16] The NAAL has a study group on the environment for worship where ongoing conversations have addressed issues such as developing criteria and methods for evaluating worship spaces, the preservation of religious buildings, and the many other research interests of colleagues.

The Federation of Diocesan Liturgical Commissions [FDLC] was also organized in the early 1970s to serve the American bishops and local commissions in matters of ongoing liturgical renewal. Although not specifically concerned with church art and architecture, the FDLC has produced valuable tools pertaining to the environment for worship. These include the filmstrip, *A House for the Church*, and two slide programs called *Worship Space* and *Places for Baptism* created by Brother William Woeger. The FDLC has also printed the *Directory of Liturgical Consultants*, Tom Stehle's *Annotated Bibliography on Worship Spaces*, and the eleven very helpful bulletin inserts on church interiors written by Norbertine Andrew Ciferni.[17]

In the mid-70s the FDLC sponsored a committee to prepare guidelines for the building and renovation of churches. Up to that time, although many dioceses had produced directives, there were no national guidelines that could be compared to the fine statements issued by the German and Irish bishops at that time. Committee members included Adé Bethune, Florian Gall, Frank Kacmarcik, Obl.S.B., Joseph Moriarity, Robert E. Rambusch, Edward A. Sövik, and Richard S. Vosko. The committee met for three years until the Bishops' Committee on the Liturgy assumed responsibility for the project and asked the liturgist Father Robert Hovda to author *Environment and Art in Catholic Worship*.[18] In 1996, a new committee was formed to develop a sequel to that statement.

In 1978, the ASCA, the GRA [both mentioned above], the Commission on Church Planning and Architecture, the National Conference on Religious Architecture, and the International Research Center all merged to create the Interfaith Forum on Religion, Art and Architecture [IFRAA]. Now affiliated with the American Institute of Architects [AIA] as a professional interest area, IFRAA promotes design excellence in religious art and architecture. Its members include artists, crafters, consultants, pastors, and architects. *Faith & Form* is its publication.[19]

In 1979, Christians in the Visual Arts [CIVA] was established to encourage those practicing the visual arts to develop their callings to the highest level, to learn how to deal with specific problems in the field without compromising faith and artistic standards, to provide opportunities for sharing work and ideas, to foster a spirit of trust, understanding and cooperative relationships between artists, the Church and society. Specifically Christian, CIVA sponsors conferences and traveling exhibits and publishes a handsomely illustrated directory of members.[20]

In June, 1979, to commemorate the first anniversary of the publication of the American Bishops' instruction, the Archdiocese of Milwaukee sponsored a National Symposium on Environment and Art where, in the words of Archbishop Rembert Weakland, O.S.B., "some of the best artists and architects of our country were assembled."[21]

In the 1980s the Georgetown Center for Liturgy, Spirituality and the Arts was founded by Jesuit Lawrence Madden. Among many other good works, the Center sponsored the Form/Reform Conferences dedicated to the design of worthy spaces for worship. Conference planner Loretta Reif has graciously and generously made Form/Reform possible for many years.[22]

The 1980s and 1990s have also seen the birth of other important allies. The Archives of Modern Christian Art was established in 1981 under the careful direction of David Ramsey. It is an ecumenical organization which exists to preserve the record of Christian religious art and architecture in the modern world, and through this work to inspire new creative achievements in the field. The Archive collections begin with the year 1400 where the Princeton Index of Christian Art ends.[23]

In 1990, the Institute for Liturgical Consultants [ILC] was founded by Gilbert Ostdiek, O.F.M. A maker of fine furniture and well known for his contributions to the liturgical movement, Father Ostdiek sought to create a training program for future liturgical design consultants using an apprenticeship model.

In addition to their course work, the participants in the program would be teamed with established designers and consultants in order to gain firsthand experience in the process of building or renovating a worship space. The Institute, the first of its kind in the United States, is sponsored by the Archdiocese of Chicago and the Catholic Theological Union. Along with Kathleen Sullivan-Stewart and Father Mark R. Francis, Father Ostdiek has tirelessly guided the continued development of the Institute from the beginning.[24]

Another organization started in the early 1990s is the Association of Consultants for Liturgical Space. Still in its formative years, the ACLS provides a network for professionals who are working in collaborative ways to build and renovate worship environments that will nurture the faith of God's people. ACLS schedules its meetings in conjunction with the Form/Reform Conferences, sponsors weekend conferences, and publishes a newsletter three times a year.

Finally, since the council, more publications than ever before are dedicated to the work of creating sacred spaces. Liturgy Training Publications publishes the monthly *E & A Letter* and the *Meeting House Essay* series which are invaluable resources for pastors, committees, architects, artists, and others.[25] The *Modern Liturgy* magazine, published by Resource Publications regularly features works of art and architecture and has its own awards program.[26]

*Image,* A Journal of the Arts and Religion, explores and illustrates the relationship between Christian faith and art in fiction, poetry, painting, sculpture, architecture, film, music, and dance.[27] *Christianity and the Arts* also celebrates Christian expression in art, dance, music and film.[28] And *Arts,* a journal of the arts in theological studies, focuses on the role of the arts in the life of the church and the seminary.[29]

This review of the good work that has been done over the past sixty years is a stimulating reminder that the reforms prompted by the Second Vatican Council took root quickly in the United States because of the prophetic vision and hard work of pre-conciliar pioneers and movements. It reveals two full generations of organizations, centers, academic programs, publications, conferences, and people passionately discussing the same issues surrounding religious art and architecture that are concerns today. Because the foundations for these interests were firmly planted, the fruits will continue to flourish for many generations. However, to employ a McLuhanism, the liturgical movement itself is the more powerful message that has shaped the public discourse on the topic of religious art and architecture. May all involved in the work of creating appropriate environments for worship be inspired by this message and strive to continue the movement.

---

[1] Marshall McLuhan and Quentin Fiore, *The Medium is the Message* (New York: Bantam Books, 1967) 74.

[2] Of course, history and research prompted the return to the earliest understanding of the liturgy as the work of the people and not the private prayer of the priest.

[3] See for example, Kathleen Hughes, R.S.C.J., *How Firm A Foundation: Voices of the Early Liturgical Movement* (Chicago: Liturgy Training Publications, 1990). Also, *Hearts in Pilgrimage: A History of the Liturgical Movement in the U.S.* This 20-minute video is available from the Notre Dame Center for Pastoral Liturgy.

[4] Susan White, *Art, Architecture and the Liturgical Reform* (New York: Pueblo, 1990) 2.

[5] Ibid., 177.

[6] *Good Work* was published four times a year. In 1965 the magazine had 1248 subscribers.

[7] See "The 1965 Convention," *Good Work,* Vol. 28, no. 4 (1965) 107.

[8] See Lawrence D. Cook, FAIA, "IFRAA: Past, Present and Future," *Faith & Form,* Spring (1995) 7.

[9] The proceedings of the conference were published as *Church Architecture: The Shape of Reform,* Washington, D.C.: The Liturgical Conference (1965).

[10] See Kevin Seasoltz, O.S.B., "Devotions and Other Uses of the Church," *Church Architecture: The Shape of Reform* (Washington, D.C.: The Liturgical Conference, 1965) 63ff.

[11] See "The Various Interests Involved in Building a Church," Ibid., 75ff.

[12] See Edward S. Sövik, "The Role of the Architect in Liturgical Renewal," Ibid., 12ff.

[13] Ibid., 85.

[14] See Lawrence D. Cook, F.A.I.A., "IFRAA: Past, Present and Future," *Faith & Form,* Spring (1995) 8.

[15] See Robert E. Rambusch, "Heaven Can't Wait: The Transcendent in the Everyday," *Faith & Form,* Vol VII, Fall (1974) 24.

[16] The NAAL is an inter-faith association of liturgical scholars and practitioners. Its members are specialists in liturgical studies, theologians, artists, musicians, and persons in related disciplines whose work affects liturgical expression and furthers liturgical understanding.

[17] The FDLC offices are located at 401 Michigan Avenue, NE, Washington, D.C., 20017.

[18] *Environment and Art in Catholic Worship* (Washington, D.C.: The National Conference of Catholic Bishops, 1978).

[19] *Faith and Form* is published three times a year. Contact IFRAA, 1735 New York Avenue, NW, Washington, D.C. 20006.

[20] CIVA, PO Box 18117, Minneapolis, MN 55418-0117.

[21] See *The Environment for Worship: A Reader* (Washington, D.C.: The United States Catholic Conference, 1980).

[22] The Georgetown Center, 3513 N Street, NW, Washington, D.C. 20007.

[23] Contact Dr. David Ramsey, College of Notre Dame, Belmont, CA 94002.

[24] For information on ILC, contact Gilbert Ostdiek, O.F.M., Catholic Theological Union, 5401 South Cornell Avenue, Chicago, IL 60615.

[25] Liturgy Training Publications, 1800 North Hermitage Avenue, Chicago, IL 60622.

[26] Resource Publications, 160 East Virginia St., Suite 290, San Jose, CA 95112.

[27] *Image,* PO Box 674, Kennett Square, PA 19348.

[28] *Christianity and the Arts,* P.O. Box 118088, Chicago, IL 60611.

[29] *Arts,* 3000 Fifth Street, NW, New Brighton, MN 55112.

# The Christmas Octave Feasts of
# St. Stephen, St. John, and the Holy Innocents

*Marchita B. Mauck*

The present Roman calendar includes within the octave of Christmas the three feast days of St. Stephen, Protomartyr, on December 26; St. John, Apostle and Evangelist, on December 27; and the Holy Innocents on December 28. Their association with the feast of the Nativity is presumed, yet a study of early calendar traditions raises a number of perplexing questions. This article offers some suggestions about when, from whence, and how the three feasts entered the Roman calendar. In addition it explores the hermeneutical web required to link these feasts with the observance of the Nativity.

In Rome the feast of the Nativity first appears on December 25 in the *Philocalian Calendar of 354*, the text of which was probably written in 335–336.[1] The feasts of Stephen, John, and the Holy Innocents do not follow the Nativity. In fourth century Roman practice apparently they were not only not associated with Christmas, they were not in the calendar at all. Why did they not appear? The Roman martyrology was exactly that, Roman; that is to say, it was local in character, and neither Stephen, John, nor the Innocents had suffered Roman martyrdoms.

Nonetheless, the feasts of Stephen, John, and the Innocents appear in their present sequence of December 26, 27, and 28, in the *Leonine Sacramentary* of the sixth century, the earliest collection of Mass prayers of the Roman rite.[2] What happened between the fourth century *Philocalian Calendar of 354* and the sixth century *Leonine Sacramentary*? For one thing, the relics of St. Stephen were discovered in Gamala, a village near Jerusalem, in 415.[3] In Rome there are ruins of a basilica of St. Stephen, founded in the time of Leo I (440–461).[4] Pope Hilarus (461–468) established a monastery dedicated to Stephen, and Pope Simplicius (468–483) built the church of San Stefano Rotundo.[5] These three monuments offer sure evidence of the cult of St. Stephen having made its way to Rome in the fifth century along with relics of the martyr.[6]

An attempt to understand the Roman developments leads one first of all to Jerusalem. Fortunately two extant documents reveal important aspects about the celebration of the liturgical year in Jerusalem prior to the sixth century. One is the fragmentary description of Epiphany in *Egeria's Travels,* the account of a late fourth century (381–384) pilgrim to Jerusalem.[7] The second is *The Armenian Lectionary,* a Typicon of the first quarter of the fifth century which enumerates the feasts according to Jerusalem practice and lists the readings for each commemoration.[8] From these documents we discover some curious and puzzling facts that immediately reveal the complexity of sorting out these feast days.

The immediate anomaly is that between Rome and Jerusalem none of the dates of the three martyrial feasts corresponds:

| *Rome* | *Jerusalem* |
|---|---|
| St. Stephen, December 26 | St. Stephen, December 27 |
| John the Evangelist, December 27 | John the Evangelist, December 29 |
| Holy Innocents, December 28 | Holy Innocents, May 9 or May 18, depending on the manuscript of *The Armenian Lectionary* |

Clearly the Roman calendar does not appropriate the calendrical assignments as customary in Jerusalem. In fact, not only does the Roman sequence differ from the fourth century pattern in Jerusalem, it is also distinct from the fourth century Syrian indications of Aphraates:[9] Nativity, December 25; St. Stephen, December 26; Peter and Paul, December 27; James and John, December 28; or the early sixth century African pattern of the *Carthaginian Martyrology:*[10] Nativity, December 25; St. Stephen, December 26; John the Baptist and James,[11] December 27. Only in the eighth-century *Gelasian Sacramentary,*[12] *Missale Gothicum,*[13] and Wurzburg epistle and gospel lists[14] does the Roman pattern of St. Stephen, John (separated from the feast of James in all but the *Missale Gothicum*) and the Holy Innocents reappear.

In comparing the Roman calendar with those of Syria, Africa, or the later western medieval examples, the feasts of St. Stephen and the others always follow directly the feast of the Nativity. In Jerusalem practice, the December calendrical feasts of Stephen (December 27), John the Evangelist (December 29), and the May 9 feast of the Holy Innocents stand independently of the January 6 feast of the Nativity.

There are no martyrial designations in *The Armenian Lectionary* for the days of the octave of Epiphany following January 6, the day on which Jerusalem celebrated the feast of the Nativity. That is not to say, however, that there are no commemorative references. To the contrary, in the course of the week's readings all the events of the Incarnation story are presented, including the Annunciation to the Shepherds, the Nativity (three times), the Coming of the Magi, the Massacre of the Innocents, the Annunciation, the Visitation, and on the eighth day, the Circumcision. Two notable exceptions to the infancy narrative citations are the account from Acts of the martyrdom of Stephen read on the second day after Epiphany, and the raising of Lazarus on the sixth day. These exceptions were governed by the designated station for the liturgy. On the second day, the liturgy was celebrated at the "Martyrium of S. Stephen," hence the Acts pericope; and on the sixth day the station was at the Lazarium, the inspiration for the non-infancy reading of the raising of Lazarus.[15] The introduction of the John 11 reading at the Lazarium reveals the precedence of the station over the course reading of Matthew, a significant gesture since the cursus for both Epiphany and Great Week in Jerusalem, as Talley points out, was built on the course reading of Matthew.[16]

The cycle of readings for the Jerusalem Epiphany octave commemorates on the second day the Martyrdom of St. Stephen, and on the third day the Massacre of the Innocents according to the Matthaean account. As noted above, the reason for the Acts citation of Stephen's death is that the station is at the martyrium of Stephen. This would seem to presume a new custom following the discovery of the relics of Stephen in 415, and thus the station differs from that in Egeria's report.[17] The story of the Massacre of the Innocents on the third day is simply the next section of a continuous reading of the Matthew text of the Nativity begun at the "Place of the Shepherds," (Matt 1:18-25); continued at the vigil at Bethlehem (Matt 2:1-12); reiterated at the synaxis in Jerusalem on January 6; interrupted on the second day by the gesture toward St. Stephen; and, finally, resumed on the third day back in the Martyrium in Jerusalem with Matt 2:13-23.[18] Thus we find in the Epiphany celebration a sequence of the feast of the Nativity followed by commemorations in the lectionary readings of the Martyrdom of Stephen and the Massacre of the Innocents. Only the account of the Holy Innocents is directly related to the Nativity as part of the Nativity cycle readings for the week. The feast of John the Evangelist is not part of the Jerusalem octave of Epiphany, and thus not associated with the Nativity, but is located in the calendar on December 29.

The Christmas octave feasts in Rome seem to derive from a conflation of elements of the Epiphany octave in Jerusalem and the martyrial feast days of December 27, 28, 29 in the Jerusalem calendar. A comparative chart more graphically illustrates the relationships (Fig. 1).

*Figure 1*

| Rome (Calendar begins with Nativity, December 25) | Egeria/Armenian Lectionary (Calendar begins with Epiphany, January 6 | Readings |
|---|---|---|
| *Octave of Christmas* | *Octave of Epiphany* | |
| Dec. 25—Nativity | Jan. 6—Nativity | |
| (2) 26—Stephen | 2nd Day | Acts 6:8–8:2 *Martyrdom of Stephen* |
| (3) 27—(vacant) [John the Evangelist inserted] | 3rd Day | Matt 2:13-23 *Massacre of Innocents* |
| (4) 28—Holy Innocents | | |
| | May 9—Holy Innocents | |
| June 29—Peter and Paul | | |
| | December 26—(vacant) 27—Stephen 28—Paul and Peter 29—James and John | |

It is perhaps helpful to look at both calendars as having a "triad" of December martyrial feasts, albeit not the same feasts. In addition there are the readings for the liturgies of the second and third days of the Epiphany octave in Jerusalem, referring to the Martyrdom of Stephen and the Massacre of the Innocents. The Roman calendar deliberately attempts a symmetrical parallelism with Jerusalem's nativity sequence and her triad of December feasts. This no doubt arises out of the Roman circumstance of a December date for the Nativity which coincides with Jerusalem's December festal cycle.

There is clearly a good deal of arbitrary rearranging in order to achieve some sort of symmetry. The Martyrdom of Stephen is commemorated on the second day of the Epiphany octave and is also the first of the triad of December feasts in Jerusalem, falling on December

27.[19] The Roman calendar thus assigns Stephen to the day following the Nativity, matching the reading on the second day of the Epiphany octave and maintaining the position of first among the triad in the December group. In Rome this day is December 26, shifting the feast one day earlier than in *The Armenian Lectionary's* December calendar.

Second, the feast of Peter and Paul, on December 28 in *The Armenian Lectionary*, the second day of the December triad, shifts in Rome out of the December sequence altogether to June 29, the traditional date of the translation of their relics *ad catacumbas* in 258 A.D.[20] The local Roman anniversary takes precedence over Jerusalem practice, thus leaving the second day of the Roman triad, December 27, vacant.

The feast of John the Evangelist, the third of the December triad in *The Armenian Lectionary* (December 29), was inserted in Rome on December 27, the second day of the triad left vacant by the relocation of Peter and Paul to June 29. But a symmetry is achieved as the third of the Jerusalem triad, St. John, now occupies the third day of the Roman Christmas octave. This symmetry takes precedence over a possible one of the third day of the Jerusalem Epiphany octave (Matthaean account of the Massacre of the Innocents) and the third day of the Christmas octave in Rome.

The feast of the Holy Innocents is celebrated on the third day of the Epiphany octave in Jerusalem by virtue of its position in the course reading of the Matthaean text. The Jerusalem choice of the Gospel of Matthew for its cursus provides a logical and compelling structure for the arrangement of its lectionary. For other reasons the feast finds a home in the Roman calendar on the fourth day of the Christmas octave, on December 28.

The analytical comparison of the sixth century Roman calendar with Jerusalem practices of the fifth century reveals a complex yet starkly logical interpenetrating of the second and third days of the octave of the Jerusalem Epiphany with their readings about the Martyrdom of Stephen and the Massacre of the Innocents, and the three December feasts of Stephen, Paul and Peter, and James and John (December 27, 28, 29), with the December Nativity octave in Rome. The Roman calendar conflates the Jerusalem January nativity context of Epiphany and the triad of feasts of December 27, 28, 29 into its own December octave of Christmas.

The Roman calendar's seemingly deliberate attempt at symmetrical parallelism with Jerusalem's January Nativity sequence as well as its corresponding December commemorations suggests a desire to include the Apostle John and St. Stephen in an analogous pattern. The care with which the Roman calendar contrives to match its second day of the Christmas octave with Jerusalem's second day of Epiphany commemoration of Stephen, rather than simply assigning the feast to December 27 as in the Jerusalem calendar, demonstrates an interest in some relationship of the feast of Stephen to the Nativity. Also, as noted above, there is a priority of the parallelism of the feast of John the Evangelist on the third day of the Roman octave to its position as the third of the December triad in Jerusalem, which prevails over the symmetry of the commemoration of the Massacre of the Innocents on the third day as in the octave of Epiphany. Though it occupies the fourth day of the Nativity octave in Rome, the inclusion of the Massacre of the Innocents in its shifted position indicates the logical connection with the Nativity.

Of these three feasts of Stephen, John, and the Holy Innocents located by the sixth century in the Roman Christmas octave, only one, the Massacre of the Innocents, really had any connection with the Nativity at the earliest stratum in Jerusalem. The self-conscious arrangement of the three days following the December 25 feast of the Nativity in the Roman calendar reveals a careful imitation of both the octave pattern of Epiphany and positions of the corresponding December feasts in the Jerusalem calendar. It does not seem unreasonable to suppose that an equally paradigmatic role might have been exerted on the Roman consciousness by the Jerusalem community's understanding of Epiphany as a unitive feast of redemption.

The manner in which the Epiphany liturgy includes the presence of the Pasch is threefold. A. Renoux points out that the very structure of the vigil for Epiphany imitates that of the Holy Saturday vigil, beginning with a psalm with its antiphon, and followed by a series of eleven readings before the eucharistic liturgy begins.[21] Second, of those eleven readings, eight refer to the Nativity, but three repeat those of the Paschal vigil. One of those three is the account of the victorious crossing of the Red Sea (Exod 14:24–15:21), which introduces a baptismal character into the Epiphany liturgy. This deliverance account, coupled with the creation story from Genesis (1:1-3, 20) and the canticle of the three youths in the fiery furnace (Dan 3:19-30), places the Nativity within the context of God's continuous story of salvation.[22] Third, Renoux points out the symmetrical stational character of the Epiphany and Paschal liturgies. The stational designations for Epiphany derive from the places of significance in Christ's coming to earth, just as the stations of Holy Thursday and Good Friday recall the last events of the story begun with the Nativity. Thus the apparent historicizing of the stational character of the Epiphany liturgy in Jerusalem actually transcends the particular events to connect with the Paschal experiences in order to express a larger view of an "idea feast" of redemption.[23]

The notion that the feast of the birth of Christ far surpasses in meaning a singular temporal moment is well expressed by Augustine in a homily for the Nativity in which he states that

> the only-begotten Word of God, the Life and Light of men, is indeed the Eternal Day, but this day on which joined to human flesh, He became, as it were, a "bride-groom coming out of his bride-chamber" is our today and passes as tomorrow becomes yesterday.[24]

Augustine goes on to say that on the feast of the Nativity we commend the Eternal Day "who so loved us that for us He by whom all time was made became Man in time," and that "He, in obedience, came into the very narrow confines of mortality so that by dying He might seek you who were dead."[25]

The structural symmetry of the Jerusalem Epiphany liturgy with that of the Paschal vigil, and the understanding that the feast of the Nativity is a unitive feast of redemption provide compelling motivation to see the Roman festal cycle as somehow expressive of these redemptive notions as well, regardless of the fact that the commemorations of the octave became skewed in the process of their assimilation into the Roman calendar. There is then a logic to the attempts to link the feasts of St. Stephen, John the Evangelist, and the Holy Innocents with the Nativity as parts of the larger mystery of redemption.

In the context of the mystery of redemption, certainly Stephen and the Holy Innocents provide powerful witness in their deaths to the passion aspect of salvation. Their martyrdoms model the notion of birth into new eternal life won by the birth and death of Jesus. Delehaye aptly describes this commitment even to death that was one of the ineluctable consequences of the birth of Jesus, a commitment which found joy in the sacrifice of their lives for those for whom dedication to Christ was preferable to the things of this world.[26]

A suffering in common for Christ provides a way to look at the disparate Roman feasts of December 26, 27, 28, to see them as a cluster portraying a catalogue of martyrdom. In his book, *The Christian Year*, Horn describes the tradition of such a catalogue of martyrdom as follows:

1) in will and deed (Stephen),
2) in will but not in deed (John),
3) in deed but not in will (Holy Innocents).[27]

Such a schema provides a way to include even John the Evangelist within the unitive feast of the Nativity, a feat with no precedent in Jerusalem.

The homiletic tradition is somewhat ambiguous in the fourth and fifth centuries concerning a direct relationship between the feast of Stephen and the celebration of the Nativity. Of course the reading of his martyrdom from Acts during the Epiphany octave as a reflection of the station for the day in Jerusalem precludes any need to link the death of Stephen to the Nativity. A laudatory speech for Stephen by Hesychius of Jerusalem (d. after 451) thus understandably makes no direct reference to the Nativity. Interestingly though, Hesychius uses the bridal chamber imagery that Augustine also used in his Nativity homily quoted above.[28]

Augustine describes Christ's becoming at his nativity a bridegroom coming out of his bride's chamber, while Hesychius uses terminology to refer to the martyr's "surveying that sacred chamber," this time the *natalis* day referring to emergence into eternal life.[29]

In a festal homily on St. Stephen, Augustine indicates that one celebrates the *natalis* of Stephen after the *natalis* of the Lord.[30] As Leclercq points out, that *natalis* refers not only to the earthly birth of Jesus, but also to the "birth" that thrusts the martyrs into glory.[31]

The interpretive document most directly relating the feast of St. Stephen to Christmas is the festal sermon of Fulgentius (d. 533) in which he explores parallel images of the "births" of Stephen and Christ:

> Yesterday we celebrated the temporal birth of our eternal king; today we celebrate the triumphant death of a soldier. Yesterday our king, dressed in the burden of our flesh considered it proper to visit the world, coming forth from the chamber of the virgin's womb; today a soldier departing from the tent of his flesh, walks triumphantly into heaven.[32]

Fulgentius considerably extends his description of the analogous images of the nativities of Stephen and Christ. Such protracted comparisons apparently formed the basis for building an entire tradition of contexts for linking the feasts of Stephen, John, and the Holy Innocents with that of the Nativity.

The mid-nineteenth century French liturgist and Abbot of Solesmes, Dom Gueranger, articulated a "visitors to the crib" image to explain the commemorations of the days of the Christmas octave. His explanation is built on past traditions. He begins by quoting an eleventh-century sermon by St. Peter Damian who describes the Virgin as leading us to the crib.[33] Gueranger accords Stephen the place of honor at the crib as the first to pay back to the Savior the death suffered by the Savior.[34] Next to Stephen at the crib stands John, the Prince of Virgins. When he left his nets to follow Jesus, he left also his betrothed, and thus offered his virginity to the Lord.[35] Gueranger is here recalling an image in the work of Notger, a monk at St. Gall in the ninth century, who described John as the Virgin Disciple as well as the Beloved Disciple, in one of his Sequences:

> O John! the dearly Beloved Virgin Disciple of Jesus!
> For love of him thou didst leave thy father Zebedee
> and his boat.
> Thou didst disdain the caresses of thy betrothed,
> and didst follow the Messias,
> That thou mightest merit to drink at the sacred fount
> of his heart.
> . . . Jesus, when conquering on his cross, entrusted
> his Mother to thy keeping;
> That thou, a Virgin, mightest protect and care for the
> Virgin in his stead.[36]

The Holy Innocents, next in line at the crib, follow "courage" (Stephen) and "fidelity" (John) who led us there, and now bid us to tarry.[37] A preface appearing in both the *Ambrosian Missal* and the *Leonine Sacramentary* acknowledges the martyrdom in deed but not in will achieved by the infants:

> Herein do we recognize how immeasurable are the gifts of thy mercy, for the splendour of thy free grace outshines the martyrs' will; and they nobly confess thy name, who are not yet able to speak. They suffer martyrdom before their bodies are ripe for martyrdom; they bear testimony to Christ before they have even known him.[38]

Gueranger's meditations in his commentary on the liturgical year revive the medieval view of Stephen, John, and the Innocents as a cortege of honor accompanying the Christ Child, the so-called *Comites Christi* as depicted by Durandus in his *Rationale divinorum officiorum* in the thirteenth century.[39] Even a cursory look at the literature suggests that it is this explanation which prevails in the West well into the nineteenth century. The "cortege of honor" motif admirably accomplishes both a linkage of the three feast days with the Nativity, and at the same time emphasizes the Paschal aspect of the feast of the Nativity, implying celebration of a unitive feast of redemption during the Christmas octave.

This study has attempted to demonstrate that the celebration of the liturgical year in Jerusalem provides the foundation for the incorporation of the martyrial feasts of Stephen, John, and the Holy Innocents in the Roman calendar. The process seems to have been twofold. On the one hand, there is the conflation of the readings from the second day of Epiphany with the Jerusalem December feasts which fall into the time span of the octave of the feast of the Nativity in the West. Second, there is the Jerusalem community's understanding of the days after the Nativity as an octave of celebration of the incarnation, an octave in which the continuous narrative from Matthew is read, to be interrupted by the readings from Acts describing the martyrdom of Stephen, and from the Johannine account of the raising of Lazarus. Both of these readings were determined by the stational designations for those days, and not because they had anything to do with the Nativity.

It is not surprising that once the feast dates had been established in the Roman calendar, the commemorations of Stephen and John, who had no real connection with the Nativity *per se* and whose feasts were outside the Epiphany octave, along with the feast of the Innocents, were understood as either having or deserving of some dignity and respect by virtue of their juxtaposition to the Nativity. Never mind the curiously mechanical manner in which those feasts found their homes in the Roman calendar within the Christmas octave. A theology was contrived to bind these feasts to the Nativity, that of the *Comites Christi*. And thus, in the West, the feast of the Nativity confronts the eschaton in the Paschal experiences of Stephen, John, and the Holy Innocents, providing perhaps, a more dramatic demonstration than the subtle reflections of the Easter Vigil liturgy embedded in the Epiphany readings of the unitive character of this "idea feast" of our redemption.

---

[1] Henri Stem, *Le Calendrier de 354* (Paris, 1953) 56–7. Thomas J. Talley, *The Origins of the Liturgical Year* (New York, 1986) 85. See also H. Frank, O.S.B., "Friihgeschichte und Ursprung des Römischen Weihnachtsfestes im Lichte Neuerer Forschung," *Archive fiir Liturgiewissenschaft* 2 (1952) 1–24; H. Engberding, O.S.B., "Der 25. Dezember als Tag der Feier der Geburt des Heren," in the same volume of *ALw* 2 (1952) 25–43; and A.A. MacArthur, *The Evolution of the Christian Year* (London, 1953) 41–3.

[2] Mario Righetti, *Manuale di storia liturgica* II (Ancora, 1946) 63.

[3] K.A.H. Kellner, *Heortology* (London, 1908) 223–5. The discovery of the relics of Stephen was made by Lucianus, a priest in Jerusalem, on December 5, 415. Lucianus wrote a report of the discovery which was translated into Latin by the Spanish priest Avitus, and sent as a letter to all the churches. See A. Renoux, *Le Codex Arménien Jérusalem 121*, (*Patrologia Orientalis* 35: 1) 176, for a

discussion of the discovery of the relics of St. Stephen. See also Righetti, *Manuale di storia liturgica* 2:64.

[4] Richard Krautheimer, *Rome, Profile of a City, 312–1308* (Princeton, 1980) 54; and also *Roma e dintorni* (Milan, 1977) 714.

[5] Krautheimer, *Rome*, 54. See also E. T. Horn, *The Christian Year* (Philadelphia, 1957) 77; and Kellner, *Heortology*, 223–5.

[6] The cult of St. Stephen spread quickly. In Book 22:8 of *The City of God*, written between 413–426, Augustine describes some dozen miracles attributed to relics of Stephen in Hippo-Regius in the two years since the relics had arrived. He says that in the interest of time he must omit many miracles, "For were I to be silent of all others, and to record exclusively the miracles of healing which were wrought in the district of Calama and of Hippo by means of this martyr —I mean the most glorious Stephen—they would fill many volumes; and yet all even of these could not be collected, but only those of which narratives have been written for public recital." Augustine, *The City of God*, tr. Marcus Dods (New York, 1950) 828.

In *The Lives of Illustrious Men,* by Jerome and Gennadius, Chapter XL, Gennadius wrote (ca. 480 or 492–495) that Orosius, a Spanish presbyter, "who, sent by Augustine to Hieronymus to teach the nature of the soul, returning, was the first to bring to the West relics of the blessed Stephen then recently found. He flourished almost at the end of the reign of the emperor Honorius," *A Select Library of Nicene and Post-Nicene Fathers of the Christian Church*, 2nd series, ed. P. Schaff and H. Wace, 3 (Grand Rapids, 1953) 393.

[7] J. Wilkinson, *Egeria's Travels* (London, 1971) 126–8.

[8] A Renoux, *Le Codex Arménien Jérusalem 121, Patrologia Orientalis* 35–36. (1971). A summary chart of the calendar with the designated stational churches and readings for the day from *The Armenian Lectionary* appears as an appendix in Wilkinson's *Egeria's Travels*, 262–77.

[9] Righetti, *Manuale di storia liturgica*, 2:63.

[10] Ibid.

[11] The reference to John the Baptist is probably a mistake of the copiest. See Righetti, *Manuale di storia liturgica*, 2:63.

[12] L. C. Mohlberg, O.S.B., *Sacramentatium Gelasianum* (Rome, 1960) 7–12; A. Chavasse, *Le Sacramentaire Gelasien* 1 (Tournai, 1958) 208; and Righetti, *Manuale di storia liturgica*, 2:63.

[13] Righetti, *Manuale di storia liturgica*, 2:63.

[14] W. H. Frere, *Studies in Early Roman Liturgy, 1 The Kalendar*, Alcuin Club Collections 28 (London, 1930) 69–70.

[15] Wilkinson, *Egeria's Travels*, 262.

[16] Talley, *The Origins of the Liturgical Year*, 132–3.

[17] Egeria's list of the stations for the liturgies (25:11) differs from that in *The Armenian Lectionary*. Since there is no reference at all to a martyrium of Stephen in Egeria's stations, the inclusion in *The Armenian Lectionary* can be presumed a new addition after the discovery of the relics in 415.

[18] See list of readings from *The Armenian Lectionary* in Wilkinson, *Egeria's Travels*, 262.

[19] Only Guerin, *Les petits Bollandistes vies des saints* 14:479, goes so far as to declare the date of December 26 as the anniversary of St. Stephen's martyrdom. He says with no hesitation, "C'était le 26 décembre de l'an 35 de Notre Seigneur." Kellner, *Heortology*, 225, points out the possibility of December 26 being a translation day rather than a death anniversary. He admits that whether December 26 or 27 is a death date is not ascertainable.

[20] Righetti, *Manuale di storia liturgica* 2:302-3; J. Stevenson, *The Catacombs* (London, 1978) 32; and Kellner, *Heortology*, 284. The tradition that June 29 commemorates a translation date is indicated by the entry in the *Philocalian Calendar of 354:* "III Kalendas Julii' Petri in Catacumbas et Pauli Ostiense, Tusco et Basso Coss," Noele M. Denis-Boulet, *The Christian Calendar*, tr. P. Hepburne-Scott (New York, 1960) 53.

[21] A. Renoux, "L'Epiphanie A Jérusalem au IVe et au Ve siecles," *Lex Orandi* 40 (1967) Noël, Epiphanie Retour du Christ, 181.

[22] Renoux, "L'Epiphanie a Jérusalem," 182–6.

[23] Ibid., 180–1. See also Dom Jean Leclercq, O.S.B., "Aux Origines du cycle de Noël," *Ephemerides Liturgicae* 60 (1946) 12. Leclercq speaks of Christmas as an "idea feast" according to Baumstark's understanding of the term, one which celebrates in all its parts the mystery of redemption.

[24] Leclercq, "Aux Origines du cycle de Noël," 12; and Augustine, Sermon 188, *Sermons on the Liturgical Seasons*, tr. Sr. Mary Sarah Muldowney, R.S.M. (New York, 1959) 18.

[25] Augustine, Sermon 188, *Sermons on the Liturgical Seasons*, 18–9.

[26] H. Delehaye, *Les Origines du culte des martyrs* (Brussels, 1933) 23: . . . il est bien clair que la chaine des marlyrs est ininterrompue, qu'ils meurent pour la meme cause, que leur témoignage est surtout un hommage à la divinite du Christ, qu'ils proclament préferer à tous les biens de ce monde et à qui ils font joyeusement le sacrifice de leur vie.

[27] Horn, *The Christian Year*, 72. The description of this catalogue of martyrdom is found in Durandus, *Rationale divinorum officiorum* (VII, 42, 2.6. 10) of the thirteenth century. See A. Adam, *The Liturgical Year*, tr. M. J. O'Connell (New York, 1981) 141–2.

[28] P. Devos, "Le Panégyrique de Saint Etienne par Hesychius de An Jérusalem" *Analecta Bollandiana* 86 (1968) 151–72. I am grateful to Rev. Vincent Fitzpatrick, S.T., for graciously translating the entire Greek text of Hesychius' encomium for me, as well as the sermons of Fulgentius on St. Stephen and the Epiphany. See also Augustine, Sermon 188, *Sermons on the Liturgical Seasons*, 18.

[29] Hesychius, in Devos, "Le Panégyrique de Saint Etienne," Paragraph 3, 158.

[30] Augustine, Sermon 317, *PL* 38, 1435–7.

[31] Leclercq, "Aux Origines du cycle de Noël," 13. Leclercq asserts that the parallelism of the death ("nativity") of Stephen and the nativity of Christ is warrant for the juxtaposition of the two feasts: "Il est precise que la fête de Saint Etienne a lieu le lendemain de Noël et que, ce jour-là, on lit le récit de la mort du protomartyr d'après les Actes des Apôtres." Our analysis has shown the issue at the most fundamental level to be the conflation of calendrical assignments and Jerusalem Epiphany custom connected with the station at the martyrium of Stephen on the second day of the octave.

[32] Fulgentius of Ruspe, "De Sancto Stephano Protomartyre et conversions S. Pauli," *Sancti Fulgentii episcopi Ruspensis opera, Corpus Christianorum* XCIA (Turnhout, 1968) 905. Fulgentius pursues a pattern in sections 4–6 of this homily in which he compares Stephen and Paul in much the same way he compares Stephen and Christ at the beginning. In section 5, page 908, he observes:

> Thus he is joined to Stephen having become a sheep where formerly he was a wolf and behold now Paul rejoices with Stephen, with Stephen he is bathed in the brilliance of Christ, with Stephen he triumphs, with Stephen he rules. Where Stephen went before, murdered by the stones of Paul, there Paul follows assisted by the prayer of Stephen.

Such an interpretation, if it reflects an older tradition, coupled with the logic of a continuous reading of the Acts account, might shed some light on the reason the feast of Paul and Peter follows that of Stephen in the December calendrical cycle in Jerusalem. It is of interest that the entry in *The Armenian Lectionary* cites Paul before Peter.

[33] Dom Gueranger, *The Liturgical Year,* 1 (1948) 233.

[34] Ibid., 1:224.

[35] Ibid., 1:250–1.

[36] Ibid., 1:269.

[37] Ibid., 1:278.

[38] Ibid., 1:290.

[39] Adam, *The Liturgical Year,* 141. Durandus, *Rationale divinorum officiorum* (VII, 42, 1).

# Secular Music in the Liturgy: Are There Any Rules?

*Virgil C. Funk*

"*Christian theology, home to many paradoxes, makes both of the follow-ing claims: worship and culture are inescapably in conversation; worship and culture are inescapably in conflict, as Christians are called to be 'in but not of the world.'*"[1]

Nowhere is the paradox described above more evident than in the work of pastoral musicians in the last quarter of the twentieth century. The Second Vatican Council's call for active participation in the liturgy, some thirty years ago, soon came to be heard as a call for Church musi-cians to develop a new repertoire that would invite and support such participation. Now, thirty years into the postconciliar reform, it has be-come possible to demonstrate the diverse ways in which national or linguistic groups of churches have approached this task of shaping a new repertoire. There are many factors that account for the variety of responses to the council's invitation: the living language in use within a country, the musicians available to play the newly composed music, the buildings in which the music is played, the readiness or lack-of-readiness to seek and receive a proper understanding of the liturgical renewal, the local or regional traditions of music in the liturgy.

In this paper I will concentrate on but one of these variables: whether or not the music of the so-called "secular culture" was seen as a usable model in the effort to develop music for the revised liturgy. The use (or non-use) of music from the secular culture became a criti-cal issue for musicians serving the liturgical renewal for two reasons: they were called to develop a repertoire which could be used as wor-ship music *by the assembly* and to do that *in their own vernacular lan-guage.*

I have chosen to focus directly on music *qua music.* As a liturgist, I am well aware of the importance of the text, even its centrality, in worship music. But I have found it both interesting and revealing to bracket the role of the text in worship music for the sake of this study and examine how various national groups have approached the use of music of the secular culture in their effort to develop worship music for the assembly to sing in their living language.

In my examination of several cultural/linguistic groups of churches I have discovered three main directions that musicians have taken; two of them are based on theoretical considerations, and the final—and most widespread direction—has been based on experience. I will describe those directions and then draw some observations based on this material. However, before examining the three directions that musicians have chosen, I have to sketch two introductory ideas that will help in understanding the data: a definition of music based on current communication theory and a description of the "cultural ear." Both are fundamental to my paper.

## Music as Communication

At the meeting of the Social Science Study Group of the North American Academy of Liturgy in 1977, Gerald Lardner presented a paper on communication theory in which he described three models of communication.[2] The classic model consists of two elements: sender and message. This model maintains that the more the sender knows about the message, the better the message is communicated. This model was used for more than 450 years to justify the proclamation of the gospel in the liturgy and, in mission nations, to the world in a "dead" language that was foreign to most of its hearers. The classic model is still used in large universities as the basis for teaching via lecture, a situation in which a professor, expert in his subject, lectures to students who may or may not understand the point of the presentation or, for that matter, may not even be present for the lecture.

The introduction of the telephone gave rise to the second communication model, in which three elements are seen to be necessary for communication: sender-message-receiver. The telephone is not of much use without a receiver to which the sending machine is connected; in the classic model, however, the receiver is not seen as essential to the act of communication.

The widespread use of the computer helped us to recognize the third model: the five elements of sender-encoding-message-decoding-receiver are all essential to communication. Semiotics[3] utilizes a version of this model; and certainly it is important to realize that in human communication the decoding process is the point at which miscommunication most often takes place. I am very grateful to Gerry Lardner for this fundamental insight into communication and I have chosen to adapt it to develop a description of the very difficult item we call "music."

Music has defied definite linguistic analysis because it is, or at least it contains, a sonic experience which is outside the rational order. Some commentators have gone so far as to say that it is fruitless to write about music, since it is a performance art form. Certainly, music *qua music* does not convey a message in the way words do. Nevertheless, by changing "message" to "medium" in adapting communication theory to an examination of music, we will find that the third model of communication described above does contribute to an understanding of the phenomenon of music.

Music, then, may be described as a sonic experience originating from 1) a sender (remotely the composer, immediately the music-maker) who 2) creates sonic experiences (performance). The sonic experience is 3) transmitted through a medium (air, acoustics, vibrations) to 4) a receiver (the listening ear) who 5) decodes the sonic experience based on his/her cultural and biological experiences and capabilities. Music is always then a relationship between sender and receiver, established through a medium and requiring an encoding process by the music-maker, and a decoding process (or audiation[4]) by the listener. All music is made up of these five parts, held in relationship to one another.

What this description reveals is that the performance, the environment, and the cultural decoding are all *constitutive* elements of music making. What is unique about music in regard to communication is that the medium (the acoustic) replaces the message or content element of verbal or rational communication. Marshall McLuhan's famous dictum that "the medium is the message" has particular relevance to music.[5] It is my opinion that insufficient attention has been paid to all five elements, both at the theoretical level and at the pastoral or parochial level, in reflections about worship music. Church musicians have too often been drawn to pay attention to the repertoire (encoding the message) and, to some extent, to the music-maker (sender), with little or no attention to the acoustic (medium), the receiver, or most importantly, the cultural ear of the listener (decoding).

When the listener and the performance of the message become one, as they do in congregational song, a unique experience in music takes place: The sender, in a sense, becomes the receiver as well. The quality of performance (encoding and decoding at the same time, in a sense) is as good or as bad as the assembly itself. As a result, the original intention of the composer and of the trained musician (encoding) become even more dependent on the ability of the assembly participant (decoding). As has often been experienced during the renewal, if the assembly does not resonate with the musical choice that a leader (musician, clergy) has appointed, there is no music made.

How the music is done, who does it, in what church environment, and how the listener (or assembly) decodes the music are as critical to understanding worship music as is the fusing of text to music or the notes on the page.

## A Word about the Decoding Process and The Cultural Ear

I want to say a brief word about the fourth element of music as communication, that is, the decoding process by the receiver. In response to the 1993 National Standards for Music Education, a number of studies on the relationship of music and the brain are now appearing. Thirty years ago, Alfred Tomatis first used the term "cultural ear" in reference to languages, theorizing that certain sonic experiences charm our individual ear, and further, that those "charming" sounds exist within our culture, thus *creating* a cultural ear.[6] These sounds come from our early childhood experiences and actually shape the way our aural mechanisms operate. His findings have recently been verified in the development of studies of the embryonic and early childhood brain. These studies actually establish the concept that our brains develop a surplus of synaptic patterns,[7] and then the brain retains those which are used while discarding those which are not used. Thus each brain pattern is uniquely built from stimulation by the environment, by use.[8] Further studies indicate that music is processed by a section of the brain separate and distinct from the area of logical and verbal processing (formerly referred to as the two-hemisphere or left-and-right-brain theory). The discovery that music is processed in the same area where concepts without words exist offers a biological explanation of why listening to music often places us in a world of imagination.[9] And "when imagination is allowed to move to deep places, the sacred is revealed. The more different kinds of thoughts we experience around a thing, and the deeper our reflections go as we are arrested by its artfulness, the more fully its sacredness can emerge."[10] The point here is that music associates itself with other codes as part of interlocked patterns in each person, and that many of these connected codes are culturally conditioned.

## Music of the Culture and Worship Music

Several factors, such as the diversity of cultures (even sometimes within the same language group), the breadth of the subject matter, and the need to narrow our focus for the sake of clarity, make it difficult to describe in any adequate way how—or even whether—music of the secular culture interacts with or informs music in worship. My approach is to examine the explicit or implicit starting points from which three national/linguistic groups have approached the question of appropriate music for worship, and then demonstrate how that starting point affects the attitude toward the use of secular music. In brief, I will try to show 1) how the Roman-Germanic School began with "sacred music" and determined that secular music could never be used in the liturgy; 2) how the French-Dutch School began with the issue of music's liturgical function and determined that the question was not relevant; and 3) how the American School began with a focus on music's pastoral function and has wrestled with this question in a way that the other two groups have not.

I have chosen to name the three approaches after the countries in which the schools grew up, knowing full well that it is an oversimplification to characterize an entire country's response based on a few examples. Nevertheless, for my purpose, and for the clarity which this approach reveals, particularly in the two theoretically rooted positions, I ask the reader's indulgence.

### The Roman-Germanic School

The Roman-Germanic School begins with the authority of the directives of Chapter VI of *Sacrosanctum Concilium*, "Sacred Music," which emphasize the requirement that worship music should be modeled on Gregorian chant and the "treasure of sacred music": "The treasure of sacred music is to be preserved and fostered with great care" (#114). "Composers, filled with the Christian spirit, should feel that their vocation is to develop sacred music and to increase its store of treasures" (#121).[11] As the council's challenge to composers to find ways of relating their new compositions—described ironically as "new treasures" to be added—to the existing music of the tradition became more difficult, a joint meeting between the *Consociatio Internationalis Musicae Sacrae* (CIMS) and the Church Music Association of America was held in Milwaukee-Chicago on August 21–28, 1966. In his letter to the Congress, Cardinal A. Cicognani admitted that there were "great problems of sacred music arising from the decisions of the council," but he stated clearly the position of the Roman-Germanic School:

His Holiness is pleased to note that in its public sessions and practical executions, the Congress will illustrate the basic principle of the conciliar *Constitution on the Liturgy,* that, namely, of inserting all new liturgico-musical elements into those magnificent achievements which the Church created and has faithfully preserved throughout her long history. The Council called these the "treasury of sacred music."[12]

So the central perspective of the Roman-Germanic School, as reflected in the writings of CIMS and of Johannes Overath,[13] is that there should be an organic relationship between Gregorian chant/sacred treasury music and the new worship music of the assembly composed for use with living languages. This theoretical position is particularly suited to factual realities of the great German tradition of sacred music, to the acoustics of their parish churches and, most of all, to the *cultural ear* of the worshiping communities in Germany. The publication of a national hymnal for German-speaking countries, *Gotteslob,*[14] in 1975, solidified this position.

In the United States, a version of this position is emerging in the thought of M. Francis Mannion. He has chosen to call the American version of this school the "modern classical school," deliberately distinguishing it from what he calls the "neo-Caecilian school," an archconservative American version of the CIMS. Mannion states that "the modern classical paradigm recognizes the 'classic' character of Gregorian chant and Renaissance polyphony as *the basis for new developments and expressions*. While the neo-Caecilian paradigm accords Gregorian chant, Renaissance polyphony and the traditional repertoire an absolute and virtually exclusive status, the modern classical recognizes that these embody a normative set of musical dynamics to be appropriated in a modern idiom."[15] He applies the general principle of the reform specifically to music. The modern classical school "takes seriously the principle of article 23 of the *Constitution of the Sacred Liturgy* that 'care must be taken that any new forms adapted should in some way grow organically from forms already existing.'"[16]

### The French-Dutch School

The French-Dutch School started not with music, but with liturgy. Joseph Gelineau had written vernacular psalm tones and, prior to the council, the texts with which these tones were to be used were translated into modern languages, including English. Gelineau was primarily interested in finding a way to adapt the liturgical psalm to the French vernacular. In 1963, in an effort to avoid the harsh musical judgments of the traditionalist musicians, Gelineau worked with Luigi Agustoni and Erhard Quack to form *Universa Laus* (UL), an independent international study group founded in 1965 for research into and reflections on liturgical music, based on a framework of international friendship, respect, and the free exchange of ideas. In spite of protests from CIMS, UL received papal recognition on May 11, 1966.[17] The musicians of CIMS have consistently argued that sacred music was being corrupted by the liturgists. Bernard Huijbers and other Dutch composers joined the UL group and brought with them the liturgico-musical experiments of the Dominican Church in Holland, together with Huijbers's theory of elemental music for assembly worship music.[18]

Gelineau and Huijbers, working with the musicologists Helmut Hucke (German) and Gino Stephani (Italian), came to the realization that the term "musica sacra" no longer adequately described their understanding of worship music. They created new terminology based on the notion of ritual function as found in the expression *munus ministeriale* [SC/CSL #112]. The notion of "Christian ritual music" was the centerpiece in the UL document published in 1980.[19] Christian ritual music, as the participants in *Universa Laus* describe it, is driven by its function in the liturgy.[20] Edward Foley, working in the United States, has noted that the development of this category parallels an interest in the ritual studies of Victor Turner and Clifford Geertz, and the emergence of the field of culturally attentive music study known as ethnomusicology.[21]

In the United States, the first glimpse of a theoretical controversy about worship music emerged in the Milwaukee/Chicago CIMS meeting in 1966. One of the most controversial papers delivered at the meeting was that by Rembert Weakland, O.S.B. (now the Archbishop of Milwaukee), who said: "There is no music of a liturgical golden age to which we can turn . . . and sacred music is not a telephone to the beyond."[22] There is no such thing as sacred music, no series of notes or progression of chords which are in and of themselves sacred. These statements reflect, of course, an effort to break through the limitations that the sacred treasury and Gregorian chant had placed on musical form, and to open the door for a fresh start on the challenge of establishing music for congregational participation without the restrictive requirement to relate the new repertoire organically to chant or the sacred treasury. Rather, this new repertoire was to be based on the demands of the new liturgy.

The Milwaukee Symposia for Church Composers (1982, 1985, 1988, 1990, and 1992), under the guidance of Theophane Hytrek, O.S.F., and Archbishop Rembert Weakland, brought the principles of the 1980 UL document to the cultural context of the United States. Driven by the liturgical renewal principle of "full, conscious, and active participation" in the liturgy through music as its starting point, the Milwaukee Statement endorsed the new language for describing worship music: Christian ritual music.[23]

After this abbreviated history, we are in a position to examine the positions of the two theoretical schools side by side and bring to bear our special consideration of how these schools relate in different and sometimes opposing ways to the use of music from the secular culture.

This chart provides an outline comparison:

|  | CIMS | UL |
|---|---|---|
| Starting Point | Treasury/Chant | New Effort |
| Foundation | Music | Liturgy |
| Nationality | German-Roman | French-Dutch |
| Terms | Sacred Music | Ritual Music |
| Sender | Large Music Forces | Parochial limitations |
| Encoding | Chant/Treasury | Ritual Function |
| Medium | Large acoustic buildings | Parochial buildings/Diversity |
| Decoding | Germanic Cultural Ear | French Cultural Ear |
| Receiver | Trained Assembly | Untrained Assembly |
|  |  |  |
| *Excluded* | *Secular Music* | *Non-Ritual Music* |
| Criteria | Treasury/Chant organic | Ritual function |
| Uncertain | Sacra Pop | Some Music |

## The Use of Music From the Popular Culture

While it is not possible to draw all the comparisons and contrasts between the notions of sacred music and Christian ritual music, notice how the shift in language results in a shift in understanding the use of music from the popular culture.

The opposite of "sacred music" is non-sacred music or "secular music." Linguistically, the use of the term "sacred music" automatically excludes secular music. The members of CIMS are, rightly so, adamant that secular music must be excluded from the category, sacred music.

The opposite of ritual music, of course, is non-ritual music. From the UL perspective, music from the secular culture can be included or excluded based on its ritual use, and the same holds true for music from the sacred treasury and Gregorian chant. It is not the music, per se, but the *use* of the music that matters, and the use of the music is further determined by the culture in which the music is found. This insight became particularly relevant as the Catholic Church was in the process of developing repertoire in more than 250 vernacular languages and as many, if not more, cultures.

From the CIMS perspective, one popular term for the use of secular music in worship music is "sacra-pop." A close examination of the term reveals that sacra-pop is not "musica" and therefore cannot be called *musica sacra*. In this school, popular music is thus excluded because of a musical criterion.

From the UL perspective, "not all musical practices in a given society lend themselves equally well to Christian celebration."[24] Some popular music is excluded because of a liturgical criterion.

The CIMS and UL do take two different, and in my opinion, valid approaches to responding to the call for congregational music in the liturgy.

CIMS is driven by the value that one should begin with the treasure of sacred music and Gregorian chant and discover how this repertoire can be adapted to congregational participation. UL, driven by the value that music for congregational participation performs a liturgical function, maintains that a fresh start must be made in musical composition in our times. After the new start is established, then the repertoire must be related to the sacred tradition and the principles of Gregorian chant.[25] In short, CIMS starts with the treasury and chant and sees how congregational music can grow from it; UL starts with no preconceived musical ideas and sees how the new repertoire relates to the principles of the music of the tradition. Both are based on values, strongly held. Similar tensions exist in other churches.[26]

## The United States: The Pastoral Practitioners

In the multi-cultural United States, the approach to the two-fold challenge of developing a music for the assembly and in the various vernaculars in current use in the U.S. was driven by trial and error. It is no accident that the organization of church musicians which formed in the United States was called "Pastoral."[27] If the Roman-Germanic School grew from its long tradition of quality music in the liturgy, and if the French-Dutch School began with a deep understanding of the history of the liturgy, the American School began pragmatically with what worked. Quite literally, music was tried out on assemblies. If they sang it, the musicians continued to use it; and if the assembly did not sing it or did not sustain it, it was discarded. In thirty years, a great deal of music has been tried and discarded.

Practitioners on the parish level in the United States, compared with their colleagues in other nations, are much more involved in the development of music in a more immediate way, although, as is the case with musicians in other nations, they are less involved in the formation of liturgical text. For the past thirty years, that is to say, local, national, and international church authorities have exercised a significant involvement in giving directions concerning ritual texts; but music has been, in the words of Mark Searle, and especially in the United States, a "soft spot" in the liturgy, a point where "the close control over text and music envisaged by the Consilium was never realized."[28]

The forces that have significantly influenced American musical practitioners are the sender: both composer and performer; the encoding process the abilities of the performer; the medium: the acoustics of the local space, the location of the musicians; the decoding process: the assembly's cultural ear.

The various starting points can be characterized, then, as musical (the Roman-Germanic), liturgical (French-Dutch), and pastoral (American). This is not to say that the French are unaware of music or that the Germans are unaware of liturgy, or that either school is unaware of the demands made by the liturgical reform. It is, rather, to say where the *musicians* in each country *began* their work of developing congregational song that would use their vernacular (text as well, in some instances, as their musical "vernacular"), that is, what became their principal filter for musical explorations.

The Roman-Germanic School has tended toward a classical model of communication and thus of music as communication. The French-Dutch School has tended toward the tripartite communication model: sender-medium-receiver. The American School, consistent with its democratic roots and its embrace of communications technology, has definitely taken on itself the task of analyzing the decoding process of the assembly as its starting point for examining and creating Christian ritual music—a most difficult task indeed.

It is my position that this decoding process, which is what is driving the American approach, is influenced by three different settings—the cathedral, the monastery, and the parish.[29]

## The Cathedral Musicians

In cathedrals (and other large buildings with "hard" resonant acoustics) the liturgical and acoustical space dramatically influences the musical choices. The resonant acoustics are well suited to chant, polyphony, and, to some extent, hymnody, and less suited to highly rhythmical musical forms. The syncopation of much popular music is acoustically ineffective in cathedral settings. In regard to the sender, cathedrals often have at their disposal larger musical forces than do the typical parishes, and also a desire for adding solemnity with music.

In regard to the decoding process, cathedrals usually host an assembly which remains physically separated from the sanctuary due to the size and proportions of the room, and in some cases, a more sophisticated musical taste. In sum, a cathedral liturgy has (1) a certain distance between the assembly and the presider (a necessity due to the size and the design of the building), (2) distinct acoustics, and (3) musicians who know what repertoire works in that acoustic and what repertoire does not.

Musicians and other members of the assembly in cathedrals are often attracted to secular music of the high culture, and are drawn to performance models because of the arrangement of the space in which the worship takes place.

## The Monastic Tradition

Musically, things are different in the monastic situation. If the cathedral model of worship is most influenced by its large resonant spaces in which festive celebrations with large musical resources take place, then we might say that the monastic model is most influenced by its theory. Monks are a symbol of a witness to a counter-cultural life-style, holding to the "higher things." And their music carries that culture. The music must be well crafted to endure repetition. And monastic music will resist music of the secular culture, deliberately.

## The Parish Scene

The situation on the parish scene is not as clear. American parishes, in their search for useful congregational song, have been greatly influenced by the *acoustic* and the *cultural ear of the assembly*.

A significant number of parish churches have been built since the Second Vatican Council. Many draw sanctuary and assembly space together. And many strive to improve the quality of the spoken word from the sanctuary, using modern acoustical techniques that deaden reverberation with acoustical tile and carpets. This in turn has increased the importance and use of microphones and strategically placed amplification. What is achieved in this new ecclesiastical environment is a preacher's ability to create a sense of intimacy with the assembly, using the slightest whisper to its most effective dramatic edge.[30] What is lost in this new environment is that the assembly song is weakened because the members of the assembly can't hear themselves sing. Musicians need amplification to be heard; sometimes even a choir is amplified.

In the experimental period in many parishes (the ten or fifteen years immediately after the council), one of the things that became obvious in this acoustical environment was that the overtones of Gregorian chant and the extended chords of traditional polyphony did not have the desired effect on the assembly's ears. It is my opinion that the people who chose to build such worship centers did so not because they were trying to exclude musical environments supportive of chant and polyphony, but because they were trying to draw the presider and assembly closer together, were trying to create a sense of intimacy or reflect a perceived new theology of incarnation. It can be argued, however, that chant and the musical treasury are not in the cultural ear of the typical American assembly in the same way they are in a German assembly. American musicians discovered this musical truth through pastoral practice.

The conditions in which the classical repertoire doesn't work (dry acoustics, microphones needed for musicians, and a sense of intimacy) provide an almost irresistible environment where musical performance techniques from some other source would have to be used. The decision to look for those other sources was not theoretical, as it was in the case of *Universa Laus,* but based in some part, at least, on pastoral necessity. And parish musicians, especially amateur parish musicians, with limited musical forces, seeking new music which would work as congregational participation music, were drawn to music that charmed the parishioners' cultural ear.

## Parish Musicians: Using Popular Music

At the time of Vatican II some parish musicians were drawn to using musical forms from the popular culture, especially arrangements, instruments, and sometimes even melodies as assembly-participation music. Music from the popular culture of the '60s with its use of guitars and assembly sing-a-long had an immediate appeal. This practice was rather quickly abandoned for two reasons: Most often the texts were unacceptable in worship settings, judged either from a traditional or a ritual functional aspect; and specific repertoire used in the popular movement of the '60s was rejected because it carried secular "codes" which proved to be unacceptable to the cultural ear of the worshipers. American practitioners discovered that banal and trite compositions cannot survive the rigorous requirement of ritual use. All theoretical positions agree.

Further, melodies drawn directly from the secular culture of the mass media (radio, TV, CDs, etc.), while attractive because they charmed the cultural ear, failed because the musical form is designed for entertainment, that is, the performer performs in such a style as to please the affections of the listener. Music performed for listeners obviously did not work as congregational song, where performer and listener are one. Msgr. Overath's warning is correct: "Congregational song is in no way to be regarded as a field for experimentation by amateur composers."[31]

## Parish Musicians: Encoding Popular Music

As a result of what we learned soon after the council, a second group of composers began to develop music that was heavily influenced by the secular culture but whose popular musical "codes" were more subtly hidden from the cultural ear by arrangement, harmony, or performance technique. When a composer was able to create music which the assembly did not recognize as blatantly drawn from the secular culture, but was nevertheless music that charmed its cultural ear, the assembly began to sing such music readily and with enthusiasm.

Through use, we know from scientific research, the brain forms and uses the cultural ear, a pathway pleasing to each individual and able to identify sonic experiences within the culture. The brain, through experience, associates sonic experiences with other symbolic elements.[32] This association sometimes has universal application, so, for example, march music with drums makes our bodies want to move (the irresistible toe tapping in the symphony hall). Some association is culturally learned: *La Marseillaise* stirs the emotion of French nationalism. Some associations are held individually, e.g., a new couple may identify "our" song.

In the United States, a group of composers has attempted to use musical techniques drawn from the popular culture, e.g., Broadway, but these composers mask the secular codes in such a way that their sources are not recognizable by the listener.[33] This technique is similar to the technique used in the transformation by J. S. Bach of the secular melody of "O Sacred Head Surrounded" into worship music.[34] Of course, not all composers are J. S. Bach. But the principle remains the same.

## Parish Musicians: Ecumenical

Another group of parish musicians has used worship music borrowed from other English and vernacular traditions: Anglican chant, Lutheran hymnody, etc. While this effort tells us little about principles for the use of secular music in worship, it is very revealing in providing information about how religious music of a particular denomination serves to reflect that particular religious culture. For example, the tune *Ein' Feste Burg* (in English: "A Mighty Fortress is Our God") by Martin Luther carries with it a Lutheran cultural identity. To introduce this music into a Roman liturgy as a gathering song in 1670 was a sign of heresy; in 1970, a sign of ecumenical openness. Music carries the culture more than even most musicians are aware, and the significance of the particular religious culture will always be part of the cultural ear.

## Parish Musicians: Eclectic

A final group of parish musicians began using music of eclectic styles.[35] They were aware of Gregorian chant and the sacred treasury, and they drew from this resource on occasion. The best of these musicians have rejected popular music as worship music, recognizing that the parishioners want something which sounds "different" from the immediate secular culture. Sometimes these better musicians use a ritual-functional model to make a musical judgment, asking: "Does the music work ritually?" Sometimes the music will be further examined to determine if it "sounds" (read "is encoded") as if it will fit the sensitivities (read "cultural ear") of the parishioners. Often this group will draw on ecumenical resources and, more rarely, on music created in a monastic environment.

## Parish Musician: A Summary

|  | CIMS | UL | PASTORAL |
|---|---|---|---|
| Starting Point | Treasury/Chant | New Effort | What Works |
| Foundation | Music | Liturgy | Practice |
| Nationality | Roman-Germanic | French-Dutch | American |
| Terms | Sacred Music | Ritual Music | Pastoral Music |
| Sender | Large Music Forces | Parochial Limitations | Parochial Limitations |
| Encoding | Chant/Treasury | Ritual Function | Multiple/Eclectic |
| Medium | Large acoustic buildings | Parochial buildings/ Diversity | Dry Acoustics |
| Decoding | Germanic Cultural Ear | French Cultural Ear | American Cultural Ear |
| Receiver | Trained Assembly | Untrained Assembly | Untrained Assembly |
|  |  |  |  |
| *Excluded* | *Secular Music* | *Non-Ritual Music* | *Banal Music* |
| Criteria | Treasury/Chant Organic | Ritual Function | Cultural Ear |
| Uncertain | Sacra Pop | Some Music | Chant |

In the last thirty years the work which has taken place at the parochial level in the U.S. has not been driven by theoretical considerations of sacred music or ritual function, as was true of the CIMS and UL groups, but by a desire for congregational participation, shaped by the building and the cultural ear. It was greatly influenced by the experience that chant and the traditional repertoire often did not work acoustically and were foreign to the cultural ear of the assembly. Some initial attempts drew directly from the popular culture, but failed due to inadequacy of the text, the rejection of the secular code associated with the music, or the inappropriateness of the musical form. Other attempts dealt with the codes associated with music. The contemporary liturgical composer, aware of the secular forms, has been masking these codes during the encoding process. The performer, of course, sometimes has respected that mask and sometimes has not. The listener/worshiper, sometimes in the decoding process, has unmasked the codes and rejected the music as "too secular." At other times, the listener/worshiper in the decoding process has responded to the music as charming the cultural ear and has found it unusually appealing for "bringing worship music into the twentieth century." The process of using secular music in the context of the parish model has a highly subjective and volatile component to its interpretation.

## Some Observations

We are now in position to begin establishing some principles regarding the use of secular music in the liturgy:

1. *Those who use the term sacred music as the official term for worship music, by definition exclude its opposite, secular music, from the liturgy: "Nil profanum."*[36] "Sacred music" and "secular music" are linguistically, mutually exclusive.

2. For those who use the term *ritual music* to describe worship music, the issue of sacred/secular is muted. Ritual music functions within a specific culture as ritual music. *If music from the secular culture can function within the ritual as ritual music then it is no longer secular music but ritual music.* Likewise, if music such as chant and music from the sacred treasury can function within the ritual as ritual music, then they are no longer sacred music but ritual music. Functional use determines the appropriateness of the music in worship.

3. Within *cathedral acoustic* settings, music from the high culture often finds a place, while music from the popular culture seems

remarkably out of place. *The acoustics of the large building, the distance between assembly and altar, and the sometimes more trained cultural ear of the assembly support this position.* Modern music using classical compositional techniques seems to be developing in this setting.

4. Within a *monastic* setting, music from the popular culture will be excluded based on a theological principle, viz., that the monastic life-style is counter-cultural.

5. Within *parochial* acoustical settings, music from the popular culture is first judged inappropriate or appropriate due to text. When approaching music *qua music*, we can establish the following observations:

   a. Music from the popular culture is excluded if it exists in an entertainment form, that is, the purpose of the music is *only* to charm the ear of the listener.

   b. Music from the popular culture is excluded from worship music if the decoding process by the assembly associates that music with cultural connotations inappropriate for worship, e.g., ballroom dancing, etc.

   c. Musical compositional and arranging techniques from the popular culture may be utilized in worship if the composer and the performer encode the music in such a way as these sources do not draw attention to themselves. This achievement seems to require the gift of a master composer.

## What does our study of various national approaches reveal?

It should be clear by now that I have barely touched on vast and complicated areas of study: music, culture, liturgy, and the ways in which they interact. I have dared, as well, to approach these topics through an examination of the various cultural prejudices or experiences that ground their starting points because of the work that has been done on the sort of filters that a "cultural ear" creates in each of us. In taking this "turn to the subject," I have deliberately omitted large areas worthy of objective consideration, such as a musical critique of the nature and quality of liturgical text and ritual structure, to name but one area worthy of extensive treatment.

Because I have kept my focus on the starting points that I hold have been assumed (deliberately or accidentally) by three culture/language groups, I have simplified my description of the work that has been accomplished subsequently in each group. It is clear, for example, that the Roman-Germanic School of liturgists and musicians has been greatly influenced in its direction by the work of the great Austrian and German liturgists such as Jungmann and Guardini, but that these liturgists and musicians have done much more than repeat the work that inspired them. French liturgists, on the other hand, have tended to be musician-liturgists, like Joseph Gelineau or Lucien Deiss, but they have also absorbed the historical-liturgical approach borrowed from Germany and, in the case of Deiss and missionaries like him, have reflected on their liturgical experiences in countries without a long history of Christianity or without a strong European heritage of ritual or music. In each case, despite different starting points, both groups of European liturgists have taken paths shaped by the pragmatic results derived from testing their ideas and insights in practice.

I am equally aware that, on this very practical side of the North Atlantic, American practitioners have held on to musical standards and liturgical principles established in Europe as guides to their understanding, principles which are judged in many instances as equal to or more important than their discovery of "what works." In fact, our foundational document for musical-liturgical development in the United States, *Music in Catholic Worship,* has developed in American musicians a sensitivity to the need for a threefold judgment about music to be used in worship. This triple judgment, in effect, names the three starting points I have examined in this paper, for it calls for a liturgical, musical, and pastoral examination of music for worship. And I agree with Edward Foley's insight that these three judgments are actually three aspects of a single act, though that insight is not yet widely shared, as he notes:

> Instead of making a judgment about worship music in terms of a convergence of a number of factors—such as the liturgical, musical, and pastoral appropriateness of a piece of music—this single, tripartite "convergence" of judgments is often fragmented into three separate decisions which alternately displace each other. Thus, a decision about the musical quality of a work is displaced by a judgment or its pastoral effectiveness or liturgical appropriateness.[37]

So what this study points to is that national communities have different starting points. Those starting points may yield wonderful results, but they may also blind liturgists and musicians in one culture to areas that are insufficiently developed from that perspective. Those same starting points may also prejudice judgments about the approaches taken by other cultures with a different starting point. An approach characterized by a strong musical focus, for example, may pay insufficient attention to liturgical/ritual concerns; the rich musical heritage of one nation or group of nations may also keep their liturgical/musical experts from recognizing that the level of commitment to that heritage in one country may differ from the interest in or understanding of that heritage in another. The ambivalence of the Roman-Germanic School toward the development of inculturated music in Africa is but one example of this truth.

Likewise, the overuse of ritual-functional criteria, when applied to music, may exclude from consideration a range of factors critical to a different understanding of liturgy as celebration. So ritual-functionalists may not understand why U.S. congregations insist on singing a final hymn, when no music is called for at that point in the Order of Mass, because they do not understand the American need to bring the celebration to a resolution for purposes of community building. On the other hand, the *exclusive* use of the pastoral judgment interpreted as a practical evaluation of effectiveness—"they sing it"—is insufficient in itself to establish any criteria for worship music beyond a somewhat cynical pragmatism.

A second lesson that emerges from this examination of starting points is that music, from each of these three perspectives, is symbolic of an entire theology of worship and thus of church that attaches itself to one or another aspect of the work of the Second Vatican Council. So the Roman-Germanic tendency to cling to and build from the heritage of chant and polyphony reveals a perspective on liturgy and on church life that emphasizes continuity with a historical past, specifically, with Christendom. Its reading of the conciliar documents would stress the historical and hierarchical aspects of *Lumen Gentium* (Dogmatic Constitution on the Church) and *Sacrosanctum Concilium*. A ritual-functional focus, on the other hand, treats music as one of many ritual tools to be used in creating a present experience. Links with the past (especially with an idealized golden age), while part of the mix from this perspective, are not as important as attention to the sacramental efficacy of liturgy in the present: liturgy as the revelation of Christ among us for the sake of the whole world (SC #7).

The American approach to ritual music, on the other hand, is part of a whole response by the U.S. Church to the conciliar recognition of the need to recover the meaning of baptism and the communal nature of worship, especially in light of our culture's overwhelming focus on individualism. From the first days of postconciliar renewal, American attention has been focused on the phrase "full, conscious, and active participation" by "all the faithful" (SC #14). The U.S. Church, in addition, did not fail to notice the next sentence in the liturgy constitution: "Such participation by the Christian people as 'a chosen race, a royal priesthood, a holy nation, God's own people' (1 Pet 2:9; see 2:4-5) is their right and duty by reason of their baptism" (SC #14). In other words, we heard the call for the assembly's participation, especially through music, as a call for the transfer of responsibility for worship from the clergy alone to the whole assembly as "their right and duty by reason of their baptism." Musical participation was recognized as the best way to symbolize that transfer and that ecclesiology.

What was often perceived from a European perspective as the unusual attention paid by the American Church to whether the assembly sang or not was, for us, a strategic, ritual (indeed, sacramental) way of expressing the sense of liturgy that has received a measure of official sanction in the statement from the *Catechism of the Catholic Church* that "it is the whole *community*, the Body of Christ united with its Head, that celebrates . . . In the celebration of the sacraments it is thus the whole assembly that is *leitourgos*, each according to [proper] function, but in the 'unity of the Spirit' who acts in all."[38] This basic insight into the communal aspect of Christian sacrament has caused us to abandon chant, not because of any dislike for chant, but because most of Gregorian chant, like most of the treasury of polyphony, was music for a small group of trained musicians, not for the whole assembly. Not only was it practically true that, in most places, the people did not sing chant when it was offered, it was also true that this repertoire could not, apart from the basic psalm tones, for example, express what was for many Americans the key insight of the conciliar reform: liturgy, like church, is something that belongs by right to all the baptized, not to a professional elite. So the assembly's inability or unwillingness to associate with a music that was composed to be sung by a musical elite was deemed reason enough to start on a different approach to music for worship.

Another movement that reveals our desire to explore the foundational aspects of our religious identity and practice—and a development that has also left some Europeans baffled—is our strong focus on, and the great success of, restoring the catechumenate and the whole process of adult initiation. This ritual has begun to shape our celebrations of Lent and the Paschal Triduum, and it is reshaping our understanding of what a parish is and what it should be about. Given such developments, is it a stretch to point out as an unsurpising sociological reality that the churches of Western Europe have in general taken an approach to music for worship that emphasizes the tradition of a (Western European) sacred treasury, while the United States has looked to a more democratic principle as its starting point? Musical participation and baptismal awareness are seen in America as symbols of the people's engagement in and ownership of the act of worship before God.

In a sense, the Catholic Church in the United States has been set adrift from its European liturgical roots by its steadfast focus on congregational involvement and baptismal responsibility and, thus, drawn to experiment with music that is not rooted in our heritage. We in the United States have paid a great price for the freedom to experiment with secular music. We have gone down some blind alleys. We have made some mistakes. So far, the rewards for exercising this freedom have not been overwhelming, for we have yet to find appropriate ways of expressing musically the sacramental and ecclesial truths that are motivating us. But we are making some progress, and experimentation is the American way. If we are to have a worship music for our times, then this is certainly not the time to stop the experimentation. What is needed, instead, is a greater exchange among nations that have each been working to express one or another facet of the multifaceted mystery that is church and, therefore, worship.

---

[1] Denis J. Hughes, "Editorial Introduction" to the issue "Worship and Popular Culture," *Reformed Liturgy and Music*, 30:2, 42.

[2] Gerald Lardner, "Communication Theory and Liturgical Research," *Worship* 51 (1977) 299–307. Gilbert Ostdiek served as chairperson of the Social Science Study Group of the North American Academy of Liturgy from 1976 to 1991, and I was an active member of that group during those years.

[3] See Jean-Jacques Nattiez, "Reflections on the Development of Semiotics in Music," trans. Katherine Ellis, *Music Analysis* 8 (1989) 22. See also Chapter III, "Philosophies and Theologies of Music" in Judith Marie Kubicki, C.S.S.F., *Jacques Berthier's Taizé Music*, unpublished dissertation, Catholic University of America, 1997.

[4] Audiation is the hearing equivalent of visualization, of hearing the sound without it being physically present. See Edwin Gordon, *The Primary Measures of Audiation* (Chicago: GIA Publications, Inc. 1979) and *Learning Skills in Music: Skill Content, and Patterns*, editor (Chicago: GIA Publications, Inc. 1993).

[5] See Marshall McLuhan's seminal works, *The Gutenberg Galaxy* (Toronto: University of Toronto Press, 1962) and *Understanding Media* (New York: McGraw-Hill, 1964).

[6] Alfred Tomatis, *L'Oreille et le Langage* (Editions du Seuil, collection Points-Sciences, 1963), English translation: *The Ear and Language* (Moulin, 1996); *Vers l'Ecoute Humaine*, tomes I et II (Editions ESF, Collection Sciences de l'Education, 1974); *L'Oreille et la Vie* (Editions Robert Laffont, Collection Reponse Sainte, 1977); *L'Oreille et la Voix* (Editions Robert Laffont, 1987); *Pourquoi Mozart* (Fixot, 1991); *Ecuter L'Univers* (Laffont, 1996).

[7] "Synaptic patterns" equal neurons, axons, and their corresponding dendrites, charged by electrical activity. At birth a baby's brain contains one hundred billion neurons and a trillion glial cells. "Electrical activity, triggered by a

flood of sensory experiences, fine-tunes the brain's circuitry—determining which connections will be retained and which will be pruned," *Time*, February 3 (1997) 51.

[8] J. Madeleine Nash, "Fertile Minds," reporting the work of neurobiologist Carla Shatz, University of California, Berkeley, *Time*, February 3 (1997). See also, in *Musica Research Notes* [http:\\www.musica.uci.edu], "The Musical Infant" and "Patterns of Opinion" (Spring, 1994); "Musical Building Blocks in the Brain" (Fall, 1994); "The Earliest Music Lessons" (Spring, 1995); "The Musical Infant and the Roots of Consonance" (Spring 1997).

[9] Don Campbell, *Introduction to the Musical Brain* (Magna Music, 1983); see also *The Mozart Effect* (New York: Avon Books, 1997).

[10] Thomas Moore, *Care of the Soul* (New York: HarperCollins, 1992).

[11] English translation of *Sacrosanctum Concilium* (Constitution on the Sacred Liturgy, hereafter SC) and other international documents issued between 1963 and 1979 is from International Commission on English in the Liturgy, *Documents on the Liturgy 1963–1979: Conciliar, Papal, and Curial Texts* (Collegeville: The Liturgical Press, 1982); hereafter DOL.

[12] DOL, document 506, #4118.

[13] I am aware that the participating organizations of CIMS vary from country to country but, for this paper, I am using the writings of Johannes Overath to represent the CIMS position. See *Crux et Cithara, Selected essays on liturgy and sacred music translated and edited on the occasion of the seventieth birthday of Johannes Overath*, Robert Skeris, trans. and ed. (Alotting: Verlag Alfred Coppenrath, 1983).

[14] Many regions and/or dioceses published a version of *Gotteslob* with regional supplements; Luxembourg renamed the hymnal *Magnificat*. The music reflects the standard established: The compositions are inspired by Gregorian chant and fit the cultural ear of the German-speaking countries.

[15] M. Francis Mannion, "Paradigms in American Catholic Church Music," *Worship* 70:2 (March 1996) 120–1.

[16] Quoted from SC #10 in Mannion, "Paradigms," 121.

[17] Letter of Archbishop A. Dell'Acqua, May 11, 1966. And this decision was questioned by CIMS.

[18] Bernard Huijbers, *The Performing Audience* (now available from Oregon Catholic Press).

[19] See footnote 5. The American musical community has developed this notion through the *Milwaukee Symposia for Church Composers: A Ten Year Report* (Chicago: Liturgy Training Publications, and Washington, D.C., The Pastoral Press, 1992). See also: J. Michael Joncas, *From Sacred Song to Ritual Music* (Collegeville: The Liturgical Press, 1997).

[20] See Gino Stephani, *Il linguaggio della musica* (Roma: Edizioni Paoline, 1982).

[21] Edward Foley, "The Ritual Function of Beauty: From Assisi to Snowbird," *Pastoral Music* 21:3 (Feb.–Mar., 1997) 17.

[22] See Rembert Weakland, "Music and Liturgy in Evolution," *Church Music in Crisis* (Collegeville: The Liturgical Press, 1966) 5, 13.

[23] "The Milwaukee Symposia for Church Composers: A Ten Year Report, July 9, 1992," in *Pastoral Music* 17:1 (Oct.–Nov. 1992) 19–50.

[24] UL Conviction #6. See Claude Duchesneau and Michel Veuthey, *Music and Liturgy: The Universa Laus Document and Commentary*, trans. Paul Inwood (Washington, D.C.: The Pastoral Press, 1992) 27.

[25] *Universa Laus Guidelines*. Initially published in *English Bulletin of Universa Laus*, 30 (1980); these guidelines are now available in Duchesneau and Veuthey, *Music and Liturgy*. See also *Aide Memoire UL*, Excepts from the UL Bulletin, 1973–1983 (Washington, D.C.: NPM Publications, 1996).

[26] "There is a common disagreement between those who believe that the only appropriate music is that which is instantly communicable to all the faithful and others who hold that an insistence on vocal participation by everybody underrates the use, demanded by much music of the European classical tradition, of mind and senses." *In Tune With Heaven, The Report of the Archbishop's Commission on Church Music*, #68 (London: Church House Publishing, 1992) 37.

[27] The association of Catholic Church musicians that formed in the United States in response to postconciliar reforms chose to name itself the National Association of Pastoral Musicians.

[28] Mark Searle, "Semper Reformanda: The Opening and Closing Rites of the Mass," in Peter C. Finn and James M. Schellman, eds. *Shaping English Liturgy: Studies in Honor of Archbishop Denis Hurley* (Washington, D.C.: The Pastoral Press, 1990) 90.

[29] Previously, I have identified five such distinctive ways of/settings for liturgy: Monastic, Cathedral, Communication, Dramatic, and Small Group: see Virgil C. Funk, "Enculturation, Style and the Sacred-Secular Debate" in Lawrence A. Hoffman and Janet R. Walton, eds., *Sacred Sound and Social Change: Liturgical Music in Jewish and Christian Experience* (Notre Dame, Ind.: University of Notre Dame Press, 1992).

[30] From a liturgical standpoint, a very questionable gain.

[31] Johannes Overath, *Crux*, 72.

[32] The literature on "associations" in music is wide and controversial. From the romantic period's use of *leitmotif* to our present-day use of background music in movies to tell us what emotion we should have, music relates to the world of the symbolic. For a recent study, see Judith Kubicki, *Jacques Berthier's Taizé Music: A Case Study of Liturgical Music as Ritual Symbol*, unpublished doctoral dissertation, 1997.

[33] J. Michael Joncas, Marty Haugen, and Christopher Walker are among the current composers to admit publicly that they deliberately encode their music with contemporary codes from Broadway show tunes.

[34] Numerous examples of this musical transformation abound, e.g., the orchestral music used by Monteverdi for the *"Deus in Adjutorium"* in his *Vespers of the Blessed Virgin* is borrowed from the prologue to his opera, *Orfeo;* Bach's *Christmas Oratorio* comes from a profane cantata, *Die Wahl des Hercules*.

[35] A wide variety of such composers exits in the United States, represented in Catholic hymnals beginning with the *Peoples Mass Book* in 1966 and continuing in publications from GIA Publications (Chicago), OCP Publications (Portland), and World Library Publications (Chicago).

[36] Johannes Overath, "Music and Faith," in *Crux*, 72.

[37] Edward Foley, "From Displacement to Convergence: Evaluating Roman Catholic Ritual Music," *Pastoral Music* 19:3 (Feb.–Mar. 1995) 21. See also a study of this concern in Ricky Manalo, C.S.P., *Music Ritual and Evaluation: A Retrieval of the Three-Fold Judgment,* unpublished master's thesis, Washington Theological Union, 1997.

[38] *Catechism of the Catholic Church,* official English translation #1140 (Washington, D.C.: United States Catholic Conference, 1994) 1144.

# Why Catholics Must Sing

*Frank C. Quinn, O.P.*

In *Catechesis for Liturgy* Gilbert Ostdiek writes:

> Two decades ago the liturgical renewal touched off some major advances and changes in our singing patterns. A comparison of our present experience with that of the days of the "low" masses is instructive. By contrast, the presider does very little singing now, and choirs may either be non-existent or play a sharply reduced role. Rather, the bulk of the singing is now done by the assembly, supported by instrumentalists and led by cantor or small choral group. When choirs do sing, it is usually in support of or in musical dialogue with the assembly. Think too, of when and what we sing. The motets and hymns in the seams have lost their pride of place to the responses and acclamations we sing during the liturgy of the word and the great Eucharistic Prayer.[1]

Singing assemblies, non-singing presiders, choirs aiding the assembly, the liturgical voices of cantors, the faithful singing music belonging to the core of liturgical rituals: the author's description of such changes from the pre-Vatican II Church is certainly correct. And such changes continue in our churches today. All one has to do is to think of what goes on in most Roman Catholic churches: Mass with a cantor or leader of song, accompanied by guitar or piano or organ. Sometimes, if the musicians are available at a particular liturgy, there is a combination of musical forces.

Further changes have taken place since the conclusions drawn by the author in the mid-1980s. In particular we note the growth in liturgical choirs in many parts of the country. In numerous churches there are one or more choirs—adult choirs, children's choirs, folk choirs, regular choirs, the variations are many—that sing at the major Sunday

Masses. Depending upon the quality of the musical and liturgical leadership these Eucharists, in which the choir sings with and for the assembly, can be the highpoints of the Sunday celebrations and draw a number of people of different stripe, depending upon the type of music chosen and the quality of celebrations themselves. Or they might continue as the "high Masses" of old, where the musical quality of the choir performance kept people from attending those particular services.

And in the 1990s we face new situations: multi-lingual and multi-cultural liturgies with the attendant demands on music and musicians.

Ostdiek's comments about the presider, that he "does very little singing now," remains quite true by and large. In fact, considering the liturgical celebrations of the Eastern Churches and even the Roman Catholic liturgies of the past, one has to admit that today a singing presider is the exception. Ironically, at a time when composers are publishing Eucharistic Prayers with full musical settings, an entirely new musical approach in terms of traditional Roman Catholic practice, where until the late 60s, the Eucharistic Prayer was the silent preserve of the priest, few presiders overall are willing or perhaps capable of attempting to sing them.

The author is also correct in his assertion that assemblies are singing in a way in which Catholics were not allowed to do for centuries. A very important point Ostdiek raises is that when assemblies sing they do so at important ritual moments rather than at the "edges and seams of liturgy."[2] And certainly the author's observation that various musical forms bespeak differing ecclesiologies is an insightful way of looking at how music is chosen for liturgical celebration, particularly in terms of balance.[3]

When twentieth century Catholics first began to sing vernacular music in worship, especially after the 1958 "Instruction on Sacred Music" was issued,[4] they usually sang four hymns or psalms at processional points in the then Latin Tridentine Mass. Not only did they not sing at the important ritual moments of the liturgy, their singing was not even considered liturgical, since it was in the vernacular.[5] After Vatican II, things began to change. Assemblies were encouraged to sing not only during processional moments but to add their voice to the praise of God within the important ritual structures of the liturgical rites, for example, during the liturgy of the word and within the Eucharistic Prayer. Such singing was now considered "liturgical." Thus, the voice of the baptized came to be heard once more in the liturgies of the Roman Catholic Church.[6]

Since Vatican II, enough has been written on the subject of music for the liturgy and popular participation that it would seem to be a foregone conclusion that (a) music is integral to liturgical performance, and (b) no matter who else sings, the assembly is the dominant voice.[7] However, despite official statements and an enormous growth industry in music for the liturgy, it seems to me that we are still very much at the beginning. The court remains out with regard to the success or failure of the post-Vatican II reforms. We may well ask the question: how far have we progressed in our understanding of liturgy essentially as sung liturgy involving assembly and ministers, since Gil Ostdiek described the liturgical situation in parishes in the mid-1980s? In assessing the roles of assembly, ministers, cantors, and choir in the majority of our parishes, how healthy is the actual situation?[8] Let us revisit the areas Ostdiek treated—assembly, musicians, worship leaders—and ask how things have changed since 1986.

## The Awakened Assembly

Lucien Deiss writes of the pre-Vatican II Church:

> In the past when one asked "Who celebrates?" the answer was "the priest." Since Vatican II, however, the answer is "the community." In the past when one asked "Who sings?" the answer was "the choir." Today, after Vatican II, the answer must be "the community."[9]

This trenchant way of putting things illustrates something that we still need to be reminded of, even this far removed from the council. The practices envisaged by Deiss have obtained in the Roman Catholic Church for well over a thousand years. The renewed stress on the liturgical role of the baptized by the *Constitution on the Sacred Liturgy*[10] was quite exciting at the time the constitution was promulgated. It offered a new vision of what official liturgy is all about: the prayer of the body of Christ, the community of the baptized. It relocated ministry as a service arising from the community and for the community, rather than a sacred office totally outside the community. Liturgical celebration was seen as the heart of Christian corporate prayer, whereby the community remembers and enters into the ever-present paschal mystery of Jesus. Rather than a "public work" done for the people by its ordained ministers, liturgy was envisaged as the "work" of the people with its ministers.

Such insights were exhilarating for several reasons. First, they transformed the way liturgy was conceived of in the Roman Catholic Church. Instead of thinking of liturgy as a kind of official religious action carried out for God's honor, whether or not the Church was actually involved, now liturgical celebration became the means whereby the baptized assembly carried out its office as the body of Christ. A corollary to this observation is the realization that liturgy really cannot be thought of as something existing in itself, with no consideration of the fact that it is an action carried out by living human beings.[11]

Second, such rethinking of the purpose of liturgy led to a renewed ecclesiology wherein the People of God constituted the primary body of the Church, hierarchical structuring being secondary.[12] Such a theology of communion, whereby the baptized are in some type of relationship as the body of Christ, is made visible in liturgical celebration in which all the baptized celebrate their oneness in Christ, but at the same time pray for all other communities that make up the Church Catholic. In liturgy all invoke God to send the one Spirit to gather all Christians into one great chorus of praise and petition.

Third, a renewed concept of the role of the assembly in worship meant that changes had to be made so that this role could actually be realized. Thus the emphasis in the *Constitution on the Sacred Liturgy* is both on the *participatio actuosa* of the liturgical assembly as absolutely essential to all future liturgical celebrations and also on the means whereby such participation could and would be carried out.

The radically new concept of the people's role, of the assembly as active rather than passive, demanded extensive catechesis. Such catechesis was made a priority in the *Constitution on the Sacred Liturgy*.[13] What probably was not fully understood at the time—and still remains to be fully actualized in the life of all parishes—is that such catechesis needs to be ongoing. Although there is a specific and formal location for such catechesis within the process of Christian initiation, for those baptized in infancy other means of formation must be found. It is here that we have failed the most.

One very important goal of such catechesis is to help the baptized to both acknowledge and, even more important, to accept their role in liturgical worship. Such a role flows directly from and is a necessary consequence to baptism itself.[14] If, as our baptismal theology suggests, the baptized participate in the charism of Christ's royal priesthood, and if the latter is exercised in the worship of God with Christ the head and in the Holy Spirit, then it is in the actualization of this aspect of our baptism along with the other baptized that we achieve that which we are baptized into: entrance into the death of Christ in baptism leading to a life of worship and work whereby we "live" into the resurrection.[15]

Since liturgy is a reality that involves the arts of music and space and sight, and especially involves the human body in motion, gesture, movement, posture, musical and spoken response, ecstatic acclamations, lyrical songs, exercising Christ's priesthood can only be accomplished in action. It is not achieved in meditating or thinking about it, nor is it accomplished in writing about it or discussing it in class. It is realized in the doing. To deepen one's life direction in Christ, the Christian gathers with others in order, as a corporate entity, to do worship. What else do we mean when we say that the Catholic view of life and worship is "sacramental"?

So important is this truth that Shawn Madigan has dedicated an entire book to the liturgy as the fundamental way in which the baptized are spiritually formed. And because liturgy, in contrast to all other methodologies, is about our insertion into the entirety of the paschal mystery of Jesus Christ so that our entire life takes on paschal overtones, Madigan concludes that the liturgy is spiritual direction, but spiritual direction of a special kind. She calls it "corporate spiritual direction," since in liturgy we are involved with the assembly of persons celebrating their corporate life in Christ, not with individuals each searching their own way.[16]

The individual baptized may not be explicitly aware of all these ramifications of living out the baptismal sacrament, but certainly there is some consciousness that Christian life is not a passive reality. The responsibility for helping the Christian faithful enter more fully into that which they have already been baptized falls on the shoulders of those who minister in the Church, ordained and non-ordained. It is demonstrated by liturgical ministers, from presider to usher, all who image full commitment to the life of worship. It is made explicit by the preacher, whether in the language of homily, a faithful preaching through the Scriptures, or in other preaching or educational events.

Some accuse the post-Vatican II liturgical reforms or the way the reforms were done of leading to a loss of mystery, a loss that ironically occurred when the assembly could finally understand what was going on! And certain groups today are demanding a "reform of the reform."[17] In listening to these critics one quickly becomes aware that their concerns are not grounded in a corporate view of liturgical celebration but rather remain interred in a past where liturgy was something to be watched from a distance by an individual who just happened to be sitting in a congregation where other individuals also carried out their "devotions." Ironically this view of liturgy reinforces the notion of rugged individualism in contemporary American society.

In actuality, the authentic mystery of the liturgy was relocated by Vatican II: there is now demanded a commitment to liturgical worship on the part of the individual, a commitment to the corporate worship of the community and the living out of that corporate worship in daily life. This corporate undertaking counters the whole thrust of American individualism, of going it alone. There is no doubt that such engagement is difficult in light of our culture. And yet it is not impossible. For here is where we work out our salvation. The mystery of God-with-us is what we are about. And so authentic liturgical mystery demands relationship, acknowledgement of the corporate body that worships, and personal commitment to be part of that worshiping body. In other words, worship demands engagement not only with God but with others. Worship is corporate activity; and there is where the mystery is really celebrated and experienced. Not only has the renewal of worship not done away with authentic mystery, it has focused on the real mystery, not simply on the "mystery" of a liturgy that was not understood and that did not involve the community.

## The Singing Assembly

An awakened assembly is a committed assembly and a committed assembly is a singing assembly. Without singing, such commitment cannot be brought into full actualization. Thus the title of the article: "Why Catholics Must Sing."[18] One may argue, as does Thomas Day, that singing is not what Americans do, particularly Irish Americans.[19] One may even claim that it is unnecessary to sing in order to carry out one's liturgical duties. And there is no doubt that when we examine the ritual texts published in the United States for use by the presiding ministers, precious little music appears in place. None of these observations, however, invalidate a fundamental principle of corporate liturgical engagement: a committed assembly is a singing assembly because corporate response is enabled through singing in a way that is impossible in spoken recitation.

The whole issue of not only who sings in liturgy, but why, is not always a central concern in discussion and writing about liturgical music because it is such a broad area of concern. In writing on liturgical music it is quite easy to deal only with the musical side—the history of liturgical music, the different styles of liturgical music both in history as well as in our contemporary multicultural universe, the ritual demands for specific forms, the kind of music Catholics sing over against the kind of music proper to the liturgies of other Christian churches—that we may forget who does the music or who should do the music. When considering the liturgical act and the type of music demanded by each ritual structure within that act, it is almost inevitable that the focus on how music shapes ritual and ritual shapes musical forms could dominate our consciousness rather than keeping to the forefront of our minds the fundamental body that worships, the assembly.[20]

It is also easy to concentrate on who sings and how much they sing —ministers, choir, congregation—and forget that liturgy is not a contest in which everyone gets an equal share of the pie. In other words, when reading the many documents that have been promulgated on the issue of music for worship, or when speaking about the topic with others, it is all too easy to stay within the rarefied atmosphere of the theoretical, forgetting that liturgy and liturgical music exist only in the doing. That is where we test our ecclesiology and our liturgical convictions.

There may, therefore, be many variations in practice in the enormous number of parishes that dot the United States. Cathedral churches will celebrate in one way, simply because of the orchestration of large spaces, smaller rural churches will realize the same liturgies in quite different ways. One parish may have a large number of musical ministries, including, for example, organ, piano, synthesizer, guitars and other string instruments, woodwinds, etc. Other churches may at times lack instruments entirely and rely on the unaccompanied voices of assembly, ministers, cantor, and choir. These variations, or better, complications, are to be expected. But none of this is important if the role of the assembly is ignored or overlooked. Some may remember the way certain composers first began to deal with the Vatican II demand for the assembly's participation. In effect, a very few nuggets were handed to the assembly while the major amount of music was given to the choir. It was immediately evident that the composer's concern was for the carefully crafted composition and its performance; to that end the role of the assembly was reduced to a minimum so that the music itself would not suffer from the singing of an untrained group.

Another factor unique to Roman Catholic parishes is the sheer number of eucharistic liturgies celebrated in them on Saturday/Sunday. In contrast to other Christian churches as well as the Orthodox churches, the number and times of celebration in Roman Catholic churches present problems unique to these churches. With all the best will in the world, liturgical musicians and ministers find it difficult to promote the worship of all the different assemblies that make up one Roman Catholic parish. And yet, in all such situations what is expected, what is even assumed, however worship is orchestrated, is the full sung participation of the assembly. Only in this way can we accomplish the vision of liturgy that has challenged us since Vatican II.

It is difficult to explain this in easy fashion to Catholic ministers, ordained and non-ordained, let alone to the Catholic faithful. Part of the reason for this is that we have come out of a lengthy period of theologizing upon the sacramental "moment" in contrast to liturgical "embellishments" of that moment—and we still find some parishes living out of that particular form of liturgical spirituality. Not only did this period concentrate on exactly when a sacrament is accomplished to the exclusion of all other "ceremonial" elements, it was a theology that concentrated in the extreme on individual "reception" of the sacraments.

Another difficulty arises from the fact that often we only pay lip-service to the ecclesiology arising from Vatican II, an ecclesiology that presents the Church as a sacramental reality. If Church as sacrament is taken seriously, then it is absolutely essential to start with the local church, the visible gathering of the body of Christ in which Christ is present. Although in Roman Catholic theology the local church is conceived of as the diocese, all people and ministers gathered around the bishop in his cathedral,[21] the sacramental principle extends to the gathering of Catholics in their local parishes, each one of which makes the Church as body of Christ visible and active. Such sacramental visibility is primarily founded in the gathering of the assembly, not in the sole appearance of the priest at the altar.[22] In recent days, however, given the worries about the shortage of presbyters as well as the change in the character of bishops being appointed to United States dioceses, it is clear that the focus is shifting from the larger vision of the way the Church is sacramentally made visible—the unique gathering of assembly and its ministers, carrying out the liturgy in a corporate fashion through movement, gesture, speech, and singing—to a narrowing intention of "protecting" the role of the priest and working out ways in which dioceses can provide such ministers for as large a number of parishes as possible. Within this worldview the necessary priority of enabling the faithful to commit themselves to sung liturgy does not always command attention.

There are also practical consequences in striving to realize the ideal of a singing congregation. In many churches the actual commitment of the assembly to fulfilling its role is frustrated by the building's architecture, its sound system, and even the very musicians whose task it is to aid the assembly. Many of our churches were built within a different ecclesial universe, where instead of focusing on the central role of the assembly, focus was on the altar and the tabernacled sacrament. Such a view of the Church and its liturgy continues even today in many of the newer churches because the builders, restorers, building committees, and clergy do not always operate out of the conviction that the assembly is primary. Such lack of conviction in the assembly is immediately evident on entering fully carpeted churches which create an intimate living room space rather than a congregational acoustical space.

Acoustically speaking, a number of churches continue to acquire sound systems on the cheap. Often, committees or pastors are sold such systems by salespeople who are not properly qualified to deal with the roles of both the singing assembly and the ministers who lead and preach to that assembly.[23]

Along with architectural and acoustical issues there is the question of the self-awareness of many of our pastoral musicians about how best to fulfill their tasks. What I mean by this is that some pastoral musicians think that by simply announcing the music to be sung and singing and playing it themselves, all will be well. Some even think this can be done without ever being seen by the congregation. Often, one or two singers and lone guitar will "lead" the assembly from a secure location in the church balcony! And even if they operate within full view of the assembly, there is still the problem of how such few forces and instruments can lead and enable the singing of the main body of the church, even if over-amplified.

It is necessary for any pastoral musician to have an image of himself or herself as a facilitator of the assembly's participation. Thus, clear directions, appropriately modest use of microphones when singing *with* the assembly, a presence which speaks of one's wanting to be there, to be with this particular group, and a conviction that every piece of music used in a celebration either contributes to or detracts from the faith-life of this congregation here and now is an appropriate beginning to effective musical leadership.

## The Assembly and Its Ministers

Of the many issues that need further discussion as well as continued implementation—the role of the choir and cantors as members of the assembly, what music belongs to the assembly as assembly, what makes good and effective liturgical music—one important area for consideration is the relation of the ministers, especially the presiding minister, to the assembly and how this is realized in musical sound. It has been my contention in this essay that a singing assembly is absolutely fundamental to liturgical celebration. But is it also necessary for the ministers to engage not only in singing with the assembly (this goes without saying) but in sung dialogue with the assembly.

What is of concern here is the recognition that if liturgical celebration is inherently musical it involves more than the assembly's voice or the choir's voice. Somehow it must involve the voice of the ministers. And since the relation of the ministers to the congregation is dialogical it seems very strange when there is a total contrast between a speaking presider and a singing congregation. One may notice this, for example, when insistence is placed on the congregation's singing the eucharistic acclamations—and emphasis among today's liturgical musicians is to add to the number of such acclamations both within the Eucharistic Prayer as well as in the great blessing prayers of other rites—while the presider engages only in speaking the Eucharistic Prayer. This creates a kind of "friction" between minister and assembly. Each inhabits different oral universes, one musical, with all the word "musical" implies, the other spoken.[24]

The renewed understanding of liturgy and liturgical participation, inaugurated by the *Constitution on the Sacred Liturgy,* was sufficiently daunting to put the musical role of ministers into the background. New and more important musical issues arose, particularly the need to get Roman Catholic congregations to sing. The need to provide music for the assembly, both in terms of publication and use, overshadowed all else. With the changes made in all the rites, the need to instruct the people, and the enormous task of transforming worshiping congregations into singing congregations, to convert audience to assembly, it is not at all surprising that certain elements of liturgical practice were not given priority.

Before Vatican II, of course, ministers were expected to sing their parts in sung Masses. But the emphasis on such singing was not on a presider's role vis-à-vis the assembly. Rather, before the mid-1960s ministerial chanting was founded in the particular status of a Mass (along with the stipendiary reward for celebration). The importance of a particular Eucharist was not based upon the presence or role of the assembly, but rather on two factors having little to do with the faithful: the number and differentiation of ministers and the amount of chanting done by the presider. A solemn Mass called for priest, deacon, sub-deacon, and acolytes, with the singing of all the ministerial texts. A high Mass called upon the priest alone to sing the readings, prayers, preface, conclusion to the Eucharistic Prayer, and the Our Father. An acolyte or other singer was necessary to answer the priest. By contrast, a low Mass was a Mass in which no singing was done by the presider; thus, it was known as a "read" Mass. It did not matter whether or not the congregation sang sacred songs. All depended upon the ordained minister. Perhaps one reason for the demise of ministerial chanting after Vatican II was a result of a reaction on the part of some priests to immediate past practice. A renewed ecclesiology insisted on the role of the faithful, of the assembly gathered for worship. The singing of the minister, realized in such a pro forma way in the past, simply did not fit into this new picture of liturgy.

After about thirty years of living with the post-Vatican II changes, the question may be posed: have we matured in our understanding and practice of liturgical celebration? In terms of actual celebration do we recognize the fact, testified to throughout the ages, that liturgy is inherently musical, not only in aesthetic terms, but in terms of how ritual celebrations are actually accomplished by a group of people? If we agree that liturgy is inherently musical, as well as being constituted by ritual actions and not simply by ritual words, are we in accord with the fact that part of the musical performance in liturgy is that accomplished by those leading the celebration, particularly in the interaction of presider and assembly? In other words, do we recognize the fundamental dialogical character of Catholic liturgy?

Again, let me add that one of the hindrances to an appreciation of ministerial singing is the perception that such singing is only pro forma or, worse, simply satisfies the ego of the presider. And yet, anyone who attends an Eastern Rite liturgy knows that the constant singing of ministers is taken for granted and, along with the singing of choir and people, enables such liturgies to be carried forward. In fact, one seldom hears a word being spoken, unless, as in the case of those Byzantine Christians in union with Rome, preaching has been restored to the liturgy. In other words, the inherent musical quality of the liturgy is first realized, not in hymns and antiphons and refrains, but in the dialogical chants shared by ministers and people and in the prose prayers belonging to the leader or, as in the case of the Our Father and Creed, to leader and people.

In some sections of the English-speaking Catholic world, there seems to be a new appreciation for singing the liturgy on the part of ministers and people. How this appreciation will evolve remains to be seen. But I do think we are at a new stage in our understanding and appreciation for doing liturgy. I realize there are a number of unresolved issues, not least of which is that many Catholic ministers, both bishops and priests, simply do not appreciate the fact that liturgy is a symbolic action and that it does not consist solely of texts and rubrics found printed in a book. And today we are faced with a new reality when discussing liturgical leadership: the role of non-ordained leaders of prayer. We have not even begun to think of how music plays a role in, for example, *Sunday Celebrations in the Absence of a Priest*.[25]

## The Assembly Today

We began this reflection on the role of the assembly by quoting from Gil Ostdiek's observations about what had occurred in the two decades since the conciliar renewal "touched off some major advances and changes in our singing patterns." Now it is three and a half decades since the *Constitution on the Sacred Liturgy* was promulgated. It has been the purpose of this essay to ask the question as to what extent we have really seized on the fundamental role of the assembly in Catholic liturgy. Have we enabled our Catholic assemblies to commit themselves to one of their primary duties, liturgical celebration? Do we understand liturgy as the "work" of assembly and the assembly's ministers? If so, how is this actualized; to what extent are our congregations singing congregations? Have we really understood what it means to say that liturgy by its very nature is sung liturgy?

As we began, so we conclude with a quotation from Ostdiek:

> If we truly sing, we do not just sing the message of the words; we sing the song "until it is all sung out and there is nothing left to sing." In that kind of singing we truly celebrate and keep feast.[26]

---

[1] Gilbert Osdiek, *Catechesis for Liturgy, A Program for Parish Involvement* (Washington: The Pastoral Press, 1986) 170.

[2] Ibid., 171.

[3] "If we stop and think about it, each of these [musical] forms implies a different ecclesiology of the assembly. Songs performed by choir or soloist stress hierarchical roles. Congregational songs sung in unison speak of the importance and self-sufficiency of the assembly. Songs with a dialogic form imply a theology of the assembly in which both the full equality of all and the ministerial roles of particular members are important. These same implications might be drawn in a larger way from the whole set of songs used in a liturgical celebration." Ibid., 172. Since the author made these remarks, other authors have written more extensively on these matters. Note, in particular, *The Milwaukee Symposia for Church Composers: A Ten Year Report* (Washington, D.C.: National Association of Pastoral Musicians, and Chicago: Liturgical Training Publications, 1992), hereafter cited as MSCC; Edward Foley, "Musical Forms, Referential Meaning, and Belief," in *Ritual Music: Studies in Liturgical Musicology* (Beltsville: The Pastoral Press, 1995) 145–73.

[4] Sacred Congregation of Rites, *Instruction on Sacred Music and Liturgy*, September 3, 1958.

[5] In the *missa lecta* or "read Mass," "the Mass could admit of vernacular, popular music, as well as the spoken Latin dialogue with the presider (giving us the so-called 'dialogue' Mass). It is important to note, however, that such music was not, strictly speaking, liturgical," Frank C. Quinn, "Hymns in Catholic Worship," *Liturgical Ministry* 4 (Fall 1995) 148.

[6] See, among others, Lucien Deiss, *Visions of Liturgy and Music for a New Century* (Collegeville: The Liturgical Press, 1996), especially the section entitled "The Songs of the Mass," 57ff.

[7] Official documents have stressed both of these points from the time of Pius X. In the latter's *Motu proprio, "Tra le sollecitudini,"* (November 22, 1904), the

pope insists, in the very first paragraph on the *participatio actuosa* of the people. But the effective mandating of the peoples' participation is found in the *Constitution on the Sacred Liturgy* [CSL], particularly paragraph 14: "The Church earnestly desires that all the faithful be led to that full, conscious, and active participation in liturgical celebrations called for by the very nature of the liturgy." The embodied character of this participation (in contrast to some who insisted that participation could be only internal) is described in paragraph 30: "To promote active participation, the people should be encouraged to take part by means of acclamations, responses, psalmody, antiphons, and songs, as well as by actions, gestures, and bearing. And at the proper times all should observe a reverent silence." The assembly's musical participation, insisted on by CSL, is implemented in the Sacred Congregation of Rites, *Instruction "Musicam sacram,"* March 5, 1967, AAS 60 (1967) 300–20, and explored in terms of the United States by the semi-official documents issued by the Bishops' Committee on the Liturgy, *Music in Catholic Worship* (MCW), 2nd edition (Washington, D.C.: NCCB Publications Office, 1982 [1972]), and *Liturgical Music Today* (LMT) (Washington, D.C.: NCCB Publications Office, 1982). The Milwaukee document, MSCC, previously referred to, was drafted in order to take into account the developments that had occurred since the publication of MCW and LMT.

[8] One easy way to appreciate the complexity of this question is by reading Francis Mannion's article on different musical/liturgical paradigms and the way they are shaped by and shape sometimes clashing attitudes to Catholic worship. No matter what one may think of the author's choice of paradigms, it quickly becomes evident that there are very different perceptions in the Church today vis-à-vis liturgical music, liturgical celebration, and the actual role of the baptized in worship. See M. Francis Mannion, "Paradigms in American Catholic Church Music," *Worship* 70 (March 1996) 101–28.

[9] Deiss, 27.

[10] CSL 14, 30.

[11] It is well to remind ourselves, considering the fact that for a lengthy period the liturgy was conceived as something existing in itself, with little connection to the Christian people, that the ancient focus was first on the assembly, and secondly on what that assembly did: celebrate its life in Christ. On this, see P. M. Gy, "History of the Liturgy in the West to the Council of Trent," *The Church at Prayer*, Volume 1, edited by A. G. Martmort (Collegeville: The Liturgical Press, 1987) 46: "During this period [from the beginning of the Church to the early Middle Ages] forms of prayer are distinguished less as liturgical or non-liturgical than by degrees of ecclesiality, the highest degree being the prayer of the local church when gathered together, especially for Sunday Mass and Christian initiation."

[12] Cf. Deiss, 27ff.

[13] CSL 41–42 and passim.

[14] Note the prayer that accompanies the [first] postbaptismal anointing, which acknowledges the newly baptized candidate's participation in Christ's priesthood. This can only become reality if the Christian actually enters into the act of worship with the rest of the body of Christ.

[15] Romans 6:3.

[16] Shawn Madigan, *Spirituality Rooted in Liturgy* (Washington, D.C.: The Pastoral Press, 1988) 12–8.

[17] This expression was used by Bishop Trautman in his address at the Notre Dame liturgy symposium in June, 1997.

[18] It is obvious, of course, that this title plays off Thomas Day's book *Why Catholics Can't Sing: The Culture of Catholicism and the Triumph of Bad Taste* (New York: Crossroad, 1990). It seems to me that Day really does not treat Catholic assemblies with much sympathy or respect; moreover, his focus, generally speaking, is on music itself, not the singing assembly.

[19] Ibid., 18–34.

[20] This is particularly the danger of the ritual school or paradigm described by Mannion in his article, 116–20, especially if the role of the assembly is ignored.

[21] The ideal envisaged by the *Constitution on the Sacred Liturgy* 41.

[22] See Kenan Osborne, *Sacramental Theology: A General Introduction* (New York/Mahwah: The Paulist Press, 1988), especially Chapter 6, "The Church as Basic Sacrament," 86–99, where the author insists that Church, the gathered body, exercises its role only insofar as it reflects Christ who is the sacrament and the "light of the world."

[23] There is often a conflict between the need to allow preaching to be clearly heard and at the same time to provide a resonant space that encourages and reinforces the congregation's singing. That is why it is so vitally important that those who are in charge of larger churches, especially, proceed with caution when deciding on sound systems.

[24] It also goes without saying that there is more than music and speech involved in the assembly's rightfully joining in their Eucharistic Prayer. Posture plays a large role also. As a consequence of the American bishops' vote on the kneeling posture during the portion of the Eucharistic Prayer that occurs after the *Sanctus,* the former have unwittingly continued to emphasize a medieval view of the Eucharistic Prayer, where the preface was but introductory to the real prayer, which was seen as belonging to the priest alone, despite the "we" language of the Roman canon! On kneeling as a posture that does not allow for one to enter fully into thanksgiving, memory, and invocation, see John K. Leonard and Nathan D. Mitchell, *The Postures of the Assembly During the Eucharistic Prayer,* A Project of the Notre Dame Center for Pastoral Liturgy (Chicago: Liturgy Training Publications, 1994).

[25] All one has to do is look at the ritual text thus named in order to see that music played little or no role in the minds of those who created this book: National Conference of Catholic Bishops, *Sunday Celebrations in the Absence of a Priest* (New York: Catholic Book Publishing Co., 1994).

[26] Ostdiek, 173.

# Psalmody as "Word of Christ"

## Margaret Daly-Denton

One of the New Testament texts most frequently invoked as the basis for the pre-eminent place accorded to the Psalter in Christian liturgy is Col 3:16. In the *New Jerusalem Bible* translation it reads:

> Let the word of Christ, in all its richness, find a home with you. Teach each other, and advise each other, in all, wisdom. With gratitude in your hearts sing psalms and hymns and inspired songs to God; . . .[1]

The problem with this, and with several other modern versions (e.g., *New American Bible, New English Bible*), is that it gives the impression of separate and possibly even consecutive actions—welcoming the word, teaching, singing psalms. Obviously, the translators have tried to alleviate the cumbersomeness of the single sentence in the original Greek, which, literally rendered, reads:

> Let the Word of Christ dwell richly in you (who are) teaching and instructing each other in all wisdom (while you are) joyfully singing in your hearts psalms, hymns, and spiritual odes to God.

The point of the passage, lost in so many translations, is that the welcoming of the word of Christ, the teaching of each other, and the singing of praise to God are three facets of the one action. The singing of praise to God becomes "the word of Christ" addressed to the community. The author of Ephesians makes the same point. Christians are to be filled with the Spirit as they address each other in the psalms, hymns, and spiritual odes with which they sing and make music to the Lord (Eph 5:19).

What exactly did the authors of Colossians and Ephesians mean by "psalms, hymns, and spiritual odes"? We tend to receive these terms as references to various different genres. In this we are influenced by our contemporary usage in which the term "psalm" usually refers to the canonical Psalter. Thus we would distinguish a "psalm" from a "hymn," the term we use for compositions of the Christian Church, traditionally metrical and rhymed. Such a distinction is not made in the New Testament and its contemporary Jewish literature. New Testament Christians who knew the psalms in Greek, used the word *psalmos*, but they also received the word *hymnos* as a translation of the Hebrew word for a psalm, *tehillah*, literally, "a praise."[2] Those in contact with Greek culture, both in the Hellenized cities of the Land of Israel and in the diaspora, would have known of the Greek cultic odes and hymns and would have seen their Psalter as the Jewish equivalent. Thus authors such as Philo and Josephus, writing to explain Judaism to "outsiders" and making the point that the Jews, too, have their cultic chants no less than the Greeks, refer to the Psalter as David's "hymns," or "odes."[3] Conversely, as we shall see, the literature of Second Temple Judaism abounds in extra-biblical compositions that are called "psalms." The terms "psalm," "hymn," and "ode" in Col 3:16 and Eph 5:19, therefore, most probably refer in a general way to the profusion of song which characterized early Christian worship. In fact, the traces that this song has left in the New Testament text indicate that the Psalter was its basic source and model.

From this it follows that when Paul invites the Corinthians to have a psalm ready to contribute to their community's worship (1 Cor 14:26), or when the author of the Letter of James urges anyone feeling cheerful to sing a psalm (Jas 5:13), we cannot assume that this necessarily refers to one of the canonical psalms. On the other hand, neither can we assume that the hymns which Paul and Silas were singing to God in prison were not from the Psalter. The *hymnos* sung by Jesus and his friends at the conclusion of the Last Supper (Mark 14:26) most certainly was. In fact, we can even pinpoint its source—the second part of the Hallel, Pss 114-118.[4]

To appreciate the early Christian experience of psalmody as "word of Christ," we need to take into account the Jewish attribution of the psalms to David. This has a long history going back to the early traditions about David's musicianship (1 Sam 16:14-23). The inclusion of Psalm (17)18 in the narrative of David's rise (2 Samuel 22) is an important landmark on the journey to the eventual attribution of all 150 psalms to him. We can take it that the early Christians accepted that David "wrote" the psalms. We need, however, to acknowledge the cultural distance between our concept of authorship and theirs.

In the Judaism contemporary with early Christianity, many more compositions were revered as psalms of David than the 150 which we know as the canonical Psalter. The most well attested of these is Psalm 151, "A psalm of David when he fought in single combat with Goliath." It is preserved in Hebrew, Greek, and Syriac versions predating the New Testament.[5] A few lines will convey something of its character:

> I was the smallest of my brothers,
> and the youngest among the sons of my father;
> and he made me shepherd of his flocks, and the ruler over his kids.

> My hands made a flute
> and my fingers a lyre;
> and I shall render glory to the Lord
> I thought within myself.[6]

The author known as Pseudo-Philo, whose writing is thought to be contemporary with the New Testament, offers two "Psalms of David," one spoken at his anointing by Samuel (*LAB* 59, 4), the other, the exorcism he prayed over Saul (*LAB* 60, 2-3).[7] The Dead Sea Scroll 11QPs[a] contains forty-seven psalms, all attributed to David. Of these, only forty are found in the canonical Psalter. The other seven are examples of the numerous "Psalms of David" which appear to have been in circulation in the New Testament period.[8] In fact, the prose note at the end of 11QPs[a] claims that David wrote a total of 4050 psalms![9]

To understand the rationale behind this proliferation of "Psalms of David," we need to look in a little more detail at the history of the attribution of the psalms to him. By the time the Hebrew Bible had reached its present form, seventy-three psalms had acquired *l[e] dawîd* superscripts attributing them to David. The Septuagint increased that number to 87. In copies of psalms found among the Dead Sea Scrolls, even more psalms appear under the heading *l[e] dawîd*.[10] The Davidic attribution presupposed a connection between David's prayers and David's career. Once in the narrative traditions he is depicted as praying in distress and fear (2 Sam 16:31). This encouraged the "discovery" of the precise occasions when David prayed particular psalms. These psalms were given "historical" superscripts associating them with incidents in David's career, e.g., for Psalm 3, "A Psalm of David when he fled from Absalom his son."[11] There were thirteen of these historical titles by the time the Hebrew Psalter reached its present form. The practice of adding these titles to psalms had become more widespread by the time the Septuagint was produced. There are indications in the Greek titles that David's "autobiographical" utterances were being received in a collective sense, as spoken in the name of Israel. Several

Syriac Psalters testify to ongoing composition of these titles. Many of them are Christian glosses, but they are in a direct line of tradition flowing from the Hebrew Bible, via the Septuagint, into early Christianity.[12]

The composition of extra-canonical psalms of David was the logical follow-through to the historical superscript tradition. If settings in David's life could be found for psalms, then psalms could be written to expand the biblical narrative and show David's interior dispositions at various critical junctures in his life. What we would regard as creative writing was seen as a searching of the Scriptures to find and bring out their inner meaning. Some of these psalms, like Psalm 151 quoted above, purported to be "autobiographical." There are also wisdom psalms which reflect the transformation of the remembered David into an imagined sapientialized figure, the holy and wise king whose Psalter taught Israel to walk in the way of *Torah* (cf. Psalm 1). Other extra-canonical psalms of David are no more than catenae of psalm quotations and allusions, their claim to Davidic "authorship" resting upon the obvious similarity of their diction to that of the Psalter. Our most valuable source for these compositions at present is the Dead Sea Scroll 11QPs[a], but there may yet be discoveries in store for us.[13]

The David who was imagined as author of all these psalms—canonical and extra-canonical—became for Israel a model of prayer. The psalms gave individual Israelites a highly personal access to him, not merely as a kingly figure, but in all of his humanity. Thus, for example, Ben Sira would emphasize David's intimacy with God who always heard his appeals for help (Sir 47:5), and the author of 1 Maccabees would cite David as an example that none who put their trust in God will lack strength (1 Macc 2:57). David's reaction to victory, failure, exultation, fear, persecution, deliverance, etc., as expressed in the psalms, would exemplify the appropriate response of a faithful Jew in similar circumstances. Thus the superscript to Psalm (101)102—"Prayer of one afflicted who is faint and pours out a complaint before the Lord"—universalizes and actualizes David's prayer in any and every new set of circumstances. One of the most moving testimonies to the contribution of David and "his" psalms to Jewish piety is found in 4 Maccabees, composed in the first century, prior to 70 C.E. The author tells how a mother encouraged her children to undergo martyrdom by reminding them of the way their father had taught them about all the great suffering figures in Israel's past. She recalled how he used to sing to his children "the psalm of David which says, 'Many are the afflictions of the righteous,'" i.e., Psalm (33)34 (cf. 4 Macc 18:15).

It was out of this understanding that the Psalter was to become a model and resource for the composition of prayers. An impressive corpus of prayers from the Second Temple period has survived. To mention just a few examples, there are the prayers of Mordecai and Esther in the Greek additions to Esther, the Prayer of Azariah and the Song of the Three Young Men in the Greek additions to Daniel, the prayers in Tobit, the Prayer of Manasseh, Ben Sira's prayers (one of these, Sir 51:1-12, found at Qumran in a Hebrew version attributed to David), the prayers in the *Liber Antiquitatum Biblicarum*, the Psalms of Solomon. Then, of course, numerous prayers are found among the Dead Sea Scrolls, a most interesting collection being the Thanksgiving Hymns, the *Hodayoth* (1QH). A common feature of all of these compositions is their literary dependence on the Psalter, as the following examples demonstrate.

1QH II, 30

But my foot stands upon level ground;
apart from their assembly
I will bless Thy Name.

Ps (26)27:12

My foot stands on level ground
In the great congregation
I will bless the Lord.

1QH IV, 11

And they withhold from the thirsty
the drink of knowledge
and assuage their thirst with vinegar.

Ps (68)69:21

They gave me poison for my food,
and for my thirst
they gave me vinegar to drink

PrMan 10

I do not deserve to lift up my eyes
. . . because of the multitude of the iniquity of my wicked deeds,
because I did evil things before you.

Ps (50) 51:4

Against you, you alone have I sinned,
and done what is evil in your sight.

David was not just a model of piety, however. The idealized David, shaped in Israel's memory and imagination, was, in a very real sense, an intimation, a prefiguration of "the one who was to come"—the ideal descendant of David, sometimes referred to in the prophetic writings as "David." "They will seek David their king" (Hos 3:5). "They shall serve the Lord their God and David their king" (Jer 30:9). "I will set up over them one shepherd, my servant David" (Ezek 34:23; cf. 37:24).

Early Christianity claimed that Jesus was that "David." Since it shared with its contemporary Judaism the conviction that David had "written" the psalms, it is not surprising that the Psalter is the most frequently cited book of the Hebrew Scriptures in its writings. While intertextual reference tends to defy quantification, we can at least say that there are very few New Testament writings that show no trace of the Psalter's presence in the form of either allusions or echoes.[14] The authority with which Davidic authorship had invested the psalms would be maximized by the New Testament authors. The tradition whereby certain psalms had become associated with incidents in the life of David was to set a precedent for them in their presentation of Jesus as a "Davidic" figure. The notion, derived from the attribution to David, that the psalms were, in some sense, prophetic, would enhance the effectiveness of psalm allusions and quotations as components of New Testament preaching, worship, and apologetic.[15]

Since the early Christians brought to their reception of the psalms the presupposition that they were the work of David, and since Jesus was their "new David" in whose name King David had prophetically written his hymns, the psalms were "about" Jesus (cf. Luke 24:44). This view of the psalms is extensively developed in the New Testament. David the psalmist is a prophet (Acts 2:30), the mouthpiece of the Holy Spirit (Acts 4:25; Mark 12:36; Matt 22:43). When David "wrote" that God would not allow him to see corruption (Ps (15)16:10), he referred not to himself, but to his descendant Jesus (Acts 25-36). It is significant that Paul develops his idea that the Jewish Scriptures were written "for us" (i.e. for Christians) in a context where he puts a psalm of David on Jesus' lips—"The reproaches of those who reproached you fell on me" (cf. Rom 15:3-4). A reception of the psalms such as this is the basis for the extensive reference to the Psalter in the gospel passion narratives. Fulfillment of the psalms in the events of the passion indicates that Jesus' death is "according to the scriptures" (1 Cor 15:3-4).

The Psalter provided the first Christians with symbolic language to express their faith. In fact the image most frequently used in the New Testament to convey the resurrection-ascension is that of Jesus seated at the right hand of God. This comes directly from Psalm (109)110, a psalm that in Jewish exegesis of the New Testament period was believed to refer to the mysterious origin of the Messiah.

> The Lord said to my Lord: "Sit at my right hand,
> till I make your enemies your footstool.[16]

In the early Christian reception, the risen Jesus is David's "Lord." This is one of several instances where the New Testament presents Jesus as the *Kyrios* referred to or addressed in the psalms. The clearest example is Stephen's final prayer, "Lord Jesus, receive my spirit" (Acts 7:59) which imitates and echoes the dying prayer of Jesus, "Father, into your hands I commend my spirit" (Luke 23:46, echoing Ps (30)31:5). Jesus addresses the psalm to God his Father. Stephen addresses the psalm to the risen Jesus, whom he has just seen in a vision at God's right hand. This is one of the earliest prayers to Christ. Like the Johannine profession of Jesus as "My Lord and my God," which echoes Ps 34:23 (My God and my Lord), it identifies the risen Lord as the *Kyrios* addressed in the psalms.[17] The exhortation in Eph 5:19 to "sing and make music to the Lord," is another case in point. It employs a familiar idiom from the Psalter,[18] making the point that the praise directed to God in the psalms finds, on the lips of Christians, a new addressee—Jesus the *Kyrios*.

The authority for this is not, of course, limited to any particular text, and not even to the Psalter. It arises out of a whole presentation of Jesus in biblical terms which have hitherto been associated only with God—forgiving sins, stilling the storm at sea, "raising the dead, showing greater authority than the Law, etc. Undoubtedly though, allusion to the Psalter has played an important part in the development of a Christology which would regard the divine title as appropriate for Jesus. The author of Hebrews, for example, finds scriptural support for such an understanding of Jesus in Ps (44) 45:7-8—"Your throne, O God, will endure for ever" (Heb 1:8-9). In this psalm, the king, understood in Jewish exegesis as the King Messiah, is addressed as "God." Clearly the Psalter was an important component of the biblical authorization for this theological development.

The New Testament evidence also suggests that this development took place principally within the context of worship. In early Christianity, as in the Judaism from which it sprung, the Psalter functioned as a model and a quarry for the composition of prayers. The high degree of allusion to the Psalter in the heavenly hymns, as "heard" in the Book of Revelation, is, no doubt, a reflection of liturgical practice in the earthly church. Luke's portrayal of the early community composing what amounts to a Christian *relecture* of Psalm 2 is another instance (Acts 4:24-30), as is the extent to which his *Magnificat* and *Benedictus* quarry the Psalter. The verbal form of the quotation from Psalm (67) 68 in Eph 4:8 probably translates an early *Targum* of the Psalter, i.e., the Aramaic version used in synagogue worship. Thus, the traces of the early Christian liturgy which the New Testament preserves—hymn fragments, doxologies, blessings, prayers, professions of faith, etc.— reveal a Church that held the Psalter in high regard among the Scriptures which bear witness to Jesus (cf. John 5:39) and found in it both the words to express its faith and the inspiration for new songs to celebrate that faith's essential newness.

It is against this background that the Psalter has been, from the beginnings of the Church, the basis of Christian liturgical song. Historically, in the celebration of the Eucharist according to the Roman Rite, psalmody occurred at the *Introit, Graduale, Offertorium, Communio.* These chants consisted of psalmody with antiphons. The antiphons were drawn not only from the Psalter and from elsewhere in the Jewish Scriptures but also from the New Testament. Thus the liturgy frequently brought the psalms into intertextual dialogue with the New Testament writings. The New Testament antiphon would function as a lens through which the psalm could be viewed on a particular Christian feast or in a particular Christian season. Even if the whole chant was from the Psalter, its insertion in the Christian context was totally transformative, since quotation, of its nature, necessarily involves reinterpretation.

Recent years have seen a considerable change. The singing of the Roman psalm-based chants is confined mainly to monasteries. In Catholic parish worship, psalmody has, to a great extent, been eclipsed by hymnody. During the early stages of the liturgical movement, Roman Catholics looked to the experience of the Christian churches which had long since established a vernacular musical repertory, notably the Anglican and Lutheran communions. From them they adopted vernacular hymns. In the days when the singing of the people was barely tolerated, as it were, on the fringes of the liturgy, the "four hymn" pattern evolved—entrance, offertory, communion, and recessional hymns. One of the side effects of this was to establish a presupposition that the hymn should comment on the liturgical action during which it is sung. Thus we had a proliferation of gathering songs for the entrance, offering songs for what was then called the offertory, "eucharistic" songs for the communion procession, and missioning songs for the recessional.

Offertory hymns have largely faded from view as we have learned to appreciate what it means to call this part of the celebration the "preparation of the gifts." We are learning, too, that it is not always necessary for the people to actually sing when they are sent from the celebration "to do good works, praising and blessing the Lord" (cf. GIRM, 57). However, in many parts of the world, the gathering and "eucharistic" songs for the entrance and communion processions still hold their ground. Texts for the communion song have moved from "eucharistic adoration" to what might be generalized as "bonding songs." The processional song has degenerated into a sort of musical "treadmill," on which the community continually rehearses its self-regarding oneness in the one body sharing the one bread.

Something valuable has been lost—the breadth, the biblical richness, the capacity of an unexpected entrance or communion antiphon to challenge and stretch us beyond our presuppositions. The Roman entrance and communion antiphons were, of course, translated for the Missal of Paul VI, but, shorn of the psalm verses to which they should have been refrains and frequently rendered in musically unworkable translations, they did not inspire significant numbers of composers. Consequently the directive in the *General Instruction* that the entrance or communion antiphon should be regarded as the first choice was "more honour'd in the breach than the observance."[19] As Aidan Kavanagh, O.S.B., has written:

> With the exception of several metrical sequences of relatively recent date, the Roman eucharist has never contained metrical hymns. Although these are now frequently included in eucharistic liturgies, especially in northern European cultures which have rich traditions stemming from non-Roman sources, the older pattern of antiphon with psalmody remains the preeminent norm in standard Roman eucharistic books. Unfortunately, the current English translations of these books make it difficult to observe this Roman tradition, except for the meditation chants between the lessons.[20]

Happily, the revision of the *Sacramentary* includes the provision of an *Antiphonary* containing over six hundred entrance and communion antiphons with recommended psalm verses to be sung with them. The work on the *Antiphonary* has been guided by the 1969 Instruction on Translation of the Apostolic See.

> Antiphons, even though they come from Scripture, become part of the liturgy and enter into a new literary form. In translating them it is possible to give them a verbal form which, while preserving their full meaning, is more suitable for singing and harmonizes them with the liturgical season or a special feast. Examples of such adaptations which include minor adaptations of the original texts are numerous in ancient antiphonaries.[21]

The application of this principle in concrete terms requires a consciousness of the christological interpretation. So the work of translating the antiphons and of allocating psalm verses to be sung with them has been guided by the Christian reception of the psalms as witnessed in the New Testament, the Fathers of the Church, and the liturgical tradition. Furthermore, a balance has been sought between the preservation of the "full meaning" and the requirements which singing imposes. The antiphons have also been designed to fulfill their liturgical function. Thus, for example, communion antiphons, to be sung in procession, are short enough to be sung by heart. The completed work demonstrates that fidelity to the original does not necessarily entail word-for-word translation. A member of the subcommittee which prepared the new *Antiphonary*, describes the "sound English . . . apt for singing" which those working on it have sought to achieve.

> "Sound English" begins with current speech, though it may be what Hopkins called "the current language . . . heightened and unlike itself." Phrases should sound natural or they will be alien to those who sing or listen to them. Fussy little words, like articles, prepositions and pronouns are not to be multiplied beyond necessity; and we have borne in mind that splendid poem by Mgr. Kevin Nichols (himself an ICEL translator) which begins: "For Lent I shall give up adjectives." It is not too much to say that the policy over antiphons has been the opposite of that over prayers. The prayers of the 1973 Missal, especially the collects, were too spare and are now much fuller. The antiphons of the 1973 Missal were too long and many of them have needed pruning.[22]

The communion antiphon for the fifth Sunday of Lent exemplifies this.

| 1973 ICEL Translation | New ICEL *Sacramentary* |
|---|---|
| Has no one condemned you? The woman answered: No one, Lord. Neither do I condemn you: go and do not sin again. | Has no one condemned you? No one, Lord. Neither will I; now sin no more. |

The psalm recommended for singing with this antiphon is Psalm (31) 32, a celebration of God's forgiveness. Ideally it should be sung in the version provided by ICEL in its *Liturgical Psalter,* a translation which presumes musical performance as the norm.[23]

It is to be hoped that over a period of years, as composers turn their hands to providing musical settings, the new *Antiphonary* will encourage that sense of psalmody as "word of Christ" that is so evident in the New Testament writings. It is also to be hoped that this new resource will inspire not only musical setting, but the composition of psalm-based texts, "new songs" on the New Testament model. Above all, the *Antiphonary* will challenge us with the "given-ness" of liturgy, its character as a received way of worshiping God. On the Twenty-eighth Sunday in Ordinary Time, for example, the *Antiphonary* will propose to us something, perhaps, unsettlingly different to our usual "Gathering song":

If you lay bare our guilt,
who could endure it?
But you are full of mercy,
Lord God of Israel.

We may find this choice unappealing at first. We have, after all, come to regard Psalm (129) 130 as a "penitential" psalm suitable for reconciliation services, Lent, etc. Yet this psalm is sung at Vespers every evening during the Octave of Christmas in joyful celebration of God's mercy to humankind, as shown in the birth of Jesus. This is just one example of how the *Antiphonary* will challenge us to look at the psalms from another angle, that of the weekly Easter of God's people, the Sunday celebration of the Eucharist. This particular antiphon may well alert us to an important aspect of the Eucharist, neglected perhaps in much modern eucharistic hymnody—that Jesus' body broken and blood shed are "for the forgiveness of sins."

Whatever the antiphon suggests to us, it will certainly expose us to psalmody as "word of God . . . living and active, sharper than any two-edged sword . . . able to judge the thoughts and intentions of the heart."[24] Thus our praise of God will be instruction of each other in all wisdom. Set to the beautiful music which the newly crafted texts will surely inspire, they will lead us to welcome all the richness of that psalmodic "word of Christ." So let us, according to our differing gifts, create, compose, commission, and learn "psalms, hymns, and spiritual odes."

---

[1] Henry Wansbrough (ed.) *The New Jerusalem Bible* (New York: Doubleday, 1985) 1948.

[2] Cf. Ps (39)40:3; (64)65:1; (71)72:20; (99)100:4; (118)119:171; 2 Chr 7:6.

[3] According to Josephus (*Ant.* VI, 214), David restores Saul to himself by singing hymns over him. In *Ant.* VII, 305, Josephus portrays the elderly David as an accomplished composer of odes and hymns to God, written in the Greek poetic metres. For Philo (*Conf.* 149), David is God's hymnodist (*hymnesas*). Philo's *Plant.* IX, 39 describes a David who speaks aloud in hymns of praise. As an example of these "hymns," Philo cites Psalm (36)37.

[4] This flexibility in terminology is reflected in the early sources of the Christian liturgy, e.g., Didascalia 2: "If you desire hymns, you have the psalms of David." In a similar vein, an anonymous work against Artemon (ca. 200 C.E.),

preserved by Eusebius, marvels at all the psalms and odes that have been composed by believers from the very first which hymn Christ as the Word of God. Cf. *Hist. Eccl.* V, 28, 5.

[5] The Septuagintal version is thought to be the nearest to the original Hebrew. The Dead Sea Scrolls (11QPs[a]) preserve a Hebrew version paleographically dated to the first century C.E. The Syriac version (5ApocSyrPs 1) derives from the Greek.

[6] Translation by J. H. Charlesworth with J. A. Sanders in J. H. Charlesworth (ed.), *The Old Testament Pseudepigrapha*, Vol. 2 (New York: Doubleday, 1985) 612.

[7] The earliest extant manuscripts of the *Liber Antiquitatum Biblicarum* of Ps-Philo (11th century C.E.) are in Latin. They are thought to translate a Greek version of a Hebrew original composed in Palestine during the first century C.E., prior to the destruction of the Temple. The author retells biblical history from Adam to David in a narrative which interweaves the biblical account with legendary expansions. Pseudo-Philo thus reflects Palestinian synagogue worship and teaching at the turn of the era. Cf. D. J. Harrington, "Pseudo-Philo: A New Translation and Introduction," in J. H. Charlesworth (ed.), *The Old Testament Pseudepigrapha*, Vol. 2, 297–377, at 299. For the Latin text, see Daniel Harrington (ed.), *Pseudo-Philon, Les Antiquités; Bibliques, Tome I, Sources Chrétiennes* 229 (Paris: Les Editions du Cerf, 1976).

[8] According to a letter from the Nestorian Patriarch Timothy 1 (780–823) to Sergius, Metropolitan of Elam, first published in *Oriens Christianus*, 1 (1901) 299–313, more than 200 psalms of David were found ca. 686–7 in scrolls discovered in caves near Jericho. Among the Cairo Geniza discoveries is a fragment of a medieval manuscript containing further extra-biblical "Songs of David." According to David Flusser, their language and style point to a composition date prior to 70 C.E. Cf. "Psalms, Hymns and Prayers" in M. Stone (ed.), *Jewish Writings of the Second Temple Period: Apocrypha, Pseudepigrapha, Qumran Sectarian Writings, Philo, Josephus.* Compendium Rerum ludicarum ad Novum Testamentum 2, 2 (Assen/ Philadelphia: Van Gorcum/ Fortress, 1984) 551–77, at 568–9.

[9] 11QPs[a] is published in J. A. Sanders, *The Psalms Scroll of Qumran Cave 11* (11QPs[a]). Discoveries in the Judean Desert IV (Oxford: Clarendon, 1965) and *The Dead Sea Psalms Scroll* (Ithaca, New York: Cornell University Press, 1967).

[10] E.g., Psalms 104 and 123 have a Davidic superscript in 11QPs[a] and Psalm (81)82 is attributed to David in 11QMelch.

[11] On this development, cf. Elieser Slomovic, "Towards an Understanding of the Formation of Historical Titles in the Book of Psalms," *ZAW* 91 (1979) 350–80.

[12] E.g., the Syriac superscripts for Psalm (21) 22—"Spoken by David in prayer when he suffered persecution by Absalom." Cf. J. M. Vosté, "Sur les titres des psaumes dans la Pesitta surtout d'après la recension orientate," *Bib* 25 (1944) 210–35.

[13] E.g., "The Song of the Lamb," mentioned in Rev 15:3 and apparently as familiar as "The Song of Moses," may be retrievable from the Tosephta Targum to 1 Sam 17, as postulated by J. C. De Moor and E. Van Staalduine-Sulman in

"The Aramaic Song of the Lamb." *JSJ* 24 (1993) 226–79. "The Song of the Lamb" may have originated as an apocryphal expansion of 1 Sam 18:7, along the lines of the many other compositions of the Second Temple Period which "imagined" the prayers or hymns mentioned in biblical narratives.

[14] According to the 25th edition of the Nestle-Aland Greek text, the Psalter is cited 55 times in the New Testament. It is alluded to and echoed much more often. Possibly only Philemon and 2-3 John lack allusions to the Psalter.

[15] David the prophet is not a Christian invention. 11QPs[a]DavComp states that David composed all his psalms "through prophecy which was given him from before the Most High." The primitive notion of prophecy as an ecstatic state involving musical activity under the influence of the spirit of the Lord (cf. 1 Sam 10:6-7) was an important factor in the development of such a perception of David. As late as the Chronicler's period, the choral singing of psalms was still being designated as "prophesying" (1 Chr 25:1). Another contributor to the view of David as a prophet was the fact that the biblical narratives about him belonged to the division of the Hebrew Scriptures known as "The Former Prophets."

[16] The "sit at my right" motif from Ps (109)110:1 appears in Matt 22:44; 26:64; Mark 12:36; 14:62; 16:19; Luke 20:42-43; 22:69; Acts 2:34-35; Rom 8:34; Eph 1:20; Col 3:1; Heb 1:3-13; 8:1; 10:12-13; 12:2. Cf. *EpBarn* 12:11 "The Lord said to Christ my Lord."

[17] It has been suggested that Thomas' address to Jesus may reflect a Christian reaction against the imperial cult under Domitian. Suetonius records that Domitian was addressed as "Dominus et Deus Noster" (*Domitianus* xiii, 2). Cf. B. A. Mastin, "A Neglected Feature of the Christology of the Fourth Gospel," *NTS* 22 (1976) 32–52, at 44. While this may be so, it is unlikely, given the extent to which the Fourth Gospel is rooted in the Jewish Scriptures, that it is merely a parody of the pagan title without any foundation in the biblical tradition. Martin Hengel explains that *Dominus et Deus* was not an official title for Domitian. Cf. his "Christological Titles in Early Christianity," in J. H. Charlesworth (ed.), *The Messiah: Developments in Earliest Judaism and Christianity* (Minneapolis: Augsburg Fortress, 1992) 425–48, at 431.

[18] Cf. Ps (26) 27:6; (56) 57:7; (104) 105:2; (107) 108:1.

[19] William Shakespeare, *Hamlet,* IV, 14.

[20] Aidan Kavanagh, *Elements of Rite: A Handbook of Liturgical Style* (New York: Pueblo, 1982) 37.

[21] Quoted in *The Sacramentary: as transmitted for consideration and vote to the member and associate member conferences of the International Committee on English in the Liturgy,* Segment Six, 74.

[22] Michael Hodgetts, "Revising the Missal: Introit and Communion Antiphons," Liturgy 19, 3 (1995) 112–8, at 115–6. The quotation from Hopkins is found in W. H. Gardner (ed.), *Gerard Manley Hopkins: A Selection of his Poems and Prose* (Harmondsworth: Penguin, 1963) xxxiii.

[23] *The Psalter: A faithful and inclusive rendering from the Hebrew into contemporary English poetry, intended primarily for communal song and recitation,* offered for study and comment by the International Committee on English in the Liturgy (Chicago: Liturgy Training Publications, 1995).

[24] It is no accident that the author of the Letter to the Hebrews had just commented at length on a psalm when he wrote that. Cf. Heb 4:12.

# Ritual Language and Liturgy

*Anscar J. Chupungco, O.S.B.*

This essay aims to offer reflections on the nature and purpose of ritual language and on how it functions in the liturgy. To develop this elusive topic I present a synthesis of the principal points raised in the works of Christine Mohrmann, Gail Ramshaw, and Gianfranco Venturi. To their expert treatment of the question I add some personal insights which are the result of my years of amateurism and tinkering with liturgical language.[1]

The essay has two parts. The first is a description of ritual language with special attention to its role in the liturgy. The second is a discussion of some disputable assumptions regarding ritual language and how they affect the current debate on the translation of liturgical texts.

## What is ritual language?

Experts on the science of linguistics understand language in its broadest sense as a system of communication through use of conventional signs, symbols, gestures, and sounds. These represent meanings that are commonly understood by the people to whom they are addressed. When applied to the realm of the liturgy, language denotes the entire system of signs and symbols, words and speech or song, moments of silence, gestures and postures, sacred images or icons, and the material elements such as water, bread, wine, and oil with which the Church celebrates the saving mystery of Christ. This type of language is called ritual, because it pertains to rites, which are the prescribed system governing the words, actions, and material things needed for a ceremony. The ceremony itself is an action, more or less solemn, which people set apart from the normal routine of the day.

Though we tend to use the word "ritual" loosely, as in the expression "morning ritual," a rite in itself is always something special, even when it is performed daily or several times a day.

In the phrase "ritual language" the word "ritual" reinforces the connotation of language as something that is performed or carried out through words, gestures, and use of material things. The phrase indicates that the liturgy, being a conjunction of interrelated words, formularies, gestures, and symbols, is by nature a ritual action.

In common usage ritual language is the type of speech used in the performance of a rite. Speech in this context refers to the system of communication which employs spoken words to express a desired message. Speech is composed of words and phrases, but these are not independent units. Rather, they combine to create a denotation, a connotation, a context or, in short, a message. It is useful to note that every word, being in the category of symbols, is plurivalent: it can signify several accepted meanings and nuances. Dictionaries normally enumerate them, carefully indicating the different contexts in which they are used. The word "foot," for example, can mean part of a living body, a system of measurement, a metaphor as in "foot of a mountain," a synechdoche as in "the feet of one who brings good tidings," or an idiomatic expression as in "foot in the door." But in combination with others, a word assumes a particular or definite meaning that is needed in order to articulate, in conjunction with the other words, the message of a text.

Thus, no word should be read singly as an independent unit, but in context, that is, in conjunction with the other components of language, including the signs and gestures that accompany the spoken word. To understand fully the meaning of a word in a linguistic unit, it is necessary to do the process of what authors call the "decomposition," "decoding," or "dehistorization" of the entire unit, in order to establish its "kernel." This process aims to discover the relationship between the kernel and the other segments of the text or, in other words, its global historical, cultural, doctrinal, and literary context.[2] It is within such context that a word, in conjunction with others, is to be understood.

Someone was mortified by the sentence "the couple pronounced their solemn vows before God's altar," because the expression "solemn vows" brought to mind the profession in religious orders! Context and the conjunction of surrounding circumstances define the meaning of a word. This explains why translations should not be done word-for-word. It must be said that those who advance such a method have, alas, a crude understanding of language.[3] Translation is the art of communicating the message in its context rather than the individual word components of the message.[4]

In the liturgy, spoken language assumes a variety of forms. It can consist of formularies, acclamations, poetic compositions or hymns, songs, and addresses in the form of homilies or instructions: in short, of anything spoken, read aloud, proclaimed, or sung. By calling this type of language "ritual" we stress the fact that liturgical language is a spoken language.[5] It is primarily intended to be performed orally in celebrations with an assembly. To a great degree liturgical language, especially formularies and hymns, has been written down. This should not lead us to regard it as a literary piece for private reading. Liturgical texts are always meant to be read aloud or sung in public. The history of the sixth-century *Veronese Sacramentary*, for example, shows that its original was a folder wherein loose pages of Mass formularies had been inserted day after day in the course of the liturgical year. They were prayers written to be recited aloud at papal Masses.

Ritual language is the language appropriate for a rite. Its function is to convey the meaning and purpose for which a ritual action is being performed. It formulates the reason and states the occasion for celebrating a rite. Thus the vocabulary and lexicon and even the grammatical construction of ritual language are shaped and developed by the rite itself. Such vocabulary and lexicon, though not necessarily reserved exclusively for a particular rite, are often understood only in the context of a ritual action.

In the liturgy, words like "blessed" and "rejoice" have a more felicitous effect than "happy" and "be happy" which can sound utterly trite and ritually uninspiring. "Behold," as in "Behold the lamb of God," is more ritually appropriate than the conversational "This is the lamb of God," which often encourages presiders to extemporize with such fashionable but obtrusive additions as "This is Jesus, the Son of Mary, our brother and friend, the lamb of God." It is a fact that ritual words are used sparingly in normal life, but one expects to hear them at liturgical rites. The following sentence, which is exclamatory, is constructed to suit the nature of a liturgical rite: "Lord, you are holy indeed, you are the fountain of all holiness." Outside the context of a rite this linguistic construction sounds contrived.

At times, ritual language also does away with normal syntactic arrangement. The formula of blessing, "May almighty God bless you, the Father, and the Son, and the Holy Spirit," is a rather unusual form of speech. But the normal construction, "May almighty God, the Father, the Son, and the Holy Spirit, bless you," lacks the tone of solemnity. Likewise the words "The body of Christ" and "The word of the Lord" are powerful statements in both English and the original Latin, but they have neither verb nor predicate, and their use can be justified only within the ritual parameter. The long and short of it is that rites produce their specific lexicon and grammar. The Latin-speaking Church witnessed this process evolve through many centuries.[6] The English-speaking Churches of today, through the agency of the International Commission on English in the Liturgy (ICEL), are happily, or should we say blessedly, approaching the day when they can claim an English ritual language.

At this point it might be useful to mention that our liturgical lexicon originates in the two fundamental concepts of Christian liturgy, namely *anamnesis* and *epiclesis*. Liturgical theologians tell us that every liturgical celebration is an ecclesial action that recalls *(anamnesis)* and intercedes *(epiclesis)*. Through the liturgical action the Church recalls the saving deeds God accomplished in Christ, presenting them before God and, as it were, reminding God thereof. As the Church performs this ritual action, it invokes the power of the Holy Spirit so that the recalled deeds may become present and bring holiness to the assembly. The mode of presence, which is considered real, has come to be known in the theology of Odo Casel as "presence in mystery."

We may say that one set of ritual vocabulary revolves around the concept of *anamnesis*. Examples are: memorial joined with praise and thanksgiving, the deeds of God in creation and history, the paschal mystery of Christ, presence in mystery, the human and Church community, the ministers and the assembly, space and time. With this vocabulary the Church speaks to God about Christ and his mystery and at the same time addresses the gathered assembly.

The Latin liturgy gives us instructive examples of how to employ ritual vocabulary. The following example from the Roman Canon is admirable for the use of Latin rhetoric: "Unde et memores, Domine, nos servi tui sed et plebs tua sancta."[7] It is a hieratic speech concerning the solemn *(unde)* memorial *(et memores)* addressed by the Church to God, the ministers serving at God's table *(nos servi tui)*, and the gathered assembly *(sed et plebs tua sancta)*.[8]

The English *Sacramentary,* newly revised by ICEL, has also choice examples of the use of ritual vocabulary. The opening line of the Roman Canon is a successful attempt to render in English the sense of the Latin original: "All-merciful Father, we come before you with praise and thanksgiving through Jesus Christ your Son."[9]

We note that the words "we come before you" expand the Latin *igitur,* which cannot be translated with one word without sounding flat and unconnected, except for the expert ears. The conjunction of these words gives the phrase the unmistakable mark of ritual language and matches the solemnity of *igitur*. On the other hand, the words "with praise and thanksgiving" serve as a "strong link between the preface (of praise and thanks) and the rest of the Eucharistic Prayer."[10]

The other set of ritual vocabulary revolves around the *epiclesis*. The pertinent concepts are: petition for God's grace, salvation, consecration, holiness, offering and sacrifice, and intercession for the needs of the Church and humankind.

The Roman Canon articulates the elements of *epiclesis* in these hieratic words: "Per Iesum Christum Filium tuum, Dominum nostrum, supplices rogamus ac petimus, uti accepta habeas et benedicas haec munera, haec sancta sacrificia illibata." The English version expresses this in typically crisp English without harm to the qualities of ritual language: "Through him [Christ] we ask you to accept and bless these gifts we offer you in sacrifice."

Because of its ritual nature the spoken language of the liturgy is consequently a literary language. While it is contemporary and hence accessible to the majority of the assembly, it uses a literary genre or style suited for solemn and formal proclamation.

We can illustrate this point, which ICEL aims to develop for the English liturgy, by reviewing the experience of the Latin Church. We are told by historians that when Latin became the liturgical language of Rome after the fourth century, several prayer formularies were authored by persons who had been formed in the school of Roman rhetoric and the classics.[11] They were bishops of Rome: Vigilius, Gelasius, Leo the Great, and Gregory the Great. Through them the literary style of that time profoundly influenced the language of the Latin liturgy. Rhetoric, which has unfortunately acquired a pejorative meaning in our day because of some grandiloquent political discourses, was actually a literary style demanded by the solemnity of the occasion. To have used another style, like the conversational, would have been regarded as trite, even irreverent. Historian Theodore Klauser describes the type of literary Latin developed by the popes for liturgical use as *Kulturlatein* in oppositon to *Volkslatein*.

Yet it would be a mistake—and some have fallen into it—to think that the rhetorical style of these Latin prayers belonged to a wholly other language, to that type of language reserved for religious purposes. Latin liturgical language is surely literary, elevated, and noble, in short rhetorical, but it is not sacred like the Sanskrit or the language used by the mystery religions. The Roman people gathered in liturgical assembly would have noted that the same style was being used by state leaders at public discourses. That is why it is not correct to regard the Latin liturgical language as sacred language. Ritual language is not synonymous with sacred language, at least in the experience of the Latin Church. Perhaps a comparison can be made with the Christian places of worship. The early Christians did not gather in temples but in houses. Sacred language is a form of ritual language, but not every ritual language is sacred language.

To press this basic point more strongly, it might help to cite a few examples of the more commonly used forms of classical Roman rhetoric.[12] An understanding of the Latin original can contribute to a greater appreciation of what ICEL tries to achieve for the English liturgical language.

Famous is the *cursus* which consists of a rhythmic arrangement of the final words of a sense line. The aim is to highlight word cadences, express sentiments of joy and wonder, and produce a sound pleasing to the ears of listeners. Scholars detect three types.[13] The first is the *cursus planus* as in *órbis exúltat*. The second type is the *cursus tardus* as in *ástra caeléstia*. The third type is the *curus velox* as in *consília respondémus*.

An example of the use of *cursus* is found in one of the Christmas formularies in the *Veronese Sacramentary:* "Deus, qui humanae substantiae dignitatem et mirabiliter condidisti et mirabilius reformasti."[14]

The lines ending with *mirabiliter condidisti* and *mirabilius reformasti* are in the *cursus velox* and are meant to evoke by their swift rhythm the sense of admiration, joy, and gratitude for God's work of creation and redemption.

The revised English *Sacramentary* has, in some of its texts, remarkably captured the purpose for which the *cursus* had been used in Latin. In the alternative opening prayer for the Mass on Christmas day, we detect the English dynamic equivalent of *cursus*. The text is concise and moves quickly but gently. Its aural effect has a comparable quality of the Latin *cursus*. The prayer elicits a response of wonder and thanksgiving: "We praise you, gracious God, for the glad tidings of peace, the good news of salvation: your Word became flesh, and we have seen his glory."[15]

Another rhetorical device is binary succession, a type of embolism which develops in pairs the principal theme of the prayer. Pope Vigilius often used this in the prefaces he authored. An example of this in the *Veronese Sacramentary* is a preface attributed to him:

> Nullis quippe forinsecus miseriis adfligemur,
> si vitia frenemus animorum;
> nec visibili dedecori subiacebit,
> qui foedis cupiditatibus obviaverit;
> nulla inquietudo praevalebit extrinsecus,
> si agamus corde sincero.[16]

ICEL's revised *Sacramentary* has preserved the concept of binary succession in the translation of the second preface of the Passion. After the solemn proem "This is the hour," the text develops the theme of Christ's victory through his passion in binary succession introduced by "when": "This is the hour when we celebrate his triumph over Satan's pride, when we solemnly recall the mystery of our redemption."[17]

A third type of rhetorical device is antithesis or juxtaposition of contrasting concepts like *ascensio* and *discessio, invisibilis* and *visibilis*. The Latin sacramentaries abound in the use of antithetical device, especially in the prefaces. The preface for the Ascension in the *Veronese Sacramentary* uses it lavishly. It reads in part: "Quia in caelos ascensio mediatoris . . . a nostra non est humilitate discessio."[18]

The ICEL translation of the second preface of Christmas is a faithful rendering of the antithesis in the Latin original: "The God we cannot see has now appeared in human form. The one begotten before all ages begins to live in time."[19]

A fourth type of rhetorical device is *concinnitas*. This consists of a balanced arrangement of the parts of an oration, which is obtained through symmetry of words and concepts. The postcommunion prayer in the *Veronese Sacramentary* is a classic example: "Quod sumit, intelligat; quod gustu delibat, moribus apprehendat; quod iustis orationibus expetit, tua misericordia percipiat."[20]

It is interesting to note that the original texts of ICEL are often characterized by symmetrical sentences. Two examples are the following alternative opening prayers:

> When we walk through the desert of temptation,
> strengthen us to renounce the power of evil.
> When our faith is tested by doubt,
> illumine our hearts with Easter's bright promise.[21]

> Lifted up from the earth,
> he is light and life;
> exalted upon the cross,
> he is truth and salvation.[22]

The foregoing discussion confirms the thinking that the ritual language used by the Church in the liturgy is literary rather than sacred. *Cursus*, antithesis, binary succession, and *concinnitas* are literary qualities of *kulturlatein* rather than properties of the sacred speech used in some religions. It is of course possible that sacred speech also uses literary devices. And while it is possible that Latin liturgical language borrowed words and phrases from the sacred language of fourth-century mystery religions, its origin and development claim a nonsacral type of language.[23]

Our discussion has also led us to believe that some traits of ritual language are cross-cultural: it is meant to be oral and aural, it forms part of a ritual action, and it employs rhetorical devices to enhance the meaning and beauty of the message. There is, to be sure, a world of difference between Latin and English syntax construction and between Latin and English literary devices. Yet both own in common such cross-cultural qualities as cadences, accents, and rhythm.

Lastly, the above discussion has shown that the new translations and original texts of ICEL are singularly attentive to the properties of formal spoken English. These are: accent on key words, avoidance of internal rhyme and of too many unaccented syllables in a row, and effort to end each line strongly on an accented syllable. The inclusion of these and other properties of modern English language in ICEL's revised *Sacramentary* has resulted, in a good number of cases, in formularies that truly match the beauty and nobility of the original Latin texts.

## What ritual language is not

There are critics who are wary of ICEL's concern for literary English, thinking that such might impinge on the faithful transmission of doctrine. The following observations are aimed to allay such a fear.

Ritual language is not intended to bear dogmatic statements on the faith of the Church. Although *lex credendi* sometimes weighs heavily on *lex orandi*, as for example in such feasts as the Holy Trinity, Immaculate Conception, and the Assumption of the Blessed Virgin Mary, it is not normal to construct ritual language with elements derived from dogmatic statements.[24] The only dogmatic formulary in the liturgy is the Nicene Creed, but we know that it was not composed originally for liturgical proclamation.[25]

We are not saying that liturgical texts do not contain doctrine. They speak about God, about Jesus Christ and his saving work, about the Church, about the rule of Christian life. As article 33 of the *Constitution on the Sacred Liturgy* affirms, "Although the liturgy is above all things the worship of the divine majesty, it likewise contains rich instruction for the faithful." The liturgy transmits to the assembly the faith of the Church. However, it does so not in the language of systematic theology and speculative philosophy, but in the language used for acclamations and narrations. The liturgy is not primarily an exposition but a persuasion: in the orations we, as it were, remind God of divine deeds *(anamnesis)* in order to persuade God to repeat them in our day *(epiclesis)*. Even the homily is not meant to be a doctrinal treatise, but a persuasive speech addressed to the assembly to regard people, events, and things in the light of God's revelation.

It is often an exercise in futility to construct doctrinal statements from liturgical formularies. While it is true that Pope Pius XII invoked the ancient feast of the Assumption as a living witness to the dogma, the liturgical formularies available then did not constitute sufficient basis for the definition. Thus those who expect liturgical texts to provide them with a corpus of Christian doctrine will be disappointed or, what is worse, might naively detect dogma where there is in reality a plurivalent symbol.[26] Dogma-hunting in every liturgical text can only be a frustrating experience. Similarly, those who are excessively fastidious about the use of abstract and technical terms in liturgical texts miss the basic premise that ritual language is more persuasive than systematic. Finally, those who demand that every doctrine be laid out fully in liturgical formularies forget that the liturgy is not a dogmatic compendium but a memorial of persons and events. To mention at every possible occasion that Mary is mother of God or that she is ever-virgin is not always catechetically helpful, nor should the omission of such titles be interpreted as a denial of Marian dogma. Liturgical formularies need not say everything that is contained in the *Catechism of the Catholic Church*. Obviously literary language should not be an excuse to ignore the requirements of orthodoxy, but it does not follow that ritual language falls under the category of systematic theology.

Ritual language is not colloquial speech. When we speak to God in public or address a community assembled in worship, we do not engage in familiar and informal conversation. The occasion is always solemn, even if it involves only two or three worshipers in the austerity of a village chapel. It is always solemn, because the object of the memorial is the sublimity of God and of Christ's saving acts.

Ritual language should be vernacular and accessible, but it should not be colloquial. Even if colloquial language is not banal or trite, it is nonetheless not ritual language. The cheery greeting "Good morning," sometimes replacing the liturgical "The Lord be with you," is at best a failure to distinguish one occasion from another. Someone has noted that it might even offend those who have suffered recent loss or misfortune. The following prayer is familiar and intimate, but hardly a ritual text for liturgical worship: "We pray to you, dear Lord, please do something quickly about this painful situation." This ritual context is often ignored by extemporized exchange of marriage vows such as this: "Annie, for so long I have searched for a partner but never found the right girl. Now at last God led me to you. I promise to be your husband, faithful as long as I live."

The ability to recite extemporaneous prayers with dignity, style, and depth is a rare gift. From the third century on, liturgical formularies began to be written down not only to ward off heresy, but also to maintain a certain literary style for solemn worship.[27] In the height of liturgical creativity authors paid detailed attention to the literary properties of the Latin language. The number of syllables were counted, accents were positioned for cadence and rhythm, and the appropriate imagery was chosen to make the text memorable.

To make sure that texts correspond to the dignity and solemnity of the liturgical occasion, ICEL goes to great lengths to revise, scrutinize, critique, and change or modify both translations and original compositions. The process of shaping the ritual language for worship is a serious enterprise involving not one but several conferences of bishops and experts in every field connected with the liturgy. ICEL has no other agenda than to communicate faithfully, nobly, and memorably to the English-speaking faithful the message of the liturgy. The following ICEL translation of the opening prayer for the seventeenth Sunday in ordinary time is remarkable for its attention to English cadence and rhythm:

> O Gód, protéctor of thóse who hópe in yóu,
> withóut whom nóthing is stróng, nóthing is hóly,
> enfóld us in your grácious cáre and mércy,
> that with yóu as our rúler and gúide,
> we may úse wísely the gífts of this pássing wórld
> and fíx our heárts even nów on thóse which lást for ever.[28]

Nothing is colloquial here, nothing is improvised: every word and every accent have been thoroughly considered.

Colloquial language should, however, be distinguished from popular religious language which we use for novena prayers. The language of popular religiosity can be solemn, though often florid, discursive to the point of rambling, and vividly picturesque. The following novena prayer is surely not colloquial, but it is not liturgical: "To whom can I turn if not to you, whose heart is the source of all graces and merits? Where should I seek if not in the treasure which contains all the riches of your kindness and mercy? Where should I knock if not at the door through which God gives himself to us and through which we go to God?"[29]

The language of popular religiosity, like that of the liturgy, is ritual, but it belongs to a different ritual genre. There is much that the former can learn from the latter, especially in its content and the use of language suited for public prayer. But in situations where people are more at ease with the language of popular worship it might not be altogether uncalled for to allow liturgical language to assimilate some characteristic traits of popular religious language.[30]

Lastly, the ritual language of the liturgy is poetic, though not subjective or without need of reference outside its inherent esthetic beauty in order to be legitimate. Liturgical language always refers to someone or something objective, namely God, Christ, the paschal mystery, the

Church, the world. It does not flow from a writer's stream of consciousness. It narrates the people's saving experience of God in their lives, and by virtue of that experience exults, breaks into song of thanks and praise, and pleads for salvation.

The liturgy often makes use of poems and poetic language in order to record the history of God's dealings with humankind. Good poetry has the power to move and touch the hearts of worshipers. The ancient Church used biblical psalms in the liturgy, and encouraged people, as third-century Tertullian informs us, to stand in the assembly to sing or recite poems, called "idiotic psalms," which narrated how Christ broke into their lives.[31] A good number of hymns composed specifically for liturgical celebrations are masterpieces of poetry. One need only recall the hymns Ephrem of Edessa, Ambrose of Milan, Fulgentius, and Rhabanus Maurus wrote for the liturgy.

Poetic context alone can explain or even justify such liturgical compositions as the *improperia* or reproaches on Good Friday. It is extremely difficult to imagine that Jesus who was led to the cross like a lamb and forgave those who crucified him would now turn to his people in words of reproach. Likewise, how do we explain, except in poetic context, such outbursts in the *Exultet* as: "O certe necessarium Adae peccatum! O felix culpa! Ut servum redimeres, Filium tradidisti!"[32]

## Conclusion

In this essay I tinkered once again with ritual, liturgical, and popular religious language. I am aware that the scholars in this delicate area of expertise might not agree with everything I have written. The only thing that I can claim with certainty to be unassailable is that liturgical action requires ritual language. The question is how to define ritual language and establish its purpose and mode of expression. I confined my discussion to two languages of liturgy: Latin and English. I am sure that the experiences of other language groups who have had to grapple with similar or perhaps more difficult points will be worth sharing for mutual help and enrichment.

---

[1] For the elaboration of this essay I am indebted to three authors who are specialists on liturgical language. They are Christine Mohrmann, *Liturgical Latin. Its Origin and Character* (Washington, D.C., 1957); *Latin chrétien et liturgique* (Rome, 1965); Gail Ramshaw, *Christ in Sacred Speech: The Meaning of*

*Liturgical Language* (Philadelphia, 1986); and Gianfranco Venturi, "Lenguaje liturgico," *Nuevo Diccionario de Liturgia* (Madrid, 1987) 1113–27. Mohrmann presents the philological aspect of liturgical Latin, Ramshaw the metaphorical, and Venturi the semiological. The three together make a fine description of this topic.

² N. Chomsky promotes this method. See *Syntactic Structures* (The Hague, 1964). See also E. Nida, *Translating Meaning* (English Language Institute, California, 1982); Idem: *Signs, Sense, Translation* (Cape Town, 1984).

³ St. Jerome attests to the absurdity of word-for-word translations. See *Eusebii Interpretata Praefatio*, Einleitung des Hieronymus, *Eusebius Werke* VII, 1, *GSC* 47, ed. R. Helm (1954) 2: "Si ad verbum interpretor, absurde resonat: si ob necessitatem aliquid in ordine, in sermone mutavero, ab interpretis videbor officio recessisse."

⁴ Consilium: *Instruction "Comme le prévoit,"* no. 12: "The translator must always keep in mind that the 'unit of meaning' is not the individual word but the whole passage." English text in *Documents on the Liturgy 1963–1979* (Collegeville: The Liturgical Press, 1982) 285. See: J. Lamberts: "Vatican II et la liturgie en langue vernaculaire," *Questions liturgiques* 66 (1985) 125–54; P. D'Haese: "Traduction et version après Vatican II; à la recherche d'une langue maternelle liturgique," *Ibid.* 73 (1992) 97–111; D. Lebrun: "Les traductions liturgiques: statut et enjeux," *La Maison-Dieu* 202 (1995) 19–33.

⁵ Oral language implies aural communication. See: K. Larsen: "Language as Aural," *Worship* 54 (1980) 18–35.

⁶ C. Vogel, *Medieval Liturgy. An Introduction to the Sources* (Washington, D.C., 1986) 293–7.

⁷ *Missale Romanum*, editio typica altera (Vatican City, 1975) 452. For background reading on the Roman Canon, see E. Mazza: *The Eucharistic Prayers of the Roman Rite* (New York, 1986).

⁸ Useful references are M. P. Ellebracht, *Remarks on the Vocabulary of the Ancient Orations in the Missale Romanum* (Nijmegen, 1966); ICEL, *A Lexicon of Terms in the Missale Romanum* (Washington, D.C.).

⁹ ICEL, *The Sacramentary* (Revised Edition), Segment Three: Order of Mass I (Washington, D.C., 1994) 33.

¹⁰ Ibid., 44.

¹¹ T. Klauser, *A Short History of the Western Liturgy* (Oxford, 1979) 18–24, 37–47.

¹² See P. G. Gülden, "Lo stile della lingua liturgica," *Le traduzioni dei libri liturgici* (Vatican City, 1966) 217–30; M. Augé: "Principi di interpretazione dei testi liturgici," *Anamnesis* 1 (Turin, 1974) 159–71.

¹³ H. Leclercq, "Cursus," *Dictionnaire d'archéologie chrétienne et de liturgie* III, col. 3193–205.

¹⁴ *Sacramentarium Veronense*, ed. L.C. Mohlberg (Rome, 1966) no. 1239, 157. See study by A. Echiegu, *Translating the Collects of the Solemnities of the Lord in the Language of the African* (Münster, 1984) 122–227.

¹⁵ ICEL, *The Sacramentary*, Segment Two: Proper of Seasons (Washington, D.C., 1994) 40.

¹⁶ *Sacramentarium Veronense*, no. 501, 66.

[17] ICEL, *The Sacramentary*, Segment Four: Order of Mass II (Washington, D.C., 1995) 10. A moderate binary succession is found in the Latin original: "Quibus et de antiqui hostis superbia triumphatur, et nostrae redemptionis recolitur sacramentum."

[18] *Sacramentarium Veronense*, no. 176, 22.

[19] ICEL, *The Sacramentary*, Segment Four: Order of Mass II, 3.

[20] *Sacramentarium Veronense*, no. 1068, 135.

[21] ICEL, *The Sacramentary*, Segment Two, First Sunday of Lent, 77.

[22] Ibid., Fourth Sunday of Lent, 100.

[23] E. Yarnold, "Baptism and the Pagan Mysteries in the Fourth Century," *The Heythrop Journal* XIII (1972) 247–67.

[24] The preface for the Holy Trinity is one clear example of dogmatic construction. The phrases *ex morte eiusdem Filii tui praevisa* (opening prayer for the Immaculate Conception) and *corpore et anima ad caelestem gloriam assumpsisti* (opening prayer for the Assumption) savor of the dogma that defined these beliefs.

[25] The formulary for baptismal profession in the third-century *Traditio Apostolica* is akin to the Creed, but does not of course include later dogmatic elements like *consubstantialis* and *ex Patre Filioque procedit*. See B. Botte (ed.), *La Tradition Apostolique de Saint Hippolyte*, no 21 (Münster, 1989) 46.

[26] Some critics of ICEL want to see dogma in such words as *mereo, mereor,* and *meritum* in practically every instance. These words, however, are plurivalent even in the Latin liturgical texts. See ICEL, *A Lexicon of Terms in the Missale Romanum*, 187–93.

[27] A. Bouley, *From Freedom to Formula* (Washington, D.C., 1981).

[28] ICEL, *The Sacramentary*, Segment One: Ordinary Time (Washington, D.C., 1993) 34.

[29] L. Lovasik, *Treasury of Novenas* (New York, 1986) 111.

[30] The IV Instruction *Roman Liturgy and Inculturation* (January 25, 1994) reminds conferences of bishops that "the introduction of devotional practices into liturgical celebrations under the pretext of inculturation cannot be allowed," because by its nature the liturgy is superior to them (no. 45). However, one thing is incorporating popular devotions wholesale into the liturgy, and another is employing their language and ritual patterns for the sake of a more popular and less classical form of worship. This may prove valuable in places where popular devotions are a vibrant element of religious life.

[31] Tertullian, *Apologeticum* 39, 18; *Corpus Christianorum* II/1 (1954) 153.

[32] *Missale Romanum*, editio typica altera, 272.

# Brother Sun, Sister Death:
# Gender, the Other, and the Liturgy

*Gail Ramshaw*

I have written long and lectured plenty on gender and the liturgy.
I think and write in American English, in which language the designation "gender," as European grammarians would understand it, no
longer exists. When contemporary Americans speak of gender, we
mean a social construct within which sexuality is manifest. We mean
the way women and men stand, the distance they stand apart, whether
they wear a necklace or a chain. But we do not mean a linguistic category that separates things more like a father from things more like a
mother. For us there is only sex: a "he" is male, a "she" is female, an
"it" is neuter. You check the sexual organs, and then you know what to
say. Perilously few exceptions are allowed. Those calling the Church
"she" are speaking an archaism, a foreign language not yet translated
into contemporary speech. And so I have taught that in the liturgy the
neighbor is not "he," the earth is not "she," and, to make our speaking
one stumbling block after another, neither is God "he" nor (I'm sorry
to say) "she," and most of us don't like God to be an "it."

Current liturgical revision has hoped to eliminate the gender bias
that characterized Western speech for three thousand years. For in an
androcentric language, from which ours evolved, not only did masculine nouns designate creatures with male sexuality and entities in
some inexplicable way male-like, but sure-as-shooting all that was
masculine was better and higher and smarter and more godly than
what was feminine. Masculinity boasted more being than femininity.
But what complicates our current editing, what changes what would
be merely a tedious task into a baffling dilemma, is that liturgical language is metaphoric as well as explicit. Metaphoric speech is not fac-
tually accurate. It alters reality by presenting things as they are not,
and in the saying renders them so. Metaphors affirm the no and the

yes simultaneously. Can then the earth, or the Church, be "she," at least metaphorically?

And the committee votes. Perhaps we let the losing side win this one.

Francis' "Canticle of Brother Sun" presents us with a classic example of our quandary. Francis wrote in a thirteenth-century Umbrian tongue: the sun is masculine, being more powerful; the moon is feminine, waxing and waning in 28-day cycles. The sun was Brother, as of the day, the moon Sister, as of the night. Francis then evoked the four elements, the core ingredients of the universe, calling them Brother or Sister: air and fire, the less corporeal of the four, are masculine; water and earth, the more corporeal, are feminine. It is a commonplace distinction in medieval minds. Recall Julian of Norwich a century later saying that the second person of the Trinity was her mother because in becoming human and taking on a body, God in Christ became feminine. Water has more corporeality than air, females had more body than males. Bleeding made God like a woman.

It is not a distinction that sits well with me. In the feminist conversation I am a minimizer, continuously interested in probing the differences between male and female, but wary lest our inadequate data and our legacy of androcentrism alter our vision and make us think we see positives and negatives that are not there. I proceed by minimizing the differences between the sexes. I judge that minimizing is the only avenue to legal equality. I doubt that we could this time around live separate but equal; and what would sexually-based laws do with the transgendered person interviewed on National Public Radio?

But more central to my work with Christian liturgical speech is my conviction that minimizing is the baptismal way. I think of the phrases in Galatians 3: "no longer Jew or Greek, no longer slave or free, no longer male and female." It took a century for Christians to heed Paul and discard the separation between Jew and Greek. It took seventeen hundred more years for the Church to reject the distinction "slave" and "free." We are finally getting around to "male" and "female." Baptism, it seems to me, recreates humans as equal under God, not as divided into two drawers stuck shut from centuries of grime, the masculine drawer filled with essays on the magnitude of the sun, the feminine drawer containing poetry on the beauty of the moon. I mean not to deny the body, only to urge that body parts and those personality tendencies perhaps attending them not constitute the categories by which even the Church separates us from each other.

But to return to Francis: that which at the end praises God is Sister Death. Is death "Sister" only because, like the nouns moon, water and earth, the words in Italian are feminine gender? Or does Francis mean rather to say that, in being the truest fact of our bodily existence and the farthest reality from God, death must be, logically, or at least metaphorically, female-like? Francis welcomes her, heading gladly into her arms, understandably, considering the unremitting physical agony he was suffering when he wrote the Canticle.

Now back to us. For us, the moon, earth, water, death, these are not female; in American English they are not even feminine. So what shall I do with the Canticle? Perhaps I shall translate Francis' poem accurately, and we will sing his words, rather than our own. We will try, even in happy health, to welcome Sister Death. But perhaps we must judge that invoking death as our Sister has got to go, for it is only more of how the male is god-like and the female dirt-like. We don't need any more of this on Sunday mornings.

Which way will you vote? We'll have to take a vote; we'll never get consensus on this one.

To force myself to think deeper (Snoopy's title for his book on theology: "Has It Ever Occurred to You That You Might Be Wrong?") I read the French feminist Hélène Cixous. She describes two kinds of writing: one closed, about the I, striving for self-definition; and one open, about the other, hoping for inclusion. Cixous decides that the first, about the I, while it has been relentlessly pursued in the West, cannot but be partial, because the I must also include the other. She asks, "Who are I?" and she writes of awe before the other, of her desire to be enlarged by the other, of the risks and rewards of opening to the other. The one is not without the other, writes Cixous. Meanings flow.

Writing in French, Cixous calls the self-referential speech about the I "masculine writing" and the speech that opens toward the other "feminine writing." But she is no hard-core maximizer. Both men and women rely on language of control, and both need language of embrace. She writes that the labels "masculine" and "feminine" represent binary distinctions which make no sense, categories that we use with care, demarcations that themselves ought to flow. Since I am a minimizer speaking American English, I appreciate her caveat: these separatist categories are no longer useful. Perhaps they are not even true. And I avoid even her reluctant use of the gendered terms.

But her focus on writing that is open to the other excites the liturgist in me. Yes, we need "I" speech, language of boundaries, in the Church as well as in the self. If I seep into you, I am no good to anyone. The Church as well needs to describe itself, this not that, Christian not Hindu, Trinity not pantheism. Both the men and the women in the Church affirm a creed and struggle over a catechism. But the liturgy inserts me into us. Western philosophy and psychology notwithstanding, in the liturgy I am not an I alone. The liturgy expresses the body of Christ. I am a fingernail—but in what a body! In the liturgy I celebrate the I-who-I-are. Even by merely showing up at the liturgy each Sunday I reconnect with the rest of my baptized self, and the metaphors in the liturgy and its rituals of greeting and eating open me further, to my Christian heritage, to the people sitting next to me, to the world's current needs, to God.

Francis knew about the other. Well-to-do, he became poor. Healthy, he embraced the leper. Taught to honor the hierarchy, he chose a lay community. In a time of monarchical display, he venerated the manger. Aware of his humanity, he communed with the animals. Electing a celibate separation, he worked with Clare and is buried alongside Giacoma. Grateful for life with brothers, he honored death as his sister. We find it troublesome to emulate him. We have no time, we need our energies to erect our boundaries, we wish no distractions from our goals, I simply must finish this manuscript, I need to construct my I— and the other is gone.

At the Sunday liturgy this collection of "I"s is invited to pray the intercessions. Perhaps your parish is not typical, but the intercessory prayers in far too many assemblies are monuments to the self, each petition about me or my parish, my attitudes, my opportunities, my fears. Gracious God, help us (read: me) to realize that I should pray once a week. Meanwhile Francis calls to us to remember the other. I would like the intercessions to be a full five minutes long, with petitions for all the others: the list of others is so long, and we need time to turn our minds from our me to the other. If coming to liturgy at all begins our opening to the other, praying a respectable intercessory prayer practices the mindset. For at least this once in the week, I attend to the I-who-I-are.

The Trinity is our paradigm for this liturgical life beyond the I. According to trinitarian doctrine, not even God is a self-contained monad. Rather, in the One of God is Three: the I of God, the you of Christ, the we of the community. As the Orthodox icon of the *Anastasis* pictures it, even in death Christ is not alone, but is grabbing onto the wrists of Adam and Eve, pulling them up, both sexes with God. I like best the depiction from 1320 in the Church of the monastery of the Chora in Istanbul: rather than looking at Adam, as is usually his stance in these icons, Christ looks straight out at us, including us in his salvation, one arm out to Eve, one to Adam, both equal, neither preferred, with us as well caught up from death into life with God. This trinitarian opening to the other is what we practice in our prayer.

There is great debate among grammarians about the origins of gender designations in speech. So why was the sun masculine? Well, it isn't, in every language and myth. But it is clear that for Francis gender was a metaphor for the other. "Brother" and "Sister" were passwords for opening his arms to the other, and for some people today sexuality remains the primary category of otherness. But simply your being of the opposite sex does not necessitate my greeting you as other. Many sexual encounters are only about defining the I, about getting you in here with me so that I am a bigger I. Even sexual intercourse can be an avoidance of the other. As well, gays and lesbians affirm that we can meet the same sex with openness to the wonder of the other. Thus while the other cannot be equated with the sex I am not, the old categories of gender might work as metaphors assisting our inclusion of the other, providing we use them with care, remembering that a metaphor, both an is and an is not, is but one example of the other included.

So, thanks to Francis and Cixous, I will now say it this way: The sun is not masculine, death is not feminine. But the baptized community wants to practice embracing the other, and our liturgical language must find ways for a culture characterized by isolation booths to open the doors. We must find the words that will superimpose the body that is Christ on the body that is me, that I may become the I-who-I-are. One way will be to sing Francis' Canticle, even with its gendered sun and moon and its medieval table of elements, for in so doing I open myself up at least to a thirteenth-century man and his mind, so very different from mine. And since we are singing metaphors, during the communion we will join in a new canticle, in which perhaps all the twelve fruits of the tree of life, each neither female nor male, all thriving on branches beyond gender, are the other that we become.

# Some Musings on the Poetry of Prayer

*Kathleen Hughes, R.S.C.J.*

"Banal," some have charged. "Flat," "insipid," "uninspiring," "too clipped," "nothing memorable"—such has been the critique of much liturgical language, especially the language of the first generation of translations, prepared in such haste after the door was opened to the vernacular by Vatican II. And often critics have added: "What we need in our prayer is more poetry."

Linking poetry and prayer seems to be a natural instinct. Indeed, there is much in common between them:

> You can't pray a lie, said Huckleberry Finn;
> you can't poe one either. It is the same mirror:
> mobile, glancing, we call it poetry,
>     fixed centrally, we call it a religion,
>     and God is the poetry caught in any religion,
>     caught, not imprisoned. Caught as in a mirror
> that [God] attracted, being in the world as poetry
> is in the poem, a law against its closure.[1]

Do we need more poetry in the language of our prayer? How is it achieved? What difference would it make if we tried to imagine liturgical prayer as poetry? And furthermore, if we want prayers which are memorable, which linger in the air, touch our imaginations and move our hearts, are we prepared to accept the demands such language might make on us? Those are some of the questions that have prompted the following musings.

For the last nineteen years I have collaborated in the work of the International Commission on English in the Liturgy [ICEL]: I am familiar with the numerous issues surrounding the translation and revision of liturgical language; I have chaired ICEL's subcommittee on original texts and produced a few of them myself; I have followed the debates about inclusive language and God language and have weighed in with one or two opinions on these topics; I am a founding member of WE BELIEVE, a movement established to counteract the forces attempting to defeat the adoption of the revised *Sacramentary*. I have, in other words, reflected a lot about liturgical language for a good number of years. Yet the poetry of prayer remains an elusive topic in discussions of liturgical language and we are far from achieving a consensus about how to address it or what it entails.

I thought of fleshing out the topic by examining the qualities of poetry that might characterize our liturgies as a whole. I considered a presentation of the many symbolic languages of prayer that make up the poetic event we call worship. I weighed the possibility of looking at some of the new texts of our prayer, but "the poetry of prayer" goes beyond the text. It takes in the full spectrum of texts, pray-ers, the numinous, and the choreography that weaves all these together with the stuff of our everyday lives.

Finally—and taking my cue from the oft-repeated desire that liturgical language be "memorable"—I decided to explore how words work in our culture and in our everyday experience as foundation for examining words in worship, words we hope will help us respond to the God of our lives and empower us to work for God's reign in our world.

In the first section, I will look at how communication happens in everyday life, how words so often fail us, but how ordinary words in ordinary time *sometimes* assume an extraordinary power. This happens, I believe, in a mysterious and often inexplicable interplay of speaker, hearer, and word spoken. Second, I will look at silence as the essential context for a word to be heard—to move, to engage, to commit. Third, having looked at ordinary communication and the silence out of which weighty words may be heard, I will turn to the liturgy and examine liturgical prayer as the community's response to the Divine Poet. Here again, I will look at the dynamic of communication, but this time asking how words work and how they make a difference in the liturgical context. Finally, I will conclude with a few words about the "memorability" of prayer and its demands.

## Word in Everyday Life

I begin, then, by asking this simple question: how do words work in our ordinary lives? What kinds of words can be heard in our world? What kinds of words enlighten or provoke? What kinds of words disturb? Do the words "peacekeeper missile" unnerve us? Does language of "ethnic cleansing" sear our very souls? What kinds of words heal or change us? give new direction to our lives? invite to a new way of being in the world? What makes the word we speak to another person a timely word? a transforming word? a liberating word? Think of the tiny phrase "Shindler's List" and how it became a word of saving power? Context matters, of course, but there is so much more.

How does a word sometimes make a real difference? What is its power—and why does it happen so infrequently? Consider, for example, the tenor of our everyday communication. How much is frivolous in our conversations? How much is chit chat, spoken to relieve the awkward silences between us? As a *Time* essay remarked some years ago: "We all know how treacherous are words, and how often we use them to paper over embarrassment, or emptiness, or fear of the larger spaces that silence brings."[2] And what of the language of public discourse? How much of it has been evacuated of meaning because words are subject to endless exegesis on our editorial pages and to reinterpretation—even revisionist history, on the six o'clock news? Words written years ago described well the present situation:

> Human perception has been dulled. We have lost our awareness of some deep and subtle things. Among them the zest for words. Words have for us now only a surface existence. They have lost their power to shock and startle. They have been reduced to a fleeting image, to a thin tinkle of sound. . . . But in our day even the sense that paradise is lost is lost. We are too superficial to be distressed by the loss of meaning, though we are more and more glib about the surface sense. We pass words from mouth to mouth as we do money from hand to hand and with no more attention to what they were meant to convey than to the inscription on the coins. The value-mark is all we notice. They signify something but reveal nothing. So far from promoting [communion between us] words clatter out of us like coins from a cash register and with much the same consciousness as the machine has of their value.[3]

T. S. Eliot captured the same idea:

> Words strain,
> Crack and sometimes break, under the burden,
> Under the tension, slip, slide, perish,
> Decay with imprecision, will not stay in place,
> Will not stay still.[4]

But once in a great while—surely you have had the experience—a word works. A word may shock us into attention. A word may strike us with all its original force, astonishing impact, intellectual insight, even power to change our hearts. We are carried out of ourselves; we experience transformation. Once in a great while, in the midst of the clatter and the clutter of words, a word is spoken which matters. It may be something that has been said to us many times before, but this time we hear it and we are different because of it.

Consider the difference a word can make in the course of a lifetime, how it can stop us in our tracks, bring us to our senses, shock us into paying attention: "I love you." "I need you." "The answer is No!" "She has six months to live." "You are ruining your life." "I'm sorry." "Go in peace." Words are able to enlighten, provoke, disturb, heal. Words can invite us to take a new direction; words can reshape our worlds.

Such a word is "a wondrous reality: form and content, significance and love, intellect and heart, a full, round, vibrant whole." That is the assessment of Romano Guardini who went on to describe the potential power of word in this way:

> It is not barren information for us to consider and understand, but a reality for us to encounter personally. We must receive and store it in all its earthiness, its characteristic style and imagery. Then it proves its power. In the parable of the sower, [the Lord] compares it to a seed in search of good ground. It possesses the power of growth, the strength to start and develop life. Hence we must not receive it as we grasp an idea with our mind, but as earth receives a grain of wheat.[5]

I wonder how, when, and why some words work. I ask myself: why is a word, which has the power of liberation, so often not effective? How is it possible that we hear the same word year after year, or from several different sources, yet only *really* and *finally* hear it, accept it, and appropriate it at a given moment, or from one person and not another? What makes us receptive to the word? What personal qualities of the speaker make the word "hear-able"? What are some qualities in us that render us as hearers hospitable to the timely word and to the person from whom it is received?

There appears to be an important and dynamic interplay among the hearer, the speaker, and the word spoken—three components of the speech act. We will examine them in turn.

First, the speaker—the person whose word is received as a timely word. We are able to hear a word from a speaker who is credible, a person who has pursued the truth and who has welcomed the word and lived it before she or he has spoken it to another. The word spoken thus becomes a revelation out of the depths of the speaker's self-understanding. The timely speaker somehow communicates that the

word spoken is not the last word nor the whole word but only a fragile attempt to voice one's truth which, though it remains incomplete,
has the full stature of integrity. The timely speaker communicates
through word and gesture that the hearer is totally free in the decision
to accept or reject the word; the speaker is aware that her own integrity
is not diminished by rejection of the word; the speaker is aware that a
forced word would find no root.

But it is not enough that a speaker be credible and trustworthy. The
word itself has to be of a certain quality. What kinds of words can be
heard in our world? What is it about a given word that makes it transforming of our lives? The word which is heard has two qualities: it is
a word of *consolation* and a word of *challenge*. The word consoles. It addresses me in my situation. It gathers up my life and identifies who I
am. It touches my everyday experience, my problems, my ambiguities,
my weaknesses. It expresses understanding. But it does not leave me
there. It is also a word of challenge or judgment in the fullest biblical
sense. It pushes me beyond where I am, inviting me into a new future,
a different way of life. It disturbs me in the best sense and it calls me
to become more authentically who I am.

Think of all of Jesus' parables. In one way or another, Jesus' words
to his followers had this double aspect: Jesus never told frivolous stories. He enthralled his hearers. He addressed them in the context of
their everyday lives and won their attention as they became caught up
in the story and its correspondence to their own experience: wedding
banquets and seeds to be sown, unjust stewards and widows' mites,
friends who knock on the door late at night, and good Samaritan
neighbors. Jesus' followers listened to his word. They found *themselves*
in the stories; this man understood them. It is a moment of consolation.
Then Jesus gently lays claim. He leads his hearers to a new and deeper
truth. He invites and summons them, in the words of the Godspell
song, "to follow him more nearly day by day."

In the manner of Jesus, the word of a timely speaker is one of consolation and challenge: consolation in the expression of solidarity and
the understanding of the boundary situation itself; challenge in the invitation to move beyond that situation to a new decision. The speaker
whose word is timely is therefore believable and trustworthy, one who
can speak the word with freedom and love.

Yet some of Jesus' followers went away sad. Not everyone receives
the credible speaker or the timely word. What can be said about hearing and the hearer? We become open and receptive to a word through
consciousness of need and our own posing of a question. An answer—
we could call it the word spoken to us—is not an answer at all until a
question has been raised. We need to distinguish, therefore, between

the timely word which finds a home and what we might call the "disturbing word" which simply rattles our cage and raises the questions. A disturbing word is a threshold word which brings a basic situation to conscious awareness, helps to pose a question and to clarify my situation as crisis or boundary, drives me actively to pursue the truth, and ultimately creates the vulnerable climate for receptivity and decision when the timely word is offered. Discovering ourselves in a crisis situation, we become consciously aware of a desire and need to hear a word which will transform that situation and bring new life, new hope, and rich possibilities.

Johannes Metz described the receptivity of hearer to word heard in yet another way. A provocative word will touch what Metz calls "the dangerous memory" of an individual or a group, not a series of trivial reminiscences but that living and life-giving memory that leads us into the future. The word, therefore, gathers up the heart of the past in such a way that it impels the hearer into the future with a faithful and transforming force. The word, then, leads and binds me to a new truth and a new vision, and it "inspirits" me to response because it holds out the hope of becoming more fully human.

This sort of reflection helps us to clarify patterns of relationships in our own lives in which we have been the speakers or the recipients of "weighty words." These reflections apply analogously to every ministry of the Word of God, whether that of catechesis, preaching, teaching, proclamation, or spiritual direction. In these various ministries of the word, a constant challenge is to be credible and trustworthy, offering a personal word that has been personally appropriated in prayer and shaped to the real historical and cultural context of the hearers, offering the word as gift and without self-interest, yet with a vigorous and compelling love of the truth.

In summary, in those instances when the "word does not return void but accomplishes the work for which it was sent" there are three important factors: the word has a certain truth and gravity; the speaker is credible; and the hearer is receptive.

Before applying this framework to the liturgy, let us pause for a moment to explore the word womb of silence.

## Word Born of Silence

There are many different kinds of silence out of which words are born. Mark Searle once categorized the variety of silences as: the fretful and fidgety silence of boredom; the silence of being and centered repose; the wordless, mutual silence of old friends; the silence of memory and recollection that quickens longing and deepens understanding; the silence of groping for words that stretch and strain and break under the weight they cannot bear; and the silence of solemn respect, "of listening carefully to another's words that matter, of knowing there is a time for speaking and that it is not now, that one must quiet oneself and listen for the word that may shape one's life."[6] In other words, "Silence is an instrument that plays in many keys, is appropriate to many moods. What all good forms of silence have in common is that they lead us to the point where we discover the limitations of speech and action, that point which is the threshold of mystery."[7]

So word is born in silence and word leads us, in turn, to silence and mystery. But here's another fact of culture. We suffer from silence deprivation! We are surrounded by noise, by Muzak, by the drone of television or the blare of news-radio. Noise envelops us; it also invades our inner selves. Our thoughts drag us in every possible direction. We replay and rewrite conversations in our heads. We deal with distraction at one event by making mental lists of "things to do" for the next. Our family, friends, and adversaries, our work and leisure obligations, our public and our private plans, what we are serving next Tuesday for dinner—all of it is a kind of inner noise at least as cacophonous as the lyrics of the latest MTV offering, and most of it is "sound and fury, signifying nothing."

Add to this noise the speed of our lives, the multiple obligations bartering for equal time and fracturing the stillness of our fragile world. "Distracted from distraction by distraction" is the way T. S. Eliot once described it. We call it noise and haste, busyness and fatigue. And all of it militates against the stillness, the composure, the attentiveness, and the serenity so necessary for genuine speech to be born.

On the other hand, sometimes the very act of silence has the power to call forth an authentic, revelatory word in another—or so Yeats tells us: "We can make our minds so like still water that beings gather about us that they might see, it may be, their own images, and so live for a moment with a clearer, perhaps even with a fiercer life because of our quiet."[8]

## The Poetry of Prayer

Here we begin to ponder the poetry of prayer, the fiercer life born of stillness, the mystery of our conversation with the divine. Those who run precipitously through life will also run precipitously through the liturgy, rushing, as Abraham Heschel once said, "In and out of the prayer-texts, as if the task were to cover a maximum of space in a minimum of time, deriving little from worship. To be able to pray is to stand still and to dwell upon a word."[9] And we would add, as Christians, that to be able to pray is to stand still and to dwell upon the

Word made flesh who is the most perfect poetry of God. Indeed, God is the Divine Poet, the one whose flawless blend of poetry and prose surrounds us, the one whom a seventeenth-century visionary captured in these lines:

> My God, my God, thou art a direct God, may I not say a literal God, a God that wouldst be understood literally and according to the plain sense of all that thou sayest? but thou art also (Lord, I intend it to thy glory, and let no profane misinterpreter abuse it to thy diminution), thou art a figurative, a metaphorical God, too; a God in whose words there is such a height of figures, such peregrinations to fetch remote and precious metaphors, such extensions, such spreadings, such curtains of allegories, such third heavens of hyperboles, so harmonious elocutions, so retired and so reserved expressions, so commanding persuasions, so persuading commandments, such sinews even in thy milk, and such things in thy words, as all profane authors seem of the seed of the serpent that creeps, thou art the Dove that flies.[10]

Even such rapturous speech cannot contain the poetry of God. Pity, then, those who forge our response to this Poet. Pity those who try to craft our prayer, who take and mold the humble stuff of light and color, of time and space, sound and smell, touch and movement, and elements of earth . . . and, most fragile of all, words. Pity those who work with words whose end is God. Could Eliot have had prayer in mind when he said:

> What we call the beginning is often the end.
> And to make an end is to make a beginning.
> The end is where we start from. And every phrase
> And sentence that is right (where every word is at home,
> Taking its place to support the others,
> The word neither diffident nor ostentatious,
> An easy commerce of the old and new,
> The common word exact without vulgarity,
> The formal word precise but not pedantic,
> The complete consort dancing together)
> Every phrase and every sentence is an end and a begin-
>     ning. . . ."[11]

We cannot help it. Sometimes we must use words, however exalted the end, however halting the beginning.

Here is my contention: If speaker, hearer, and word spoken each is an *essential* part of the dynamic of the word that is actually heard in our world, the word which makes a difference, surely the *same* dynamic is operative when we gather for prayer. The word, the speaker, and the hearer are *all* essential to the word-event of worship.

First of all, word spoken. The word of prayer must be a weighty word, a language capable of expressing the voice of the Church at prayer. One of the chief criticisms of the *Sacramentary* now in possession is that its language is ordinary or in the wrong language register. It is no secret that this first generation book was done at break-neck speed. Some of it is inelegant, flat, and monosyllabic.[12] At the same time, some of the prayers, particularly some alternative opening prayers are too complex for aural comprehension on a first reading.[13] Some of the prayers, especially the present alternative opening prayers, include a war of images competing for attention. Similarly, some liturgical texts incorporate too many scriptural allusions while others seem oddly disconnected from the Scriptures. Suffice it to say that much of the present *Sacramentary*, especially its collect prayers, is decidedly *not* memorable.

Happily, in the revision of the *Sacramentary* there are new texts and fresh translations whose meter and rhythm have been more carefully weighed. Our new texts will help us pray with words of force and texture, the whole a careful choreography of sense and sound. I think it safe to say that what has been produced in the second-generation *Sacramentary* is something beautiful for God. But word is only one component of the poetic communication of liturgy.

The speaker, in this case the presider (and analogously the lector, the homilist, the cantor, and the proclaimer of intercessions), must possess certain qualities and skills in order to be credible and trustworthy in giving voice to our prayer. In worship, the presider is like the poet described by W. H. Auden, uttering the word, and in so doing, teaching each of us to pray:

> Follow, poet, follow right
> To the bottom of the night,
> With your unconstraining voice
> Still persuade us to rejoice
>     With the farming of a verse
>     Make a vineyard of the curse,
>     Sing of human unsuccess
>     In a rapture of distress;
> In the deserts of the heart
> Let the healing fountain start,
> In the prison of his days
> Teach the free man how to praise.[14]

The reformed liturgy, product of the council, now places enormous requirements on the one who would lead us in prayer. By having the presider face the community, the ritual now demands a range of skills of communication and expression. And what's more, to be credible and trustworthy, presiders must sound like they *mean* what they say. A story told me by one of my students illustrates this well:

There was a young man who belonged to a praying Christian community, and he felt he was called to become a man of the cloth, one who would lead his community in prayer. He brought this desire to the congregation and they supported his decision by contributing to his formal education in the ministry. After he completed his studies he returned to the community when it was at prayer. They were so pleased to see him and asked him to pray with them by reciting the twenty-third psalm. And recite he did, and very eloquently, too. He pronounced each word carefully and with dignity, giving each phrase the oh-so-right inflection. He finished with just the right flourish. The assembly thought it was so wonderful and they applauded loudly. He was touched.

Then one of the old deacons of the church got up and asked the young man, "Is this what you said, son?" The deacon then proceeded to say the twenty-third psalm in his own way. It was not with the eloquent language of the young man. The old deacon's English was broken, he didn't pace it well, it wasn't exactly as it was written in the Good Book, he didn't stand up properly. But the congregation was spell-bound. Some openly cried. There was a "speak it, deacon," an "Amen," an "I hear you."

The young man was openly moved, too. When the old deacon finished, the young man came to him and said, "I don't understand! I studied for six years, attained a Doctor of Divinity degree, and they only applauded for me, but they wept for you! How do you do it?"

"Son," the old deacon replied, "You know the psalm, but I know the Shepherd."

So, we need words that matter and we need believing and believable presiders. But having said this much about word and speaker it seems undeniable that after thirty plus years of liturgical reform, new texts and well-trained presiders won't make the slightest bit of difference unless we, hearers of the word spoken in our name, recognize that *we* are the third party in the speech act of prayer.

Some of us have placed a great deal of attention and energy on the new texts of the liturgy and we genuinely delight in the hope that we will have a revised *Sacramentary* soon. Many of us have recognized, as we implemented the liturgical reforms of the council in our dioceses and parishes, the need for careful, prayerful preparation of presiders who will speak the poetry of our prayer. But how much time, energy and critique, did we spend on ourselves as hearers? To use a time-honored phrase: it is a question of active participation; it is a question—once the liturgy is prepared—of spending at least as much time preparing ourselves.

If, today, we can barely hear a word above the din inside us and around us, if we have barely time for listening with the hectic pace we keep, what would make us think that better texts and prayerful proclamation are the real issues, or the only issues? In the last analysis, we are a part of the poem or it doesn't happen in us:

> See
> how in silence and peace
> the poem grows:
> a dazzling tree that rises
> skywards
> —and we, words of the poem.
> leaves of the tree.[15]

The poetry of prayer is not something we hear, nor something we observe, but something we create each time we gather for the liturgy. We must bring to bear all the attention we can muster, all the stillness and composure, all the knowledge of our present situation, all the vulnerability and need, all the dyings and the risings below the surface of our lives in that place where we may meet the Divine Poet.

"Strange," says a character in a recent novel,

> Strange, the places in yourself you don't know about, the deep places inside you that can be weeping all the time that your mouth is talking or laughing. The inside of you is like a well about which you know very little. That must be your soul where all the real things take place. And if it is a right deep place and has been tended by your hand, then [God will be] deep down in there, whispering to you always about the realities."[16]

## Conclusion

We have looked at word in everyday life and noticed the essential interplay of credible speaker, receptive listener, and a word that matters. We have discovered the importance of speechlessness—of silence—for a true word to be spoken. We then returned to the trinity of word, speaker, and listener as ingredients in the poetry of prayer which we call the liturgy, ingredients which in care-full and balanced choreography make prayer "memorable."

Now there is one thing left to do, namely, to be explicit about why it is important that prayer be memorable at all. Implicitly throughout this essay we have been talking about "memorable" language. Implicitly we have been talking about a word-event which makes a difference. Implicitly we have been talking about liturgy that does not leave us unmoved and uncommitted, but rather shocks us into attention, places a claim upon us, sends us to live a fiercer and more focused life, and invites us again and again into a new way of being in relationship with God and with the world God so loves.

In his ninth elegy, Rilke tells of the traveler who returns from the mountain slopes into the valley. "He brings, not a handful of earth, unsayable to others, but instead some word he has gained, some pure word. . . . *Here* is the time for the *sayable,* here is its homeland." Rilke urges his traveler: "Speak and bear witness."[17]

Maybe that is a way to imagine what memorable prayer is all about: it is a charge to speak and bear witness to the word we have heard on the mountain slopes.

---

[1] Les Murray, from *The Daylight Moon,* Persea Books, Inc., cited in Missy Daniel, "Poetry is Presence: An Interview with Les Murray," *Commonweal* 119:10 (May 22, 1992).

[2] Pico Iyer, "The Eloquent Sounds of Silence," *Time* 141:4 (January 25, 1993) 74.

[3] Romano Guardini, *Sacred Signs,* trans., Grace Branham (St. Louis: Pio Decimo Press, 1956) 103–4.

[4] T. S. Eliot, "Burnt Norton," *The Collected Poetry and Plays 1909–1950* (New York: Harcourt, Brace and World, Inc., 1971) 121.

[5] Romano Guardini, *Meditations Before Mass,* trans., Elinor Castendyke Briefs (Westminster: Newman Press, 1956) 67.

[6] Mark Searle, "Keeping Silence," in *Liturgical Gestures, Words, Objects,* ed. Eleanor Bernstein (Notre Dame: Notre Dame Center for Pastoral Liturgy, 1995) 10–11.

[7] Mark Searle, "Silence," in *Assembly* (September, 1982).

[8] W. B. Yeats, *The Celtic Twilight* (London: A. H. Bullen, 1912) 128.

[9] Abraham Heschel, *Man's Quest for God* (New York: Simon and Schuster, 1954).

[10] John Donne, *Devotions Upon Emergent Occasions* (Ann Arbor: Ann Arbor Paperbacks of University of Michigan Press, 1959/1965) 124.

[11] T. S. Eliot, "Little Gidding," *Collected Poetry and Plays 1909–1950* (New York: Harcourt, Brace and World, Inc., 1971) 144.

[12] E.g., Opening Prayer for the Ninth Sunday in Ordinary Time.

[13] E.g., Alternative Opening Prayer for the Seventh Sunday of Easter.

[14] W. H. Auden, "In Memory of W. B. Yeats" in *Collected Poetry of W. H. Auden* (New York: Random House, 1945) 51.

[15] Catherine DeVinck, "That I May See," in *A Time to Gather* (Allendale, N.J.: Alleluia Press, 1967) 35.

[16] Walter Macken, *Seek the Fair Land* (London: Pan Books Ltd., 1959).

[17] R. M. Rilke, "Duino Elegies," in *Selected Poetry of Rainer Maria Rilke*, ed. and trans. by Stephen Mitchell (New York: Vintage, 1989) 199–200.

# The Language of Ministry in Contemporary Roman Catholicism

*John F. Baldovin, S.J.*

Language shapes reality. Recently a friend reminded me of the axiom popular among some feminist theoreticians: "Those who control the vocabulary, control the conversation." The saying was particularly apt in the context of a discussion with a diocesan environment and art commission in which an architect's plan for a chapel of reservation in a proposed church was described as locating the chapel in a *corner*. It was suggested that the perception of the plan would be altered considerably were the placement to be described as a *niche*. Language shapes reality. It is, in the famous phrase of Martin Heidegger, "the House of Being."

This profound insight into the way language affects our perception of reality is also true in terms of persons. We can easily understand that a vastly different appreciation of function applies to persons when they are called "ushers" and when they are called "ministers of hospitality." The former connotes keeping order and taking people to their seats, whereas the latter points to a welcoming attitude on the part of a gathered assembly. The very same actions may be performed by ushers and ministers of hospitality, but the perception that the different names give makes a world of difference.

Such attention to vocabulary is not mere quibbling or sophistry. What we call things or persons has a profound affect on how they are conceived and how we relate to them. If twentieth century philosophy and contemporary experience have taught us anything, they have taught us that language is of the utmost importance, especially when it comes to religion, where words can not only *describe* things and states of affairs but *do* them. "I take you to be my wife or husband . . . I baptize you in the name . . . Be sealed with the gift . . ." The purpose of this essay is to analyze the language that contemporary Roman

Catholics use about ministry (especially in the official liturgical texts) in the hope that some clarity about the meaning of ministry in the Church might ensue. We shall do this by discussing the changes in vocabulary and imagery in the reformed liturgies of the Roman Catholic Church, with particular attention to the rite of ordination for deacons, presbyters, and bishops, and to the rites performed by lay persons.

## The Language of the Pre-Vatican II Books

Before dealing with the changes in vocabulary and perception brought on by the reforms of the Second Vatican Council, we shall make a brief survey of the language used in the pre-Vatican II books. Let us start with the *Ritus Servandus* of the Tridentine Missal.[1] Throughout this guide to rubrics, the presider is referred to as either *sacerdos,* or *sacerdos celebrans,* or simply *celebrans.* The Latin transliteration of the Greek *diakonos, diaconus* is used for the deacon (as *subdiaconus* is employed for the subdeacon). The servers are called *acolythi,* but sometimes the more generic title *ministri* is used. The title for the presider is not differentiated between presbyter and bishop, since the missal was intended for use by anyone in presbyteral or episcopal orders. The same terminology found in the rubrical *Ritus Servandus* is employed in the rubrics throughout the missal.

Turning to ordination in the pre-Vatican II rites, we shall begin with the instruction given to the candidates. This instruction by the bishop contains language of priesthood, consecration, and elevation in status. It makes clear that priests, deacons, and subdeacons occupy a "lower rank" than bishops.[2] Presbyters (priests) are called "to a rank so exalted no one should approach without feelings of dread."

In the first prayer of consecration, the bishop prays that God will "pour forth on these servants of thine the blessing of the Holy Spirit and the power of priestly grace." In language similar to the instruction, the bishop addresses God as the "author of hierarchical grades." The form of the sacrament (at least since Pius XII declared it to be so) is: "We entreat thee, almighty Father, to give these servants of thine the dignity of the priesthood." At the handing-over of the chalice and paten (which had been in the theology of St. Thomas Aquinas the matter and form of the sacrament) the bishop says to the new priest: "Receive the power to offer sacrifice to God and to celebrate Masses for both the living and the dead in the Lord's name." A second imposition of hands with a formula for receiving the power to forgive sins follows after Communion.

In the terminology that Mary Collins has adopted in an important study, "The Public Language of Ministry," we are dealing here with ideas about status orientation and particularly status elevation.[3] Collins summarizes well the process of sacralization that produced the traditional Roman ordination rites. It is precisely the notion of sacralization and how it fits into a modern Catholic world view that is at issue today. There can be little doubt that Christian faith moved from a rather non-cultic and non-sacral self-understanding to one that adapted the sacral world view of late antiquity. This process began in the third century and was completed in all its main lines by the time of the Carolingian reform of the ninth century. In this world view the priest is a sacred person, set apart to offer sacrifice, albeit the sacrifice of the New Law, the Eucharist. He is differentiated by his powers, the greatest of which is the power to consecrate at the Eucharist and to "offer sacrifice for both the living and the dead." These are the ideas reflected in the language that the rites employed prior to the Second Vatican Council. They are made all the more complex by the ideal of sexual continence imposed upon priests beginning in the fourth century.[4]

The very language of priesthood and celebrant (not to mention sacrifice and power) carries resonances that inevitably color the perception of the person of ministers and of their activity, especially at worship. In some ways the Second Vatican Council and subsequent reforms attempted to redress this situation. To that reform we shall now turn.

## Vatican II and the Reform

Vatican II's *Dogmatic Constitution on the Church (Lumen Gentium)* addressed a number of important ecclesiological issues that had been left unresolved with the abrupt adjournment of Vatican I in 1870. Among these issues was the relative status of bishops and presbyters. Bishops are now clearly differentiated from presbyters as members of a different *ordo* in the Church.[5] Presbyters form a kind of college in each local church to aid in the bishop's ministry, and as pastors the presbyters exercise a similar three-fold office of ritual leadership (priest), governance (pastor), and preaching (prophet).[6] In fact, by placing the ministry of proclamation of the Word first, the council Fathers seem to have been emphasizing the last of this triad.

In terms of the question we are asking about language, perhaps the most important statements of the council reflect on the distinction between the priesthood of the ordained and that of the baptized. *The Decree on the Ministry and Life of Priests* reflects a sentence found in *The Dogmatic Constitution on the Church* #10, which states: "Though they differ essentially and not only in degree, the common priesthood of the faithful and the ministerial or hierarchical priesthood are nonetheless ordered to one another; each in its own proper way shares in the one priesthood of Christ."[7]

The constitution does not say explicitly what the essential difference between the two forms of this one priesthood is. It should be noted, however, that the intent of the sentence is to emphasize the unity of priesthood in Christ and the essential difference is mentioned in a subordinate clause. Perhaps the *Catechism of the Catholic Church* can be of some help. The Catechism inverts the sentence we have just cited. I will cite the whole paragraph for the sake of completeness:

> The ministerial or hierarchical priesthood of bishops and priests, and the common priesthood of all the faithful participate, "each in its own proper way, in the one priesthood of Christ." While "being ordered to one another," they differ essentially. In what sense? While the common priesthood of the faithful is exercised by the unfolding of baptismal grace—a life of faith, hope, and charity, a life according to the Spirit—the ministerial priesthood is at the service of the common priesthood. It is directed at the unfolding of the baptismal grace of all Christians. The ministerial priesthood is a *means* by which Christ unceasingly builds up and leads his Church. For this reason it is transmitted by its own sacrament, the sacrament of Holy Orders.[8]

Notice that the emphasis here is put on the difference rather than the fact that the two forms of priesthood are ordered to one another, an indication of the Catechism's pre-Vatican II approach to Catholic faith and practice. On the other hand, the essential difference is described in terms of serving the priesthood of all the faithful, which is a direction that many would want to see ordained ministry take. Moreover, even though lay persons are not mentioned in the Catechism's section on ministry in the Church (#871–896), they are described as having ministries in the section on the lay faithful:

> Lay people who possess the requisite qualities can be admitted permanently to the ministries of lector and acolyte. When the necessity of the Church warrants it and when ministers are lacking, lay persons, even if they are not lectors or acolytes, can also supply for certain of their offices, namely to exercise the ministry of the word, to preside over liturgical prayers, to confer Baptism, and to distribute Holy Communion in accord with the prescriptions of law.[9]

It is interesting to note that although lay persons may exercise ministries, nowhere are they said to be *ministers*.[10] I suspect that this distinction is deliberate in the Catechism and that it reflects a desire to keep the ordained ministry as separate as possible from the laity, given the acknowledgment of the fundamental unity and equality of all the faithful. This is precisely where the debate is today.

What of the liturgical books of the reformed rites? *The General Instruction of the Roman Missal* replaces the *Ritus Servandus* of the pre-Vatican II *Missale Romanum*. From the beginning the General Instruction maintains the distinction of the ministerial priesthood which it claims is "clear from the prominent place the presbyter occupies and the functions he takes in the rite itself," namely, offering the sacrifice in the person of Christ and presiding over the assembly.[11] Throughout the Instruction the presider and assistants are referred to as "priest" and "ministers."

Multiple ministries are recommended for the celebration of the Eucharist: acolyte, reader, cantor.[12] In concelebrated Masses the presider is referred to as the principal celebrant. Similarly, in the text of the Eucharist of the Roman Rite the presider is generally called "the priest *(sacerdos)*." During the Eucharistic Prayer at concelebrated Masses a distinction is made between the "celebrant" and "concelebrants." The major difference between the pre- and post-Vatican II rites lies in the fact that for the first time in the history of the Roman liturgy provision is made for the participation of the people, in accord with the desire of the *Constitution on the Sacred Liturgy*.[13] Apart from this important departure the language of ministry is stable in the Sacramentary.

What of the ordination rites? As mentioned above, Mary Collins has done a great deal of work on the language in the reformed ordination rites. Jan Michael Joncas has pursued her work further in light of the 1990 second edition of the *Rite of Ordination of Bishops, Presbyters and Deacons*.[14] Employing the analysis of anthropologist Victor Turner, Collins had found that in the reformed rites of ordination the language of sacerdotal theocracy prevails. After an historical analysis she found that it represents the product of an arbitrary process of sacralization—arbitrary in the sense that it resulted from historical circumstances that differed from the original gospel message. Therefore, the language of the ordination rites promotes a world view that in her view can be characterized as pseudo-sacralization. After careful analysis of the changes in the language of the 1990 revision, Joncas maintains that "[c]oncerns about the language employed to designate ordained ministry remain."[15] This is the case even though the revisions emphasize service above honor and rank. While it is true that the language of rank and dignity remains, the language of promotion to the presbyterate has been altered to that of "admission."[16] It could be argued that the proposed English translation attempts to soften the hierarchical language of the Latin original in a way that remains faithful to it. It remains, however, that the language of the rites expresses a world view of sacralized power and authority.

One more set of rites needs to be discussed before we can turn to the contemporary situation of the language of ministry. In a significant move in 1973, Paul VI suppressed the subdiaconate and other minor orders in favor of the institution to two traditional ministries: lector and acolyte. The document *Ministeria Quaedam* makes it clear that (male) lay persons may be instituted into these ministries. It seems unfortunate that formal admission to these ministries has been reduced to a stepping-stone, the equivalent of the old minor orders, for seminarians. In any case, in principle, one might argue that ministry in the broad sense is open to lay persons in the Church.

Finally, we can consider the application of this principle in liturgical rites as they are currently celebrated. In the *Order of Christian Funerals* provision is made for funeral liturgies outside of Mass. In the absence of a priest or deacon a lay person may preside.[17] Throughout the rite the rubrics make reference to "the presiding minister." In addition, the document *Sunday Celebrations in the Absence of a Priest* naturally provides for the presidency of lay persons at Liturgies of the Word (with Holy Communion) or the celebration of the Liturgy of the Hours (with Holy Communion) when priests and deacons are not available to preside. "These ministers carry out their responsibilities in virtue of their baptism and confirmation."[18]

On the basis of this data it can be argued that lay persons are legitimately called "ministers" when they preside at the rites of the Church.

## The Current Situation

Our survey has opened the way for a number of considerations about the language of ministry. First, we shall deal with the language of priesthood. Although the word "priest" is derived ultimately from "presbyter" or elder, it has come to have sacerdotal connotations, relating to sacral character and the offering of sacrifice. Thus, in English the word "presbyter" can be translated either as "presbyter" or "priest." The second term applies equally as well to presbyters and bishops. On the other hand, the post-Vatican II reforms have clearly emphasized the sacerdotal character of the entire body of the baptized, i.e., as a corporate entity, offering the sacrifice of the New Law, which is very unlike sacrifices of old. Christians do not offer animals or things to God. They offer themselves in union with Christ, who offered himself to the one he called "Father." Thus, the Eucharist is indeed a sacrifice, but of a different sort from traditional sacrifice. The terminology of priesthood for the ordained complicates this issue for it inevitably connotes a sacral character for certain Christians. I believe that it is possible to retain the function and personal identity of the ordained without sacralizing them. I do this on the basis of a definition of ordained ministry that stresses both their own discernment of a call to ministry as well as a number of gifts or charisms discerned by the Church: holiness of life and ability to lead the community, preach the gospel, and preside at public prayer.[19] Both Catholic tradition and common sense require us to retain distinct categories and language for the ordained but they do not require us to use language implying that they inhabit a sacred sphere.[20] The title "presbyter" carries less sacral connotation and would therefore be preferable. It is somewhat unfortunate, therefore, that even the proposed ICEL translations of the Eucharistic Prayers for the new edition of the Sacramentary employ the terms "bishops, priests and deacons" in their intercessory sections.[21]

By the same token one can question the use of the term "celebrant" for the presider at the Eucharist. To celebrate connotes doing an action—and in this case in distinction from others present. "Mary and John are celebrating their wedding anniversary" means that those who party with them are not celebrating in the same sense. It would, however, be preferable to understand the eucharistic action (sacrifice) as the act of the entire assembly, acting of course in Christ by the power of the Holy Spirit. Thus the traditional and universal avoidance of the singular first person pronoun in the Eucharistic Prayers. The presider speaks in the name of the community in offering its prayer to God and though he may (should) have the charism to pray in this way it need not distinguish him from the community as a celebrant. Given the importance of language for forming our attitudes (which is, after all, the point of this essay) the assembly's attitude toward its own participation in the eucharistic action will remain passive as long as the language of "celebrant" for the presider predominates.

Related to the question of language about the ordained is the issue of lay ministers and the definition of ministry in general. Ministry has been defined so broadly that it could apply to almost any activity of the Christian life.[22] On the one hand there is value here in that service to others is an inherent aspect of the life of discipleship. On the other hand, the term "ministry" seems emptied of content when one applies the word loosely. I suggest differentiating "ministry" at four levels:

1. The ministry that belongs to all Christians in virtue of the challenge to live out the implications of their baptism.

2. Any public service undertaken on behalf of the Church, for example, visiting the sick, a variety of liturgical ministries.

3. Professional ministry (religious education, pastoral care) undertaken after training and sanctioned by the local community or diocesan church.

4. The ministry of the ordained: bishops, presbyters, and deacons.

One of the difficulties today is that the requirements for ordained ministry outlined above are so often applicable to the third category of ministers. Thus the phrase "lay presider" used in more and more situations of necessity seems to be somewhat of an oxymoron.[23] This situation creates inevitable conflicts in role expectations and the exercise of authority. We can hope, however, for creative outcomes of this tension and conflict. In the meantime, the third category surely merits the appellation "minister." For the sake of clarity we would do better to refer to the activities of the first and second categories as "ministries" while avoiding the terminology of "minister" for individuals undertaking them. We should continue, as do the liturgical books, to call those who do pastoral and liturgical service "ministers" in the course of their specific activity. On the other hand, little is served by calling them ministers in general.

What of the term "extraordinary minister" when used of lay persons ministering Holy Communion? The word "extraordinary" may have had some use at the onset of this practice but seems unnecessary today when the practice of having lay ministers of communion has become common. The more we understand the Eucharist to be the activity of the gathered assembly rather than the assembly's assistance at the action of the "celebrant," the more anomalous it seems to have presbyters or deacons, who are not participating in the liturgy, "imported" into the assembly solely for the purpose of distributing communion.

## Conclusion

Ministry remains a controversial topic in the post-Vatican II era. This situation is reflected in confusion and debate around the language used for ministers of the gospel. The view of the Church as the body of the baptized exercising their charisms in service of God, one another, and the world, will continue to inform the expression of ministry in ways that have been outlined in this essay. In turn, our language will continue to shape our attitudes about the baptismal call that each has received and will also shape our understanding of the relation of the baptized to those ordained and otherwise appointed to office in the community. There is no such thing as a perfect theology, set in stone for all time. Nor does there exist perfect language that can adequately capture the Holy Mystery we call "God." It is likely, in my opinion, that new language and terminology will develop for ministerial tasks and persons, for theology is an ever-new and ongoing attempt to express our experience of the life of the gospel in ways that are faithful to our tradition as well as to contemporary experience.

---

[1] The proper name of this rubrical guide that served as the equivalent of today's *General Instruction on the Roman Missal* is *Ritus Servandus in celebratione Missae* in *Missale Romanum ex decreto concilii Tridentini restitutum summorum pontificum cura recognitum* (Rome: Vatican Press, 1962 edition).

[2] Though the distinction between bishops and presbyters was not clarified as a difference of order until the Second Vatican Council *Dogmatic Constitution on the Church (Lumen Gentium)* #18–27. See Norman Tanner, ed. *Decrees of the Ecumenical Councils, Vol. 2: Trent to Vatican II* (Washington, D.C.: Georgetown University Press, 1990).

[3] Mary Collins, "The Public Language of Ministry," in *idem., Worship: Renewal to Practice* (Washington, D.C.: Pastoral Press, 1987) 137–73. This study was first published in *The Jurist* 41 (1981).

[4] For further reflection, see John F. Baldovin, "Eucharist and Ministerial Leadership," in *Proceeding of the Catholic Theological Society of America 1997.*

[5] See *Lumen Gentium* #26.

[6] See *Lumen Gentium* #28; *Decree on the Ministry and Life of Priests* (Presbyterorum Ordinis) #4–6.

[7] *Lumen Gentium* #10: "Sacerdotium autem commune fidelium et sacerdotium ministeriale seu hierarchicum licet essentia et non gradu tantum differant, ad invicem tantum ordinantur."

[8] *The Catechism of the Catholic Church* #1547. Emphasis in the original.

[9] *Catechism* #903 (see #1143).

[10] For an excellent commentary and study on the whole question of the institution of ministers other than the ordained, see David N. Power, *Gifts That Differ: Lay Ministries Established and Unestablished* (New York: Pueblo Publishing Co., 1980).

[11] *General Instruction of the Roman Missal*, 2nd ed., in *The Liturgy Documents: A Parish Resource*, 3rd edition (Chicago: Liturgy Training Publications, 1991) #4.

[12] *General Instruction* #78.

[13] *Constitution on the Sacred Liturgy (Sacrosanctum Concilium)* #31.

[14] Jan Michael Joncas, "The Public Language of Ministry Revisited: *De Ordinatione Episcopi, Presbyterorum et Diaconorum," Worship* 68 (1994) 386–403. Like Father Joncas, I am indebted to Peter Finn of the International Commission on English in the Liturgy for providing me with both the Latin 1990 text and the provisional ICEL translation of these rites.

[15] Joncas, 401.

[16] E.g., in the proposed English translation *ascensuri* and *prohevendus* in the bishop's homily to candidates for the presbyterate has been altered from "raised" and "promoted" to "admitted" and "exercise." See *Pontificale Romanum ex decreto sacrosancti oecumenici concilii vaticani ii renovatum auctoritate pauli pp. vi editum ioannis pauli pp. ii cura recognitum: De Ordinatione Episcopi, Presbyterorum et Diaconorum, editio typica altera* (Vatican City: Vatican Polyglot Press, 1990); and *Rites of Ordination of Bishops, Presbyters, and Deacons,* Proposed revised translation by International Commission on English in the Liturgy (Washington, D.C., 1993).

[17] *Order of Christian Funerals,* prepared by the International Commission on English in the Liturgy and approved for use in the dioceses of the United States of America by the National Conference of Catholic Bishops and confirmed by the Apostolic See (Chicago: Liturgy Training Publications, 1989) #182.

[18] *Sunday Celebrations in the Absence of a Priest,* approved for use in the dioceses of the United States of America by the National Conference of Catholic Bishops (New York: Catholic Book Publishing Co., 1994) #21. See also *A Ritual for Laypersons* (Collegeville: The Liturgical Press, 1993), where the title "minister" is used throughout.

[19] See my "Eucharist and Ministerial Leadership."

[20] At the same time, since the language of priesthood has been so enshrined in English usage, I do not imagine that our use of the term will change any time soon.

[21] The Latin has *toto clero,* which could legitimately be translated as "all those who minister." But this is precisely the question at issue. There is a fear that translating *clero* simply by ministers will blur the distinction between ordained ministers and others.

[22] On the question of defining ministry, see John N. Collins, *Are All Christians Ministers?* (Collegeville: The Liturgical Press, 1992) as well as his longer, more scholarly treatment, *Diakonia: Interpreting the Ancient Sources* (New York: Oxford University Press, 1990).

[23] That is, if presidency is one of the most important gifts one looks for in a candidate for ordination, then presidency by definition should be exercised by the ordained. Present ecclesiastical discipline and the shortage of ordained ministers makes this impossible. But this is a question that cannot be solved on the level of language.

# *Lex Orandi:*
# Memorial in the Eucharistic Prayers
# of the Roman Missal

## *Patrick McGoldrick*

The Church celebrates the Eucharist because it must. This obligation arises from the words of Jesus at the Last Supper recorded by Paul and Luke: "Do this *eis ten emen anamnesin*"—as my memorial, as a memorial of me, in memory of me. Eucharistic Prayer III acknowledges this as a "command," but it is not a merely external imposition laid upon the Church. Rather, it represents, and indeed constitutes, an inner compulsion, a necessity that springs from the very nature of the Church. The Church would cease to be the Church if it ceased to remember, to keep the memorial that is the eucharistic celebration.

If the word "memorial" or "memory" is at the heart of the Eucharistic Prayers, this reflects the importance that the reality of memorial, in a broad sense, has in the prayer as a whole. Memorial takes a variety of forms and expressions and it relates closely to the other major dimensions and themes of the Eucharistic Prayer. It is the aim of this paper to consider under some different aspects this major theme or, better, dimension of the four Eucharistic Prayers of the Roman Missal. Attention is focused particularly on the fourth of these since this is the text in which the memorial is most richly developed.

It is the whole of the eucharistic action that is the memorial celebrated by the Church, and the Eucharistic Prayer can never be detached from this action, of which it is an integral and constitutive part. Nevertheless, this is the prayer that reveals most explicitly the significance of the full eucharistic action, and within this context it is legitimate to focus attention on the prayer.

While memorial is a dimension of the fourth Eucharistic Prayer—as of all these prayers—in its entirety, it is more evident at a number of points: in the long opening proclamation of thanksgiving, in the *epicle-*

*sis* (partly), in the institution narrative, and in the *anamnesis*. Finally, God is asked to remember those presented in the intercessions.

## To Proclaim in Thanksgiving the Memorial of the Lord

At the Last Supper Jesus gave thanks, and from that time the Church has never ceased to give thanks in imitation of him. The great Eucharistic Prayers of the broad Christian tradition are prayers of thanksgiving, not in a narrow sense of gratitude merely but, as many Eastern *anaphoras* show, extending over praise, blessing, confession, acknowledgment, glorification. While for the most part the prefaces of the pre-Vatican II *Roman Missal* mentioned only thanksgiving ("Gratias agamus . . . semper et ubique gratias agere"), the inclusion of Eucharistic Prayer IV, following an Eastern model, expanded the range of the traditional Roman vocabulary and so helped to enrich our understanding of the attitude that underlies the prayer and is expressed in it. Faced with the mystery of God and with the generosity of God revealed in Jesus Christ, the Christian people can only give thanks and praise in glorification of so great a God. This thanksgiving and praise will find expression in different ways: in a more restrained form and more economically in the Roman preface and the rest of the Canon, more expansively both in range and in expression in the case of Eastern *anaphoras* generally.

If our thanksgiving is usually expressed, in part at least, through an evocation of a deed or deeds of God in the past, this is not always the case. Not all the prefaces recall the past; several proclaim God's continuing action, and others combine past and present in expressing the reasons for our outpouring of praise. In the case of the Canon this proclamation of thanksgiving is not continued after the *Sanctus,* but in Eucharistic Prayer III the *Vere Sanctus* extends our praise by proclaiming the pattern and the purpose of the continuing action of God, the all-holy creator, in the world. In its confession of God's praise, the Eucharist moves easily and diversely between past and present.

While the Roman preface chooses one or other aspect of the mystery of salvation appropriate to the occasion, or evokes briefly God's work of creation or Christ's paschal mystery or a similar theme, Eucharistic Prayer IV develops very skillfully a long account that takes its beginning in the transcendent reality of God and follows God's great design through creation and the stages of the history of salvation to the sending of the Holy Spirit from the Father by the risen Christ. It is a magnificent hymn of thanksgiving, praise, and glory for God and God's work.

This memorial of the fourth Eucharistic Prayer has a strong sense of a great divine purpose for the entire creation, at work from the beginning, extending through the passing aeons, and effective in the whole movement of human history. The prayer itself will later look forward in hope to the fulfillment of this plan in God's kingdom.

Though a memorial may not be essential at this point in all cases, nevertheless that it should occur in most cases is significant. In general it is important that the liturgical assembly should rehearse the history of God's great deeds both in its broad sweep and in its individual episodes. At one level this serves to keep fresh in our minds the tale of the major events and figures that have given us our past and so have helped to make us what we are in the present. It is *our* history, then, and it reminds us that we are part of a movement towards a future that is indeed ours but finally is not of our making. The Christian account of creation and salvation allows the particular assembly to unite itself with all those who share this story, to enter into both the history and the great community of past and present of which it is part. At this level, the memorial is important for the sense of the identity of the Church (both universal and local), since the story it tells reveals where the Church has come from, why it exists, and by what power it functions. Viewed thus, the memorial is not merely a recital of past events but it brings this past for those who proclaim it into their present.

Important as this first level is, however, the point of this memorial of God's mighty deeds is not to heighten the self-awareness of the assembly. Our memorial is not addressed to ourselves but is made in a prayer of thanksgiving offered to God and, as we have seen, is an expression of our praise. While it is indeed *our* history that the prayer recounts, it is ultimately and more truly *God's* history, in the sense that it is God who has created it. Moreover, we are not simply recalling it to God, as if it were an account or address or encomium. In accordance with a biblical pattern of prayer, to proclaim the memory of what God has done for us, to make memorial of it together before God is to give thanks for what we have received and to praise the one who gave it. To commemorate and to proclaim the mighty deeds of God should lift the mind and voice in wonder and worship: "Lift up your hearts. We lift them up to the Lord." The fundamental Christian attitude towards God our creator and our savior finds expression in our calling these things to mind, and this attitude in turn should be deepened by such a prayer. Whatever the particular form and expression the Eucharistic Prayer may take, this is the spirit that animates us: "Let us give thanks to the Lord our God." Thus our memorial is made in a prayer of the Christian people, and so in a prayer that is made through Christ in the Holy Spirit, or—to look at the same reality in another way—in *the* prayer of Christ made through us, catching us up in its movement, in the Holy Spirit. In this light, our memorial cannot be understood as simply an acknowledgment of merely *past* events but rather as a proclamation of deeds that are somehow glimpsed as *present* in God, deeds that are somehow understood to endure in the divine economy.

Since the Eucharistic Prayer is a proclamation of God's great deeds and of the one whose deeds they are, it must be a proclamation of faith: a profession of faith, not recited as a series of statements of doctrine, but made in doxology—in thanksgiving and praise and, as the prayer progresses, in invocation and supplication and intercession. The Eucharistic Prayer is the great expression of faith at the heart of every Eucharist. Assembled in fulfillment of Christ's will, and carrying out in his memory the pattern of action that he left it, the Church proclaims its faith in him and in the whole mystery that is focused in his Last Supper. To gather in his name and to do the eucharistic action in obedience to his command is already an act of faith, and that faith finds its most developed expression in the great central prayer of thanksgiving that is itself made in imitation of Jesus' own action on the day before he suffered.

While this section of the paper has used the heading of proclamation to consider the opening part of the Eucharistic Prayer, it should be noted that this heading will remain relevant to later parts also.

A question can be raised about this first section of memorial in the Eucharistic Prayer. Has this memorial a specifically eucharistic reference or application? A proclamation of thanksgiving and praise is appropriate for many occasions, and there is nothing in itself that would render the first half or so of a text such as Eucharistic Prayer IV unsuitable for use in private prayer or at a non-eucharistic gathering of the Christian people. The same could be said for a preface and *Sanctus* together with the *Vere Sanctus* of Eucharistic Prayers II or III. Is the Eucharist just another suitable occasion for such a prayer or is there a closer link between this memorial and the Eucharist? The fact that in three of the four Eucharistic Prayers (and see the two Prayers for Masses of Reconciliation) the section of thanksgiving, including the *Vere Sanctus* or *Post Sanctus*, leads into the first *epiclesis* suggests that the articulation of these two may provide some answer to our question.

## We Celebrate the Memorial of Our Redemption

Towards the end of the section of thanksgiving in Eucharistic Prayer IV, after the paschal mystery of Christ's death and resurrection has been evoked, the prayer goes on to speak of the gift and the work of the Holy Spirit. In literal translation the text reads: "And that we might live no longer for ourselves but for himself, who died and rose for us (2 Cor 5:15), he [the risen Lord] sent the Holy Spirit from you, Father, as the first fruits to those who believe, to complete *(qui . . . perficiens)* his work on earth and bring all sanctification to fulfillment *(omnem sanctificationem compleret)."* The Holy Spirit is the first gift of the risen Christ, and the role of the Holy Spirit is to complete the work of Christ on earth, that is, to bring the whole work of sanctification to its final goal. The Spirit, who has been at work in the incarnation ("made flesh by the Holy Spirit"), and so in the whole life and ministry of Jesus, is now presented as the first fruits for us of the paschal mystery. Thus the Spirit, active in the economy of salvation, is also the fruit of that economy, the culminating gift of God's great work, and the Spirit is to bring that work to its divinely willed fulfillment.

The *epiclesis* follows, in literal translation: "We pray then, Lord, that the same Holy Spirit may sanctify these gifts so that they may become the body and blood of our Lord Jesus Christ." And the second *epiclesis* will ask the Father to gather all who share the one bread and one cup into one body, a living sacrifice in Christ. The use of the connective "then" *(igitur)* suggests that there may be a deeper connection of thought.

That Holy Spirit who is to bring the whole work of sanctification to fulfillment is to sanctify these gifts; that Spirit whose task it is to complete the work of Christ on earth is to make of the bread and wine Christ's body and blood (and to make of those who will partake of them the body of Christ) "in order that we may celebrate this great mystery which he [Christ] left us as an everlasting covenant." Three related points may be noted. First, the thought of the prayer establishes a close link between the great divine economy of salvation and this particular Eucharist celebrated by this group of Christians with these gifts of bread and wine. The Eucharist, *this* Eucharist, is seen to be inserted into the onward movement of God's history of salvation; or, to put it somewhat differently, the Eucharist is a point of focus in which the lines of the history we have been proclaiming can be seen to converge. Second, the mystery that by the working of the Holy Spirit has been accomplished in the humanity of Jesus Christ is by the working of the same Spirit to be realized both in the Eucharist and, through the Eucharist, in the participants. Third,—though in part this is to anticipate—the memorial that we celebrate in obedience to Christ is made possible, given effect, actualized by the Holy Spirit.

This line of thought suggests that the opening memorial such as of Eucharistic Prayer IV is more than just a suitable proclamation for the Eucharist as for many other occasions. It has indeed a genuine eucharistic function; it sets the broad context of the mystery of God, creation, history of salvation in which the Eucharist is celebrated, and thus which gives meaning to the Eucharist. Each Eucharist celebrates the divine plan in all its breadth; it enters into the enduring work of Christ; it brings the participants into the depths of God's trinitarian life.

A somewhat similar pattern can be seen in Eucharistic Prayer III. The theme of thanksgiving and praise proclaimed in the preface breaks into acclamation of God in the *Sanctus,* and this is prolonged in the *Vere Sanctus.* Two threads join this bloc to the *epiclesis.* The first is the theme of holiness: the all-holy God, acclaimed by heaven and earth in the *Sanctus,* who makes all things holy "through your Son, Jesus Christ, our Lord by the working of the Holy Spirit," is asked therefore *(ergo)* to make our gifts holy by the same Spirit. Thus each Eucharist springs as a gift from God's holiness, as part of the divine economy of salvation. The second thread is the theme of offering/gift: the Lord, who never ceases to gather together a people "so that from the rising of the sun to its setting a pure offering may be made to the glory of your name," is asked therefore to make holy the gifts that we have brought into the divine presence to be consecrated. Later on this prayer will develop this theme of offering, but here we are clearly invited to see that, following the enduring pattern and purpose of the divine action, God in *this* Eucharist is continuing to gather together a people so that a pure offering may be made. Since the time of the *Didache* and St. Justin, Christians have liked to find the fulfillment of the text of Mal 1:11 in the Eucharist. Thus, though Eucharistic Prayers III and IV have a somewhat different structure, in their development and articulation of the elements we have examined they show that that divine will and saving power which the Church proclaims in its memorial touches the participants in each eucharistic action.

Of importance is the shift that occurs within these and similar prayers between the opening memorial and the *epiclesis.* The former is a proclamation of thanksgiving for all that God is and all that God has done; the latter is a prayer of supplication. God's gifts are gratuitous, totally undue to us. What we have received is to be acknowledged with praise and gratitude; what we need for present and future is to be sought with humble but confident petition. Humble, because we are never to take God's gifts for granted and because we must develop an attitude that will respect this fact and give expression to it. Confident, because God remains faithful: what God has done God will continue to do among us now and in the world; and God will bring to fulfillment the design of salvation we have just proclaimed.

While the *epiclesis* can be seen as linked to what has preceded, it has a more obvious connection with the narrative and the actions that are to follow.

All four accounts of institution have a brief introduction, which situates the actions and words of Jesus being narrated. While the first three prayers place these in relation to his suffering or his being handed over, the fourth, echoing at greater length John's account of the Last Supper, presents as setting the hour of Jesus' glory and his love for his disciples right to the end (13:1; 17:1; cf. 12:23). Thus the slightly differing contexts established by these introductions invite us to see the purpose and meaning of Jesus' action and of the eucharistic action in which we are engaged in differing lights.

This part of the Eucharistic Prayer is frequently called the "Account of Institution" or the "Institution Narrative." In our present texts it functions clearly as more than a simple narrative of past events, and this becomes more evident still in the actual celebration of the Eucharist. *Epiclesis* (or *Quam Oblationem*), institution narrative and *anamnesis* are closely connected. In the Roman tradition the account of Jesus' actions and words is preceded by a petition seeking God's blessing on our gifts of bread and wine so that they may become that body and blood of which the account speaks. The account is then followed by a memorial offering which we make in accordance with Jesus' command. This sequence suggests that the central part, though narrative in form, is engaged dynamically in each eucharistic action.

This is confirmed by two facts. First, the priest accompanies his proclamation of the narrative by actions that correspond in part with the word he is speaking, and so that imitate in part the actions of Christ; he also performs the gestures of bowing, showing the bread and the cup to the participants, and genuflecting before these elements. Second, the institution narrative is not an account directed primarily at the participants. As an integral part of the Eucharistic Prayer, it is addressed to the Father, and Eucharistic Prayers I, III, and IV show this explicitly ("to you, his almighty Father . . . he gave you thanks"; "to be glorified by you, Father most holy . . ."). Our memorial, in other words, is made before God; it continues our proclamation of thanksgiving to God and it looks to God to give effect to what we do. Our commemoration of the Last Supper, then, is not merely an account of past events. The direction and the context of the institution narrative in the Eucharistic Prayer and the manner of its proclamation in the eucharistic assembly show that our memorial is a dynamic one that carries the events commemorated into effect in the present. This is not to be attributed to the effort of human memory merely or to the power of the ritual itself. Rather, the memorial is directed to God and the effect is sought from God, and this effect is brought about by the sanctifying action of the Holy Spirit.

The *anamnesis* throws further light on the nature of our eucharistic memorial, as its name suggests.

Reference to memorial would be expected here, just after the account of Jesus' actions and words at the Last Supper and his command, "Do this as a memorial of me." The Roman Canon establishes a connection, with the phrase *"unde et memores,"* while Prayers II and III begin *"Memores igitur."* As Jesus commanded, so we are remembering in this Eucharist. *Memores* is not a particularly strong word—"mindful" or "remembering"—and should not be made to bear an excessive theological burden (which, as we shall see, can be distributed more evenly). What we remember in essence is the paschal mystery, expressed most simply in Eucharistic Prayer II ("his death and resurrection") and drawn out in each of the other texts. In treating of the Eucharist, St. Paul says that we "proclaim the death of the Lord" (1 Cor 11:26); similarly St. Justin speaks of it as the memorial of Christ's passion. However, from the time of Hippolytus and the earliest version of the Canon the Roman tradition of the Eucharistic Prayer—supported by the great Eastern *anaphoras*—testifies that in celebrating the Eucharist we commemorate not merely Christ's death but his paschal mystery. The acclamation of the mystery of faith, introduced into the Roman rite in the late 1960s, confirms this.

If this first theme of the *anamnesis* is to be expected, the second is perhaps more surprising: offering. The Roman prayers link them tightly, as the very structure of the *anamnesis* shows. The Eucharistic Prayer of Hippolytus, followed by Eucharistic Prayer II, set the pattern *memores . . . offerimus,* and the Roman Canon, from its primitive version cited by St. Ambrose to the present text of the *Roman Missal,* has used the same words in the same grammatical and syntactical arrangement. This is also the construction of some Eastern *anaphoras,* though many do not have the theme of offering at this point. The more usual objects of this verb of offering seem to be the bread and cup, or the gifts that are God's, or the sacrifice. Eucharistic Prayers II and III use expressions similar to these; the Canon adds *hostia,* and Eucharistic Prayer IV is unusual in designating Christ's body and blood as the offering. Though this sacrificial theme is probably not a primitive feature of the Eucharistic Prayer, its early inclusion here and the close relationship in which it is placed to the memorial *(memores offerimus)* suggest that it reflected a growth in the Church's understanding of the commemoration it was making, a commemoration that sought expression in an act of offering. The Church's memorial of Christ's paschal mystery is such that it can be expressed in terms of offering. Perhaps it would not strain the evidence to conclude that at its deepest level the Eucharist is a sacrifice in that it is the memorial of Christ's sacrifice.

Such a development in the early Church might well have been related to some loss in understanding of the full force of the biblical memorial, so that the theme of sacrifice, of an offering being made to God, was felt appropriate to sustain the movement towards God that was part of the sense and experience of the early Christian memorial with its Jewish roots.

Eucharistic Prayer III follows this classical Roman pattern but Prayer IV has an interesting difference, following upon Christ's command, "Do this as a memorial of me": "And so we too, celebrating now the memorial of our redemption, recall Christ's death . . . profess his resurrection . . . and offer. . . ." To celebrate the memorial of our redemption involves recalling and offering. The liturgical memorial is expressed at once in the proclamation of the paschal mystery and the offering of the sacrifice. This confirms and makes more explicit the understanding that seemed to underlie the older formulation of the Roman tradition. Our commemoration gives rise to an offering, our offering is an act of memorial. As was pointed out, it is not necessary to overload the word *memores:* in the Roman tradition the intimately related theme of offering already carries much of that weight. When Roman texts wish to speak of "celebrating the memorial," they have the Latin resources to express this, as Eucharistic Prayer IV shows (and both prayers for Masses of Reconciliation confirm). Eucharistic Prayer III shows that the original theme of thanksgiving has not disappeared but has continued to underlie the whole prayer: "Memores . . . offerimus tibi, gratias referentes. . . ." In the eucharistic memorial our proclamation of thanksgiving has become a sacrificial offering. Even our expression of praise is itself God's gift.

The final point of interest from the *anamnesis* is its reference to Christ's second coming.

## Until He Comes

All the Eucharistic Prayers in a variety of ways bring out the eschatological dimension of the Eucharist, as is seen in the *Sanctus,* for example, or in the references to our communion with the saints, or in the hope we express to enjoy the vision of God, or in our prayer that we be made an everlasting gift to God. Of more direct relevance to our topic is the reference in the *anamnesis* of the third and fourth Eucharistic Prayers to the second coming of Christ, with which can be linked a similar reference in the acclamation of the mystery of faith.

Most prayers, as we have seen, expand the simple mention of passion and resurrection. Many Eastern *anaphoras* add at this point a reference to his second coming, and do so in such a way as to make it a mystery that we commemorate. The eschatological thrust of the Eucharist was already evident in Paul's words, "you proclaim the death of the Lord until he comes." But while Paul seems to understand the Eucharist as straining towards the coming of the Lord in glory, these *anaphoras* present it as part of our memorial. So the *anaphora* of Basil, to take just one example: "We too, then, mindful of his holy sufferings, his resurrection from the dead, his ascension into heaven, his sitting at your right hand, God and Father, and his glorious and fearful second coming. . . ." This manner of speaking suggests that the Second Coming was taken in the context of the paschal mystery and was seen as already contained or begun in Christ's glorification.

Neither the Roman Canon nor the prayer of Hippolytus has such a reference to the Second Coming. However, when new eucharistic texts were being prepared, it was thought important to include this fuller expression of the total mystery of Christ. So in the third and fourth prayers a participial phrase speaks of our awaiting *(praestolantes)* or looking forward to *(exspectantes)* Christ's coming in glory, a wording—and a conception of our relation to the *parousia*—that is more familiar to the western mind: "calling to mind . . . and eagerly awaiting . . ., we offer . . ." The *anamnesis* of Eucharistic Prayer IV sums up a number of our points:

> And so, Lord God,
> we celebrate the memorial of our redemption:
> we recall Christ's death and his descent among the dead;
> we proclaim his resurrection and his ascension to your right hand;
> and, looking forward to his coming in glory,
> we offer you. . . .

This memorial of our redemption is not concerned with something that is simply past: the mystery we commemorate is also of the present and of the future, and to celebrate it is to be engaged with it in the present and for the future. The Eucharist celebrates the whole mystery of Christ, a mystery that in the glorified humanity of the risen Lord transcends all limits of time. For us, however, this mystery can be expressed only in terms of past and present and future, celebrated in the present as a memorial of God's culminating deed in the paschal mystery of Christ and as a promise, pledge, anticipation of its fulfillment in us, in the Church, and indeed in the world at the glorious coming of the Lord Jesus. Our Eucharist takes place in and as part of the dynamic, historical realization of God's great design. We celebrate the accomplishment of that plan in the glorified Lord, and in our celebration it is actualized among us, as we work for its accomplishment in all creation and move towards its final fulfillment in God.

Our texts show clearly that the mystery they proclaim is at once of eternity and of time, fulfilled beyond time and still to be worked out in history.

The realization of the divine purpose in history and its fulfillment at the end of time are the gift of God, and so, as we have seen, must be sought in humble but confident petition. The second *epiclesis* asks of the Father that through our participation in the body and blood of Christ the Holy Spirit may make of us one body in Christ, a living sacrifice in Christ to the praise and glory of God's name. The work of Christ on earth is still to be completed by the Spirit: we have not yet grown into the full Christ, and his sacrifice has still to become ours. Such petition is continued in the intercessions, and here again there is a hint of memorial: God is asked to remember the universal Church and the world, the faithful departed and all who have died in God's friendship. Eucharistic Prayer IV, harking back to its earlier account of God's plan for all created things, prays for its final fulfillment in the kingdom, where all creation will have been set free and we shall join with it in singing God's glory, through Christ our Lord. Joined with all creation in the Eucharist in the praise of God, we pray that, with all creation, we shall ourselves become that praise in God's kingdom.

The memorial of the Eucharist has at its center the mystery of Christ. In celebrating this mystery, our prayer can reach back in faith, in thanksgiving, to the very beginnings of God's design, and can thrust forward in hope, in petition, to its fulfillment. The eucharistic memorial is focused on Christ but its field of vision is the whole divine economy.

# Observant Participation: Ethics, "Hard Words," and Liturgical Inculturation

*Anthony J. Gittins, C.S.Sp.*

## Understanding People

When the twentieth century was young, intrepid anthropologists ventured to distant lands, lived with exotic people, practiced the arcane art of participant observation, returned home to write objective accounts, and spent their last decades introducing students to the mystery-religion of anthropology, imprinting them with vicarious experiences of disappearing worlds.

As the century waxed and the world was tamed by international airlines, and as local knowledge became less exotic but more sought-after, other academic disciplines discovered the lure of participant observation: intensive, detailed, small-scale studies in fields from folklore to phonology and on topics from reputation to ritual, with a view to disclosing the native's point of view[1] and to capturing something like objective reality. But the anthropological bandwagon became increasingly overcrowded with enthusiasts, and many of the original passengers were suffering from travel sickness; some had already disembarked or left the parade. Anthropology, no longer captivated by the siren named *Objectivity*, and increasingly sensitive to its own ethical responsibility and to the people whose lives it affected, began to reinvent itself.

As the century waned, the quest for dispassionate participant observation became the pursuit of reflexivity[2] and observant participation,[3] which profoundly affected the anthropologist, the information gleaned, and the very interpretation placed on the ethnography.

## Reflexive Ethnography and Moral Responsibility

The shift to observant participation highlights an increased respect for the formative interaction between outsider and insider, researcher

139

and practitioner. It acknowledges that anyone who encounters a society seeking to understand and explain its dynamics, must be prepared to be changed by the encounter;[4] that any group infiltrated by however benign an outsider will be markedly affected by his or her presence;[5] and that when the researcher reports to a wider community, questions of ethics and propriety will inevitably arise.

With these considerations in mind, this essay builds on a bedrock of "thick description,"[6] attempting several things: to identify dilemmas and possibilities at the heart of any attempts to understand human social behavior and motivation; to emphasize the researcher's moral responsibility (whether theologian, anthropologist, or missionary) to local people and to a wider community; to urge that in an age of inculturation and contextualization theologians be as aware of the ethos of particular cultures as of the Christian tradition; and to assert that those who prepare ecclesial ministers must be no less apprised of how the faith is locally received and transmitted than of the way it is discussed in the academy.

Recently this writer spent time studying the missionary presence in a Pacific island.[7] The focus was family life and the local church, but it soon became apparent that a clarification of the role and status of the local priest, of his liturgical style and the ecclesiology that underpinned it, was central to any interpretation of the dynamics of local church and family life. The only way to interpret daily behavior and the unformalized belief which was its foundation, was first, to understand the moods and motivations of the resident missionary, and second, to make them explicit.

This immediately raises ethical questions. On the one hand, guests should be respectful of hosts, clergy should be a loyal fraternity, missionaries should close ranks, and anthropologists should be protective of the people under scrutiny. On the other hand, visitors are not blind, clergy are not clones, a conspiracy of silence is incapable of promoting proclamation of the Word, and researchers may not repudiate moral responsibility. If contextualization is an imperative, and if the integrity of local churches is a priority for a contemporary ecclesiology and pastoral theology, how can any visitor committed to teaching principles of inculturation remain silent on encountering a local church which is palpably a foreign import and whose pastor is an unapologetic patriarch? If the renewal of the liturgy and the full and active participation of the community are constitutive of a living church, how can a teacher of theology pretend that every Christian minister is committed to this, in the face of overwhelming evidence to the contrary?

The turn from imagined objectivity, ethical neutrality, and participant observation, to reflexivity, moral responsibility, and observant participation, allows us to respond to such questions candidly rather than disingenuously: in fact it urges us to greater honesty and social responsibility. The issue is wider than that of protecting informants, maintaining anonymity, and not affecting the status quo. And the problem is not simply how to remain objective and academic. One effect of globalization has been to convince us that we *are* involved in each other's lives and that we *do* bear responsibility for our actions or omissions. We must inquire whose interests are being protected and at what cost, and whose are being compromised, as a result of ethnographic and pastoral undertakings.

Pastoral theology need not even claim the academic distinterestedness of the social sciences: pastoral agents are part of the pastoral problem and part of its solution. Similarly, those committed to preparing future generations of ministers are themselves part of the ministry. Their expertise must include more than theoretical knowledge. They must be wise mentors capable of helping others to avoid the more egregious pastoral errors with which they are familiar.

### Italian and Marian:
### Local Church or Expatriate Imposition?

The case-study below focuses on a funeral,[8] but we must also characterize my host.[9] From Europe and ordained priest in 1965, he had spent the decades since then in various placements from South America to the South Pacific. Never in one place for much longer than five years, he claimed to have "no time" for local languages, managing with his heavily accented English. He was dedicated, perhaps obsessively, to the missionary vocation as he understood it, yet local people found him difficult, and not only linguistically. His English was often incomprehensible to people of this remote and technologically rudimentary island. He always and unvaryingly referred to himself in the third person as "the Father." Taking the weight of the world on his shoulders, he was generally unsmiling and maintained a stiff and uneasy relationship with all. He treated the people like stupid children, reproached them for "putting the Father on the Cross," and frequently spoke of them as "devils." Bluntly dogmatic, he listened only very selectively, and appeared a stranger to true dialogue or pastoral collaboration.

The women religious, indigenous and expatriate, were tolerated rather than trusted, and treated as parish workhorses. Burdened with menial tasks, they were criticized constantly by a sexist cleric who took no advice and allowed no initiatives. Though his tenure as pastor was shorter than that of most of the sisters, and though their combined pastoral competence far exceeded his own, he kept a tight rein on ecclesial authority. When the convent closed soon after my arrival, it was as clear that he would shed no tears as it was that the local people were desolate.

The core of his piety was Marian, epitomized in his devotion to the apparitions in Medjugorje. On the very day of my arrival he announced to me: "we will say the rosary together at nine o'clock every night; and we will recite the Divine Office at six o'clock each morning with the sisters." Having neither rosary nor appropriate edition of the Divine Office, and being disinclined to take such orders, I contrived every evening of the coming weeks to retire early to bed or to absent myself.

Each morning found me in the back of the church with the worshipers while the priest led an accelerated Morning Prayer, the sisters gamely following some distance behind. Clearly, life with "the Father" was, for everyone, cast in the form of competition or uneasy deference. Mass followed immediately. Apart from the charming sight of the altar server (always male)[10] wearing only a wrap-around skirt and perhaps a flower in his hair, there were no other concessions to local custom or style. On the contrary, liturgy began with an ostentatiously recited decade of the rosary, after which the pastor's beads were draped around the crucifix which stood on the altar between priest and people. Then signing himself in exaggerated fashion, he began, "In the Name of the Father . . ." and I wondered how many of the congregation thought he was referring to himself![11] The Eucharist, without homily or Prayers of the Faithful, lasted hardly twenty minutes and never included Communion from the chalice or appropriate music. On Sundays one sensed that devotional hymns were allowed: rarely were more than two verses sung. Yet these Pacific people clearly loved singing, produced natural harmonies, and were accomplished polyphonists. The liturgy stifled participation, rhythm, and movement. When these exuberantly embodied and wholesomely physical people gathered in church, they became inhibited and stiff, quietly accepting what "the Father" ordained.

## Death, Burial, and Liturgical Inculturation

When Andrew, esteemed leader of the Catholic community, died of old age, people from many villages, including "Big Men" and representatives of the United Church[12] began to assemble.

> Seasonally cold,[13] it has been raining for more than twenty-four hours. People's progress is slow, but they gather loyally and in large numbers, shivering in their poor clothes and huddling under

umbrellas of pandanus fronds. They sit, mostly, in absolute silence: almost no movement, no shuffling, no noise. Although pressed together, they are respectful, deferential, and very tolerant of others invading their space. Rather different from people like me who claim lots of personal space and are not good in crowds.

Some of Andrew's adult children, educated professionals in the world of politics and education, are coming by air. The small inter-island plane had not landed when the priest arrived—in his four-wheel-drive truck, at a time convenient to himself—and proceeded with the funeral liturgy!

As people gathered outside Andrew's modest house, the priest went inside. Barging in, dressed in his priest's outfit, he makes straight for the room where Andrew is laid out and where the immediate mourners are wailing in conventional chorus. He tells them to be quiet! He "shoos" people away from the bedside and starts the Prayers for the Dead, including the *De Profundis* in an unfamiliar English translation and at such a speed that no one could possibly understand. Mass follows almost immediately, [the priest] having attempted to convince everyone that it should be so, because "this is the best gift we can give Andrew" and "you can do your own celebrations later when the Father has gone."

It is very noticeable that [typical Western males'] grief tends to be repressed whereas here it is clearly expressed. It is brought to the surface very effectively, albeit in a formal way: keening and sobbing rather than ululating, it is somewhat rhythmic.

[Note: This society is matrilineal. Andrew's matrilineage includes his brothers, his sisters and their children, his (deceased) mother, her siblings, and her sisters' children. The matrilineage (by convention) does not mourn at this time, but the assembled community, including Andrew's own children (who do not belong to his matrilineage but their mother's), are expected to be spontaneous in expressing their grief.]

The grief is real, but orchestrated. Nothing appears random, much less chaotic. Some people (members of the matrilineage) are chatting quietly. Others are sewing as they offer a "ministry of presence." Others again are organizing food or preparing the very important and communal meal for later. There is an excess of food even in this season of scarcity: food is life. This stratified society is built upon institutionalized gift-exchange, and food, like all forms of wealth, must circulate rather than be hoarded. Everyone who comes must be fed. Not to provide liberal amounts of food is shameful. At this time of year, people are hungry much of the time. A funeral actually provides an opportunity for the family of the deceased to cooperate in feeding the wider community! A funeral is a good feed! [It goes without saying that everyone is expected to participate. Not to participate is to insult one's prospective hosts].

Others are organizing the team (Andrew's sons and members of his brothers' families) who will dig the grave in front of Andrew's house. There is a buzz of activity, some of which is maintaining the normal flow of daily life so that it is not totally suspended or even seriously disrupted. Life continues, literally in the midst of death. Children are everywhere. They are not kept away from death any more than they are kept away from life. But they know how to behave: with decorum.[14]

[The missionary] by contrast, seems quite out of place. He blusters and is quite unable to move to the rhythm established prior to his arrival. He wants movement and he wants it now! He is wrapped up in his own schedule, driven at his own frenetic pace, determined to impress on everyone just how busy he is. Unfortunately they know, only too well! He dominates, and determines what will happen from now on. Too bad one of the two plane-loads of Andrew's family have not arrived.

He departs to get more tools for digging the grave, ordering people [oblivious of protocol and his own inappropriateness] to start digging, and effectively disrupting the established process. He sends a message to the adjacent parish, summoning the other missionary, who arrives in very short order. When both are ready (though the grave is unfinished and some of the family have still not arrived) he begins *The Christian Rite of Funerals* with a rosary!

Not only is such devotionalism inappropriate for this local community in general, but specifically so today, with so many fellow-Christians from the United Church, not to mention the non-Christians in attendance. If the United Church chose, it could validly claim that Catholics put Mary at the center, even of Eucharist! The priest ostentatiously declaims the rosary, beads held high in his outstretched hand and with dramatic gestures as he invokes Mary's holy name.

Just then a group of family mourners arrives from the airstrip, naturally moving directly to pay respects to Andrew's body. The priest, however, perceives this as disruptive of his liturgy! Just then Andrew's oldest daughter, with a piercing scream, bursts through the crowd and entirely dominates the proceeding for several minutes. Marcy, a highly-educated woman, by her own admission "educated out of her culture," is an important figure married to an influential politician. Short of stature and large of frame, acknowledged as very beautiful and dignified, she is magnificent in her voluminous dress and high-piled head-scarf. Marcy is now the clear focus of attention for everyone except the bemused priest. Completely absorbed, deaf to the rosary, and quite oblivious of [the priest], she launches into a ritualized ululation accompanied by rhythmic movements and bold, sweeping gestures, embracing the community and expressing heart-rending grief at the death of her father.

The priest, having tried to ignore the interruption, now raises his voice in competition with Marcy, who continues as if in trance. [Later she explained that she had never really been trained for this act of filial piety, and was actually very self-conscious yet determined to acquit her obligation to her father and the community]. As she finished, one of the sisters, a local woman and long-time friend, came from the crowd and very beautifully embraced Marcy in her grief, only accentuating the absence of sympathy on the part of [the presider].

Meanwhile, as the missionary adamantly continued his rosary, a bizarre touch underlined the incongruity: during the Fourth Glorious Mystery, as the Blessed Virgin Is Taken Up Into Heaven and as the heavily accented words "blessed is the fruit of thy 'oom Jesus" roll on, a pack of village dogs catch a bitch in the space between priest and people, and proceed to mount her, successfully and successively, in full view of the quite unperturbed mourners . . . [With pained expression the priest ignores the interlude and continues the recitation].

The rosary completed, the Eucharistic Liturgy begins without preamble.

Raising the round, anemic, flat host, and the golden chalice, the priest prays: "we have this bread and wine to offer, fruit of the vine and work of human hands." Of course it is simply not true. Philip, Pastor of the United Church, and educated in Rabaul, New Britain [in a previous conversation] actually used the word "contextualization": the only time I heard it. He said he uses juice and taro [for Sunday Eucharist], and I don't entirely blame him. There is a huge separation between the words and gestures of this liturgy and the life-experience of this community!

And then it is over. The people are told, "we have just done the very best thing for Andrew," that "the Father is praying that Andrew will soon get out of Purgatory and the time of purification," that "he cannot help himself now, but our prayers can help him and we must pray for him." [Days later he assures the community that "we can get Andrew out of," or "quickly through," Purgatory, "by this Mass." I learned that traditionally people saw the priest as relevant precisely insofar as he could use his "prayer-magic" to improve people's lives. By this criterion, the current priest holds out much promise to the people].

The concelebrants leave, the second without a word and with absolutely no sign of pastoral concern or involvement. The pastor had "talked at" the people, done the "magic thing," waved the hand of blessing, and then continued his life. Neither missionary even stayed for the meal![15]

Yet this is certainly a community, a vibrant community. There were impressive signs that it is also an ecclesial community, thanks to Andrew's pioneering and appropriate leadership. But the presider failed to speak a homily or panegyric; did not invite the community's response or involvement in any way [apart from disrupting the grave-digging arrangements]; did nothing to strengthen the bonds of the community of believers; and did not reach out to those beyond it. The following day I revisited Andrew's village, and was impressed by several things. Marcy, now quite rational and low-key, touchingly recalled her father's vision of Jesus some six months previously. A son, former politician, local celebrity, and quite antagonistic to Christianity and missionaries, spoke movingly about his father's integrity, and about his (the son's) hope that it would not be forgotten. Andrew's sister explained that in the coming months, everyone who had participated in the funeral would receive doba, a ceremonial exchange of gifts, to acknowledge their presence and support.

One of the women was teaching the schoolchildren. She was conducting a religion lesson/ prayer service/Bible study. She explained that we are all one family, and that we, as Christians, should try to live as such. We should not allow ourselves to be provoked, to get angry, to judge others.[16] She retold the story of the prodigal son, glossing it very well, turning it into a story in the context of the local culture. She instructed the children to "forgive those who have done wrong to you. Show love." I think to myself: life goes on; the good news is proclaimed; and blessed are those who do not lose faith!

## A Delicate Counterpoint:
## The Harmony of Sisters and Catechists

The embarrassing account of Andrew's funeral represents the most public and official face of the Church, but the inspiring vignette of the village catechist doing her best is fortunately replicated across the wider parish: to this we now turn.

The pastor claims as virtue what really is necessity: he delegates local catechists to preach on Sundays. However, not knowing the language and thus lacking control over what is actually said, he effectively cedes moral influence to his catechists. Andrew and one of the sisters were chiefly responsible for catechist-training. Now, with Andrew dead and the sisters no longer present, the matter of quality control is acute.

Most of the formal training in catechesis and liturgy had been the sisters' primary responsibility.[17] One sister, trained in Eldoret, Kenya, fifteen years previously, was pivotal. With an elderly church-member she created hymns using biblical texts, trying to incorporate some movement and dance, especially for Good Friday, Easter, and Pentecost, when the pastor was less likely to object. She created Entrance and Offertory hymns for Sundays.[18] She maintained a very good rapport with the people.

Every village with a Christian community had a local, unpaid catechist responsible for funerals the pastor failed to attend. A good thing as far as inculturation was concerned, this was also problematic, for the catechist could only do what he had learned from the sister, who in turn was dominated by the pastor. However, in the (routine) absence of the pastor there was some experimentation, and significant gatherings of people, for whom funerals were of major importance. The sister had succeeded in Christianizing funerals in a very sympathetic way until the pastor, suspecting that she tolerated belief in spirits, publicly condemned her.[19] The pastor's view of funerals was that the local people had little respect for the dead and for their burial. Local people contended that the pastor disapproved of their behavior, and thus often did not seek either his presence or a formal church funeral.

Several respected church members indicated that if there was any creative innovation, it was in spite of rather than due to the priest; and the example of the United Church also provided alternative possibilities, some of which had been copied. Their pastor explained that to him funerals were extremely important. He attempted to create an appropriate liturgy for every single person who died, and to visit the family and share food with them several times after the funeral. Sisters and respected elders explained to me that the Catholic priest did not integrate Christian worship into the people's lives, but superimposed Mass and rosary wherever he could. He was widely seen as irrelevant to, and ignorant of people's lives.

## Local Churches, "Hard Words," and the Challenge of Inculturation

Our case study and its context, though abbreviated, must serve as the basis for concluding reflections. Though comparative data are needed, even short ethnographic descriptions can help to generate questions and items for an emerging pastoral agenda.

First, there are difficult pastoral situations and difficult pastoral agents. In the former case it is difficult to find appropriate personnel: in the latter there are personnel for whom it is difficult to find placements; there is a tendency for one to attract the other. Pastors who have been moved around perpetually, or who seem to persevere *in spite of* local people or conditions, are pastorally dangerous. Bishops faced with declining personnel and vacant parishes are in an invidious position: but "square pegs for round holes" can never be a pastoral solution.

Second, some missionaries are theological dinosaurs. No professional lawyer or surgeon would be allowed to practice without updating and peer review. Justice demands similar standards for pastors if Vatican II is not to be a dead letter.

Third, in principle it is insiders who will implement inculturation. But they must be facilitated and encouraged by outsiders. This is urgent. Bishops and pastors must be made aware of their pastoral responsibility. Risks must be taken and mistakes allowed, prudently.

Fourth, where the local bishop is an inveterate "institutional man,"[20] true loyalty to Church and people is only served when there is loyal dissent. There must be a constant ground swell against ecclesiastical autocrats. Outsiders or short-term visitors, including theologians, have a duty to speak out. Silence is not golden: it may be collusion in injustice.

Fifth, pusillanimous silence dressed as loyalty to the Church serves no one. The pastoral need of people and the integrity of all requires not only that we work for the building up of Church and Realm of God, but that we address impediments on our own doorstep. New case studies are needed. We absolutely must stand up for authentic inculturation. Whether in teaching, publications, or conversation, we must speak truth and create a new conversation in a new climate.

And finally, is it legitimate to generalize from a single case? A delicate question: but if the case is not a caricature and the matter is not trivial, if it illustrates a situation of pastoral need and if it is replicable in terms of other case studies, thus offering a baseline for future studies, then it is not only legitimate but urgent: the good of people, the credibility of theological training, and the hope for the inculturation of the gospel and the liturgy depend on it.

As for "hard words": perhaps there are some in reflections such as these. But they just may need to be uttered.

---

[1] Clifford Geertz, ambassador of cultural anthropology to surrounding disciplines, crafted many a fine phrase and memorable title, including an essay, "From The Native's Point Of View," in a book entitled *Local Knowledge* (N.Y.: Basic Books, 1983).

[2] Judith Okely and Hellen Callaway (eds.), *Anthropology and Autobiography*, ASA Monographs, 29 (London: Routledge, 1992).

[3] Barbara Tedlock, "From Participant Observation To The Observation Of Participation: The Emergence Of Narrative Ethnography," *Journal of Anthropological Research*, Vol. 47, No. 1 (1991) 69–94.

[4] David Young and Jean-Guy Goulet (eds.), *Being Changed By Cross-Cultural Encounters: the anthropology of extraordinary experience.* (especially pp. 209–36) (Ontario: Broadview Press, 1994).

[5] Okely and Callaway, 1992.

[6] The term, coined by philosopher Gilbert Ryle and given wide currency by Clifford Geertz, refers to a careful, detailed and layered ethnographic account, of fairly narrow focus. See his "Thick Description: Toward an Interpretive Theory of Culture," in *The Interpretation of Cultures* (N.Y.: Basic Books, 1973) 3–30.

[7] In 1996. For confidentiality, the precise location is withheld. Call it Doba Island. It is, however, important that I identify myself here as an anthropologist, missionary, and currently teacher of cross-cultural ministry: unequivocally involved *in* this text, as well as *behind* it and *in front of* it.

[8] Funerals are extremely important social and religious occasions which cry out for a sensitive pastoral-liturgical response on the part of the Catholic Mission.

[9] Given the nature of the essay, this is unavoidable. I do not want to caricature, but to illustrate, from field notes and interviews, the impression the pastor created in the community and myself.

[10] When a church was blessed a few years previously (before this pastor arrived), the sisters had prevailed, and the liturgy was dramatic: the bishop was welcomed by a festive procession of the people in native dress, including women in ceremonial grass skirts and little else. The bishop was not amused and forbade any repetition! And this, among a people with as fine a sense of modesty as of display. They were insulted, and the sisters humiliated, by episcopal high-handedness.

[11] This is no joke; sometimes I wondered what sense people could derive from, for example, the bald—and quite meaningless—exhortation to "Fasta-Abstinence" *(sic)*, repeated but not explained, on Ash Wednesday.

[12] A member of the World Council of Churches, the United Church derived originally from the Australian Methodist Church. Its membership is perhaps

five times as numerous as the Catholic community. The pastor and his wife (and delightful family) are local people, theologically and pastorally sensitive, and loyally discreet when asked about the Catholic missionary (see note 16).

[13] The material indented as an extract comes from my fieldnotes, surreptitiously recorded on microcassette and transcribed immediately afterwards. This is part of the "thick description," foundation of the ethnographic record.

[14] Note this natural liturgy: *leitourgia,* "work of the people." It is important that we understand the cultural basis of behavior if we are ever to inculturate the liturgy.

[15] Eucharistic and gift-exchange themes, crying out for development and integration, were ignored. Common courtesy was disregarded. [See my *Bread For The Journey: the mission of transformation and the transformation of mission.* Maryknoll, N.Y.: Orbis Books, 1993].

[16] There is a very important cultural convention, strongly upheld, according to which people will never attempt to interpret another person's motivation. They simply say that no one can know what is in another person's heart and one must not give voice to "hard words." I am convinced this kind of conventional behavior has allowed missionaries to survive otherwise major criticism: their rudeness in respect of the funeral meal discussed here, is a case in point. Annette Weiner, "From words to objects to magic: hard words and the boundaries of social interaction," *Man,* Vol. 18, No. 4 (1983) 690–709. "Speaking what one truly thinks about something is called 'hard words.' Saying 'hard words' is perceived to be extremely dangerous and produces immediate and often violent repercussions. 'Hard words,' once spoken, cannot be recalled; apologies do not carry any power to mute their effects. The warnings were always the same: do not say the words in your mind; the words you say to someone are not the words you think," 693–4.

[17] The pastor organizes a catechists' day every three months. He reads sections of the *Catechism of the Catholic Church* which fit within his pastoral horizons. Otherwise the sister runs the proceedings.

[18] The effect of this excellent initiative, however, was mitigated both by the pastor's begrudging support, and by the fact that the sister had minimal language skills and therefore was entirely reliant on an elderly church member for translation and theological content. My interviews with him left me with serious misgivings in these areas.

[19] When a corpse is laid out, people traditionally gather round and throw stones at it, to chase the spirit to the Isle of the Dead (Tuma). The sister attempted to modify this practice and teach the theology of Purgatory and the Communion of Saints. The pastor evidently interpreted this as "accommodationism."

[20] A phrase of theologian Charles Davis, describing those who vote "The Party Line" rather than according to the demands of justice and pastoral need.

# Ritual Moment and Pastoral Process: Rethinking Pastoral Theology

*Herbert Anderson*

In his vice-presidential address to the North American Academy of Liturgy in 1992, Gilbert Ostdiek made a vigorous plea for the renewal of unfinished conversations among various disciplines of ministry.[1] The partners he proposed for those conversations included liturgics, religious education, homiletics, pastoral care, and justice ministry. Evangelism and parish administration or church development are other aspects of ministry that might well have been included on that list. These conversations are necessary, Ostdiek argued, because each aspect of ministry has become an isolated, autonomous discipline supported by methods and criteria from the human sciences and often disconnected from other aspects of pastoral practice.

The fragmentation of ministry has been exaggerated in our time because the various aspects of ministry are no longer held together in the person of a pastor. In larger parishes, there are commonly a host of people, both paid and volunteer, who identify themselves as ministers with a specialization. One aspect of ministry may dominate because of the preferences of the pastor and the traditions of the parish, or the ministry of a parish may be a collection of specializations each vying for primacy. Even if pastoral practitioners plan together at staff meetings, they do not have an accessible pastoral theology coherent enough to hold the various ministries of the Church together in a systemic whole. Without coherence, authenticity suffers. Conversations between and among the disciplines of ministry are therefore not only useful: they are needed in order to rethink pastoral theology for the sake of unity in the Church's ministry.

Bilateral conversations are not new in pastoral theology. Over the last decades, each discipline in ministry has had a partner in dialogue from the human sciences. These conversations have enlarged our understanding of human experience and refined the skills needed for the practice of ministry. The alliances have not been without difficulty, however. For pastoral care, the dependence on psychology has sometimes eclipsed the place of theology and led to a focus on the human story to the exclusion of God's story. Parish administration was dominated for a time by management techniques. Those who hold that liturgy ought to be taught in the department of dogmatics regard the conversations with anthropology with suspicion.[2] While some disciplines may need to recover their theological identity, the dialogue with human sciences should continue.

Within the Church, ministry disciplines have assumed for a long time that their partners should be bible or theology or ethics. These bilateral or interdisciplinary conversations need to continue and become more reciprocal. What Gilbert Ostdiek has proposed (and I am seconding) is that the disciplines of ministry themselves need to become conversation partners with one another: between preaching and pastoral care, between education and preaching, between administration and worship, between worship and evangelism, and so on. The focus of this essay is on the conversation between worship and pastoral care.[3]

These bilateral conversations will be enhanced 1) if all disciplines of ministry are regarded as potential partners for conversation in a web of shifting, interdependent alliances without dominance; 2) if we attend to the multiple layers of those conversations because each discipline is modified by the social location of the practicing minister; and 3) if there is an organizing metaphor for the Church's ministry inclusive enough to encompass differing acts and methods. A wholistic or systemic theory of church and its ministry is needed to frame these bilateral conversations.

What is missing is a pastoral theological method for unifying the functional specialties of ministry. Such unity is necessary because the complexity of pastoral ministry today requires greater coherence and wholeness so that the witness of faith communities will be credible and authentic at the end of Christendom.

## The Need for Unity in Ministry

The urgency of these conversations across disciplines is also pressed upon us by the context of ministry today. Although there are many ways to read the signs of the times, they all point to cataclysmic changes in the world and in the Church. Among other agendas, the Church will need to learn how to live as a partner and neighbor in a world in which Christianity and Western enlightenment categories no longer dominate. Canadian theologian Douglas John Hall insists we are the last generation to inherit the presumptions about Church that began in the fourth century of the common era under the reign of Constantine.[4] What the Church gives up at the end of Christendom, he says, is the presumption of rulership and power in the Western world.

According to Hall, the gift at the end of Christendom is humility. The Church is free to disestablish itself in order to become "the disciple community described by the Scriptures and treasured throughout the ages by prophetic minorities."[5] If Hall's analysis is correct, and I think it is, *the relation between the Church and the world will be different and pastoral theology, the practice of and reflection on the ministry of the Church, will need to be different as well.* Patterns of ministry, developed when the remnants of Christendom were still in place and when the vestiges of the Enlightenment still governed theology, will change. When new narratives are applied to the practice of ministry for the sake of the whole, pastoral disciplines will need to let go of customary habits, entrenched divisions, and cherished positions of dominance. The gift of humility that governs our response to the world is equally appropriate within the Church. A pastoral theology governed by that same humility will provide a new framework for integrating the Church's ministry fragmented by specialized disciplines during privileged times.

*The Arts of Ministry*, edited by Christie Cozad Neuger and written by women, adds another dimension to our reflection on these conversations between pastoral disciplines. The arts of ministry, as the authors envision them, consist of those theories, theologies, methods, and practices that make up the everyday life of the pastoral practitioner within a parish context. What I found particularly helpful is the feminist and womanist angle of vision on the Church's ministries, "especially as it articulates the shared goals of inclusivity, radical social analysis, the transformation of destructive power arrangements, and the healing and empowerment of the Church."[6] *Bilateral conversations are not simply between disciplines.* The contexts in which we do ministry are also part of the dialogue. Therefore we need to be attentive to the impact of the social location or standpoint of each person in bilateral conversations about ministry.

A second contribution to rethinking pastoral theology after Christendom is more metaphorical. In a recent essay, Bonnie Miller-McLemore used the idea of *the human web* to reflect on the transformation of pastoral theology. The image of human web is a critique on the individualistic focus of pastoral care. "The world of parish ministry has offered a little-recognized wealth of insight for teaching, and recent congregational studies have also begun to confirm the congregational nature of pastoral care."[7] It is a legitimate critique and a worthy vision. The vision of a web suggests that the parish is a *living communal web* made up of interdependent parts. A parish works best when care, administration, education, worship, proclamation, and evangelism work interdependently. Because the complexity of the task of ministry requires a coordinated and interdependent effort with many foci and many perspectives in each foci, bilateral conversations are necessary in order to weave and reweave the web in creative and life-affirming ways. What I am proposing, with this borrowed image of a *living communal web,* is that pastoral theology provides the theoretical framework for sustaining and modifying the interdependent functioning of those interdependent parts for the unity of parish ministry. I will suggest later that this image of a communal web is not unlike the experience of communitas that is formed during periods of liminality.

## A Common Dialectic in Ministry

Bilateral conversations on topics of mutual interest in ministry, even if they are attentive to social location, will not by themselves take us beyond our individual disciplines unless they are grounded in a common method and unifying theology of pastoral practice. This is the place where pastoral theological conversation often deteriorates. The methods of worship, care, education, and administration are different enough to resist easy correspondence. One alternative is to look for common themes such as transformation or narrative or suffering to which aspects of ministry might find common cause. For Ostdiek, all ministry is an expression of "the seamless care of God" and "each moment of ministry attends in its own way to the one journey we are making."[8] As a unifying principle for ministry, God's care is necessary but not sufficient. The task is to determine more clearly *how* each moment of ministry attends to the one journey in faith.

Because this dialectic of moment and journey or process is a dynamic common to all aspects of ministry, it has the potential to be common ground for the bilateral conversations between the disciplines of ministry. We experience this dialectic in daily living whenever we are encouraged to bracket enough time to smell the roses or listen for the sound of a bird or watch a child's first steps—to savor the moment in the midst of the process. Those moments have meaning, however, because of the context in which they occur. In the practice of ministry, we are aware of teachable moments in the midst of a lifelong process of learning or a moment of conversion or commitment within a larger and longer process of transformation. A committee's decision to repair the roof on the parish school is made within a process of deliberation. If that moment of decision is not congruent with process that precedes it, the roof may be repaired but people will be diminished. Fostering reciprocity between ritual moments and pastoral processes strengthens both. It may also provide a methodological framework for uniting the sometimes fragmented aspects of pastoral ministry.

This essay explores one aspect of moment and process in the journey of faith and the practice of ministry: the reciprocity between ritual moments and the human or pastoral process.[9] Sacramental rituals are human rituals. Because that is so, we need to understand the ritual moments, and most especially the sacraments, as both human and saving. Ritual moments, as they are referred to in this essay, include both sacraments and other social symbolic actions that may be formal and repeatable or informal and situational.

Examining the relationship between ritual and process is important because ritual moments are often disconnected from the human processes that surround them. The baptism of an infant, for example, may not reflect the dynamic family process of welcoming a child in which the ritual moment occurs; a wedding may not embody the alternate processes of leaving and cleaving that are necessary to become married; a funeral process may not provide a model for the grieving that precedes and follows it. If ritual moments are attentive to the human processes in which they occur, there is greater likelihood that the rituals will contain symbols that can carry the weight of human ambiguity. When the correspondence between ritual moments and pastoral processes is made explicit, rituals of faith become a pastoral resource of unusual richness. The human ills of fear, doubt, and despair drive us back to moments in the journey that are signs of God's presence with us. When the reciprocity of moment and process is practiced in our ministry, it not only strengthens faithful living: it becomes a vehicle for enhancing the coherence of pastoral theology.

## Moment and Process

A moment, as I am using it here, is not meant to be understood literally as a fraction of clock time but a segment of time we lift out of the human process in order to mark or analyze it. Each moment of experiencing is reflective of previous moments, but not determined by them. As a segment of time, a moment is more than a transition from the past to some predetermined-determined future reality. The past may be settled but the future is open. Human process is the continuous unfolding of new possibilities that are shaped by the choices we make and the actions we take in each moment. Life may be understood as a process punctuated by these critical moments of transition. We are regularly transformed as we traverse these moments of transition.

Process points to change, coming to be, flux, and interaction rather than permanence, fixity, being, and substance. When the focus is on process, change becomes the fundamental characteristic of all reality. All of life is caught up in motion and change. And because God is still creating, nothing that lives is finished or complete. If we formulate the future strictly on the basis of the present or the past, we prematurely restrict the future for humankind that God is continually making new. Sometimes the change is so imperceptible that it goes unnoticed. Other times, the change is discontinuous enough to be disruptive of personal or social stability in the present moment. When we are betwixt and between, we are in liminal time without place or position. We travel through these transitions by means of prescribed rituals until it is safe or until the routine behavior necessary for social life is restored.

For Victor Turner, society itself seems to be a "dialectical process that involves us with successive experience of high and low, communitas and structure, homogeneity and differentiation, equality and inequality, phases of structure and communitas."[10] Because the spontaneity, immediacy, and equality of communitas cannot be sustained over time, according to Turner, "communitas itself soon develops a structure, in which free relationships between individuals become converted into norm-governed relationships between social personae."[11] Although human life is a dialectical process between structure and anti-structure, Turner still regards structure as the norm. What remains in contemporary culture is a deep need to transcend the *chronos* of ordinary space and time.

Near the end of *Ritual Process*, however, Turner hints at the kind of rapid change that is now common in our time. He writes, "The very flexibility and mobility of social relations in modern industrial societies, however, may provide better conditions for the emergence of existential communitas, even if only in countless and transient encounters, than any previous forms of social order."[12] What Turner anticipated nearly thirty years ago is more and more the reality of our time. Transition has become a permanent condition. Change in patterns of social interrelatedness, educational needs, equal regard among people, and role expectations in family and work all occur with such rapidity that we are in *perpetual liminality*. Charles Handy presents a similar picture of constant change under the rubric of *second curve thinking*. Contrary to the old adage that "if it ain't broke, don't fix it," Handy suggests that we initiate change before what is currently in place "peters out."[13] In an age of turbulence and rapid change, constancy is maintained by allowing the past and the future to coexist in the present. Moment and process are permanently and reciprocally linked in regular transitions, and constant change characterizes social interrelatedness. In rethinking pastoral theology, we need to attend to the relationship between moment and process in order that our ministry will be responsive to a time of perpetual liminality.

If perpetual liminality is one of the characteristics of our time, then communitas, as Turner understands it, is potentially a more common expression of human relatedness. And if communitas is possible because old rigid patterns or hierarchies can not endure a time of rapid change, then the living communal web is a realistic vision for ministry and a viable framework for pastoral theology. That vision also means that bilateral conversation between equal partners in ministry is more necessary and more possible in our time. It is necessary because communities of faith after Christendom will need to cohere to endure. It is possible because the gift of humility helps us understand that interdependence is not an option. Everything is connected to everything else, including ritual moments and pastoral processes.

## Ritual Moment and Pastoral Process

With this discussion of the reciprocity of moment and process in mind, we can understand more clearly the significance of three questions Gilbert Ostdiek has asked about the connection between human and ritual processes. 1) What process, he asked, is implied in a particular sacrament or ritual moment? 2) Are there significant moments or marker events in the process that need to be ritualized? 3) How are communities affected by ritual processes?[14] Ostdiek uses RCIA to illustrate ways in which the Christian communities as a whole are reshaped by a ritual process. The second is an important question that Ostdiek has explored under the rubric of "human situations in need of ritualization."[15] Because new situations and novel conditions reveal gaps in our ritual repertoire, we need to create new rituals that foster growth and help us through previously uncharted waters.[16]

Here I want to respond to the first question: what human process is implied in a particular sacrament or Christian ritual and how do ritual moments correlate with the pastoral process?

One way to examine this reciprocity is to identify pastoral moments that occur in relation to a ritual process. A pastoral moment may be at an administrative intervention of advocacy with a hospital that made it possible for the entire family to be at bedside for Eucharist with a dying grandparent. It may include several conversations to diminish wedding anxiety or hear grandpa's life story before the Eucharist. The pastoral moment may be baptismal catechesis to help Jennifer Marie's parents understand why she could not be baptized in

the birdbath in their back garden. It may include efforts to seek reconciliation between conflicted family members so that the wedding
can proceed peacefully. Frequently, these pastoral moments are not
explicitly connected to the ritual process in which they occur. As we
expand existing sacramental rituals into ritual processes, conversations across disciplines become even more necessary in order to in-
sure appropriate correspondence with the human journey. When the
ritual process parallels the human process, it will evoke our common
desire to hear ourselves named and our life journeys told within safe,
hospitable frameworks.

Even if we come to understand ritual as a process, there will still be
moments or segments of time within that process to be marked and reflected upon. Because change is the norm for this time of perpetual
liminality, a ritual moment may be more than a rite of passage from
one status to another or from one journey to another. Because of the
complexity of our time, ritual moments also need to be paradoxical
enough to carry the ambiguities of the human story.

- *A ritual moment* may bring closure to a previous process, status,
  or relationship while the future remains open. Something that
  has been must end or be recognized as other and something new
  must begin. A ritual for miscarriage marks the reality that creation of a human life had begun and ended before a child was
  born.

- *A ritual moment* may initiate a new status altogether or facilitate
  patterns of acting that will forge a new future. A blessing from
  parents in the process of leaving home ritualizes a change in
  membership in the family but not severance from it. Through it,
  the family acknowledges that a son or daughter is a separate and
  distinct individual, worthy of respect, and sent into the world
  with the promise of God's presence.

- *A ritual moment* is a proleptic reality when it seeks to embody the
  future towards which an individual, couple, or community in-
  tends to move. From the Christian perspective, this understanding of ritual is grounded in God's promised faithfulness in the
  future.

- *A ritual moment* is an embodied or incarnate reality. It is not surprising that the present interest in spirituality parallels a resur-
  gence of interest in ritual. We long for concrete moments in
  which our experience of the Mystery touches our skin. Ritual is a
  social strategy that builds community. It is also bodily action that
  transforms how we think about ourselves and God.

The life cycle ritual moments of baptism, marriage, and burial each occur in the midst of a process that precedes and continues after the ritual moment.[17] Infant baptism happens in the process of welcoming the child that begins long before the birth and continues after baptism. Although baptism has many other meanings, it is a ritual of hospitality by which a child is named and incorporated into the community of Christ's Church. Baptism is a crucial sign of hospitality if a child enters a home that is already too cluttered with occupational, recreational, and personal commitments, and perhaps other children, or if the child is expected to fill a vacuum in the family. In either case, the child often suffers unless the ritual moment of baptism is allowed to transform the process of welcoming a child. Part of the significance of baptism is in its unfolding. It will have more impact on the subsequent growth of a child if the stories of family expectations or the story of birth or the significance of the name given at baptism are told and retold.

The process of becoming married has begun before the wedding and will continue after the wedding. There are two principal parts to that process: one is leaving and the other is cleaving or forming a marital bond. If the ritual event that occurs in the midst of this process is to enhance becoming married, then it needs to be attentive to leaving home as well as bonding. When the moment of betrothal was ritually separate from the wedding, it was easier to see becoming married as a process with two parts. A wedding is not magic but it can be a significant moment in a process if more attention is given to embodying the processes of leaving and cleaving that precede and follow it in the ritual.

This principle of reciprocity between moment and process also applies to the relationship between the funeral and the grieving process within which it occurs. The funeral is witness to and celebration of God's triumph over death that we remember in the resurrection. It is more, however. It is public ritual by which a community of family and friends mark the end of a life. It is also an occasion for remembering a human story that has ended. If the funeral ritual is to enhance the grieving process, it needs to embody good grieving principles. The experience of baptism is not what saves us; a wedding does not make a marriage; but how a funeral is conducted is essential to the pastoral process. Each of these ritual moments in the cycles of life is enriched by taking seriously what we learn about the human story through pastoral care. When that occurs, the ritual moment will in turn have more impact on the process within which it occurs. In this way, worship needs pastoral care because of the stories it hears. On the other hand, pastoral care needs worship as a reminder that our story has significance in God's story.

## Forging a Common Vision

The moment/process dialectic is not, however, an end in itself. It is an essential dimension of faithful living because it helps weave together the human and the divine. Connecting the human story and God's story is a unifying theology for bilateral conversations between pastoral disciplines. Moments when we encounter divine presence occur in the midst of ordinary human processes. The Emmaus story, often employed to illustrate the integral connection of "moments" in the unfolding faith journey, begins as an ordinary meeting of strangers who pass the time by telling stories on the road and ultimately becomes a ritual process of breaking bread and telling stories in which the human and divine narratives intersect and human community is reborn. Emmaus is about "a rendezvous with Yahweh on the road to surprise," as a friend observed recently. Unifying the diverse ministries of the Church and establishing the reciprocity of moment and process have this larger, common purpose: weaving together the human and divine narratives as we *rendezvous with Yahweh.*

The common commitment that brings together the disciplines in pastoral theology and determines the aim of our ministry is a response to the human longing to find God in my story and locate my story in God's narrative. The challenge for ministry in our time is to connect our lives, our stories, our morality with God's life, God's word, God's way; to connect God's grace with the challenges of daily living. The bilateral conversations are an essential vehicle for fashioning forms of ministry through which we might be reminded of the power of God's ongoing sustaining presence in human life. Pastoral theology after Christendom will need to sustain two contradictory modes of conversation toward the world and within the disciplines of ministry: listening to the other with respect and for the sake of understanding rather than conversion; and speaking clearly of God when we are not sure anybody is listening.

If the aim of ministry is to help individuals and communities fashion narratives that weave together divine and human stories into a single fabric, the relationship between worship and pastoral care gains special significance. In pastoral care, the human story predominates while in worship the human story has often been eclipsed by God's story. "For that reason alone, pastoral care needs the perspective of worship to avoid becoming stuck in a horizontal view of experience without transcendence. Worship, on the other hand, needs the pastoral care perspective to keep its praise and intercession grounded in the lives of real people."[18]

Worship and pastoral care are not only reciprocally linked: they become paradigmatic of every pastoral theology conversation aimed at weaving together divine and human stories. Among the many alliances that sustain the Church's ministry and provide grist for pastoral theological reflection, the link between worship and pastoral care is at the core.

---

[1] Gilbert Ostdiek, O.F.M. "Unfinished Conversations," in *Proceedings of the North American Academy of Liturgy* (1992) 3–14.

[2] Louis A. Smith, "Lathrop's Holy Things: A Review Essay," in *Lutheran Quarterly*, Vol. XI, No. 2 (Summer, 1997) 224–9. "What liturgy is about is to be determined by exegesis of the biblical words that deal with the commanded rites of the liturgy. But Lathrop's thoroughgoing anthropological approach is not able to make distinctions like this" (228).

[3] This essay is written affectionately as a tribute to Gilbert Ostdiek who is, I submit, a pastoral theologian at heart in the Rahnerian sense of the term. His instincts are to bring isolated fields of study into a larger whole through a vision that unifies all forms of pastoral ministry. Rahner defines pastoral theology as theological reflection on the Church's ministry. "Pastoral theology deals with the action of the Church. It is pastoral because it engages concrete circumstances; it is theological because it reflects systematically on the nature of the Church and analyzes the circumstances which confront the Church today." See Karl Rahner, *Theology of Pastoral Action* (New York: Herder and Herder, 1968) 25.

[4] Douglas John Hall, *The End of Christendom and the Future of Christianity* (Valley Forge, Penn.: Trinity Press International, 1997).

[5] Hall, *op. cit.*, 51.

[6] Christie Cozad, Neuger, ed., *The Arts of Ministry: Feminist-Womanist Approaches* (Louisville: Westminister/John Knox Press, 1996) 9. In her conclusion to the volume, Neuger makes this observation. "No practice can be sustained as liberating and transforming without a continual process of critical reflection about the practitioner's and the congregation's social locations, about the kinds of interpretive and ethical norms that emerge from those experiences, and about the kinds of resources that continue to generate new insights into theory and practice" (197).

[7] Bonnie J., Miller-McLemore, "The human web: Reflections on the state of pastoral theology," in *Christian Century*, Vol. 110, No. 11 (April 7, 1993) 367.

[8] Ostdiek, *op. cit.*, 11.

[9] Gilbert Ostdiek loves schemas and paradigms of ritual process. I have a file folder full of creative, graphic productions from his computer that chart moments in a journey or identify events in the process of human life and pastoral ministry. I am grateful for what I have learned from Gilbert about the reciprocal relationship between moment and process.

[10] Victor Turner, *The Ritual Process* (New York: Aldine de Gruyter, 1969) 97.

[11] Turner, *op. cit.,* 132.

[12] Turner, *op. cit.,* 203.

[13] Charles Handy, *The Age of Paradox* (Boston: Harvard Business School Press, 1994).

[14] Ostdiek "Ritual Process and the Human Journey," in *Disciples at the Crossroads: Perspectives on Worship and Church Leadership,* Eleanor Bernstein, ed. (Collegeville, The Liturgical Press, 1993). These three questions from an earlier draft became five statements in the published chapter (129–34). Although the statements more or less answer the questions, I have continued to use the questions because they sharpen the focus of this exploration.

[15] Ostdiek, "Human Situations in Need of Ritualization," in *New Theology Review* Vol. 3, No. 2 (May 1990) 36–50.

[16] Herbert Anderson and Edward Foley, *Mighty Stories, Dangerous Rituals: Weaving Together the Human and the Divine* (San Francisco: Jossey-Bass, Inc. Publishers, 1998). See 125–48 for an elaboration of this thesis.

[17] Anderson and Foley, *op. cit.,* For an extensive discussion of these three life cycle moments, see 57–122.

[18] Anderson and Foley, *op cit.,* 53.

# Ethics and Ritual:
# Lessons from Freud

*Lawrence A. Hoffman*

It seems self-evident that we scrutinize ideas as to their truth. But theories of ritual are rarely provable; they are more akin to art talk or literary criticism than to physics and chemistry. On what grounds, then, do we accept or reject them?

My case in point is the celebrated view of Sigmund Freud, for whom ritual is "like" an obsessional neurosis. Now if (as Freud thinks) ritual really *is* neurosis, then maybe (as he further thinks) we should all be cured of it. But what if ritual and neurosis just "look" the same on occasion? What if the statement, "Ritual is like neurosis" is akin to "Hamlet is like a man consumed with passion"—a metaphoric piece of literary criticism rather than a scientific pronouncement, and, therefore, intended to imply no more that we should cure people of ritual than that we should cure Hamlet of passion?

A theory of ritual may be just plain wrong, of course. But its truth value may be indeterminable, or, at the very least, it may have to be judged along with some other criterion beyond "true/false." I think even Freud knew that. Though his account of ritual's origins committed him to reject ritual on scientific grounds, his final criterion was not scientific, but ethical.

I want, therefore, to apply Freud's own ethical considerations to that part of his theory that is not scientifically demonstrable. To do so, I will situate Freud's theory in the backdrop of his time, and then return to the ethical considerations that should guide us in our evaluation of the master's work—indeed, of the master himself, as we shall see.

Sigmund Freud (1857–1939) was an Austrian Jew, part of the current of Jewish intellectuals that pulsed through Europe as the twentieth century arrived. Thorstein Veblen, himself an intellectual son of

Norwegian immigrants, identified with these Jews whom he called the "vanguard of modern inquiry."[1] By contrast, T. S. Eliot, who bemoaned the demise of old-time upper-class Christian cultural hegemony,[2] advocated a "homogeneous" class of leaders, with a "unity of religious background. Reasons of race and religion" he thought, made "any large number of free-thinking Jews undesirable."[3] With others, Eliot could have had Freud in mind when he cited the "clever Jew undergraduate mind at Harvard." He thought Jews operated with "chilly detachment,"[4] blithely dismantling old certainties for liberal universalistic causes. They were cultural corporate raiders cornering the market on Europe's intellectual capital and selling it off cheaply without regard to its long-term shareholders.

There is some truth to Eliot's charge. Freud was an outsider, never fully at home in a society that was still Christian, and becoming increasingly antisemitic besides. He was heir to a century or more of German Jewish intellectuals who had been baptized, some out of conviction, others because (as Heinrich Heine had proclaimed) it was the "admission ticket to European culture." Not so Freud, however, who practically began his autobiography (1935) by saying, "My parents were Jews and I remained a Jew myself." He was, however, stridently irreligious, even forbidding his wife (a granddaughter of a rabbi) to practice Jewish ritual in their home.[5] He preferred the gentleman's club, B'nai B'rith, to the synagogue. But fearful that psychoanalysis would be branded a Jewish science, he opted publicly to bleach out signs of Jewish identity, and to present himself as the epitome of the very dispassionate scientist that conservatives abhorred.

### Freud's Theory of Ritual

Freud returned again and again to his particularly trenchant critique of religion, beginning with a 1907 monograph likening religious ritual to obsessive-compulsive behavior. In 1913 *(Totem and Taboo)*, he expanded his views, unveiling religion's origin in a putative primal playing out of the Oedipus conflict. *Future of an Illusion* (1927) evaluated religion's future rather than its past, and *Moses and Monotheism* (1939) applied (as Freud put it) "the theme of *Totem and Taboo* to Jewish religious history."[6]

Freud's most telling observation holds, "Hysteria is a caricature of a work of art; an obsessional neurosis is a caricature of religion and paranoiac delusion is a caricature of a philosophic system."[7] I leave two-thirds of this pithy synopsis to artists and philosophers, while I tackle the middle term, Freud's theme from 1907, revisited. Both religious rite and obsessive-compulsive neuroses are punctiliously defined behavior regimens that are dysfunctional to the psyche. Freud sought their origin in taboo, especially the taboo of touch. In both instances, individuals feel obliged to touch something, but only at certain times and places, and only in certain ways. Each culture has its own taboos, but Freud noted one that is universal: incest. *Totem and Taboo* establishes the origin of ritual in forbidden sexual drives (especially of a man toward his mother) which are controlled by taboos on touch. Since the drive is too strong to abandon altogether, the touching impulse is displaced onto a surrogate object and the act of touching it is controlled with picayune but strongly held strictures.

Freud's illustrations sometimes ring embarrassingly true. The traditional synagogue that Freud would have known,[8] features to this day the presentation and reading of Torah scrolls which are ceremoniously touched in a fashion that is ringed round with rules. In a famously argued case study, Theodor Reik[9] remembered as a child feeling uneasy while the men around him read the Torah with such respect. Later he realized that the Torah is referred to in the feminine, that it is ritually "undressed," and that a pointer known as a *yad*, literally a "hand," is inserted within it as it is read—as if it is being violated by the all-male group gathered around it.

Freud himself submitted the Eucharist to a similarly scathing attack. He believed, with Jean Baptiste Lamarck, that cultural forms can be inherited across generations, but from Charles Darwin he drew the hypothesis of a primal horde of humans who had once populated the planet. In each band a strong male surrounded himself with women, and used brute strength and threats of punishment to hold at bay the desire of the younger males for them.[10] Freud now argued that once upon a time, the younger males had killed and devoured the primal father before sleeping with his women, their mothers. Hence the universal taboo against incest, which showed up also in Australian totemism, a system that had attracted recent scientific interest.

Australian tribes are divided such that men are prohibited whole categories of women as sexual partners, whereas logic would deny only immediate blood relatives (mothers, primarily) to them. All women of one's own clan (the kangaroo clan, let us say) are known as mother or sister (much as Christians might say "sisters in Christ," Freud points out).[11] Kangaroo males may not marry kangaroo females (their "mothers" and "sisters"), and in addition, the kangaroo itself is said to be the tribal patriarch, who is studiously guarded from becoming the object of the hunt. However, at a single annual ceremony, kangaroos are not only hunted, but are sumptuously consumed in sacred feasting. For Freud, it seemed self-evident that the whole thing was a cultural residue of the days when a single male called many women his "wife," and the younger males were forbidden access to them. The fear of hunting the totem, coupled with the ritualized (= obsessive) eating of it once each year, recalled the time the clan actually did kill and eat its tribal father. From that, it was but a short distance to the obvious parallels of the crucifixion and communion with bread and wine as Christ's body and blood.

To be sure, there is much that is wrong with Freud's etiology of ritual, including the fact that the primal horde is entirely a fiction of his and Darwin's imagination, but it was enough to convince him that religion, like neurosis, is a disease for which psychoanalysis is the cure.

He returned to his theory late in life with *Moses and Monotheism*, which argues (by now predictably) that the Israelites had been saved by an Egyptian named Moses, whom they had then killed—a repetition of the primal crime. They appointed a new Moses, probably a Midianite who had initiated them into the cult of the thunder-God of the desert. The first Moses had been a monotheist, however, influenced by the religious breakthrough of Amenhotep IV (Ikhnaton, 1375–1358 B.C.E.). Feeling overwhelmingly guilty over the patricide, the Israelites became fanatic monotheists—as the prophets regularly demonstrate.

## Enter Freud's Jewishness

Freudian research, a veritable cottage industry by now, has sought the roots of psychoanalysis in Freud's Jewishness. Freud himself attributed his theory to his marginalization in Gentile circles,[12] but also (as the Lamarckian he was) to Jewish cultural-hereditary endowment. When Reik criticized Lutheran psychoanalyst and pastor Oskar Pfister, with whom Freud had been in close relationship, Freud labeled Reik's censure "too good for those *goyim [sic]*." Freud apparently posited an unbridgeable difference between Jews and Aryans; he had internalized the racism of his era.[13]

He was driven, however, by fear that psychoanalysis would be branded a "Jewish" heresy. His dismay at Jung's defection, for instance, though motivated partly by a bruised ego, and partly (so it is said) by Jung's symbolic denunciation of Freud "the father,"[14] derived from the fact that Jung had been a token Christian in a band of Jewish disciples. The most regularly cited evidence here is Freud's letter to disciple Karl Abraham, Jung's rival.

> It is really easier for you than for Jung to follow my ideas, for . . .
> you are closer to my intellectual constitution because of racial kinship, while he, as a Christian and a pastor's son, finds his way to
> me only against great resistance. His association with us is the

> more valuable for that. I nearly said that it was only by his ap-
> pearance on the scene that psychoanalysis escaped the danger of
> becoming a Jewish national affair.[15]

Freud had reason to fear the marginalization of "Jewish" science. Europe was becoming marginal for Jews. Austrian Jewry had been granted official "toleration" in 1782, and by 1848, Jews and Christians were dying together at revolutionary barricades. In 1867, hoping to enlist a loyal citizenry in the wake of Austria's defeat by Prussia the year before, Emperor Franz Joseph completed the work of granting Jews citizenship rights.[16] Freud's childhood hopes were nurtured by that liberal era. He recalled his father decorating the house for the liberal ministers elected that year, as he (aged 10) joined "every industrious Jewish schoolboy [in carrying] a minister's portfolio on his knapsack."[17] By the time Freud was 23 (1880), Jews were ten percent of Vienna's population, but forty percent of its medical school, twenty-five percent of the law school, and virtually one-hundred percent of its journalists.[18] Arthur Schnitzler, Stefan Zweig, Gustav Mahler, Arnold Schoenberg, Theodor Herzl and Freud all grew up in *fin de siecle* Vienna.

But Vienna was being reshaped by Georg von Schoenerer (1842–1921) and Karl Lueger (1844–1910). The former entered Parliament in 1873, where he introduced German pan-nationalism, and lobbied against immigration of Slavs, and then of Russian Jews particularly, following the Czarist pogroms of 1881. The latter hammered together the conservative Christian Social Party in 1889 and was elected mayor of Vienna in 1895. Two years later he entered office, bringing official antisemitism with him.

Freud, just turning 41 in 1897, had followed Lueger's progress, writing to Wilhelm Fliess, his Jewish friend and colleague, about his joy when Lueger was (temporarily, it turned out) blocked from being confirmed in office.[19] Lueger threatened not just Freud's Judaism but his liberalism as well. When World War I erupted, he flirted with optimism once again, announcing, "For the first time in thirty years . . . I feel like giving this not very hopeful Empire another chance." But twelve years later, the Austrian empire in shambles, and antisemitism rising, he conceded, "Whenever I feel an inclination to national enthusiasm, I strive to suppress it as being harmful and wrong, alarmed by the warning examples of the peoples among whom we Jews live."[20]

Privately, Freud remained passionately Jewish throughout it all, albeit not religiously or ideologically—just (he thought) racially! Since he held that "the Christian religion was every bit as bad as the Jewish," conversion was out of the question, and in any event, the growing racist definition of identity made conversion beside the point, both in the eyes of his enemies and in Freud's view as well. Freud saw himself a "specific member of a tribal community" who shared willy-nilly a "common mental construction,"[21] a "persistent character" that was racially immutable.[22] Ironically, Lueger and Freud would have agreed on that fact, merely evaluating it differently. Echoing his growing pariah status, Freud would later recall in a lecture to his B'nai B'rith lodge, "I was a man outlawed, shunned by everyone. The longing arose in me for a circle . . . who would receive me with friendliness. Your society was pointed out to me. . . . That you were Jews only suited me the more, for I myself was a Jew, and it always seemed to me not only shameful, but downright senseless to deny it."[23]

He had never been converted to Zionism either, though he had to have known it, since Zionism's father, Theodor Herzl, was a well-known journalist in Freud's Vienna. But when General Allenby marched British troops into Palestine in December, 1917, Freud admitted, "My sole joy at the moment is the occupation of Jerusalem and the experience that the English are undertaking with the chosen people." He recognized "the great potential of a Jewish center in the world [as a] rallying point for Jewish ideals."[24] His well-known introduction to the 1934 Hebrew edition of *Totem and Taboo,* saying he "could not take part in nationalist ideals" yet had "never repudiated his people" reads like an apology for not having supported the Zionists more. If he were to be asked (he says), "What is there left to you that is Jewish?" the answer would be, "A great deal, and probably its very essence."[25]

But what does that mean? If religiously estranged and no active Zionist, what kind of Jew was he? Peter Gay differentiates four possible answers: professional, intellectual, tribal, and sociological.[26]

A professional Jew would be one whose entire professional life is bound up with other Jews. Freud worked hard at *not* being a professional Jew.

An intellectual Jew is one whose principal intellectual debts lie within Jewish tradition. Now a case has been made for Freud's having harbored talmudic aptitude from his Jewish upbringing.[27] Freud does indeed allude to a residue of talmudic casuistry that he thinks he displays on occasion, saying (for instance), "Our Talmudic way of thinking cannot disappear just like that. Some days ago a small paragraph of *Jokes* strangely attracted me. When I looked at it more closely, I found that, in the technique of apposition and in its whole structure, it was completely Talmudic."[28] But Freud is just repeating his racist conviction that all Jews are unconsciously talmudic of necessity; talmudism is an "inherited" cultural endowment that emerges on occasion. Gershom Scholem, a Jewish contemporary of Freud's children, who grew up in a religiously marginal home as they did, testifies to how common it was then to characterize the thinking of even the most un-Jewish Jews as "talmudic." His case is sociologist Georg Simmel "whose parents had left the Jewish fold before 1850 and who was totally estranged from everything Jewish and yet was widely regarded as the quintessence of a talmudist"—this despite the fact that Martin Buber, who knew Simmel well, said that he had heard Simmel say "we" of being Jewish only once.[29] It is actually very hard to find any Talmud in Freud's work: his reasoning seems no different from other German scholarship of the time. David Bakan has argued also that Freud operated (unconsciously, at least) with Jewish mysticism's antinomian tendencies: he unseated Moses, the lawgiver; identified with the figure of Satan; and even collected god- and goddess-figurines.[30] Bakan's thesis has psychoanalytic attractiveness, perhaps, but Freud explicitly claimed (like other Jewish *Wissenschaft* masters) to despise Kabbalah. He excused Jung from fully understanding psychoanalysis because, "It is easier for us Jews, as we lack the mystical element."[31]

Freud's Lamarckian diagnosis of Jung confirms Gay's conclusion that Freud was a tribal and sociological Jew: tribal because he identified with the Jewish people; sociological because he operated on Europe's intellectual and social margins. Europe's rising racism guaranteed both. Take Simmel again: Despite complete assimilation as an accomplished German scholar, he was denied a full professorship because, as he once admitted, *"Hebraeus sum."*[32] *Hebraeus* (!) note; not *"Judaeus."* Simmel kept trying to pass; Freud did not. Freud was, he admitted, even "a fanatical Jew," much to his own surprise.[33]

But how important was a tribal or sociological Jewish identity in the development of Freud's theories? As Gay notes, the world is filled with marginal intellectuals who accomplish nothing, and the only other genius of comparable stature and accomplishment is Darwin, who was a distinctly non-marginal British country squire.[34] By contrast, John Murray Cuddihy avers that without Freud's tribal and sociological Jewishness, he would have discovered nothing at all. Freud committed the classic error of thinking that if only he dazzled the world with his brilliance, he would "make it" on intellectual merit alone. But Europe was closed to Jewish parvenus, whose intellectual excellence could not hide the Jewish mannerisms that even the enlightened Freud carried around with him. Underneath his gentlemanly exterior there lurked the old "Jew," the *Yid*. When European culture kept reminding him that his inner Yiddish core belied his outer Victorian shell, Freud charged the Victorians with having even more to hide: the deep dark secrets of sexual fantasies, repressed urges, and slips of the tongue that ought to make a gentleman blush. Freud's mortal sin was not the truth he told, but the fact that he dared to tell it. Victorians did not do that. Jews, apparently, did. Cuddihy asks, rhetorically, "Was Freud revealing a secret of nature or was he breaking a secret of polite society. . . . Was he the first to *discover* the sexual etiology, or the first to publicly *mention* it?"[35] And he responds, over and over again, that without Freud's inner *Yid,* he would never have revealed the inner id.[36]

As we have seen, however, Freud's tribal Jewish identity is unquestionable. He was genuinely proud of the "Jewish" traits that he thought he had inherited. His biographer, Jones, relates how "characteristically he [Freud] gave his advice in the form of a Jewish anecdote," even to non-Jews (in this case, it was Madame Maria Bonaparte, and the anecdote was apparently one of many that Freud customarily used, since Jones alludes to it by saying, "It was the one about . . .").[37] Jews who want to pass do not cite Jewish proverbs.

Yosef Yerushalmi grapples with the theme of Freud's tribalism, preferring the term, "psychological Jew," meaning people who "evince no special need to define themselves as Jews or to embrace any particular form of Jewish commitment, but feel themselves to be somehow irreducibly Jewish nonetheless."[38] I think Freud did have a need to define himself as a Jew, but the rest of Yerushalmi's definition is apt. As Yerushalmi sees it, Freud was more Jewish than he let on. He knew enough Hebrew to name his dog "Jofie," a never-before known animal name, but a Germanization of the Hebrew "Yofie," meaning "Beautiful." Then, too, there is a gift he received from his father in 1891, a family Bible inscribed in a run-on mosaic of obscure allusions to the Bible and rabbinic literature. "Why" asks Yerushalmi, "if Freud knew no Hebrew, did Jakob [his father] write this elaborate Hebrew inscription to him?"[39] Indeed, as Bakan maintains, he *did* know some Hebrew—he had been taught it as a child, says Jones, even though he later forgot it;[40] or, equally likely (it seems to me), he read traditional Hebrew, although not the modern variety.

I suspect that Jakob's own Jewish identity had been sharpened by the success of Lueger's Christian Social Party in Vienna, where Jakob lived. Yerushalmi tracks down the inscription's veiled references, and concludes that Freud had studied the Bible at age seven, but abandoned it later. Now, Jakob was calling his son to return to his spiritual biblical home—which he did, but only years later with *Moses and Monotheism.*

*Moses and Monotheism* is *Totem and Taboo* applied to Judaism, but also Freud's response to the pending Holocaust, and once again, to Jung. In January, 1933, Hitler had become Chancellor of the Third Reich. The following December, Jung referred publicly to "the differences which actually do exist between Germanic and Jewish psychology" and which can "no longer be glossed over." Shortly thereafter (1934) he contrasted "the Jewish race as a whole" whose unconscious was still not "weaned from barbarism" with the "creative and intuitive depth of soul" that the "Aryan unconscious" displays.[41] Still in Vienna, but watching Hitler's success and Jung's implicit collusion, Freud turned finally to his father's Bible, penning his first draft of *Moses*. Already in 1933, he had despaired of help, "especially the Christian-Aryan variety."[42] With the *Anschluss* (1938), he fled to England, where he further lamented the absence of denunciations of what was happening across the channel.[43] He had published part of *Moses* in 1937, but now he completed the book which appeared in its entirety the next year.

## Enter Freud's Ethics

Yerushalmi reads *Moses* as a defense of Judaism's ethical superiority over Christianity. We have seen how Freud saw the Christian Eucharist as an implicit admission of the primal crime. *Moses* confirms the Jewish failure to acknowledge the horrid event. Judaism had repressed the memory of murdering the first Moses, turning it instead into a neurotically intransigent monotheism. In Freud's view:

> Christianity acknowledged the murder of the Father through the expiatory sacrifice of the Son but lost the Father by deifying the Son and soon its Jewish monotheism degenerated into a virtually Egyptian paganism. Judaism stubbornly clung to the Father and thus retained a pure monotheism, but it paid for its continual repression of the Father's murder with an unending consciousness of guilt. And yet, precisely because it could not find release in the Christian myth of salvation (Freud calls it the "fantasy of atonement"), this very guilt was channeled into ever more rigorous ethical imperatives and so enabled the Jews to reach "ethical heights which had remained inaccessible to other peoples of antiquity."[44]

Yerushalmi's analysis of Freud is compelling. Freud converted his theory of ritual's origins into an ethical diatribe against Jung and the Christian world for their silence in the face of the Holocaust.

Freud did not need the Holocaust to awaken him to an ethical impulse, however, as we see by looking more closely at how Freud's ideas arose. In general, great ideas emerge from what I will call a "presumptive state," by which I mean the construction of the world that a thinker takes as axiomatic. Moreover, ideas constitute part of a thinker's "personal project," the goal or end by which a thinker justifies the work of a lifetime, the explanation that would be given either by the thinker (or by an outside observer) to the question, "What is it that you think you have accomplished?"

Freud's presumptive state is his rationalistic nineteenth-century notion of religion being a crutch for the needy, and ritual a sickness of the immature. His personal project was making humankind better; he thought he could rescue people from their childish reliance on ritual. His project, then, was scientific only accidentally: scientific as to means alone. As to ends, it was wholly ethical, an insistence on bettering the world. Here, however, his pessimism about the human condition dampened his expectations: That is the gist of his *Future of an Illusion* (1927) and also *Civilization and its Discontents* (1930). In the end, he says,

> It is not true that the ego is psychologically capable of anything that is required of it . . . [for] the id cannot be controlled beyond certain limits. . . . At this point the ethics based on religion introduces its promises of a better after-life. But so long as virtue is not rewarded on earth, ethics will, I fancy, be preached in vain. . . . A real change in the relations of human beings to possessions would be of more help in this direction than any ethical commands."[45]

Freud saw his life's work as part of an ethical project. His real indictment of ritual is that it blunts the necessary work of righting economic wrongs. Shades of Karl Marx (another of my sometime Jewish ancestors)! Claude Levi Strauss (still another) claimed both Freud and Marx as ideological mentors because they heralded what I call the theology of Gilbert and Sullivan—as Little Buttercup puts it, "Things are seldom what they seem/Milk can masquerade as cream." So, for Freud, neurosis masquerades as ritual, and for Marx, bourgeois domination masquerades as theology. These two ideological giants shared a moral vision of a better age. Marx had known poverty first-hand—in England he depended on Engels to support his writing habit. But Freud, too knew financial difficulty. Though married late (at age 30, 1886), he quickly fathered six children, with no clear way to support them. In 1900 he had practically no income at all. He therefore watched the Communist system unfurl with more than academic interest, and in 1927 he still spoke assuredly of "the great experiment in civilization that is now in progress in the vast country that stretches between Europe and Asia," adding, "What is in preparation there is unfinished."[46] In 1930, thinking still of Soviet policy, he advocated socialist economics and free love, but concluded that "human love of aggression was not created by property. It reigned almost without limit when property was still very scanty." Do away with property, and people will fight over sexual prerogatives; establish free love, and they find some other excuse to exercise "this indestructible feature of human nature."[47] By 1939 (Did he have in mind Hitler's pact with Stalin?) he had to admit that his fear was realized: the Soviet state had subjected its citizens "to the most cruel coercion and robbed them . . . of freedom of thought."[48] So social remedies might prove helpful, but only the unlikely possibility of analyzing every last human being would do the trick.

Taking Freud's ethical mandate as the most serious way to judge him, we can say that our final word on Freud the ritualist should be an ethical one. And here, Freud's theory (and Freud himself) fail the test. A half a century after Freud's own death, it is not clear that ritual mires the oppressed in their own oppression. That position is still argued on occasion,[49] but we are more likely to view ritual as a neutral thing, able to be put to good or bad use. Similarly, it is not clear that Freud's own patients use their gift of new-found reason (if that is what it is) to make the world a better place. Freud's presumptive state, like that of Socrates, held that reason was enlightenment; it would automatically outfit its owner to become a moral agent. Alas, we know better today. Freud's grand explication of ritual is both right and wrong on scientific grounds: right in the case of people for whom ritual is indeed an obsession; wrong for the vast majority who are properly drawn to ritual, but not obsessively, and not to resolve an oedipal conflict arising from a primal crime centuries past.

More to the point, it is wrong on ethical grounds suggested by Freud's own personal project; treating ritual like obsession, and then curing people of the need for it did not add to the world's good.

Finally, given Freud's belief in the obligation to pursue a moral life, we must pass judgment on how well his personal project with its ethical imperative determined his own behavior. And here he fails, as Yerushalmi decisively demonstrates. In 1934 he told German novelist Arnold Zweig that he was afraid to be totally candid about his beliefs because a certain Pater Schmidt (an ethnologist and confidant of the pope), had closed down the *Italian Journal of Psychoanalysis* and might ban psychoanalysis in Austria.[50] In the first publication of *Moses* (1937), he held back the argument that linked it to *Totem and Taboo* and to Christianity, because the Austrian Church might turn against him. Only in England, the *Anschluss* completed and the Church powerless before the German invasion, did Freud publish the missing part.[51]

Freud was constantly worried about telling the world too much truth, and in 1939, the truth he didn't tell had ethical consequences. He now chose prudential silence over moral outcry. Polish Jews asked him for an article on psychoanalysis for a proposed Polish-Jewish encyclopedia because, "We have in Poland a difficult struggle for existence and want to demonstrate our achievements." Freud refused on the dubious grounds that it was for Christians, not Jews, to speak out. Or (as Yerushalmi maintains), did he just not want psychoanalysis to be perceived as Jewish?[52]

His failure to denounce antisemitism publicly, or even to contribute an article for Polish Jewry, must constitute our final ethical judgment. Yerushalmi cites historian Salo Baron as remarking, "If a thinker of Sigmund Freud's stature takes a stand on a problem of vital interest to him, the world is bound to listen," and adds, "Just so!"[53] We are left with an enormous appreciation of Freud the prodigious genius, even as we fault him, scientifically and ethically, for a theory of ritual that is almost certainly wrong, a Lamarckian (and racist) view of ethnicity that is equally incorrect, and a personal failure to act with full moral character when it mattered. Freud was self-analyzed, after all. On his own testimony, and by his own standards, he should have been among the lucky few to behave better. And he didn't.

---

[1] David A. Hollinger, *Science, Jews and Secular Culture* (Princeton: Princeton University Press, 1996) 25.

[2] T. S. Eliot, *The Idea of a Christian Society and Other Writings* (Faber and Faber, ed., 1982).

[3] T. S. Eliot, *After Strange Gods* (Faber and Faber, 1934); quoted in Anthony Julius, *Anti-Semitism and Literary Form* (Cambridge: Cambridge University Press, 1995) 159.

[4] William Carlos Williams and Paul de Man, cited in Julius, 147.

[5] Yosef Hayim Yerushalmi, *Freud's Moses* (New Haven: Yale University Press, 1991) 11.

[6] Letter to J. Dwossis, Dec. 11, 1938, cited by Peter Gay, *A Godless Jew* (New Haven: Yale University Press, 1987) 152.

[7] *Totem and Taboo*, James Strachey, ed. (New York: W.W. Norton, 1913[1950]) 73.

[8] Though it is not clear how well he knew it. See David Bakan, *Sigmund Freud and the Jewish Mystical tradition* (New York: Schocken, 55–7); Peter Gay (*A Godless Jew* [New Haven: Yale University Press, 1987]) notes that his son, Martin, professed never to have been inside a synagogue, and when he got married he did not even know the custom of covering his head there. Freud himself was circumcised, married by the noted Reform rabbi Noah Mannheimer, but celebrated no Bar Mitzvah.

[9] Theodor Reik, *Pagan Rites in Judaism* (New York: Gramercy Publishing, 1964) 66–79.

[10] *The Descent of Man* (1971), cited in *Totem and Taboo*, 125–6.

[11] *Totem and Taboo*, 7.

[12] "The Resistances to Psycho-Analysis" (1925).

[13] Sander L. Gilman, *Freud Race and Gender* (Princeton: Princeton University Press, 1993); citation, 34–5.

[14] Jung actually refers to Freud that way, as in his letter confessing an affair with a patient: "My action was a piece of knavery which I reluctantly confess to you as my father." Cited in Yosef Hayim Yerushalmi, *Freud's Moses* (New Haven: Yale University Press, 1991) 44.

[15] Freud to Abraham, May 3, 1908, *Collected Letters*, 34. Cited frequently, e.g., Peter Loewenberg, "Sigmund Freud as a Jew: A Study of Ambivalence and Courage," *Journal of the History of the Behavioral Sciences* 7 (1971) 365.

[16] For Austrian Jews, especially Freud's circle, see Hannah S. Decker, *Freud, Dora, and Vienna: 1900* (New York: Free Press, 1991). After centuries of devastating pariah status, Emperor Joseph II emancipated Jews in a famous "Edict of Toleration" (1782). Until 1848, however, they were still unduly taxed and officially banned from inhabiting Vienna. The Freuds moved to Vienna in 1869, when Sigmund was four.

[17] Carl E. Schorske, *Fin-de-Siecle Vienna* (New York: Vintage, 1961).

[18] Decker, *Freud, Dora*, 26.

[19] M. Bonaparte, A. Freud, E. Kris., eds., *Origins of Psychoanalysis: Letters to Wilhelm Fliess, 1887–1902* (New York: Basic Books, 1954) 133.

[20] Jones, *Life and Work*, vol. 2, 171, and "Address to Society of B'nai B'rith," May 6, 1926; cited by Loewenberg, 366.

[21] Cited in Sander Gilman, *The Case of Sigmund Freud* (Baltimore: Johns Hopkins, 1993) 93, 89. On the "common mental construction," see Gilman, *Freud, Race and Gender* (Princeton: Princeton University Press, 1993) 25.

[22] The term is Philip Rieff's (*Freud: the Mind of a Moralist* [New York: Viking, 1959] 261).

[23] Cited by David Bakan, *Sigmund Freud and the Mystical tradition* (New York: Schocken, 1965) 47–8.

[24] Jacquy Chemouni, *Freud et le Sionisme* (France: Solin, 1988) 88, 91.

[25] "Preface to the Hebrew Translation," Vienna, December, 1930.

[26] Gay, *Godless Jew*, 127–33.

[27] Ernst Simon, "Sigmund Freud the Jew," *Leo Baeck Institute Yearbook* 2 (1957). Cf. Ken Friedman's study of *Freud's Dream of Interpretation* (Albany: SUNY, 1990).

[28] Hilda C. Abraham and Ernst L. Freud, eds., *A Psycho-Analytic Dialogue: The Letters of Sigmund Freud and Karl Abrahams* (New York: Basic Books, 1965) 36. Cited by Loewenberg, 365, and Gilman, *Freud Race and Gender*, 34.

[29] Gershom Scholem, *From Berlin to Jerusalem* (New York: Schocken, 1980) 67–8. On reading Buber's first book on Chasidism, Simmel had remarked, "We Jews are certainly a very strange people."

[30] David Bakan, *Sigmund Freud and the Jewish Mystical Tradition*.

[31] Freud to Abraham, July 20, 1908; cited regularly, e.g., Loewenthal, 365.

[32] Scholem, *Berlin to Jerusalem*, 67.

[33] Josef Philip Hes, "A Note on An As Yet Unpublished Letter by Sigmund Freud," *Jewish Social Studies* 48 (1986) 322; cited by Gilman, *Freud, Race and Gender*, 35.

[34] Gay, *Godless Jew*, 140–7.

[35] John Murray Cuddihy, *The Ordeal of Society* (New York: Basic Books, 1974) 83, 90.

[36] Ibid., 20, 23, 28, 65, 70.

[37] Reported by Janet Malcolm, *In the Freud Archives* (New York: Vintage, 1985) 21.

[38] Appropriating Philip Rieff's "Psychological man." Yerushalmi, *Freud's Moses*, 10.

[39] Yerushalmi, 71.

[40] Bakan, 50–1.

[41] Translation by Yerushalmi, *Freud's Moses*, 48–9. See positive interpretation of Jung by Ernest Harms, "Carl Gustav Jung: Defender of Freud and the Jews," in Aryeh Maidenbaum and Stephen A. Martin, eds., *Lingering Shadows* (Boston: Shambhala Press, 1991) 31–49.

[42] Yerushalmi, *Freud's Moses*, 48.

[43] Cf. his "Comment on Anti-Semitism" (*Complete Works*, vol. 28, 291) where he gives a precis of some anti-Nazi remarks, calling them "unusual"; and his "Anti-Semitism in England" (letter dated November 16, 1938, *Complete Works*, vol. 28, 301) where he turns down an invitation to write an article on anti-semitism, but invites non-Jews to write it. "I had to leave my home, saw the Scientific Society I had founded dissolved, our institutions destroyed, our printing press taken over by the invaders, the books I had published confiscated or reduced to pulp, my children expelled from the professions. Don't you think you ought to reserve the columns of your special number for the utterances of non-Jewish people, less personally involved than myself?"

[44] Yerushalmi, *Freud's Moses*, 50–1.

[45] *Civilization and Its Discontents*, James Strachey, trans. (1930: New York: W. W. Norton, 1961) 90.

[46] *Future of an Illusion*, James Strachey, trans. (1927: New York: W. W. Norton, 1961) 9.

[47] *Civilization*, 60–1.

[48] *Moses*, 67.

[49] Cf. Work of Marvin Harris and Maurice Bloch.

[50] Ibid., 27.

[51] *Moses*, "Prefatory Notes," 67–8.

[52] Ibid., 96–8.

[53] Ibid., 82.

# Announcing God's Reign:
# Liturgy, Life and Justice

## *Mark R. Francis, C.S.V.*

Is the historic liturgical tradition in which we worship capable of calling us to live just lives?[1] Unfortunately, the intrinsic relationship between proclaiming God's Reign in worship and the call to justice is not always evident to Christians who gather for worship every Sunday. Many do not readily see the connection between the faith announced and celebrated liturgically and the ethical decisions they are called upon to make in the course of their daily lives—decisions that not only affect themselves and their families but also contribute to justice or injustice in the United States and the larger world. With Michael Warren I would agree that "the most serious questions affecting those in pastoral ministry is the question of spirituality. Liturgists and catechists face an enormous dilemma: how to help middle-class and upper middle-class Christians find a gospel-centered spirituality that will affect their lifestyle."[2] This lack of a conscious connection between what we celebrate and how we live severely compromises the ability of the Church to offer a credible alternative to a worldview in the United States that increasingly sees the Church as irrelevant to the ultimate concerns of humanity.

Has this gap between how we worship and how we live always existed? I believe it would be helpful to begin this essay by reviewing how our ancestors in faith have seen the connection between communal worship and just living. I will then discuss aspects of our present situation that impede our making the connection between how we worship and how we live our lives informed by the justice that flows from faith in Christ. Finally, I will propose two possible strategies for helping our liturgies to bridge the gap between worship and life.

## The Historic Connection between Liturgy and Justice

In the tradition of Israel to which Christians are heirs, the prophets consistently saw the relationship between religious observances and justice. Deutero-Isaiah, for example, speaks of justice *as* religious observance:

> Is not this the fast that I choose:
> to loose the bonds of injustice
> to undo the thongs of the yoke,
> to let the oppressed go free,
> and to break every yoke?
> Is it not to share your bread with the hungry,
> and to bring the poor into your house;
> when you see the naked to cover them,
> and not to hide yourself from your own kin? (Isa 58:6-7)

Words like this, of course, are not addressed to a people who have no problem relating their ritual/religious practices to ethical behavior. Time and again the prophets call Israel to greater faithfulness to the social ideals set forth in the Torah by insisting that their worship will never be pleasing to God if it does not reflect interior conversion. It is also important for Christians to acknowledge that the failure to make the connection between liturgy and ethical life was not resolved by the coming of Christ. The evangelist Luke—despite his idyllic portrait of the first Christian community in Jerusalem painted in Acts (their coming together for worship in joy with one mind and heart)—goes out of his way to recount the fate of that cagey couple Ananias and Saphira. They both failed to see the connection between the power of God proclaimed by the apostles and the new order of human relationships—the *koinonia*—established in Christ. As the narrative recounts, this lack of vision was fatal (Acts 5:1-11).

It is significant that the first account written about the Lord's Supper in the New Testament deals with the relationship of liturgy and justice. In his first letter to the Corinthians, the apostle Paul called the whole Corinthian community to task for not recognizing the ethical implications of their eucharistic worship. He reproved the more wealthy members of the Church because of their unwillingness to wait for their poorer sisters and brothers before beginning the Lord's Supper, to the point that he questioned the very identity of the supper celebrated under those conditions. While the Corinthians claim to be celebrating a memorial of the Lord's dying and rising, their exclusion of the poor, their failure to "discern the body" of Christ which is the Church, led Paul to state quite starkly: "When you come together, it is not really to eat the Lord's supper" (1 Cor 11:20). Paul's is the first critique of Christian worship cut off from its connection to just living.

Later Christian writers will restate this ancient prophetic insistence on the integral connection between acceptable worship and justice. In the middle of the second century Justin Martyr began his description of the Sunday *synaxis* by stating, "Those of us who have resources come to the aid of all who are in need, and we are always assisting one another."[3] He concludes his discussion of the liturgy with another social action note: "The wealthy, who are willing, make contributions, each as they please, and the collection is deposited with the president, who aids orphans and widows, those who are in want because of sickness or some other reason, those in prison, and visiting strangers—in short, he takes care of all in need."[4]

The early third century document, the *Apostolic Tradition*, attributed to Hippolytus, exhorts those who have received alms for the poor: "Let those who receive (the gifts) serve with zeal. The one who has received (gifts) to bring to a widow or sick person or someone who is working for the church is to bring them on that same day. If they have not brought them on that day, they will bring them on the next day, adding something of their own, because the bread of the poor has stayed in their possession."[5]

One of the most dramatic statements regarding worship and justice is found in the exhortation given to bishops in the third century *Didaskalia Apostolorum*. The writer, echoing the letter of Jas 2:2-4, demands that the poor not only be tolerated, but accorded a place of honor in the liturgical assembly itself.

> If a poor man or a poor women comes, whether they are from your own parish or another, especially if they are advanced in years, and there should be no room for them, then make a place for them, O bishop, with all your heart, even if you yourself have to sit on the ground. You must not make distinctions between persons if you wish your ministry to be pleasing to God.[6]

Despite the hyperbolic nature of such a rubric, one wonders if the day will ever come when such a subversive ceremonial directive will ever be enacted. For example, to see Cardinal O'Connor of New York give up his throne to one of the many bag ladies who occasionally "crash" solemn Masses at St. Patrick Cathedral would indeed be a powerful ecclesial symbol of respect for the poor and a proclamation of the radical equality of all human beings in God's presence.

The concern to make the connection between liturgy and just living—although often obscured once the Church became one of the established pillars of the social order—was never totally forgotten. Great Christian thinkers of many ages continued to make reference to the intrinsic link between liturgical prayer and justice for the poor: St. Augustine, Pope Leo the Great, St. John Chrysostom, St. Thomas Aquinas, Martin Luther, John Calvin, John and Charles Wesley, Dorothy Day, and Bishop Oscar Romero. While the Church often aided and abetted the forces of social and political oppression, the tradition of justice found in the Scriptures continued to challenge the worship of the Church to attend to the plight of society's poor and marginated.

One such voice was heard on our own continent. On the eve of the Reformation, in April of 1514, Bartolomé de las Cásas, the first priest ordained in what the Spaniards called the new world, underwent a conversion while preparing a homily for Mass. He was an *encomendero*—a person who was *encomendado* or "entrusted" with Indian slaves as a reward for his help in subduing the island of Cuba by "blood and fire." The Scripture reading that changed his life was from the Book of Sirach:

> Like one who kills a son before
>     his father's eyes
> is the person who offers a
>     sacrifice from the property
>     of the poor.
> The bread of the needy is the life
>     of the poor;
> whoever deprives them of it
>     is a murderer." (34:24-25)

After meditating on this passage he could not celebrate Mass—the eucharistic offering—until he freed all of his slaves. From that moment he became a tireless worker for Native Americans in the face of the brutality and avarice of many of his compatriots.[7]

Five years later, on the other side of the Atlantic, in his *Treatise on the Blessed Sacrament*, written in 1519, Martin Luther made much the same connection between the eucharistic reception and its ethical consequences when he wrote:

> When you have partaken of this sacrament, therefore, or desire to partake of it, you must in turn share the misfortunes of the fellowship . . . all the unjust suffering of the innocent, with which the world is everywhere filled to overflowing. You must fight, work, and—if you cannot do more—have heartfelt sympathy.[8]

These examples from our history indicate that the concern to link Christian worship with God's call to promote justice in the world was never totally eclipsed. It is noteworthy though, that in returning to the sources of the Christian liturgy during the last century, the concern for social justice reflected in the writings of the early Church became an important part of the liturgical movement's agenda. Those who sought to renew worship in both Protestant and Catholics circles saw the concern for justice as an essential part of their program of renewal. Leaders of the movement like the Anglican tractarian E. B. Pusey and Roman Catholics like Lambert Beauduin and Virgil Michel saw the Church's liturgy as the indispensable means of rebuilding a truly Christian society amid the social ruins of the industrial revolution. In an eloquent address to the Anglo-Catholic Congress of 1923, Bishop Frank Weston carefully grounded liturgical renewal in Anglicanism with justice concerns:

> If you are prepared to fight for the right of adoring Jesus in his Blessed Sacrament, then you have got to come out from before your tabernacle and walk, with Christ mystically present in you, out into the streets of this country, and find the same Jesus in the people of your cities and villages. You cannot claim to worship Jesus in the tabernacle, if you do not pity the Jesus in the slum . . . And it is folly—it is madness—to suppose you can worship Jesus on the throne of glory, when you are sweating him in the souls and bodies of his children. It cannot be done . . . You have got your Mass, you have got your altar, you have begun to get your Tabernacle. Now go out into the highway and the hedges . . . Go out and look for Jesus in the ragged, in the naked, in the oppressed and sweated, in those who have lost hope, in those who are struggling to make good. Look for Jesus. And when you see him, gird yourselves with his towel and try to wash their feet.[9]

There have also been many Christians of good will, however, who have legitimately questioned the time and effort spent on liturgical renewal in a world beset by desperate poverty and social injustice. To many social activists, the Church appears out-of-step and preoccupied with non-essentials, much like the Russian Orthodox ecclesiastics who met in St. Petersburg to debate the length of stoles and other liturgical vesture in 1917, while several blocks away Lenin and his followers readied themselves for the October revolution.

There have always been honest voices raised to remind those engaged in liturgical reform that their efforts must be set in a context that goes beyond mere aesthetics—they must be integrally related to the values of the gospel. In the height of the Nazi barbarity in Germany, Dietrich Bonhoeffer summed up this critique well when he wrote: "Only he who cries out for the Jews dare permit himself to sing in Gregorian."[10]

## What Prevents Our Liturgy from Announcing the Reign of God?

Notwithstanding the fine tradition of the liturgical pioneers in linking a renewed liturgy with social justice, we must ask why many Christians today still have a very difficult time relating their worship to any practical commitment to the advancement of God's reign in ways that go beyond the merely individual quest for salvation. Those who are convinced that both the gospel and the best of Christian tradition promotes the integral connection of liturgy and justice must somehow answer the questions posed by the Sri Lankan theologian Tissa Balasuriya in relation to the Eucharist. "Why is it that in spite of hundreds of thousands of eucharistic celebrations, Christians continue as selfish as before? Why have the 'Christian' peoples been the most cruel colonizers of human history? Why is the gap of income, wealth, knowledge and power growing in the world today—and that in favor of the 'Christian' peoples?"[11] These are hard questions, and ones that cannot be satisfactorily addressed with simple solutions. While few Catholics would question the change of the bread and wine into the body and blood of Christ during our eucharistic celebrations, we have a much more difficult time understanding that this transformation of the sacramental elements ultimately takes place in order to change us—in order to conform us to Christ Jesus and to give us the strength to announce God's reign in word and deed.

I would propose that at least part of the solution rests in two characteristics of liturgy that may appear at first glance to be contradictory. First, we must strive to help people see the connection between our everyday life and what we do in worship. Second, we must also accentuate the potential our liturgical traditions have for helping us see the world in a more honest fashion. The liturgy, by placing us in a liminal or threshold position vis à vis the existing structures of society (and Church), has the potential for helping us see where we need to address the injustice in both society and Church.

## Liturgy and Life

A good friend of mine who has ministered for years in church-related work once confided to me that one of the things she most enjoys about going on vacation every year is that she can get away from "church people." It is not that she dislikes the people with whom she works—on the contrary, she is loved in her parish as a person who gets along with everyone, a woman of great faith and compassion. What she enjoys escaping from, however, is the almost unavoidable "in language" or jargon of a pastoral staff that works together and has its own vocabulary and particular way of looking at reality, almost as if it is unaware that there is a larger world outside the doors of the church. While some of this is necessary—and even based on gospel values—much of the time we mistake "a pious demeanor" for the Good News of Christ and this separates us from the hurley-burley of the modern world and the lives of ordinary men and women who live there. While Catholic clergy, especially those of us who live together in community, are often sheltered from the stark realities of working in the marketplace, of marriage and raising children, my Protestant relatives and friends assure me that the problem of ministers being out of touch with the wider world is not unique to the Roman Catholic communion.

I believe that this has everything to do with how we prepare liturgy in our parishes. As Msgr. Jack Egan wrote several years ago, the effects of such a disconnection can be devastating.

> To the extent liturgy is unconnected with daily life it leads us either to a premature withdrawal from this world as beyond hope or to passive accommodation which confines love, peace and justice to Church gatherings, but allows them no role in public life, in work, in economics, politics or culture.[12]

What helps liturgy make the connection with daily life? Attention to the everyday symbols employed in worship seems to be a good start. Our panoply of liturgical symbol and gesture did not fall from the sky, no matter how stylized it often appears in the execution. The actions of coming together, listening to stories, eating and drinking, embracing, are all human actions that we do in our lives apart from specifically "churchy" settings. The fact that people might be uncomfortable performing these actions may indicate a lack of human living outside the Church—but it might also indicate that the hieratic way they are being carried out allows little connection with the real life conditions that led the Church to adopt them as liturgical symbols in the first place. But it seems impossible for Christians of the twentieth century to present themselves as compelling visionaries of a just world order if we cannot even bridge the gulf between the language we use in worship and our experience. As the English liturgist Christopher Walsh points out, it is really difficult to take Christians seriously, especially because of the way we worship. He underscores the fact that there is a discrepancy,

> between language and experience, between description and reality, between ideology and fact. Thus "families" whose members know nothing of each other, "communities" which are nothing of the sort, "songs" which are recited, "acclamations" which are muttered by one voice, baptisms where people are "bathed" and "buried" with Christ under 10 ml. of water and "welcomed into a community" which has not bothered to turn up or even been informed of the event, "meals" at which no one drinks and where "sharing one bread" means simultaneous consumption of 500 individual breads, "gifts of the people" which are the joyless and perfunctory discharge of an obligation. The list is depressing and almost infinitely extensible.[13]

In addition to paying more respect and attention to the symbolic side of worship that flows from human experience, how can we help worshipers make the connection between liturgy and life? Certainly, homilies that are pertinent to the situation of the people listening, petitionary prayer that voices the concerns of the community in living the Christian life in their community, hymnody that speaks of God in Christ passionately involved with our world and its suffering would all go a long way in bridging the chasm between how people are experiencing God during the week and their hour or two of worship on a weekend.

I do not mean to suggest, however, that we should start churning out "theme liturgies"—those products of the 60s which were (and in some places continue to be) the bane of Catholic worship. Just after the reform of the liturgy began, Catholics had a new liturgical minister called a "commentator" whose job it was to tell the bewildered assembly what do to. Often, the commentator would greet the assembly at the beginning of the celebration with the dreaded "seven first words": "The theme of our Mass today is . . ." Many times, stating the theme was rather superfluous. On Passion Sunday, for example, the theme would be the "suffering of Christ" (despite the fact that the procession with palms is usually a dead "give-away" that we're going to read the passion). As the decades of the 60s and 70s wore on, however, and peace and justice committees were set up in many parishes, it was not unusual for the eucharistic celebration to take on themes "to educate the people." These themes ranged from those of a political nature like "Peace in Vietnam" to ecological concerns such as "Save the Whales." The United States Catholic bishops also got into the act and designated several Sundays throughout the Church Year as theme Sundays: National Catechetical Sunday, National Vocation Sunday, National Mission Sunday, and the list, unfortunately, continues to grow.

This eucharistic thematizing, though, reached its logical conclusion in 1988. In a book by a well known "creation theologian," his proposal for making our Sunday eucharistic liturgy more relevant, more life-giving, more "in touch" revolved around choosing meaningful themes. One of his suggestions was the need for white middle-class congregations to get in touch with their bodies. Therefore he suggested that we jettison the traditional celebrations of the liturgical year and devote our Sunday gatherings to themes of body parts like the brain, pancreas, and liver. He described the service this way: "A scientist or doctor could tell us how our livers serve us; a dancer could perform a liver dance and elicit everyone's participation; a poet could proclaim an ode to the liver."[14] This, he contended, would help us appreciate our bodies. This suggestion met with less than universal support.[15]

The major problem with these theme celebrations is that they are superimposed on the liturgy since they are unrelated to the scriptural readings proclaimed and have little to do with the purpose of the gathering. While certainly not opposed to peace, ecology, mission, catechetics, vocations—or even the body—the Christian community does not come together to advance a particular political or social agenda or even a fine new church program. Rather, we gather each week to celebrate the suffering, death, and resurrection of Christ—to confess the paschal mystery that we experience not simply as a past event, but as a present reality that gives hope to our future. We need to continue to remind ourselves that any real insight we might have into the issue of justice flows from our relationship with Christ, the Just One we proclaim in our liturgy. This proclamation, though, must also be tempered with humility, since we know that our assimilation of the Good News is not complete, that there are still parts of our lives that remain wounded and untouched by God's justice and love. For that reason, no matter how righteous the cause, our moral myopia sometimes limits our ability to see all of the implications of the justice for which we work. Thomas Shephard describes well our liturgical worship as a "rehearsal" for the definitive banquet of God's Reign.

> The Liturgical Assembly, then, is the place where justice is proclaimed, but it is neither a classroom nor a political rally nor a hearing. It is more like a rehearsal room where action must be repeated over and over until they are thoroughly assimilated and perfected—until, that is, the actors have totally identified with the part assigned to them. The liturgical action is a rehearsal of the

utopian kingdom first enacted upon the human stage in meals which Jesus shared with the outcasts and sinners. In it we learn to understand the drama of God's justice as it unfolds in our world and to identify with the role assigned us so that we can play it effectively in our lives and eventually before the throne of God for all eternity, when [God's] justice will be established beyond all compromise.[16]

## Liturgy and Liminality

The second characteristic of liturgy that will help believers connect justice with their worship is that of liminality. The term "liminality" is derived from the Latin word *limen* meaning threshold. It was a term coined by anthropologist Arnold van Gennep who spoke of the ability of religious ritual to place the participants outside of their normal set of social references and reflect on their position in the world. Like a "retreat" that allows us to step out of our normal routine and obligations in order to get a better vantage point from which to evaluate them, liturgy is meant to place the community of believers on the "threshold" in order to see reality as it truly is. In stripping away what another anthropologist, Victor Turner, calls the "status incumbencies"—the roles we play out in our everyday life such as parent, child, teacher, student, boss, worker—the liturgy helps us contemplate "the mysteries that confront all human persons, the difficulties that peculiarly beset their own society, their personal problems and the way in which their own wisest predecessors have sought to order, explain away, cloak or mask these mysteries and difficulties."[17]

Indeed, this liminal characteristic of worship has much to do with announcing God's reign and how things ought to be. It is an acknowledgment of reality to which God calls humanity—the real state of affairs. It is an acknowledgment, however, that is only possible for a Christian once one has been enlightened by the paschal mystery of Jesus Christ. This is the dynamic of transformation that the liturgy offers us. Not manipulating us to act justly out of guilt, but inviting us to a transformation in Christ through the rich ambiguity of our liturgical symbols. As Kathleen Hughes has pointed out, it is through the ordinary words, gestures, signs, and symbols of our liturgical tradition, placed in the liminal setting that is the liturgy, that we are effectively called to transformation in Christ.

> The liturgy provides numerous invitations to transformation. The language of ritual prayer, reflecting as it does God's saving encounter with humankind in and through Christ, deliberately shat-

ters our ordinary categories, using ordinary words and gestures in extraordinary ways, often presenting logic-defying irreconcilables in juxtaposition. At one and the same time the community is sinner and saved, powerless and graced by God, active subject of the praise of God and needy receiver of empowering grace.[18]

Attending to the liminal nature of our liturgy might also help us to critique not only the unjust world we live in, but the very liturgical forms themselves that often unintentionally contribute to injustice. How we present the Holy in our worship should be attended to very carefully for, in this, injustice of all kinds can creep into the liturgy and render our worship a stumbling block rather than a reason for embracing Christ.

This point is graphically brought home by a memorable scene from the movie *Malcolm X*. While in prison, Malcolm attends obligatory services led by a white prison chaplain who preaches to a predominantly African-American group of inmates a gospel of obedience and submission. Behind the pulpit, prominently displayed, is one of those highly sentimentalized portraits of Jesus popular in the nineteenth century—and Jesus is blond and blue-eyed. Clearly, the message the film wishes to convey is that in this setting, a white Jesus is indeed a sign of oppression rather than liberation—hence the attractiveness of the Black Muslims to someone like Malcolm X who rejected Christianity because it purported to speak the truth about God, yet perpetuated the holiness (and dominance) of one race over another.

The call to announce God's reign also demands that we attend not only to what we say, but how we say it. The issue of inclusive language, therefore, is not simply a fight over semantics, but is also revelatory of how we envision the very holiness of God and how God's grace touches us here and now. If our liturgical language excludes women or those with disabilities, if it leads to harmful stereotypes of others, it needs to be corrected to help all people claim the human dignity that is theirs. The African-American Catholic bishops, in a pastoral letter written several years again, expressed this point well when they stated categorically that: "All people should be able to recognize themselves when Christ is presented, and should be able to experience their own fulfillment when these [liturgical] mysteries are celebrated."[19]

We proclaim a God who knows no partiality (Acts 10: 34), who has called us in Christ through baptism and in whom there is no longer "Jew or Greek, there is no longer slave or free, there is no longer male or female" (Gal 3:25). The truth of our oneness in Christ must be expressed in our liturgical celebrations—else we leave the Church open to a just charge of hypocrisy.

## Conclusion

As Catholics, we worship in an historic tradition. In so doing we draw upon the wisdom of previous generations of faith-filled people who responded with sacrifice and joy to the wonderful news of redemption in Christ. They, like us, proclaimed Christ in such a way that his good news became a powerful catalyst for redressing wrongs and satisfying ancient hungers for justice. Part of this historic tradition, and one that makes our worship ever new and vital, is that our tradition is also capable of responding to the stirrings of the spirit—to the movements in the Church and the world that challenge us to find ever more eloquent and effective ways of proclaiming the Lord's death until he comes again. In being attentive to these movements, in reading these signs of the times, we are also called to embark on a journey of conversion in order to announce God's reign of justice to the world.

----

[1] As both colleague and collaborator, Gil Ostdiek has always shown a lively interest in the relationship between worship and living a just life. Much of his teaching and writing, especially his interest in liturgical catechesis, has focused on the need to relate liturgy to daily life in order to lead believers to a more authentic Christian discipleship—a discipleship that lives out the intrinsic relationship between proclaiming the reign of God in worship and the call to justice. See his "Liturgical Catechesis and Justice," in H. K. Hughes, M. R. Francis (eds.), *Living No Longer for Ourselves: Liturgy and Justice in the Nineties* (Collegeville: The Liturgical Press, 1991) 170–84.

[2] Michael Warren, "Culture, Counterculture and the Word," in Blair Glimer Meeks (ed.), *The Landscape of Praise: Readings in Liturgical Renewal* (Valley Forge Penn.: Trinity Press International, 1996) 283.

[3] Cf. L. Deiss, *Springtime of the Liturgy,* trans. by M. J. O'Connell (Collegeville: The Liturgical Press, 1979) 93.

[4] Ibid., 94.

[5] Ibid., 145.

[6] Ibid., 176.

[7] See the excellent discussion of Las Casas and his conversion by Enrique Dussel in "The Bread of the Eucharistic Celebration as a Sign of Justice in the Community," in M. Collins and D. Power (eds.), *Can We Always Celebrate the Eucharist?* Concilium 152 (New York: Seabury, 1982) 56–65. For a wider historical context see also Justo L. González, "Voices of Compassion," *Missiology* 20 (1992) 163–73.

[8] *Treatise on the Blessed Sacrament,* 1519. Quoted in J. Frank Henderson *et al.,* 101.

[9] "Our Present Duty," *Report of the Anglo-Catholic Congress* (London, 1923) 185–6.

[10] Quoted by Ebehard Bethge, *Dietrich Bonhoeffer, Person und Werk.* (Münich: Chr. Kaiser Verlag, 1955) 23. (Trans.)

[11] Tissa Balasuriya, *The Eucharist and Human Liberation* (Maryknoll: Orbis, 1979) xi–xii.

[12] John Egan, "Liturgy and Social Justice: We've only Just Begun," *Origins* 13 (September, 1983) 252.

[13] Christopher J. Walsh, "Task Unfinished," in J. D. Chrichton, H. E. Winstone, J. R. Ainslie, eds., *English Catholic Worship. Liturgical Renewal in England since 1900* (London: Geoffrey Chapman, 1979) 139–40.

[14] Matthew Fox, *The Coming of the Cosmic Christ* (San Francisco: Harper and Row, 1988) 222.

[15] See John Allyn Melloh, "Forum: One Sunday Would Be Liver Sunday," in *Worship* 64 (1990) 259–64.

[16] Thomas B. Shephard, "Liturgy and Social Justice," reprinted in Federation of Diocesan Liturgical Commissions Newsletter 12:5 (Sept.–Oct., 1985) 38–9.

[17] Victor Turner, "Passages, Margins and Poverty: Religious Symbols of *Communitas*," *Worship* 46 (1972) 402.

[18] Kathleen Hughes, "Liturgy and Justice: An Intrinsic Relationship," in *Living No Longer for Ourselves*, 48.

[19] "What We Have Seen and Heard." A Pastoral Letter on Evangelization From the Black Bishops of the United States, *Origins* 14, No. 18 (Oct. 18, 1984) 285.

# Liturgy and Spirituality:
## Making Some Sense of a Whirlwind

*Richard N. Fragomeni*

This essay examines three questions. What is Christian spirituality? What is Christian liturgy? What is the correlation or intersection of the two? These questions are pertinent for several reasons.

First, in the United States of America, at the close of the twentieth century, there is strong evidence of a swell of interest in things spiritual. One need only enter a bookstore to witness the number of volumes that have appeared with the word spirituality in their titles. From spiritual masters to soul matters, the market is flooded with texts that address themselves to an audience that is ready to buy anything claiming to assist in the ways of the spirit, especially when life is confusing or in disillusion and cultural transition. These books deal to a great extent with the emotional aspect of people, with personal memories and with the interpersonal, without demanding, however, much by way of belief or creed. The plethora of this kind of literature has made the meaning of the word spirituality unclear. Some clarity of thought seems necessary.

Second, the questions are pertinent because the liturgical renewal in the Roman Catholic Church has reached a moment in which interest in the meanings and significance of the renewed liturgy in the lives of the people are being studied. It is not uncustomary, for instance, for participants in liturgical celebrations to be surveyed or interviewed in order to ascertain the level of personal meanings that have been appropriated from the enacted rites. Those who are engaged in the pastoral implementation of the rites, as well as those who train them, believe that such information will assist in the actual development of the rites and their power to engage the assembly in conscious and active participation. Others, claiming the bankruptcy of the liturgical reform, use this evidence to demonstrate the superficiality of the changes that have occurred in the liturgy. These interpreters point to the impotence of the revised rites to instill holiness in the lives of believers, In both cases, this sort of interest may be classified as a particular understanding of the mystagogical dimension of liturgy, which places the accent on the affective response of the participants. That is, liturgical renewal is happening with greater accent placed on the how and the what of the way the rites affect the consciousness of persons. Another way of interpreting this level of the renewal is to say that it is a turn to the spiritual aspect of the liturgy, to the ways in which the liturgy makes the community grow in sanctity of life. In any case, the question of what sanctification is and how it shows up in people's lives is confused. What virtues and activities are put forward as the hallmarks of sharing in the paschal mystery of Christ? How do we evaluate the impact of the liturgy to instill these? Holiness of life has been the goal of the liturgical renewal from the beginning. Is it working?

Third, these questions are pertinent because, when probed, they can lead to deeper insight and appropriation of both the Christian spiritual and liturgical traditions. Many committed believers sometimes settle for the status quo thinking about spirituality or liturgy. Others may think that the final word has been spoken about these matters and the conversation is over. Our point of departure in this essay is the conviction that the conversation must continue; no synthesis has yet been reached. The following pages offer a way of thinking about the questions so as to further the conversation, seeking to make some sense of a whirlwind.

## What is Christian Spirituality?

It is commonplace at conferences that draw religious people to find keynote presentations and workshops that address the topic of spirituality. Some have said, and not without reason, that one need only to place the word spirituality into a title of a workshop and the room will be filled. In view of its current usage, what does the word spirituality mean? Is it a study of the lives of the saints and their ways of living the mandates of the gospel? Is it a matter of academics, analyzing the varieties of consciousness that humans can attain? Is it the study of the lives of holy people? Or, perhaps, can spirituality best be defined as the refinement of certain mental abilities, so as to perform more efficiently in sports, sex, or selling automobiles?

An author in the field of contemporary spirituality defines the word this way, as he introduces his thesis and begins his book on Christian spirituality:

> In what follows, I shall take it (spirituality) to mean the intrinsic, self-transcending character of all human persons and everything that pertains to it, including, most importantly, the ways in which that perhaps infinitely malleable character is realized concretely in everyday life situations. For, drawing on ancient metaphors for "breath" in Hebrew, Greek and Latin, "spirit" itself refers to the essential human capacity to receive and transmit the life of God, our unlimited openness to being, life, and conscious relationship.[1]

This definition claims that spirituality 1) is a mode of being human, open to self-transcendence; and 2) is a way of realizing this identity in the behaviors of one's life. In other words, spirituality is the capacity of the human person to be fully alive in the gift of life.

Appealing to the same sources of etymology, Jean Leclercq defines the word with the accent on the Christian dimension of spirituality as he introduces a collection of essays on the topic:

> What is, in fact, this "spirituality" examined by eight scholars extending their research over more than ten centuries? . . . For St. Paul and the early fathers of the Church, the "spiritual" was opposed not to "corporeal" but to "carnal," in the equally pauline sense of the word: the whole man, body and soul, under the law of sin but capable of grace. The first Latin writers from North Africa coined the word spiritualitas to designate all the activities of life according to the Holy Spirit, and this tradition remained unchanged up to and through the monastic middle ages. Later under the influence of scholasticism and the sharp dichotomy between spirit and matter, the word spiritual started to be distinguished not from what is carnal, in the pauline context, but from what is corporeal matter.[2]

This definition places the emphasis on the uniquely Christian origin of the word and on the way that it is a life lived in and through the Holy Spirit, within the context of corporeal existence, in whatever way this later context is understood. What is noted in this definition is the important presence of the Holy Spirit in the life of persons, and not simply their capacity for self-transcendence. The Pauline origin of this definition, noted by Leclercq, cannot be underestimated. St. Paul's theology of the Spirit leads the way for the understanding of spirituality as the vital life of Christ, living within the actions and disciplines of believers. Romans 8 and Galatians 5 are chapters from the Pauline epistles that give testimony to this way in the Spirit. Gal. 5:15-26, specifically, contrasts the life of the flesh with that of the Spirit.

Thus, Christian spirituality is 1) a life lived in the power of the Spirit, and 2) a life that is characterized by certain behaviors that manifest this being.

Michael Downey picks up the early definition of Christian spirituality as life lived in the power of the Holy Spirit, conformed to the person of Christ. He goes on to develop this understanding in distinction to a more psychological and therapeutic one, popular in much of the literature.[3] Placing the accent on the divine workings of the Spirit, Christian spirituality is situated within the realm of gift, which is given to those whose desire it is to live in discipleship with Christ.

In an extensive collection of essays entitled *The Study of Spirituality*, the editors offer a "Note on 'Spirituality'" in which they present the many definitions of the word that are used in their edited volume. Among the attempts to define spirituality are: "the forms and structures of the life of prayer"; "the spiritual life is life"; "some kind of wholeness"; "a search for meaning and significance by contemplation and reflection on the totality of human experiences in relation to the whole world which is experienced and also to the life which is lived and may mature as the search proceeds."[4]

This brief survey of some of the definitions of Christian spirituality show the diversity of meanings that are given to the term. For the sake of the conversation, four modes of defining spirituality are offered as an attempt to summarize and clarify these meanings. This typology is presented as a tool for a clearer discussion of the subject:

*Spirituality I* (S1)—this term understands spirituality in the original sense that it is given in the Christian tradition: Life in the Holy Spirit, offered by Christ to the glory of God. The accent is on the way of being in the Spirit, with characteristic behaviors that demonstrate this way of being. S1 is Christian spirituality. In this way of understanding, there is only one Christian spirituality, since there is only one life in the one Spirit of God.

*Spirituality II* (S2)—designates the varieties of disciplines and practices that have evolved over the Christian centuries by saints, mystics, religious leaders, and popular religiosity. These disciplines and practices, sometimes called *spiritualities,* have been designed to assist believers to yield to the gift of the Spirit, making themselves vulnerable, as it were, to the ravishing presence of God. Thus, we have Ignatian, Carmelite, Franciscan, Dominican, Biblical, and Marian spiritualities, to name a few. The S2 variety demonstrates the need for multiple genetic, cultural, and gender based ways in which the person and the community can access the gift of the Holy Spirit. These Christian practices are not to be confused with the actual life in the Spirit which they promote and cultivate. All of these disciplines are optional, in that none of them is the essential way to salvation. Salvation is found in the gift of the Spirit (S1) that enlivens the heart and transforms human desire. Nevertheless, Christians have found these disciplines helpful in their engaging this transformation, wrought by God.

*Spirituality III* (S3)—this designation would define spirituality with the accent placed on the human subject. In this case, spirit denotes the human spirit, with its capacity of self-transcendence, rather than the Holy Spirit, and her capacity of transforming the human. S3 is associated with human development and the achievement of the fullness of human potential. Certainly this mode of spirituality cannot be called Christian since there is no appeal within it to the power of the divine Spirit. However, that is not to say that S3 cannot become a threshold for the realization of S1. The Christian tradition has always held the human in highest esteem. The distinction between the human spirit (S3) and the Holy Spirit (S1), however, must be maintained.

*Spirituality IV* (S4)—defines the practices that have been created to assist in the work of developing the human spirit. These practices include therapy groups, Twelve-Step programs, and other psychological techniques that assist one with self-knowledge, such as the Ennegram and the Myers-Briggs psychological profile test. Many of the New Age practices fall into this type of spirituality. Hypnotic regression and past-lives investigation certainly are popular forms of S4. The use of crystals and pendulums are presently techniques that are claimed to assist with personal growth. The goal of these techniques is efficiency. S4 is directed to the achievement of human potential, and is employed towards that end whether it be efficiency in productivity, relationships, health, or some combination of these.

S2 and S4 are similar in that they are techniques employed for a way of wholeness. The former accents the ways of divine access, while the later leads to the shaping and wholeness of the human spirit. In S1, what is found is the Other, whose presence transforms the human. What is found in S3 is the strength of human potential, armed to face the world.

In summary, these four types are offered as a tool to clarify the meanings of the word spirituality, with a view to understanding the unique character of Christian spirituality. This typology, however, does not consider the ways of other religious traditions, such as Judaism or Buddhism. It is of recent usage also to associate the word spirituality with these religious traditions. Other categories are needed to understand the complexity of the meaning of an originally Christian word now associated with other religious traditions. Such a differentiation is beyond the scope of this present essay.

With these four ways of understanding spirituality, we can approach our second question about the meaning of Christian liturgy.

## What is Christian Liturgy?

It is commonly held that the word liturgy comes into English usage from Greek. The root meaning of the word associates it with the work and activity of people. Thus, it has come to signify the full, active, and conscious participation of the people in a godly action. In the earlier days of the liturgical renewal, this signaled greater responsibility on the part of believers to celebrate and adapt the liturgical books that were being produced.

Other authors, aware of the divine action that is part of the liturgy, began to adjust the original meaning of the word liturgy, giving it a kind of theological twist. For instance, Peter Fink boldly states "We are humbled when we realize that—our newly rediscovered definition of liturgy notwithstanding—liturgy is not the work of the people; it is first and foremost the *work of God in the people* transforming them, us, and all human life into God's own glory."[5]

From the point of view of anthropology, Ronald Grimes makes a similar remark when he defines liturgy as that which believers do in the hope that the divine would do something in them.[6] In other words, the ritual activity of the community becomes an aperture for the divine activity. The theological word for this is mediation. The liturgy mediates a godly presence that transforms.

Both writers demonstrate a concern for defining the liturgy as the action of God in the midst of human affairs, rather than accenting the human action as primary. Liturgy is the way of a divine disclosure of presence that enlivens the community of faith and acts as the power of God's self-communication.

Liturgy is understood as an act of divine activity. It is the action of communication, the way in which the community of believers finds itself enraptured by the gift of God, communicated first among us in the flesh of Jesus of Nazareth. Thus, the liturgy falls into the field of language,[7] specifically the language of symbol, metaphor, story, gesture, and silence, which Christians have inherited as their vocabulary from the past. By virtue of this kind of symbolic language, the Christ-event is celebrated and the significance of the paschal mystery announced. The communication is made as an appeal to the community to share in the gift by an appropriation of its power into their lives and relationships. The symbolic language of the liturgy is a powerful dynamic of

God's action that continues to "event" among those who are ready to receive it.

The nature of any symbolic language is such that it appeals to deep levels of human desire and prompts a response. Involved in this response, the human imagination is funded and shaped by the non-discursive symbols which are received. When symbols thus activate desire and imagination, they have made their way to the core of human consciousness. From this center, world views and values are constructed and decisions emerge. Decisions, in turn, direct our behaviors which pattern our relationships with others and the world. Relationships determine our well-being or demise, for humans are social beings and can survive only in communion.

While the nature of the symbolic is powerful within any context, Christian liturgy claims that symbolic language gains new power by virtue of the one who inspires it, namely Christ, by the power of the Holy Spirit. In the thirty years of post-conciliar liturgical reform, there has been a renewed emphasis on the importance of the epiclesis. This invocation has been retrieved from earlier liturgical forms, and places the community and its symbols at the disposal of the Holy Spirit. Thus, the community, in faith, is invited to believe that what is heard, shared, touched, seen, felt, and tasted, comes from God. The gift is the sacrament. It is communicated in the liturgy. The sacrament is the divine encounter with the Christ-event in the power of the Spirit. Entering the community in the rich symbols it brokers, future visions are imagined, godly values are communicated, decisions of justice and mercy are encouraged, and relationships of covenant communion with God, others, and the cosmos become the living sacrifice of praise. Gratitude heralds the way of being-in-the-world. All of this is the work of God among us. Thus, the liturgy becomes the official place of the community's knowing of God. Without the liturgy, the sacrament of the divine self-manifestation and gift are neither known nor received.

From this perspective, we return to our second question: What is Christian liturgy? The following points offer a summary.

1. Basically, the liturgy is an activity of symbolic communication. In the liturgy, the community is engaged in various modes of language (word, gesture, silence, activity, music, and so on) which keep the memorial of the Christ-event alive. The liturgy brings this event into the midst of the community of faith as both an offer and a gift. In this, the community engages in the liturgical action as the premier engagement with God who invites and initiates communion.

2. These language modes shape and disclose the divine self-gift and render the community available to receive it. By verbal and non-

verbal language, the community is engaged in an action that renders the participants receptive to the gift. Passivity is the enemy of any kind of liturgical appropriation.

3. The gift is the sacrament of the divine communion, which the community can encounter and receive. The sacrament is wrought among us not by our activity, but by the activity of the Holy Spirit, whom the liturgy invokes. The sacrament engenders within the community a deep response of gratitude that is displayed in relationships of compassion with all.

4. The liturgy is the public and ecclesial action of the community of faith; it is the center and source of Christian life. From this point of view, it is an official action of the community, from which no one can be lightly excused. In faith, it is the access place to God.

5. Since the liturgy communicates in symbolic language, the question of how to critically examine the quality of the symbolic language that is used in the liturgy is an important one. Intelligent examination of the liturgy might show how the liturgy may camouflage and promote the "disvalues" of exclusivity and bondage. That which can unite us in the Spirit may be filled with the bones of demons. While we cannot further elaborate this fifth point, awareness of the quality of symbolic language and its power is essential as we move to the third question of this essay.

## What is the Connection between Liturgy and Spirituality?

To answer this question, we return to the types of spirituality which were proposed above, with special attention given to S1 and S2. The first type of spirituality defined the specific Christian dimension of living life in the Holy Spirit. This mode of being can be understood as the very essence of Christian life: the life of holiness which comes from communion with God. In turn, the second type of spirituality defined ways in which living in the Holy Spirit can be welcomed. These spiritualities, S2 as they were called, are the disciplines and techniques by which Christians avail themselves to the Holy Spirit. Thus, as disciplines, they are not to be confused with the reality of holiness. In other words, religious practices do not substitute for religious being.

As recounted, throughout the Christian centuries a variety of the S2 disciplines were created to assist believers. These disciplines grew up at historical and cultural moments when life in the Holy Spirit was difficult and perilous. Emerging from the needs of the community, these spiritualities shaped the religious consciousness of their practitioners, and gradually became associated with a way of life. It is not difficult to

understand how such a close association and devotion to certain disciplines and practices caused the word spirituality to be synonymous
both for these practices (S2) and the way of being in the Holy Spirit (S1).

We also claimed above that the liturgy is in the mode of language
and communication, a discipline of symbolic activity that engages the
community in the memory and experience of the Christ-event. In this,
the liturgical renewal, over the past thirty years, has been an endeavor
to make liturgical language speak in such a way that God communicates among us. Thus, in response to the third question of this essay,
what is the connection or intersection of spirituality and liturgy, we
offer the following: The liturgy is the official and public discipline of
the Roman Catholic Church (S2) that seeks to engage the community
in the dangerous action of appropriating the divine gift (S1). As such,
it is the ecclesial way of coming to live in the Spirit. It is the premier
discipline that leads the community into a knowing of God. This discipline is neither formally doctrinal nor cognitive. Rather, it is a discipline of the heart and the memory, that profoundly seeks to prepare
the community to yield to the sacramental gift that is offered. The
liturgy, as a spiritual discipline, impacts the members of the community, rendering them receptive to divine communication.[8] In reality,
like all spiritual disciplines, the liturgy is a formative activity of Christian discipleship.

Unlike the other S2 disciplines of the tradition, moreover, the
liturgy holds a unique origin. Franciscan disciplines of life owe their
origin to Sts. Francis and Clare. The thirty-day retreat experience was
crafted by St. Ignatius of Loyola. The liturgy, however, holds pride of
place in the tradition because it claims the actions and life of Jesus as
its origin. That means that it is by Jesus' own example that the community of faith comes together to share the sacramental gift of God.
Christian spirituality, as the way of being in the Spirit, was inaugurated among us by the one upon whom the Spirit rested. In his ways
of eating, drinking, reconciling, healing, relating, and being, we are
disciplined into the tranformational gift that makes the people the
beloved daughters and sons of God. Jesus set into motion patterns of
surrender to God that we come to celebrate and inhabit in the liturgies
of the Church. Because of its origin, the liturgy is given the place of
honor among S2 traditions. It is called, and it is in fact, the source and
summit of the Church's life.

There are six implications of the connection between spirituality
and liturgy:

1. Since the liturgy holds such prominence in the Church, other spiritual disciplines are to be evaluated in view of the liturgy. Other spirit-

ual disciplines (S2) sometimes focus on one aspect of the Christ-event at the diminishment of the whole mystery. For instance, a Marian spirituality must include a sensitivity to the various ways of Christ and the Church. No Marian devotion can place Mary in the center where God alone belongs. The liturgy balances the focus of other spiritualities by situating them in relation to the paschal mystery and tempering them in view of the larger understanding of life in the Spirit.

2. It is to be remembered, nevertheless, that before the Second Vatican Council, while the liturgy was centered on the role of the presbyter, and for the most part was considered by many to be his action, the other spiritual disciplines were the essential ways of holiness. Since the community had little part in the official liturgy, that for the most had become Baroque court ritual, the other disciplines served the community in its growth in holiness.[9] The great value placed on these other S2 disciplines became apparent at the beginning of the liturgical renewal. At that time, believers either were reluctant and belligerent in leaving behind these disciplines, or the more attuned to change discarded them completely and quickly attempted to make the liturgy the *only* discipline available for spiritual living. In fact, a healthy community includes a variety of other ways of discipline to accommodate the various needs of its members. This does not mean that any and all disciplines of spirituality are appropriate. Pastoral criteria need to be developed to evaluate the appropriateness of some disciplines.

3. We have now entered an era of the liturgical and spiritual renewal of the Church in which other practices of S2 are being retrieved (such as perpetual adoration, benediction, novenas). Retrieval is not, however, an easy task. It implies that these spiritual disciplines be garnered within the context of a renewed understanding of the Christian life, of contemporary theology, and the relationship that Christians must have with the post-modern world. The challenge for leaders in the Church is to recognize that spiritual disciplines of the past grew out of certain cultural and historical periods, with their own needs and interests. They also grew out of specific world views. Simply to import them back, without an examination or concern for the new contexts of this era is tantamount to an uncritical resuscitation of the past, driven by nostalgia. This does not mean that such S2 phenomena cannot be retrieved. The retrieval, however, must be a reinterpretation of the disciplines in view of the shifts in culture and in the Church. At this juncture, we are in the discussion of the inculturation of spiritual disciplines, including the liturgy.

4. The liturgy is considered to be the central S2 of the Roman Catholic community. Nevertheless, it does not stand alone. We mentioned

above that the liturgy is the only official spiritual discipline of the Church. The accent is on official. In other words, one can still officially be alive in the Holy Spirit and never say the rosary or attend a thirty-day retreat. However, this is not the case when it comes to the celebration of the Eucharist, as an example. Without communion in the bread and wine, without communion in the assembly of believers who are affected by word and song, the claim is that there is very little life in the Spirit possible. The Roman Church places such an essential importance on the liturgical access to the Spirit and to the way of holiness that it remains seriously sinful to absent oneself from the liturgical activity of the Church.

On the other hand, it seems that the liturgy cannot do it all. That is, the liturgy cannot impact the lives and hearts of persons by itself. Access to the living God and life in the Spirit require other disciplines, both personal and communal. That is why, while the liturgy is the official spiritual discipline of the community, persons who are serious about life in holiness are encouraged to consider other forms of spiritual practices that can help open the heart for the ravishment of God and its consequences.

There is one caution, however. In the liturgical renewal, the liturgy has sometimes been seen as a S4—something I do in order to get something out of it for me. Thus, the liturgy, rather than being a discipline that leads to life in the Holy Spirit, may be seen as a mode of personal fulfillment of the S3 type. There can also be the distortion of other S2 disciplines. They may become ways of deception—ways of using spiritual practices for narcissistic ends. The consequences of living in the Spirit become the point of verification.

5. The consequences of living in the Holy Spirit have already been mentioned above. Paul articulates them at the end of the fifth chapter of the Letter to the Galatians. They are relational consequences that reflect the communion of the Trinity: love, joy, peace, patience, kindness, goodness, fidelity, gentleness, and self-control. Believers are not to be conceited or jealous. Rather, the life in the Spirit is manifested in carrying the burdens of others and living the beauty of God.

6. Life in the Holy Spirit (S1) is the aim of the liturgy. The liturgy impacts the community and sets it alive with the gift of God. The truth of the liturgical renewal is found in the lives of the community that are lived in the mystery of the Christ-event—lives that manifest the gift to the world. The truth of the liturgy as a spiritual discipline (in fact, all the disciplines find their truth here as well) is the reality of the community transformed into Christ. The liturgy disciplines the community to receive the Spirit and to live deeply in the gift. The gift that is

received is thus given away in order joyfully to carry the burdens of others. In the practice of love we find the truth of any spirituality.

Christian spirituality is vital and passionate life in the Holy Spirit. Such life is the true worship of God. The liturgy affords us the way to render it.

---

[1] Richard Woods, *Christian Spirituality: God's Presence through the Ages* (Chicago: The Thomas More Press, 1989) 3. The author credits his debt for this understanding to J.A.T. Robinson, William Earnest Hocking, Kenneth Leech, Reginald Garrigou-Lagrange, and Gerald Hughes, among others.

[2] *The Spirituality of Western Christendom*, ed. E. Rozanne Elder, intro. by Jean Leclerq (Kalamazoo, Michigan: Cistercian Publications, Inc., 1976) xxix.

[3] Michael Downey, "Christian Spirituality: Changing Currents, Perspectives, Challenges," in *America* (Apr. 2, 1994) 8–12. See his development of this thesis in his recent book, *Understanding Christian Spirituality* (Mahwah, N.J.: Paulist Press, 1996).

[4] *The Study of Spirituality*, ed. C. Jones, G. Wainwright, and E. Yarnold (New York: Oxford University Press, 1986) xxv–xxvi.

[5] Peter E. Fink, S.J., "Liturgy and Spirituality: A Timely Intersection," in *Liturgy and Spirituality in Context: Perspectives on Prayer and Culture*, ed. Eleanor Bernstein, C.S.J. (Collegeville: The Liturgical Press, 1990) 61. This is an excellent collection of essays which examines several aspects of liturgy and spirituality.

[6] Ronald Grimes, *Beginning Ritual Studies* (Lanhan, Md.: University Press of America, Inc., 1982) 43–5.

[7] For the development of the understanding of liturgy in the genre of language, see David N. Power, *Unsearchable Riches: The Symbolic Nature of Liturgy* (New York: Pueblo Publishing Co., 1984). See also Louis-Marie Chauvet, *Symbol and Sacrament: A Sacramental Reinterpretation of Christian Life*, trans. P. Madigan, and M. Beaumont (Collegeville: The Liturgical Press, 1995).

[8] The interest in the formation of consciousness and the liturgy has been taken up by catechists. This is not a new awareness for liturgiologists. Cf. Aidan Kavanagh, "Teaching Through Liturgy," in *The Notre Dame Journal of Education* 5 (1974) 35–47. See also Mark Searle, "The Pedagogical Function of the Liturgy," in *Worship* 55 (1981) 332–59.

[9] Note the fine development of this point in the classic work by Louis Boyer, *Liturgical Piety* (Notre Dame: University of Notre Dame Press, 1955).

# St. Francis of Assisi's *Canticle of Creatures* as an Exercise of the Moral Imagination[1]

## *Thomas A. Nairn, O.F.M.*

David Tracy explains that "every classic contains its own plurality and encourages a pluralism of readings."[2] This aspect of the classic aptly refers to Francis of Assisi's short vernacular song, *The Canticle of Creatures*. After nearly eight centuries, commentators continue to attribute a variety of meanings to the song. This short study will investigate three contemporary interpretations of the *Canticle*, those by Eric Doyle,[3] Eloi Leclerc,[4] and Roger Sorrell,[5] to ascertain how contemporary authors view the song. It will then suggest that another possible interpretation, one which demystifies nature, may be more adequate to the medieval world view and to the circumstances of the song's composition. Since this demystification also entails an assertion of true human freedom, one may properly describe the *Canticle* as an exercise in *moral* imagination.

I need to express one caution, however, as I begin this project. I am viewing the poem from the point of view of a moralist, not that of a historian. Although I believe that the interpretation I offer corresponds with what Francis says about the origin of the *Canticle*, as well as with what a person of his culture and world view might understand, this interpretation is as much an *exercise* of moral imagination as it is a description of that moral imagination I claim was exercised by Francis. Nevertheless, I do believe that an overlooked interpretation of the *Canticle*, one which at least complements those mentioned above, is a call to moral conversion.

## The *Canticle* and the Early Biographies

Although the *Canticle* is mentioned by Thomas of Celano and possibly by Bonaventure,[6] detailed descriptions of Francis' composition of the song are found primarily in the *Legend of Perugia* and the *Mirror of Perfection*.[7] According to these latter sources, St. Francis composed the *Canticle* in three parts at three distinct times during the last two years of his life. The first, dealing with nature (or, as I will suggest, with the cosmic elements), was composed while Francis resided at San Damiano during the winter of 1224–25; the second part, dealing with reconciliation, written to heal a feud between the archbishop and the *podestà* (mayor) of Assisi; and the final part, calling upon "Sister Death," written shortly before Francis died.[8]

If one accepts the account of the *Legend of Perugia,* the event which occasioned the composition of the original section of the *Canticle* was a dream or vision that St. Francis experienced in which God assured him of salvation. The following day he explained this dream to the brothers:

> God has given me such a grace and blessing that he has condescended in his mercy to assure me, his poor and unworthy servant, still living on this earth, that I would share his kingdom. Therefore, for his glory, for my consolation, and the edification of my neighbor, I wish to compose a new "Praises of the Lord," for his creatures. These creatures minister to our needs every day; without them we could not live; and through them the human race greatly offends the Creator. Every day we fail to appreciate so great a blessing by not praising as we should the Creator and dispenser of all these gifts.[9]

He went on to tell his brothers the manner in which they were to sing the new *Canticle:*

> His heart was then full of so much sweetness and consolation that he wanted Brother Pacificus, who in the world had been the king of poets and the most courtly master of song, to go through the world with a few pious and spiritual friars to preach and sing the praises of God. The best preacher would first deliver the sermon; then all would sing the "Praises of the Lord," as true jongleurs of God. At the end of the song, the preacher would say to the people: "We are the jongleurs of God, and the only reward we want is to see you live a truly penitent life."[10]

Thus by Francis' own admission (according to the *Legend of Perugia*), the purpose of the composition was simply to thank God for the creatures, who minister to human needs and through whom humanity offends God through lack of proper appreciation, and to lead people to penitence.

## "A Pluralism of Readings"

Given the fact that the *Legend of Perugia* portrays Francis as giving such a straightforward explanation regarding his purpose in composing the *Canticle,* it may seem pointless to search for another meaning. Yet, if Tracy's understanding of a classic's plurality of meanings is appropriate, each generation must be involved in the task of interpretation.[11] Thus, in spite of a basic agreement among themselves, the three commentators in question have each developed somewhat different interpretations of the meaning of the *Canticle,* ranging from a response to ecological problems (Sorrell) to an expression of the deepest archetypes of the human unconscious (Leclerc).

The authors all acknowledge a dependence of the *Canticle* upon the Liturgy of the Hours as it would have been recited during the time of Francis. They recognize the parallels between the *Canticle* and two liturgical texts which were frequently repeated during the hour of Lauds: Psalm 148, recited every morning, and the *Canticle of the Three Young Men* (Dan 3:56-88), recited every Sunday and feast day.[12]

According to these commentators, Francis' special contribution is in his use of the titles of "brother" and "sister" by which he addresses the creatures. Sorrell explains that by means of these titles Francis "enfraternizes all creation in God—accepting the creatures into his spiritual family as brothers and sisters. . . . The tenderness and feeling in this action should not be doubted, since Francis, in an emotional and final way, had given up his first family and reached out in turn to his friends, followers, and fellow creatures as his second family."[13] For Doyle, the terms disclose the "structure of reality," a brotherhood and sisterhood that "transcends all barriers and becomes a primarily spiritual relationship, founded upon recognition of a common origin in the sovereignly free, all-loving, creative will of God."[14] Leclerc speaks of these titles as "rooted in, and inseparable from, a profound affective and esthetic experience. . . . [expressing] a genuine love and a 'sense of union with the being and life of Nature' (to use Scheler's words)."[15]

When trying to ascertain Francis' specific purpose for composing the *Canticle,* however, each comes to a different conclusion. Doyle suggests: "It was not only the attractiveness and loveliness of creation that moved St. Francis . . . it was also the selfishness of human beings. . . . [The *Canticle*] is a protest against the misuse of creatures."[16] For Sorrell, the message of the *Canticle* is similarly "appreciative and ecological":

> It is appreciative in that people are instructed to value creation on
> at least three levels: the symbolic (the sun as signifying God), the

aesthetic (Brother Fire as beautiful), and the utilitarian (the sun gives light, the earth feeds people). It is ecological in that it explicitly rejects a view of creation that would objectify it and take it for granted as being worthless and irrelevant unless it proves serviceable to humanity.[17]

Leclerc concentrates on the mystical, contemplative aspect of the song:

> The *Canticle of Brother Sun* is both praise of the cosmos and a hymn to the inner depths. When read according to its full meaning it proves to be the expression of the spiritual experience. What this brotherly praise of creatures, to the honor of the Most High, ultimately reveals to us is an approach to God that involves the saint simultaneously in a humble, fervent communion with all creatures and in the soul's opening of itself in its own innermost depths.[18]

Thus these commentators share what I believe are somewhat modern presuppositions, on the one hand an aesthetic vision of nature and on the other, at least for Doyle and Sorrell, the understanding that material creation is being threatened by humanity.

## The Medieval World-View

The expositor of medieval popular culture, Aron Gurevich, has suggested that "whenever we come across something in medieval texts that seems to point to an aesthetic relationship with nature, we have to ponder very carefully the specific complex of ideas and feeling underlying the case in point."[19] To the extent that this is true with the interpretations in question, one may ask whether they correspond either to the world view of Francis or to the circumstances in which Francis apparently composed the *Canticle*. If the creatures described in the song are actually threatened material creation, then the song is indeed ecological and appreciative. But what if the creatures mentioned in the *Canticle* meant something else to Francis and his contemporaries?

### The Cosmic Elements

A striking feature of *The Canticle of Creatures* is, in fact, the sorts of creatures that Francis chooses to call "brother" and "sister." Those familiar with the early biographies know of Francis' fondness for calling both animate and inanimate creatures by these titles.[20] Yet the *Canticle* limits itself only to the cosmic elements of sun, moon, stars, earth, air, fire, and water. This limitation seems deliberate, especially given that the apparent liturgical models of the song, Psalm 148, and *The Canticle of the Three Young Men,* continue the praise of God in animate creation. Sorrell seems to miss this point, explaining that the song refers to "physical creation" in a way that "reveals a deep appreciation of the natural environment."[21] Leclerc (and to a lesser extent, Doyle) is better here, acknowledging that the song indeed names the cosmic elements. However, following Erhard-Wolfram Platzeck, he indicates that medieval cosmology cannot explain the *Canticle.*[22] Although I agree with Leclerc that the song is not simply reducible to a hymn praising the medieval cosmos, I believe that the medieval understanding of a foundational place of the cosmic elements in the then known universe is an essential backdrop for Francis' enterprise.

How would the educated or uneducated contemporary of St. Francis view the cosmic elements described in the *Canticle?* Characteristic of the agrarian culture of the time, people used water, earth, and fire as remedies to heal illness.[23] For the educated, Aristotle's astronomy[24] and his natural philosophy[25] already enjoyed a popularity in the twelfth century. The sublunar universe was seen as composed of various mixings of the four elements, each of which in turn was reducible to various combinations of two pairs of contrary qualities (hot/cold and moist/dry). Air resulted from the union of the qualities hot and dry; fire, hot and moist; earth, cold and dry; and water, cold and moist. As philosophers used the qualities to explain motion and change, they also believed that the elements themselves were composed of "opposing powers which maintain an inherently unstable equilibrium."[26] It was this fundamental instability in the elements themselves that allowed a general transmutation from one substance to another and became the basis for the science of alchemy.[27] Brother Elias, Francis' successor as Minister General of the Order, was said to have pursued alchemy "with enthusiasm," ensuring that other friar alchemists were attached to his residence in Assisi.[28]

### The Cosmic Elements and the Human Person

Gurevich explains that our contemporary perspective of disjunction between subject and object did not exist in the Middle Ages. He speaks of "a world-view which makes no clear distinction between the human body and the world it inhabits. . . . [A person's] properties as an individual and as a member of a group, on the one hand, and the properties of the earth he tilled within the confines of that group, on the other, were not sharply delineated, but remained intertwined in the social mind."[29] The boundary between the self and the world was a fluid one. In viewing the world, the medieval person was also viewing the self.

Thus, in the early Middle Ages, not only philosophers and theologians but also troubadours and poets saw the person not merely as a part of the larger world but rather as a "microcosm" reflecting the larger "macrocosm" and revealing a parallelism between the person and the world. The four elements whose combinations were responsible for the world humanity inhabits were the same four elements that constitute the human person. Gurevich shows this parallelism in a variety of ways:

> Repeatedly, medieval thinkers strove to embody the idea of the microcosm and macrocosm in graphic illustrative form. In the allegorical drawings illustrating the works of Abbess Hildegard of Bingen, the macrocosm is represented in the shape of the symbol of eternity—a circle, which Nature holds in her hands, while she in her turn is crowned by divine Wisdom. Within the circle is placed the human form—the microcosm. He bears within himself heaven and earth, says Hildegard. . . . In one of the miniatures decorating the words of the Alsatian Abbess Herrad of Landsberg, man-microcosm [sic] is surrounded by the planets and the four cosmic elements—fire, water, earth and air.[30]

If the cosmic elements were the foundation both of the world and of the person, it would seem that an appropriate reading of the *Canticle* would not be that of ecological awareness or of a response to human alienation from nature. Such readings would seem to demand a separation of the person from nature that was simply not part of the medieval mind. Yet if this is not the case, what then is the misuse of creation to which Francis attempts to respond by composing the *Canticle?* Perhaps the elements should not be seen as exploited *by* humanity but rather as influences *upon* humanity.

For the typical person in the Middle Ages, the elements of sun, moon, and stars would not have been seen as creatures inferior to humanity but rather as powers which affected human fortune:

> That . . . power emanated from the heavens and affected the earth was made virtually self-evident to Ptolemy and almost everyone else by the behavior of the Sun and the Moon. By analogy with, and extrapolation from, these two most prominent celestial luminaries, the other planets and stars were also assumed to cause a never-ending succession of terrestrial effects. Because celestial

bodies possessed different powers and had different positions, their effects also varied. Depending on a complex set of relationships, planets and stars could cause either beneficial or harmful effects.[31]

Similarly, earth, air, fire, and water affected the very identity of the person. Gurevich notes:

> The elements of the human body were identical, it was held, with the elements forming the universe. Man's [sic] flesh was of the earth, his blood of water, his breath of air and his warmth of fire. Each part of the human body corresponded to a part of the universe: the head to the skies, the breast to the air; the stomach to the sea; the feet to the earth.[32]

Combination of the contrary pairings of the qualities of hot/cold and moist/dry were the foundation of human temperament, and thus the four elements were related to the four humors: earth related to the melancholic temperament, air to the sanguine, fire to the choleric, and water to the phlegmatic.[33] Imbalance among the four created illness and disease, both physical and mental. The constant goal of medicine in the Middle Ages was the same as that of natural philosophy, to restore balance among the elements.[34]

## Another Possible Interpretation:
## An Exercise of Moral Imagination

It is Leclerc who describes the *Canticle* as a creation of the religious imagination. He suggests that it is the imagination that "makes us 'see' the physical reality in a certain way by imposing on it an existence created by the imagination itself."[35] Referring to the *Canticle*, he claims that the song "contains a selection of material images whose 'imaginary' character, though not thrust upon us, is definitely asserted."[36] Thus Leclerc maintains that it is through the imagination that Francis adds value to creation: "Matter to which a value has been given is matter that as it were expands under the action of unconscious interior values."[37]

Having investigated how people of the Middle Ages understood the cosmic elements, one must ask whether this interpretation of adding value (or of defending threatened creation) coheres both with the medieval world view and with the circumstances of the composition of the song. If we return to the *Legend of Perugia,* we see that the *Canticle* was born of a particular religious experience of Francis, his profound realization that he would share in the reign of God. This experience became the occasion for a composition "for the glory of God, for my consolation, and for the edification of my neighbor." By means of the song, he also wanted to acknowledge that through creatures humanity has offended God because of lack of proper appreciation. Finally, he asked that the friars sing the *Canticle* as a means to move their audiences "to true penitence." In thanksgiving for his own salvation and to lead to *human* penitence, Francis speaks of the creaturehood of the cosmic elements.

Noting these circumstances, one needs to discover what factor this exercise of the imagination created that led Francis' contemporaries to "see" differently and thus be moved to penitence. Analyzing the brief strophes that name the elements, one sees in each a movement toward God and a movement toward humanity. Brother Sun, for example, bears the likeness of God, yet he brings day to the human race. Sister Water is both useful to humans and precious, a term Francis normally reserves for the Eucharist.[38] Brother Air and all the weather's moods are means by which God cherishes all creation. Sister Earth is our mother through whom God feeds humanity. Thus Francis characterizes the cosmic elements in relation to God and in service to humanity. But these images of the *Canticle* are vastly different from the portrayal of the cosmic elements in the previous section. This choice of images, when seen against the background described above, is significant. Could Francis be making the claim that, when confronted with the cosmic elements, humanity must remember that they are *merely* creatures of God? If this is a plausible interpretation, then the use of the terms "brother" and "sister" in referring to the elements performs not only a relational function but a relativizing function as well. The terms may not "add value," imaginatively bringing nature up to the level of humanity, but rather bring the cosmic elements, understood as elements which influence humanity, down to human level.

By means of the concrete images of the song, Francis stressed that his contemporaries should see the value of the elements as inseparable from humanity on one hand and from God on the other. Gurevich explains that this was a persistent theme in the Middle Ages: "In so far as nature did not contribute to knowledge of God, it was devoid of value; if it hindered [humanity] from drawing near to God, then it was seen as evil, a manifestation of satanic powers."[39] When read in this context, the *Canticle* is a proclamation regarding the proper place of the cosmic elements. The focus of the song remains the praise of God. In fact, the lack of appreciation which Francis decries is not the lack of appreciation for creation but rather for creation's God. The elements are misused when they do not move humanity to such praise of God.

If the proper role of the elements points humanity to God, then God and not the elements is the true influencer of humanity. If this explanation is at all adequate, however, the *Canticle* says more about humanity than it does about the elements. Creation, which includes even the cosmic elements, serves God in serving humanity. But as humanity accepts its place as the microcosm of this universe it must also appreciate its own vocation in serving God. It is in this calling that humanity finds true freedom. It is noteworthy that Thomas of Celano relates: "He called all creatures *brother,* and in a most extraordinary manner, a manner never experienced by others, he discerned the hidden nature with his sensitive heart, as one who had already escaped into the freedom of the glory of the sons of God."[40] Can the moral vision of the *Canticle* be a call to such freedom achieved in conversion? Such an interpretation may also show more adequately than the others described above the coherence of this original section of Francis' song with those sections he added later, addressing reconciliation and the welcoming of Sister Death. The entire *Canticle* becomes a proclamation of praise to God in humanity finding its true freedom in serving God.

## Conclusion

The notions of vision and moral imagination are becoming more and more a part of the vocabulary and methodology of Christian ethics. When applied to the *Canticle,* they enable one to see the song in a manner different from other contemporary interpretations. *The Canticle of Creatures,* by demystifying the cosmic elements and by examining the basis of human freedom, becomes a call to moral conversion.

## Appendix

*The Canticle of the Creatures*[41]

Most high, all-powerful, all good Lord!
     All praise is yours, all glory, all honor
     And all blessing.
To you alone, Most High, do they belong.
     No mortal lips are worthy
     To pronounce your name.
All praise be yours, my Lord, through all that you have made,
     And first my lord Brother Sun,
     Who brings the day; and light you give to us through him.
How beautiful is he, how radiant in all his splendor!
     Of you, Most High, he bears the likeness.

All praise be yours, my Lord, through Sister Moon and Stars;
  In the heavens you have made them, bright
  And precious and fair.
All praise be yours, my Lord, through Brothers Wind and Air,
  And fair and stormy, all the weather's moods,
  By which you cherish all that you have made.
All praise be yours, my Lord, through Sister Water,
  So useful, lowly, precious, and pure.
All praise be yours, my Lord, through Brother Fire,
  Through whom you brighten up the night.
  How beautiful is he, how gay! Full of power and strength.
All praise be yours, my Lord, through Sister Earth, our mother,
  Who feeds us in her sovereignty and produces
  Various fruits with colored flowers and herbs.
All praise be yours, my Lord, through those who grant pardon
  For love of you; through those who endure
  Sickness and trial.
Happy those who endure in peace,
  By you, Most High, they will be crowned.
All praise be yours, my Lord, through Sister Death,
  From whose embrace no mortal can escape.
Woe to those who die in mortal sin!
  Happy those she finds doing your will!
  The second death can do no harm to them.
Praise and bless my Lord, and give him thanks,
  And serve him with great humility.

---

[1] I know Gilbert Ostdiek less as a liturgist than as a teacher, colleague, and brother in community—one whose imaginative and playful creativity has often challenged me to imagine in new ways. I therefore dedicate this essay dealing with St. Francis and the moral imagination to him in thankfulness for this gift of the imagination that he has shared with me.

[2] David Tracy, *The Analogical Imagination: Christian Theology and the Culture of Pluralism* (New York: Crossroad Publishing Company, 1981) 113.

[3] Eric Doyle, *St. Francis and the Song of Brotherhood* (New York: Seabury Press, 1981).

[4] Eloi Leclerc, *The Canticle of Creatures: Symbols of Union* (Chicago: Franciscan Herald Press, 1977).

[5] Roger D. Sorrell, *St. Francis of Assisi and Nature: Tradition and Innovation in Western Christian Attitudes Toward the Environment* (New York: Oxford University Press, 1988).

⁶See *1 Celano* 80 and 109; *2 Celano* 213 and 217; and a possible allusion to the *Canticle* in St. Bonaventure's *Major Life of St. Francis* 9, 1. Quotations from the early Franciscan sources are from Marion Habig, *St. Francis of Assisi, Writings and Early Biographies: English Omnibus of the Sources for the Life of St. Francis* (Chicago: Franciscan Herald Press, 1972).

⁷*Legend of Perugia* 43–4, 50, and 100; *Mirror of Perfection* 100–1 and 118–23. Since contemporary authors suggest that the *Mirror* is dependent upon the *Legend of Perugia*, I will use the *Legend* as my basic source. See Sorrell, *St. Francis and Nature*, 120.

⁸Sorrell, *St. Francis and Nature*, 98.

⁹*Legend of Perugia*, 43.

¹⁰Ibid.

¹¹Tracy, *Analogical Imagination*, 115–24.

¹²Sorrell, *St. Francis and Nature*, 99; see also Leclerc, *Canticle of Creatures*, 4. Raphael Brown also acknowledges a "possible indirect liturgical source in an eleventh-century Advent hymn. See "Appendix VIII" of Omer Englebert, *Saint Francis of Assisi: A Biography* (Chicago: Franciscan Herald Press, 1965) 441.

¹³Sorrell, *St. Francis and Nature*, 127.

¹⁴Doyle, *St. Francis*, 63.

¹⁵Leclerc, *Canticle of Creatures*, 11–12.

¹⁶Doyle, *St. Francis*, 67.

¹⁷Sorrell, *St. Francis and Nature*, 123.

¹⁸Leclerc, *Canticle of Creatures*, xiii.

¹⁹Aron J. Gurevich, *Categories of Medieval Culture* (London: Routledge and Kegan Paul, 1985) 65.

²⁰See, for example, St. Bonaventure's *Legenda Major* 8, 6–11.

²¹Sorrell, *St. Francis and Nature*, 125.

²²According to Leclerc, the ordering and the values given to the elements are contrary to that followed by medieval cosmology. See Leclerc, *Canticle of Creatures*, 21. See also Erhard-Wolfram Platzeck, *Das Sonnenlied Des Heiligen Franziskus von Assisi: Zusammenfassende Philologisch-Interpretative Untersuchung mit Aeltestem Liedtext und Erneuter Deutscher Ubersetzung* (Werl: Dietrich Coelde Verlag, 1984) 29.

²³Aron J. Gurevich, *Medieval Popular Culture: Problems of Belief and Perception* (Cambridge: Cambridge University Press, 1988) 83.

²⁴Prudence Allen, "Hildegard of Bingen's Philosophy of Sex Identity," *Thought* 64, no. 254 (September 1989) 233.

²⁵Gurevich, *Categories*, 56–7.

²⁶Gad Freudenthal, *Aristotle's Theory of Material Substance: Heat and Pneuma, Form and Soul* (Oxford: Clarendon Press, 1995) 2.

²⁷See Titus Burckhardt, *Alchemy: Science of the Cosmos, Science of the Soul* (Baltimore: Penguin Books, 1967).

²⁸Wilfred Theisen, "The Attraction of Alchemy for Monks and Friars in the 13th–14th Centuries," *The American Benedictine Review* 46, no. 3 (September 1995) 242–3.

²⁹Gurevich, *Categories*, 45.

³⁰Ibid., 59.

[31] Edward Grant, *Planets, Stars and Orbs: The Medieval Cosmos, 1200–1687* (Cambridge: Cambridge University Press, 1994) 572.

[32] Gurevich, *Categories*, 57.

[33] Scott Russell Sanders, "Ancient Quartet," *Parabola* 20, no. 1 (February 1995) 8.

[34] See, for example, Urban T. Holmes, *Medieval Man: His Understanding of Himself, His Society, and the World* (Chapel Hill: North Carolina Studies in the Romance Languages and Literatures, 1980) 34–6.

[35] Leclerc, *Canticle of Creatures*, 7.

[36] Ibid., 5–6.

[37] Ibid., 7.

[38] Ibid., 8.

[39] Gurevich, *Categories*, 64.

[40] Thomas of Celano, "The First Life of St. Francis," 81. Celano alludes to Rom 8:21.

[41] Habig, *Omnibus*, 130–1.

# From the *Rubricae Generales* and *Ritus Servandus* of 1570 to the *Institutio Generalis* of 1969

## Frederick R. McManus

More than a quarter century after the publication of the reformed Roman Missal of 1969–1970, it is worthwhile revisiting its front matter and comparing the chief elements of the preliminaries in this liturgical book of Vatican II and Paul VI with its predecessor, the missal of Trent and Pius V.[1]

The front matter is an integral part of the revised liturgical books of the Roman rite, which were gradually published beginning in 1968. Called *praenotanda* or, in the case of the Roman Missal and the Liturgy of the Hours, *institutiones generales*, these preliminaries are descriptive, explanatory, authoritative.[2] More important, the front matter is doctrinal, liturgical, pastoral, and rubrical. With good reason the conciliar constitution on the liturgy required that, when particular (national or regional) liturgical books in harmony with the Roman Ritual are to be created by the local churches, the Roman *praenotanda* may not be omitted—whether these introductions are pastoral, rubrical, or with special social (ecclesial) significance.[3]

The *institutio generalis* of the new Roman Missal (IGMR) was first published in 1969 along with the revised Order of Mass.[4] It is as important for the ritual reform of the eucharistic celebration as are the text and running rubrics of the Order of Mass itself. The purpose of this paper is to describe the sixteenth-century antecedents of the IGMR, offer a broad and selective view of the IGMR's eight chapters and 341 sections,[5] and speak of needed development after nearly three decades.

## *Missale Romanum* of 1570

The first liturgical book for the Eucharist that was imposed on all the churches of the West—at least on those churches that did not have their own rite or use of two hundred years' duration—was the Roman Missal of 1570.[6] The book had the following material prefixed to the

214

body of the text:[7] Bull *Quo primum; Rubricae generales Missalis; Ritus servandus in celebratione Missarum; De defectibus Missae; Praeparatio ad Missam; Gratiarum actio post Missam; Tabula literarum Dominicalium; Calendarium; Tabula perpetua festorum mobilium.*[8]

Matters in the above list that were related to the Church year had to be altered in the light of the reformed Gregorian calendar of 1582.[9] Aside from this development, however, the front matter of the Roman Missal changed very little until certain twentieth-century papal documents were added.[10] Until then only editorial changes were made, some as minor as the introduction of numbering of paragraphs. During that period of more than three centuries the body of the missal had been much augmented with new formularies as new feasts were incorporated in the calendar. On the other hand, both in substance and in form the front matter of a nineteenth-century edition of the Roman Missal was recognizably the same as that of 1570.[11]

Three parts of the front matter of the 1570 missal are the direct antecedents of the IGMR of 1969: *Rubricae generales Missae; Ritus servandus in celebratione Missarum; De defectibus Missae.*

Of these three, the *Rubricae generales* had the purpose of describing the ranks and relationships of feasts and occasional Masses; the liturgical texts, especially the variable texts, with directions for their use; and such matters as the proper hour for celebration, the several tones of voice of the priest, and other practical matters.

The second preliminary document, the *Ritus servandus*, was prepared as a ceremonial or ritual description of the rite itself. It offered much greater detail than was provided in the Order of Mass found in the body of the missal.

It is usually said that the *Rubricae generales* and the *Ritus servandus* of the 1570 Roman Missal were derived from the 1502 *Ordo Missae* of Johannes Burchard (or Burckard), a celebrated papal master of ceremonies.[12] True, there is often a verbal dependence on Burchard's *Ordo*, a text which had appeared in various Roman Missals prior to 1570 (that is, in missals never imposed throughout the West).[13] But this 1502 source was different in several ways: Burchard's *Ordo* combined liturgical norms and ceremonial directions. Matters later to be treated separately in the 1570 *Rubricae generales* and *Ritus servandus* were given by Burchard in a single running text. Even where the 1570 front matter clearly depends on Burchard, the earlier material was thoroughly recast and edited. The 1570 texts, moreover, omit entirely Burchard's treatment of the medieval dry Mass and what we call bination and trination, as well as the rite for the offering of gifts by the people.

In the twentieth century another Burchard, Dom Burckhard Neunheuser of Maria Laach,[14] has drawn attention to the several references in the 1502 text to the role of the assembled faithful, which left no traces in the Roman Missal of 1570. He mentions, among other things, directions that the faithful *(circumstantes seu interessentes)* should pay devout attention rather than say prayers different from the Mass, should be able to hear clearly the prayers and readings, and should have the opportunity to offer their gifts, as noted already. He concludes that Pius V "eliminated almost completely the references to the faithful."[15] It would be anachronistic to suggest that Joannes Burchard was delineating a vigorous congregational participation, but he does mention the assembly repeatedly—while the people are just about absent from the later description of the eucharistic celebration that was the norm from Pius V to the eve of the Second Vatican Council.

The relationship of the 1570 material to Burchard's *Ordo Missae* is nonetheless considerable. The later work amounts to a rewriting and expansion, as evident in places where the verbal dependence is apparent. Both Burchard and the Roman Missal are primarily concerned with the recited or low Mass, although the 1570 *Ritus servandus* adds, section by section, full, ancillary directions for solemn and sung liturgies. Both Burchard and the Roman Missal fail, from our contemporary viewpoint, by not offering any doctrinal, liturgical, or pastoral guidance—not even to the extent found in the parallel *praenotanda* of the Roman Ritual of 1614.

The third section of the 1570 Roman Missal that is in some sense an antecedent of the IGMR is the lengthy tract "De defectibus Missae."[16] This treatment of the *pericula* or defects which might conceivably occur in the minister, the material elements, or the celebration itself, is the culmination of such tracts and the concerns expressed in them during the medieval period.[17] Only two or three paragraphs of the 1969 IGMR were needed to deal with matters that had occupied nearly fifty paragraphs in the Roman Missal ever since 1570.[18]

It is not necessary to dwell upon this lengthy section of the 1570 front matter, except to say that it deserves the reputation of dealing with potential defects in such minute detail as to encourage the worst kind of scrupulosity in priest celebrants, sometimes in matters that were hardly significant enough to warrant church legislation. Yet one example is worth quoting: it enters into the area best left to moral theology (the determination of the gravity of transgressions), but at the same time reveals a certain reasonableness about a central text of the eucharistic prayer:

> V. 1. . . . If any omission or alteration is made in the formula of consecration of the Body and Blood, involving a change of meaning, the consecration is invalid. An addition made without alter-

ing the meaning does not invalidate the consecration, but the Celebrant commits a mortal sin.[19]

## Content of the 1570 *Rubricae Generales*

After a brief introductory note about the relation between the Mass and the Office of the day, the general rubrics had some twenty sections or chapters:

1 Double [as a rank of celebrations]
2 Semidouble and Simple
3 Weekday and Vigil
4 Votive Masses of Saint Mary and Other Saints
5 Masses of the Dead
6 Transfer of Feasts
7 Commemorations
8 Introit, Kyrie Eleison, and Gloria in Excelsis
9 Prayers
10 Epistle, Gradual, Alleluia, Tract, and the Gospel
11 Creed
12 Offertory, Secret Prayers, Prefaces, and Canon
13 Communion, Prayers after Communion, Ite Missa or Benedicamus Domino, Blessing, and Gospel of Saint John
14 Arrangement of Mass from the above Rubrics
15 Hour for Celebrating Mass
16 What Is To Be Said Aloud, and What Inaudibly, at Mass
17 Order of Genuflecting, Sitting, and Standing
18 Colors of the Vestments
19 Use of Vestments
20 Preparation of the Altar and Its Ornaments

Of these sections, the first seven have to do with the choice of the Mass formularies according to the calendar, the next seven are concerned with the choice and numbers of texts, and the remainder are self-explanatory. What is characteristic of the document is the failure to offer rationale or guidance: these are for the most part bare norms, without expressed doctrine or theory and hardly a reference to the assembly. An exception is a pastoral exposition on the tones of voice that is worth quoting:

> XVI. 2. The priest must take great care to pronounce the words that are to be spoken aloud distinctly and becomingly. He should

not read so fast, that he cannot attend to what he is reading; nor so punctiliously, that he becomes tedious to his hearers. The voice should not be so loud as to disturb others who may be celebrating in the church at the same time, nor so low that those present cannot hear. A mean should be observed. The delivery must be impressive enough to arouse devotion, and the pitch suited to the hearers, so that they may be able to follow what is being read.

The words that are to be said inaudibly must be pronounced in such a manner as to be heard by the celebrant himself, but not overheard by those present.[20]

It is equally rare that the general rubrics offered any counsel. A single instance is that "as far as possible, the Mass should agree with the Office" of the day unless there is a "reasonable cause" for another choice of Mass.[21] For the rest, it is a matter of rules, often complex, governing prayer texts that are sometimes multiple: three *orationes collectae* and other presidential prayers on lesser feasts and weekdays, but with as many as five or even seven such prayers at choice.[22]

## Content of the 1570 Ritus Servandus

If the general rubrics provide norms for choice of Mass formularies, the *Ritus servandus in celebratione Missae* was written as a descriptive and prescriptive regulation of the ritual acts of the Order of Mass, more detailed than the rubrical directions of the *Ordo* itself. It would be wearying to describe the succession of ritual acts, and the numbered sections indicate the content in sequence:

1 Preparation of the Celebrating Priest
2 The Priest's Approach to the Altar
3 Beginning of Mass and the Confession
4 Introit, Kyrie Eleison, and Gloria in Excelsis
5 The Prayer
6 Epistle, Gradual, and Other Parts to the Offertory
7 Offertory and Other Parts to the Canon
8 Canon of the Mass to the Consecration
9 Canon after the Consecration to the Lord's Prayer
10 Lord's Prayer and Other Parts to the Communion
11 Communion and the Prayers after Communion
12 Blessing at the End of Mass and the Gospel of Saint John
13 Omissions in Masses for the Dead

## Twentieth Century

This account of these parts of the front matter of the Roman Missal, almost unchanged after the first edition of 1570, can be quickly completed by mention of important developments prior to the 1962–1965 council.

1. First, there is the document added to the 1920 edition of the Roman Missal, *"Additiones et variationes in rubricis Missalis, ad normam bullae 'Divino afflatu' et subsequentium S. R. C. decretorum."*[23] Its purpose was to incorporate the partial liturgical reform decreed by Pius X in 1911 and 1913,[24] a reform that had been introduced into the Roman Breviary in 1914. It was intended (at least as a first step) to purge the Roman liturgy of the accumulations of the ages—*tamquam deterso squalore vetustatis.*[25] The reform touched such matters as the regular use of the entire psalter in the canonical hours, the restoration of the Sunday and weekday offices (especially Lenten weekdays), and a radical diminution of the pervasive saints' days and votive celebrations.

In the Roman Missal the purposes of the reform of Pius X were achieved, at least in an initial and limited way, by the inclusion of the supplementary document, *Additiones et variationes.* This considerably altered the *Rubricae generales* of 1570, although the earlier document continued to be printed in the missal. The old *Ritus servandus* was left intact, since the ritual or structural revision of the Order of Mass was hardly opportune at the beginning of this century: the *Additiones et variationes* simply did not address ritual changes.

2. The next steps of the reform initiated by Pius X were not taken for four decades. But in 1960, as one of the fruits of the general liturgical commission established by Pius XII in 1948,[26] a series of efforts culminated in a new code of rubrics for both breviary and missal issued by authority of John XXIII.[27] Once again, a substantive reform—affecting a simplification of the church calendar, with another pruning of saints' days, as well as shortening of the canonical hours, limitations upon votive Masses and Masses for the dead, etc.—did not greatly affect the Order of Mass as enshrined in the *Ritus servandus* of 1570.

There were exceptions, some of them significant: the omission of the "prayers at the foot of the altar" and of the "last gospel" on occasion, the suppression of the duplicative readings of texts by the presiding priest when these were sung by others, the prohibition of preaching and the distribution of holy Communion superimposed upon the rite of Mass (that is, while the Mass continued), the omission of the penitential rite before Communion, and the like.

3. For completeness, mention should be added of a somewhat earlier reform in the 1950s, but affecting the services of Holy Week only.

Also the work of Pius XII's commission, this was a clear and strong indication of what was to come, with or without the intervention of an ecumenical council, something not expected during the time of Pius XII. In the experimental Easter Vigil of 1951 and in the overall reform of Holy Week in 1955, the Order of Mass was affected in ways that would be reflected in the code of rubrics just mentioned. The principal element was the first introduction into the liturgical books of extensive directions concerning the participation of the assembly, especially sung and spoken participation. Another notable development in the Holy Week reform, again a forerunner of the broader reform, was the clear distribution of liturgical roles, in particular by the suppression of the duplication of readings and chants by the presiding celebrant (above).

In effect, the 1960 code of rubrics, for both Eucharist and Office, might be characterized as a lengthy and thoroughgoing replacement of the old *Rubricae generales* of 1570 and the *Additiones et variationes* of 1920. The minutiae of the document are no longer of immediate interest except as indications of progress made by the 1948 commission and, equally, of continuity with what was to come: the conciliar constitution of 1963 and the Roman Missal of 1969–1970. In fact, perhaps the chief landmark of John XXIII's apostolic letter of promulgation was his statement:

> After we had decreed [in January 1959], under the inspiration of God, that the ecumenical council should be convoked, we frequently considered what should be done concerning this work [the codification of the rubrics of office and Mass] begun by our predecessor. After long and mature examination, we have come to the decision that *the more basic principles affecting the general liturgical restoration should be proposed to the fathers of the ecumenical council,* but that the correction of the rubrics of the breviary and missal, already mentioned, should not be delayed any longer.[28]

In some sense this was the genesis of *Sacrosanctum Concilium (SC)* of the Second Vatican Council and of the liturgical reform carried out in harmony and in continuity with the conciliar decree (and with the decisions made by Pius XII beginning in 1948).

We may quickly pass over the conciliar mandate to reform the Order of Mass—and thus a mandate to redo the front matter of the existing missal. This was the clear and forceful purport of *SC* 50:

> The Order of Mass is to be revised in a way that will bring out more clearly the intrinsic nature of its several parts, as also the connection between them, and will more readily achieve the devout, active participation of the faithful.

> For this purpose the rites are to be simplified, due care being taken to preserve their substance; elements that, with the passage of time, came to be duplicated or were added but with little advantage are now to be discarded; other elements that have suffered injury through accident of history are now, as may seem necessary or useful, to be restored to the vigor they had in the tradition of the Fathers.[29]

A full explanatory *declaratio* describing the projected revisions was submitted to the conciliar fathers before the vote on *SC* 50, already amended in the light of the debate.[30]

## The *Institutio Generalis* of 1969

Likewise, there is no need to describe the process by which the IGMR was developed in 1967 and 1968.[31] This has been recounted in an article, "Punti qualificanti della 'Institutio generalis Missalis Romani,'" by Carlo Braga, who headed the study group of the Consilium of implementation which prepared the IGMR text, on the basis of the Order of Mass and the other parts of the new Roman Missal.[32] The text was published by decree of the venerable Congregation of Sacred Rites, April 6, 1969, in a volume containing the reformed *Ordo Missae* in its entirety, to be effective on November 30 of that year. In addition, the book included Paul VI's apostolic constitution *Missale Romanum.*[33]

The function and authority of the new IGMR are succinctly expressed by Paul VI in this apostolic constitution of promulgation:

> Now, however, our purpose is to set out at least in broad terms the new plan of the Roman Missal. We therefore point out, first, that a General Instruction, for use as a preface to the book, gives the new regulations [*normas*] for the celebration of the eucharistic sacrifice. These regulations cover the rites to be carried out and the functions of each minister or participant as well as the furnishings and the places needed for divine worship.[34]

*Introduction (Proœmium)*

A preliminary note of some significance is this: The IGMR has 341 numbered sections arranged in eight chapters, but it is preceded by an introduction or proem of fifteen separately numbered sections. This addition was prefixed to the IGMR a year after its initial publication, when the full sacramentary volume of the Roman Missal was promulgated on March 26, 1970.

The introduction may best be understood as a kind of historical and doctrinal response to the critics of both the Order of Mass and the IGMR, especially those within the Roman Curia who were dissatisfied with the papal constitution but could hardly attack it directly. This introduction can be understood as an expansion of the constitution *Missale Romanum*, which had broadly but carefully delineated what had been changed in the reform, while asserting its justification in the decisions of the Second Vatican Council.[35]

Even the subheads of the fifteen-section introduction suggest that it is defensive in tone while solid and factual in content: "A Witness to Unchanged Faith," "A Witness to Unbroken Tradition," and "Adaptation to Modern Conditions." The initial assertion of the Church's "great care, faith, and unchanged love" for the Eucharist, as well as "its coherent tradition, continuing amid the introduction of some new elements" is supported throughout the introduction. Historically, it calls upon the authority and intent of the Council of Trent as well as of the Second Vatican Council.

Nothing of this sort appeared in the front matter of the 1570 missal, nor may we suppose there was any need for it. To begin with, the "new" Order of Mass as represented in the *Rubricae generales* and *Ritus servandus* was not notably different from the medieval rite—however great the efforts made at scholarly investigation during the new missal's preparation after Trent. Moreover, whatever dissent there may have been among the fathers of Trent, there was not an articulate "liturgical" minority within the Roman Curia of that period—surely not one that would have challenged Pius V as the "traditionalists" of the 1960s and 1970s (and now even in the late 1990s) have challenged Paul VI.

Nevertheless this introduction goes beyond its immediate setting. It offers a well thought out justification for the reform in a sound canonical, as well as doctrinal and catechetical, tradition. In the 1990s it might well serve, along with the conciliar constitution *Sacrosanctum Concilium* (chapter 2) and the apostolic constitution *Missale Romanum*, as a continuing, solid response to the dissident minority in the Church today, whether within ecclesial officialdom or not.

When the IGMR appeared in somewhat emended form in 1970, over and above the new introductory section, it was necessary for the new Congregation for Divine Worship to make a formal presentation in these terms:

> After its publication as a preliminary to the 1969 *Ordo Missae*, the General Instruction of the Roman Missal became the object of many different doctrinal and rubrical comments. Some points in it

did not come across clearly, mainly because of the difficulty of keeping all the contents in mind, since many points are covered in different sections of the Instruction. Some complaints, however, were based on prejudice against anything new; these were not deemed worthy of considering because they are groundless: a review of the General Instruction both before and after its publication by the Fathers and *periti* of the Consilium found no reason for changing the arrangement of material or any error in doctrine. . . .[36]

### *Chapters 1 and 2:*
### *Nature and Structure of the Eucharistic Celebration*

The first two chapters of the IGMR (nos. 1–6 and 7–57) can be described together, both because they are fundamental and because they are in sharpest contrast to what appeared in the 1570 Roman Missal. Such background and doctrinal material (entitled "Importance and Dignity of the Eucharistic Celebration," chapter 1), and such a thorough treatment of the Order of Mass ("Structure, Elements, and Parts of the Mass," chapter 2) have simply nothing comparable in the old missal.

The brief opening chapter deals successively with the nature of the Mass as the action of Christ and the people of God, and the need that it be arranged or planned to achieve its effects (1–3).[37] Then sections are devoted to the ecclesial nature of the celebration plainly shown in the people's participation (4), the choice of forms and elements to foster that participation (5), and national or regional authority (6). It is no. 6 that best expresses the responsibility (and power) of cultural adaptation or liturgical inculturation and indeed the overall purpose of the IGMR as a whole:

> The purpose of this Instruction is to give the general guidelines for planning the eucharistic celebration properly and to set forth the rules for arranging the individual forms of celebration. In accord with the Constitution on the Liturgy [*SC* 37-40], each conference of bishops has the power to lay down norms for its own territory that are suited to the traditions and character of peoples, regions, and various communities.

It has to be confessed that later papal and curial documents have not had the breadth of this affirmation, neither documents addressing adaptation directly[38] nor the 1983 Code of Canon Law of the Latin Church.[39]

Chapter 2, a lengthy exposition of the structure, elements, and parts of the eucharistic celebration, does include in its fifty sections some disciplinary or rubrical norms. Examples are the regulation about inaudible prayers of the presiding priest (13), the enumeration of Masses or days when the Gloria (31) and the profession of faith (44) are obligatory additions, and similar matters. Nevertheless the chapter is basically descriptive of the Order of Mass, with doctrinal or theoretical explanation of each part or element. As is evident, nothing corresponding to this material is found in the predecessor front matter of 1570 or, for that matter, in the limited twentieth-century additions and variations prior to the Second Vatican Council.

This chapter's definitions of each element of the celebration, although prepared by the experts in pastoral liturgy of the Consilium and issued by authority of Pope Paul VI, are not necessarily absolute in a twentieth-century structuring of the Roman liturgy. The latter has had an extraordinarily broad and eclectic development. As an example, some might argue that the opening prayer or collect might be better understood as a prayerful introduction to the Liturgy of the Word rather than as the most venerable part of the general introductory rites, often called gathering rites in other churches. The prayer is explained as the culmination of the introductory part and thus as a kind of introduction to the entirety of Word and Eucharist (32). Explanations of this sort are still authoritative and also highly significant for any understanding of reformed structure and relationship of elements as of this time. Put differently, there is a basic presumption that these doctrinal explanations are the surest source of sound liturgical catechesis—unless and until they are changed by further Roman reform or by inculturation.

Much the same can be said of the succeeding chapters of the IGMR. They can now be summarily described, with very selective quotations or references to illustrate the thesis of this paper, that the document is admirably concerned with the meaning and rationale of the celebration, not merely with rubrical directions or norms.

## Chapter 3:
### Offices and Ministries in the Mass

This chapter is a relatively brief treatment of the participants in the celebration, with special attention to ordained ministers and special ministers in the course of the rite. Happily the opening paragraph begins, as do the *praenotanda* of other reformed liturgical books, with the entire assembly and its members, each one with the "right and duty" of participation. In particular, it embraces the rationale of the so-called distinction or distribution of roles (58). This element of official reform, as has been repeatedly noted, dates back to the Holy Week rites revised by Pius XII in 1951 and 1955, but the IGMR cites only the *Constitution on the Sacred Liturgy*.[40]

After the introduction, the chapter deals successively with those in holy orders (59–61), the whole people of God (62–64), and the special ministers who have particular functions or offices to carry out during the celebration (65–73).

Attention should be drawn to the way in which the relationship of bishop and presbyters is described. First the general principle is asserted, dating from antiquity or at least from the period when bishops and presbyters became clearly distinct: "Every authentic celebration of the Eucharist is directed by the bishop, either in person or through the presbyters, who are his helpers" (59). Corresponding to *SC* 41, the assisting or concelebrating role of the presbyters is explained: "not to add solemnity, but to express in a clearer light the mystery of the Church, which is the sacrament of unity" (59).[41]

The presidency of the bishop himself at the head of the local church assembly or, in his absence, that of a presbyter whom he deputes or designates remains clear and intact in the IGMR. The alternative presidency of the presbyter—always in dependence on the bishop of the local church—is then explained (60), in full accord with *SC* 42.[42]

In this same section, the order of deacons is described in its eucharistic office (61), a matter that will be mentioned again below.

The second part of chapter 3, on the "office and functions of the people of God," is almost entirely theory or doctrine, aside from an injunction against "any appearance of individualism or division" (62). Altogether it is an impressive exposition, with special attention at the end to the liturgical function of choirs, which is said to include encouragement of "active participation of the people in the singing" (63–64).

The final part of the chapter, more clearly directive or normative, deals with a series of special ministers—not fully admissive of women, given the period of the IGMR's composition, and not yet providing for special ministers of the Eucharist. New developments include the office of commentator (68 a)[43] and, far more important, the liturgical planning or preparation process, which will also appear in later parts of IGMR. Here a simple concluding direction is given:

> All concerned [i.e., those persons with special ministries] should work together in the effective preparation of each liturgical celebration as to its rites, pastoral aspects, and music. They should work together under the direction of the rector of the church [that

is, the one who will preside at the Eucharist] and should consult the faithful (73).

## Chapter 4:
## The Different Forms of Celebration

The fourth chapter, dealing with the diverse forms which the Roman eucharistic liturgy may take, begins with an eloquent reaffirmation of SC 41–42 (74–75) and then speaks of the conventual Mass of religious within the context of the Liturgy of the Hours (76). In large part, however, it is a lengthy expression of rubrical minutiae, elaborating on the running rubrics of the Order of Mass (77–252). It is thus largely regulatory, with the text of the preceding chapters providing the rationale. In a sense it may stand in direct succession to the ritual description in the 1570 *Ritus servandus*—but with all the reforms and revisions enjoined by the Second Vatican Council.

The first and fundamental part is on "Mass with a Congregation" (77–153), in particular the basic form *(forma typica)*: a "sung celebration, with a reader and at least one minister, with a schola or at least one cantor, and with the people singing."[44] It is followed by a sequence of paragraphs on the functions of the deacon (127–141), the acolyte (142–147), and the reader (148–152).[45]

In what may now seem an anomaly, the basic form of celebration does not include the deacon's role, although a prefatory note explains that "a deacon may exercise his office in any of the forms of celebration" (78). The omission (or rather postponement of the deacon's office entirely to the next part) is the more notable because the Order of Mass, which this chapter of the IGMR describes, has repeated mention of the deacon's role.[46]

The apparent anomaly is easily explained: Although the restoration of an authentic diaconal order was authorized by decree of the Second Vatican Council in 1964,[47] implementation had to await papal action in 1967[48] and then the respective decrees of the conferences of bishops for their territories, country by country.

A generation later, with nearly twelve thousand "permanent" or stable deacons in a country like the United States,[49] with comparable numbers elsewhere, any description of the basic form for parochial or similar celebration should include the diaconal functions—even though most of these functions may well be exercised by the non-ordained. Day to day in the church community, deacons exercise the *diakonia* and witness of charity and also the *diakonia* of the Word, but when they are present at the eucharistic celebration, above all the Sunday Eucharist, they are to undertake their appointed liturgical ministry.

Like the treatment of the lesser ministers, the second part of chapter 4, "Concelebrated Masses" (153–208), is largely a matter of bare rubrical directions, lengthy and complex. Only at the very beginning is there a brief doctrinal note: "Concelebration effectively brings out the unity of the priesthood, of the sacrifice, and of the whole people of God" (153).[50] As in most canonical norms, the reason for each direction can generally be discerned and understood, although it is not directly articulated.

It is nonetheless important to see how the failure to integrate at least summary mention of assisting priests into the basic form of Mass creates a faulty concept of concelebration as a distinct species of eucharistic celebration. The possibilities of triumphalism and clericalism with excessively solemn or large "concelebrations" were noticed rather soon after the introduction of the rite in 1965 in accord with *SC* 57–58. For example, in the United States a June 1966 statement of the national episcopal liturgical commission[51] asserted how

> regrettable would be the use of the rite of concelebration as a means of adding solemnity to holy Mass. Neither priests nor laity should be given the notion that concelebration is an impressive liturgical display, intended to enhance a special feast or occasion. A number of priests concelebrate at one altar, not for reasons of solemnity, but in order to signify the unity of the Church.[52]

Subsequent problems have been studied in a balanced way by Gilbert Ostdiek.[53] But even the technical term, "concelebrants," may now be misleading since the whole community "concelebrates" with the presiding bishop or priest. It is hard to say whether a reform of the elaborate rite would resolve the problems, with all the ordained bishops, presbyters, and deacons who assist at any Eucharist taking the places assigned to their respective orders, wearing the simplest of vesture, and with the bishops and presbyters no longer obliged to so-called verbal or formulated concelebration.[54]

For the rest, chapter 4 has summary parts on "Mass without a Congregation" (209–231) and "Some General Rules for All Forms of Mass" (232–252), with rather exacting rubrical directions. Attention should be drawn, in the final part, to the careful description of the rites for Communion under both kinds—largely repeated from a 1965 ritual.[55] The development of Communion *sub utraque* from the examples cautiously given in *SC* 55 is evident in the somewhat broader list of occasions (242), but even the limited concessions of the IGMR are now obsolete in many places where Communion may be given from the cup (and even in other modes) without limitation of persons or communities.[56]

Today it would be appropriate to integrate the regular (and not exceptional) practice of Communion under both kinds into the basic form of Mass at the beginning of chapter 4 (and indeed into the usual Order of Mass).

Finally, the IGMR's doctrinal introduction to this rite should be mentioned, especially the following:

> Holy communion has a more complete form as a sign when it is received under both kinds. For in this manner of reception a fuller light shines on the sign of the eucharistic banquet. Moreover there is a clearer expression of that will by which the new and everlasting covenant is ratified in the blood of the Lord and of the relationship of the eucharistic banquet to the eschatological banquet in the Father's kingdom (240).

In summary, this chapter is somewhat limited to directives and ritual norms of celebration, but the occasional expository texts are valuable in themselves. In this of course it differs radically from the *Ritus servandus* of 1570.

*Chapter 5:*
*Arrangement and Furnishing of Churches for the Eucharistic Celebration*

This chapter is much briefer than chapter 4, consisting of some 28 paragraphs (253–280). These deal successively with principles, church arrangement, chancel or sanctuary, altar, altar furnishings, chair for the priest and seats for the ministers, ambo or lectern, places for the faithful, placement for choir and organ, reservation of the Eucharist, images, and the church plan. About half the paragraphs are explicitly doctrinal or expository and thus supportive of the norms affecting what has come to be called the environment of worship. As has been made clear repeatedly, nothing comparable to this kind of exposition is found in the front matter of 1570.

Derived from chapter 7 of *SC*, the text of chapter 5 has the same openness to diverse forms of art (254), strong preference for "noble simplicity, not ostentation" (280), facilitation of active liturgical participation (257), limitation upon the number of images of the saints (278), and the usual demand that eucharistic reservation be in a private and separate chapel: "Every encouragement should be given to the practice of eucharistic reservation in a chapel suited to the faithful's private adoration and prayer" (276).[57] This misunderstood matter perhaps needs even sharper definition.

*Chapter 6:*
*Requisites for Celebrating Mass*

For the most part, like chapter 4 this is a chapter of directives rather than doctrine concerning sacred or liturgical furnishings in general, vessels, vesture, and other requisites (287–312). But principles affecting church architecture in chapter 5 are reiterated: a welcome to "the artistic style of every region" with acceptance of "adaptations in keeping with the genius and traditions of each people . . ." (287); efforts "to respect the canons of art and to combine cleanliness and a noble simplicity" (312). In a couple of instances there is a certain regression from *SC* 128, which leaves certain decisions, especially in regard to the material and design of sacred furnishings and vestments, to the enactments of conferences of bishops, subject to confirmation by the Roman See; in the IGMR, however, adaptations of the design of vestments (304) and their color (308) may only be "proposed" for the consent of the Roman See.[58]

By far the most important part of the chapter is found in the opening paragraphs on the elements of bread and wine (281-286). No. 283 provides a substantive statement, for example, on the nature and authentic sign value of the element of bread:

> The nature of the sign demands that the material for the eucharistic celebration truly have the appearance of food. Accordingly, even though unleavened and baked in the traditional shape, the eucharistic bread should be made in such a way that in a Mass with a congregation the priest is able actually to break the host into parts and distribute them to at least some of the faithful. (When, however, the number of communicants is large or other pastoral needs require it, small hosts are in no way ruled out.) The action of the breaking of the bread, the simple term for the Eucharist in apostolic times, will more clearly bring out the force and meaning of the sign of the unity of all in the one bread and of their charity, since the one bread is being distributed among the members of one family.[59]

This of course is not unrelated to the principle enunciated earlier in IGMR 56 h:

> It is most desirable that the faithful receive the Lord's body from hosts consecrated at the same Mass and that, in the instances when it is permitted, they share in the chalice. Then even through the signs communion will stand out more clearly as a sharing in the sacrifice actually being celebrated.

In turn, this is derived from the strong endorsement given in *SC* 55 to receiving "the Lord's body from the same sacrifice" as "that more complete form of participation in the Mass."[60]

Of great interest is an exception that was omitted in the promulgated text of IGMR 262. The latter requires that the bread be unleavened "according to the tradition of the Latin Church."[61] Nevertheless, in the several drafts or schemata of the IGMR, in December 1967, in February 1968, in March 1968, and in July 1968,[62] the following appears:

> Where it may seem more suitable to a conference of bishops in particular circumstances, however, that leavened bread [*panis fermentatus*] should be used, whether in the ordinary way or in some cases, the matter should be proposed by the conference itself to the Apostolic See.

The language prepared by the Consilium and only omitted in the very last period before promulgation of the IGMR recognized that the use of unleavened bread, following the more ancient and venerable tradition of the Eastern Churches, would indeed be a more profound adaptation[63]—but it did not rule out the possibility for the Roman rite of the Latin Church.

*Chapter 7:*
*Choice of the Mass and Its Parts*

Both chapters 7 (313–325) and 8 are largely pragmatic directions for the choice of the variable texts for the eucharistic celebration, when choices are made available. To begin with, the breadth of such choices, alternatives, and options at the discretion of the presiding celebrant is vastly greater than in the 1570 Roman Missal. In general, not much explicit rationale is offered, but much of what is given by way of direction reflects the greatly enlarged corpus of prayer texts, the principles of chapter 5 of the *Constitution on the Sacred Liturgy*,[64] and the new *Lectionary* for Mass developed by decree of the Second Vatican Council:

> The treasures of the Bible are to opened up more lavishly [in the reform of the eucharistic celebration] so that a richer share in God's word may be provided for the faithful. In this way a more representative portion of holy Scripture will be read to the people in the course of a prescribed number of years.[65]

Chapter 7 deals in succession with the choice of Mass, that is, the Mass formularies for a given day (314–316), and with the choice of texts, that is, for the individual parts: readings, prayers, and songs (317–325). No elaborate explanation is given for the detailed norms, but the overall principles of choice are expressed in a significant prefatory statement:

> The pastoral effectiveness of a celebration will be heightened if the texts of readings, prayers, and songs correspond as closely as possible to the needs, religious dispositions, and aptitude of the participants. This will be achieved by an intelligent use of the options described in this chapter.
>
> In planning the celebration, then, the priest should consider the general spiritual good of the assembly rather than his personal outlook. He should be mindful that the choice of texts is to be made in consultation with the ministers and others who have a function in the celebration, including the faithful in regard to the parts that more directly belong to them.
>
> Since a variety of options is provided for the different parts of the Mass, it is necessary for the deacon, readers, psalmists, cantors, commentator, and choir to be completely sure beforehand of those texts for which they are responsible so that nothing is improvised. A harmonious planning and execution will help dispose the people spiritually to take part in the celebration (313).

This consciousness that the Eucharist is the action of Christ and of the whole assembly, whatever the offices of the presiding priest and others, is apparent elsewhere, for example:

> If he celebrates with a congregation, the priest should first consider the good of the faithful and avoid imposing his own personal preferences. In particular, he should not omit the readings assigned for each day in the weekday lectionary too frequently or without sufficient reason, since the Church desires that a richer portion of God's word be provided for the people (315).

Yet another paragraph reveals the ambiguity and even controversy in restoring the valuable tradition of an Old Testament reading on Sundays and holydays, a matter not explicitly mentioned in *SC* 51, but treated here:

> Accordingly, it is expected that there will be three readings [on Sundays and holydays], but for pastoral reasons and by decree of the conference of bishops the use of only two readings is allowed in some places. In such a case, the choice between the first two

readings should be based on the norms of the Lectionary and on the intention to lead the people to a deeper knowledge of Scripture; there should never be any thought of choosing a text because it is shorter or easier (318).[66]

The next chapter is anticipated by proposing that Masses for the dead be employed "sparingly." The text continues: "Every Mass is offered for both the living and the dead and there is a remembrance of the dead in each eucharistic prayer" (316). Thus the excesses of the past are corrected but in moderate language.

*Chapter 8:*
*Masses and Prayers for Various Needs*
*and Occasions and Masses for the Dead*

The final chapter of the IGMR (326–341) is again largely a matter of practical directions, covering the similar area of Mass formularies and the like, in this case those outside the system of the liturgical year and its calendars, both general and particular calendars. Again it reflects a concern for the preeminence of the temporal cycle and, at the next level, the major observances of the sanctoral cycle—the same concern that was demonstrated by Pius X at the beginning of the century, as already noted.

The initial paragraph is worth quoting for its balance:

> For well disposed Christians the liturgy of the sacraments and sacramentals causes almost every event in human life to be made holy by divine grace that flows from the paschal mystery. The Eucharist, in turn, is the sacrament of sacraments. Accordingly, the Missal provides formularies for Masses and prayers that may be used in the various circumstances of Christian life, for the needs of the whole world, and for the needs of the Church, both local and universal (326).

The chapter deals first with diverse Mass texts: ritual Masses (related to sacraments and sacramentals), Masses for various needs, and votive Masses (related to mysteries of the Lord or in honor of saints). This makes up the first part of chapter 8 (326–334), and the injunction that they be used sparingly (327) is included—similar to that in chapter 7 about Masses for the dead. The second part of the chapter offers regulations for requiem celebrations (335–341), beginning with a doctrinal explanation:

> The Church offers Christ's paschal sacrifice for the dead so that, on the basis of the communion existing between all Christ's members, the petition for spiritual help in behalf of some members may bring others comforting hope (335).

The statement is one final illustration of the manner in which throughout the IGMR such expository material precedes or is intermingled with the norms or directions, in sharp contrast to the bare regulations of the 1570 missal, as described at the beginning of this paper.

## Conclusions

*The Present*

Conclusions of different kinds may be drawn or developed from what has been said.

1. The thesis advanced by the survey of the front matter of the two missals, late medieval and modern, marks the latter as a remarkable part of the liturgical reform mandated by the Second Vatican Council. The contrast between 1570 and 1969 is no less than extraordinary. It suggests the clear wisdom of the conciliar fathers: they recognized the grave weaknesses of the medieval rite[67]—not substantially changed in the post-Tridentine reform, and practically static from then to the mid-twentieth century. In particular, the bishops also recognized, in the context of ritual books, the importance of pastoral, rubrical, and ecclesial "prefatory instructions."[68] Much as the front matter needed and needs to be supplemented by the national or regional churches as a function of inculturation, in accord with IGMR 6, it still stands as an invaluable contribution to understanding and thus to enriched celebration by worshiping assemblies.

2. Of course, much more can be said. Study and commentary on the IGMR, itself a commentary on the Order of Mass, should go on. There is nothing absolute or sacrosanct about many of the judgments made in the IGMR, any more than in the ecclesiastical texts of the missal itself—despite the rule, *lex orandi [supplicandi] statuat legem credendi.* The prayer texts are not divinely inspired by any means. Much additional investigation into the "legislative history" of the IGMR remains desirable, in itself and as basis for ongoing reform.

3. Yet the most pastorally useful dimension seems to be in the area of liturgical catechesis, whether this is the instruction and formation of the ordained ministers or the catechesis which the ministers and others who share in the teaching office of the Church—that is, all the baptized—communicate to others. The wealth of explanatory material in

the front matter is often the necessary key both to sound forms of celebration, its immediate purpose, and to the kind of liturgical formation that is essential to the complete reception of the reform by the Church even after three decades.

## The Future

1. The next question is the potential for revising the IGMR text of 1969 after years of pastoral liturgical experience. It is equally the ongoing need for greater reform, whether in the nuclear rite or Order of Mass or in the early stages of inculturation, region by region.

There could well be a polishing, reworking, and reordering to update the IGMR, certainly to recognize changed situations such as the spread of Communion under both kinds—which might now well be treated as typical and regular, with allowable exceptions. In an updating, some of the minutiae in describing the ritual acts of Communion under both kinds or those of concelebrating priests might be radically abbreviated as already obsolete.

2. One development that goes beyond the scope of this paper is a further reform of the Order of Mass itself—which would obviously involve a revision of the IGMR as well. This should be a further progression to a fresh level or plateau, certainly not any regression from the reform arising from the traditional and ancient conciliarity embodied in the Second Vatican Council or the primacy exercised in turn by Pius XII, John XXIII, and Paul VI.[69] Among other things a representation that was made to the conciliar fathers in 1963 concerning the simplification of several areas of the Mass "in the greatest need of revision" ("at the beginning, at the offertory, at the communion, and at the end") was inadequately achieved and now needs reappraisal.[70]

3. This survey of the IGMR has already spoken of some substantive areas for correction or change. Chief among these are the integration of the deacon's role into the basic rite (namely, the Sunday parochial liturgy) and the integration of the role, in much simplified form, of concelebrating bishops and presbyters (and, for that matter, deacons) who assist at the Eucharist and should not be thought of as creating a new species of celebration. Along the same lines it now seems desirable to develop somewhat the concept of greater or less solemnity of celebration; this might be done for weekday parish or community Masses, for celebrations with small and special groups (much too cautiously approached in the 1969 instruction on the subject),[71] with small children (more generously and wisely embodied in the 1973 directory),[72] and even with adolescents and young people generally.

4. Perhaps above all, there is some need to supplement the basic or typical form with attention to the bishop as presider, with some ritual and theoretical material beyond the teaching in nos. 74 and 75. This is not to denigrate the 1984 Ceremonial of Bishops, although that volume is often repetitious of what is found in the missal or other ritual books. The need arises from the fundamental notion of the eucharistic gathering as manifesting the Church assembled and actualized—and, as explained in *SC* 41, preeminently manifested in the whole participating assembly presided over by the bishop together with the orders of presbyters and deacons.

One author regretted that this stational Eucharist as it is now called was not chosen as the *forma typica*.[73] Realistically and pastorally, the Sunday parochial liturgy better serves this purpose of the basic form, but the IGMR needs to be enriched by some inclusion of the principal elements of the episcopal liturgical office, perhaps using a 1968 Roman instruction on this matter,[74] as well as very limited material from the Ceremonial of Bishops itself.

5. The introduction of variations and adaptations, whether cultural or simply contemporary and regional, is primarily the work of the local churches and especially of the bishops assembled in conciliar fashion as conferences, in accord with IGMR 6, that was noted above as fundamental. The same is true of the pastoral and other guidance that the conferences of bishops may adopt to supplement the IGMR.[75] That document, however, can be augmented to be more supportive of and encouraging to national and regional creativity, especially the composition of new prayer texts that will become the voice of the Church and the *lex orandi*.[76]

6. A general review of the IGMR suggests possibilities that would greatly enhance the document, particularly where today the best ritual choices seem not to be made by bishops, presbyters, and deacons. Where ritual options or alternatives are properly given, some preference—whether for authenticity of rites or for sign value—should be indicated, perhaps strongly and with explanation. Examples include the preference for the priest's inaudible recitation of the prayers as he places the bread and cup on the altar;[77] for the proclamation of the gospel, in the absence of a deacon, by a priest other than the presiding celebrant (34)—who remains at his seat and listens to the gospel before he gives the homily; preaching from the chair of presidency rather than from the ambo (97); etc.

To these may be added preference to be given to the preparation of the cup at the side table by the deacon (133)—even by another minister or indeed by the priest himself—as well as to the preference for purifying the vessels after Communion (by priest or deacon or other minister) at the side table or, even better, "after Mass when the people have left" (120, 138, 147). In one sense these are minutiae, but in another the actions in question are entirely secondary and are distractions to the assembly when done at the altar in full view of the community. They may also be at the expense of the assembly's periods of religious silence.

There is no need to pursue these matters further, but a minute scrutiny of needed improvement in the IGMR should now be undertaken, a generation later. In turn this brings us to saying again that the 1969 front matter of the Roman Missal is vastly different from and superior to its 1570 predecessor. Whatever the weaknesses or compromises it may show, its exposition of doctrine and theology, liturgical principles, pastoral orientation, and in fact good sense is of high quality.

The General Instruction of the Roman Missal reflects an appreciation of and commitment to the best traditions of the Roman rite. It is an organic development coupled with the best insights of the pastoral liturgical specialists of the period during and after the Second Vatican Council. Open to the creativity of the Spirit-filled community, it truly needs to have the attention of that Christian community and especially of the ordained and other ministers of the eucharistic celebration.

-------

[1] This paper is a tribute to Gilbert Ostdiek, O.F.M., in praise of his contributions as scholar and teacher, as religious and presbyter. In particular, it is a sign of appreciation of his invaluable efforts in support of the International Commission on English in the Liturgy, as a member of ICEL's Advisory Committee. At the same time, it recalls the memory of Annibale Bugnini, C.M., by any count the chief and revered architect of the 1948–1975 reform of the Roman rite and in some sense the twentieth-century Alcuin.

[2] The *praenotanda* differ in quantity and quality. As will be seen, the *institutio generalis* of the revised Roman Missal is of very high quality, like the similar document for the Liturgy of the Hours as well as the *praenotanda* for Christian initiation and the Lectionary for Mass. The first full liturgical book of the reform, for ordinations (1968), lacked such an introduction; the second edition (1989) has extensive introductory material but hardly of the same quality as some of the other books. See Frederick R. McManus, "*Praenotanda* of Ordination: The Doctrinal Content of the Liturgical Law," *The Jurist* 56 (1996) 487–526.

[3] Second Vatican Council, constitution *Sacrosanctum Concilium*, December 4, 1963 [= SC], no. 63 b. The English translation of the constitution, as well as of other documents including the *institutio generalis*, will be taken from *Docu-*

ments on the Liturgy 1963–1979: Conciliar, Papal, and Curial Texts [= DOL], ed. International Commission on the Liturgy (Collegeville, Minn.: The Liturgical Press, 1982). The 1963 constitution is DOL 1.

[4] Institutio generalis Missalis Romani [=IGMR], Congregation of Sacred Rites [=SRC], decree, Ordine Missae, April 6, 1969, in Ordo Missae (Vatican City, 1969); Notitiae 5 (1969) 147; DOL 203. The full sacramentary volume of the Roman Missal, incorporating this material, was promulgated the following year: Congregation for Divine Worship [= CDW], decree Celebrationis eucharisticae, March 26, 1970: AAS 62 (1970) 554; DOL 213.

[5] An introduction or proem of fifteen separately numbered sections was added in 1970 and is explained below. Because of the 1972 suppression of the subdiaconate in the Latin Church and creation of the lay ministries of acolytes and readers, nos. 142–52 were replaced by sections on acolytes and readers, but the overall numbering of the document was not altered. There is a useful index of the IGMR by Gaston Fontaine, "Institutio generalis Missalis romani concordantia verbalis," Notitiae 5 (1969) 304–22.

[6] Pius V, Quo primum, July 14, 1570. The undertaking had been mandated on the final day of the Council of Trent, December 4, 1563.

[7] Shortly after Pius XII initiated the preconciliar Roman liturgical reform (1948), an English translation of the front matter of the 1570 missal was published: Joseph Francis, The Laws of Holy Mass: Being the General Rubrics and Other Preliminaries of the Roman Missal (New York: Sheed & Ward, 1949). The contents are substantially those listed here, along with a supplementary document promulgated at the beginning of the present century (below).

[8] Missale Romanum ex decreto Sacrosancti Concilii Tridentini restitutum, Pii V Pont. Max. jussu editum (Rome, 1570).

[9] This appeared in later editions of the Roman Missal as a distinct section, "De Anno et ejus Partibus," which preceded the liturgical calendar itself.

[10] Briefs of Clement VIII (Cum sanctissimum, July 7, 1604) and Urban VIII (Si quid, Sept. 2, 1634) had been added early on.

[11] For example, Missale Romanum ex decreto Sacrosancti Concilii Tridentini restitutum, S. Pii V Pontificis Maximi jussu editum, Clementis VIII. et Urbani VIII. auctoritate recognitum (Ratisbon, 1861) 3–80.

[12] Text in J. Wickham Legg, ed., Tracts on the Mass (London, 1904) 119–74, together with other late medieval texts of similar character. See J. A. Jungmann, The Mass of the Roman Rite (New York: Benziger, 1951) 1:135, where the English translation "taken almost bodily from the Ordo Missae" of Burckard is an overstatement; see idem, Missarum Sollemnia (2nd ed., Vienna, 1949) 1:172.

[13] See Legg, Tracts, xxvii–xxviii. The myth of a "Tridentine" or post-Tridentine Order of Mass notably different from the late medieval Roman rite is only a myth. Present day references to a "Tridentine Mass" by traditionalists are to preconciliar usages, ordinarily those of 1962 or, by traditionalists who do not accept the reforms of Pius XII and John XXIII, to the usages decreed by Pius X.

[14] "The Relation of Priest and Faithful in the Liturgies of Pius V and Paul VI," in Roles in the Liturgical Assembly (New York: Pueblo, 1981) 207–19.

[15] Ibid., 208–9.

[16] In later editions, "De defectibus in celebratione Missarum occurrentibus."

[17] See Thomas Aquinas, *Summa Theologica*, III, q. 86, art. 6, for an example of a much briefer and less complex treatment of the *pericula*. The 1570 text shows how greatly these concerns had increased (and been refined) in the intervening centuries.

[18] IGMR 285–286; see also 239.

[19] Translation from Francis, *Laws of Holy Mass*, 132–3.

[20] Translation from Francis, *Laws of Holy Mass*, 49–50. This is the kind of comment or exhortation that is found in the pastoral and canonical prenotes of the 1614 Roman Ritual, but it is entirely exceptional in the 1570 missal.

[21] IV, 3.

[22] IX, 12.

[23] The edition was promulgated by SRC, decree *Evulgata editione*, July 25, 1920: *AAS* 12 (1920) 448–9.

[24] Apostolic constitution *Divino afflatu*, November 1, 1911: *AAS* 3 (1911) 633–8, including appended rubrics. Motu proprio *Abhinc duos annos*, October 13, 1913: *AAS* 5 (1913) 449–50.

[25] *Abhinc duos annos.*

[26] May 28, 1948; Annibale Bugnini was secretary of this commission. For the chronology see Thomas Richstatter, *Liturgical Law: New Style, New Spirit* (Chicago: Alba House, 1977) 182; for a full account, see Bugnini, *The Reform of the Liturgy 1948–1975* (Collegeville: The Liturgical Press, 1990) 7–13. Although the code of rubrics did not appear until the time of John XXIII, it had long been in preparation by Pius XII's commission.

[27] Motu proprio *Rubricarum instructum*, July 25, 1960: *AAS* 52 (1960) 592–3. (This had been preceded by a moderate simplification of rubrics prepared by the commission and promulgated by SRC, decree *Cum nostra*, March 23, 1955: *AAS* 47 [1955] 218–24.) For a contemporary commentary on the 1960 code of rubrics, see McManus, *Handbook for the New Rubrics* (Baltimore: Helicon, 1961).

[28] *Rubricarum instructum.* Emphasis added.

[29] See also *SC* 25, which decreed a collaborative procedure for the reform of all the Roman liturgical books.

[30] The vote on *SC* 50 was 2249 affirmative, 31 negative, 4 null. This makes it all the more unseemly that in the 1990s a high curial official should publicly attack Paul VI—and through him the ecumenical council held under his presidency—for the reform of the Roman liturgy. For the *declaratio* submitted on October 8, 1963, see *Acta Synodalia* II, 2: 289; also below, at note 70.

[31] See Bugnini, *Reform*, 386–91, 394–6. There were five schemata or drafts of the IGMR: no. 250 (*de Missali* 41, IGMR 1), October 12, 1967; no. 264 (*de Missali* 43 bis, IGMR 2), December 18, 1967; no. 273 (*de Missali* 46, IGMR 3), February 15, 1968; no. 282 (*de Missali* 48, IGMR 4), March 21, 1968; no. 301 (*de Missali* 52, IGMR 5), July 15, 1968. Piero Marini has prepared a list of the hundreds of (mimeographed) schemata in the lengthy process of the Roman revision: "Elenco degli 'Schemata' del 'Consilium' et della Congregazione per il Culto Divino (Marzo 1964–Luglio 1975)," *Notitiae* 18 (1982) 455–722.

[32] In R. Kaczynski, G. Pasqualetti, and P. Jounel, eds. *Liturgia, opera divina e umana. Studi sulla riforma liturgica offerti a S. E. Mons. Annibale Bugnini* (Rome: CLV, 1982) 243–61.

[33] April 3, 1969: *AAS* 61 (1969) 217–22; *DOL* 202. The texts of the related documents are in *DOL* 202–9. The IGMR is *DOL* 208; the translation incorporates variations and amendments through the second edition of the Roman Missal, promulgated by the CDW on March 27, 1975.

[34] *Missale Romanum.* See preceding note.

[35] For an account of the opposing forces, see Bugnini, *Reform,* 394–5 (on the introduction as such) and 386, footnote 53 (on pressures which resulted in changes in the body of the IGMR, especially no. 7). Bugnini treats the introduction as a distinct document (as its content suggests), but it appears in the Roman Missal as a simple prefatory section of the IGMR.

[36] Presentation, May 1970: *Notitiae* 6 (1970) 177; *DOL* 205. This brief explanation is followed by "Variationes in 'Institutionem Generalem Missalis Romanae' Inductae," 177–90. The majority of the changes were for clarification; only nos. 7, 48, 55 d, 56, 56 b, and 60 are listed as involving (minor) "doctrinal" questions.

[37] The numbering of articles in the IGMR (1–15 in the introduction just described) is begun again in the first chapter and runs continuously from 1 to 341. The numbers will be indicated in parentheses.

[38] From the instruction of CDW, *Liturgicae instaurationes,* September 5, 1970 (*AAS* 62 [1970] 692–704; *DOL* 52) to the instruction of the (current) Congregation for Divine Worship and the Discipline of the Sacraments on the Roman liturgy and inculturation, *Varietates legitimae,* January 25, 1994: *AAS* 87 (1995) 288–314. This has the subtitle, "Instructio Quarta 'ad exsecutionem constitutionis Concilii Vaticani Secundi de Sacra Liturgia recte ordinandam' (ad Const. art 37–40)."

[39] Canon 838, §3 and canon 841 do not begin to do justice to the responsibility of the conferences of bishops, as enunciated in *SC* 22, §2, and in *SC* 37–40 in respect to liturgical adaptation or inculturation. This weakness of the canons in no way diminishes the ecclesial power of the conferences as determined by the ecumenical council; see canons 2 and 6, §1.

[40] *SC* 28: "In liturgical celebrations, each one, minister or layperson, who has an office to perform, should do all of, but only, those parts which pertain to that office by the nature of the rite and the principles of liturgy."

[41] This is an improvement on *SC* 57, §1. The latter mentions only one aspect of concelebration: it "aptly expresses the unity of the [ministerial] priesthood."

[42] The first sentence of no. 60, speaking of the presbyter's possession of "the power of orders to offer sacrifice in the person of Christ," was added (properly enough but needlessly) in the 1970 edition of the IGMR, doubtless to pacify the disaffected who sought to have the presbyteral office enhanced.

[43] This office as such seems to have become close to obsolete in places like the United States, although there may be occasional use of such a person to make announcements or the like. The practical disappearance of this ministry may reflect a concern over the excessive verbalization of the rite.

[44] This is the language employed for the basic or exemplary form of celebration, originally called the *Missa normativa* in 1965; it is a kind of nuclear rite, susceptible of contraction and amplification, simplification and elaboration, according to circumstances. See Consilium, schema no. 106 (no. 12, *de Missali*),

"Schema Primum 'Ordinis Missae Normativae,'" September 19, 1965; "Schema Primum Ordinis Missae 'Normativae' Patribus 'Consilii' Proponendum," October 9, 1965.

[45] As already noted, the paragraphs on the functions of the subdeacon were omitted in 1972, with the suppression of that order.

[46] In the Order of Mass the deacon is mentioned in relation to the introductory *monitio* of Mass, the proclamation of the gospel (including his blessing by the priest beforehand), the preparation of the cup, the incensation of the priest and people, the invitation to exchange the sign of peace, the distribution of Holy Communion, the purification of the plate and cup, the invitation to bow before the blessing, and the dismissal. No mention is made of the deacon giving the invitation to the memorial acclamation (found in at least the German language missal), although this is logical, given the removal of *Mysterium fidei* from the institution narrative and its new use as an invitation to the people ("ad fidelium acclamationem veluti aditum"—Paul VI in the apostolic constitution *Missale Romanum*).

[47] Dogmatic constitution *Lumen gentium*, November 21, 1964, no. 29.

[48] Paul VI, motu proprio *Sacrum Diaconatus Ordinem*, June 18, 1967: *AAS* 59 (1967) 697–704; *DOL* 309.

[49] As of January 1, 1997, the *Official Catholic Directory* (New Providence, N.J.: Kenedy) gives the figure of 11,788 deacons, as compared to 31,977 diocesan priests and 16,120 religious priests (page 2109).

[50] The material is derived from an early ritual booklet on concelebration and Communion under both kinds. See SRC, decree *Ecclesiae semper*, March 7, 1965: *AAS* 57 (1965) 410–12; *DOL* 222, 223, 268.

[51] Then called the Bishops' Commission on the Liturgical Apostolate, now the Bishops' Committee on the Liturgy, National Conference of Catholic Bishops.

[52] The text of the statement is in McManus, ed., *Thirty Years of Liturgical Renewal: Statements of the Bishops' Committee on the Liturgy* (Washington, 1987) 48–52. See also IGMR 59.

[53] "Concelebration Revisited," in *Shaping English Liturgy*, eds. Peter C. Finn and James M. Schellman (Washington: Pastoral Press, 1990) 139–71.

[54] The most succinct if rigid exposition of this position was given, in the light of allocutions by Pius XII, in a *dubium* on valid concelebration from the Supreme Sacred Congregation of the Holy Office on May 23, 1957: *AAS* 49 (1957) 370. The text seems to be still in possession, although it needs revisiting in the light of history and sacramental theology: ". . . whether several priests validly concelebrate Mass, if only one of them expresses the words 'Hoc est corpus meum' and 'Hic est sanguis meus' over the bread and wine, but the others do not express the words of the Lord but, with the knowledge and consent of the celebrant, have and manifest intention of making their own the celebrant's words and actions. *Negative:* for, *by the institution of Christ*, he alone validly celebrates who pronounces the consecratory words" (emphasis added). See Jean Carroll McGowan, *Concelebration: Sign of the Unity of the Church* (New York: Herder and Herder, 1964) esp. 72–109: "Dogmatic Problems Concerning Concelebrations." The practice of the Eastern Churches needs to be taken into consideration; see ibid., 39–53.

[55] See above, note 50.

[56] In the United States, the gradual extension of Communion from the cup to any and all eucharistic celebrations was finally marked by the publication, *This Holy and Living Sacrifice: Directory for the Celebration and Reception of Communion under Both Kinds,* by the Bishops' Committee on the Liturgy (Washington, 1985).

[57] For a fuller exposition, on which the text of the IGMR is based, see SRC, instruction *Eucharisticum mysterium,* May 25, 1967: *AAS* 59 (1967) 539–73; *DOL* 179. No. 55 of this instruction explains the successive unfolding of the modes of Christ's presence: in the assembly, in the word, in the person of the minister, and finally in the sacrament. "Consequently, on the grounds of the sign value, it is more in keeping with the nature of the celebration that, through reservation of the sacrament in the tabernacle, Christ not be present eucharistically from the beginning on the altar where Mass is celebrated. That presence is the effect of the consecration and should appear as such." Put differently, the tabernacle should not be in sight of the assembly during the eucharistic celebration; if there cannot be a separate chapel of reservation, at least the Eucharist should be removed from the chancel of the church before Mass. "Environment and Art in Catholic Worship" of the (U.S.) Bishops Committee on the Liturgy (Washington: NCCB, 1978) easily remains the best set of guidelines on the questions raised in chapter 5 of the IGMR.

[58] See the careful distinction made in *SC* 40, where Roman consent is required for more profound adaptations, which can only be "proposed" by the conferences of bishops. Other variations or adaptations, listed in the liturgical books, fall within the legislative competence of the conferences of bishops and require only the *recognitio* (review, recognition) or confirmation of the Apostolic See. The canonical distinction was explicitly explained by the conciliar liturgical commission (before the vote on the text) as embodying a *valde diversus processus* at the two levels; see *Acta Synodalia*, I, 4:289.

[59] The addition, in the 1970 edition, of the words "and baked in the traditional shape" may seem a slight attenuation of the sign value of the community's sharing in the one loaf, but it may only reflect an anxiety not to promote bread or breads in shapes other than round.

[60] Along with similar, earlier urging from popes like Benedict XIV and Pius XII, without much success.

[61] The promulgated text is carefully crafted to call the bread wheaten *(triticeus)* without any qualification, thus leaving open the possibility of unleavened bread with some slight addition such as salt or flavoring. This door was later closed, and the 1983 Code of Canon Law of the Latin Church reaffirms that *only* wheat *(mere triticeus)* may be used (canon 924, §2).

[62] See above, note 31, for a list of the schemata of the IGMR.

[63] See above, note 61.

[64] Reference should be made to documentation on the calendar, also in the missal: Paul VI, motu proprio *Mysterii paschalis,* February 14, 1969: *AAS* 61 (1969) 222–6; *DOL* 440. The apostolic letter approved the *Normae Universales* for the liturgical year as well as the general Roman calendar itself (SRC, decree *Anni liturgici ordinatione,* March 21, 1969: *Notitiae* 5 [1969] 163–4; *DOL* 441–2), all incorporated in the front matter.

[65] *SC* 51. The lectionary of readings (first issued in 1969 in the form of a list, *Ordo lectionum Missae*, with its own *praenotanda*) is a volume separate from the *Missale Romanum's* sacramentary volume of presidential prayers.

[66] For an account of this controverted matter, whether all three readings should be obligatory, as recorded in the schemata of the Consilium, see McManus, "Ecumenical-Liturgical Convergence: Sunday Lectionary," *Studia Liturgica* 26 (1996) 168–77.

[67] See *SC* 50 especially, quoted above at note 29. Its somewhat euphemistic language does not disguise the sorry situation after four centuries (and more) of an unchanged Order of Mass in most of the Latin Church.

[68] See *SC* 63 b.

[69] For a canonical appraisal of the potential for progress in ritual reform, see McManus, "The Possibility of New Rites in the Church," *The Jurist* 50 (1990) 435–58, esp. 444–58; idem, "Vision: Voices from the Past," in *National Meeting Addresses 1990–1995* (Washington: Federation of Diocesan Liturgical Commissions, 1996) 308–32, esp. 326–32.

[70] See the *declaratio* related to *SC* 50, above, note 30.

[71] CDW, instruction *Actio pastoralis*, May 15, 1969: *AAS* 61 (1969) 806–11; *DOL* 275.

[72] CDW, directory for Masses with children *Pueros baptizatos*, November 1, 1973: *AAS* 66 (1974) 30–46; *DOL* 276; also appended to the IGMR in American editions of the *Sacramentary*.

[73] See Aimé-Georges Martimort, "Le Ceremonial des Eveques," *Notitiae* 21 (1985) 196–206; English translation in *The Bishop and the Liturgy* (Washington: Bishops' Committee on the Liturgy, 1986) 9–18.

[74] SRC, instruction *Pontificalis ritus*, June 21, 1968: *AAS* 60 (1968) 406–12; *DOL* 550.

[75] This is the nature of the pastoral notes or introductions, as well as the outlines, format, and arrangements of presidential prayers that ICEL regularly proposes to the eleven member and fifteen associate member conferences that sponsor ICEL. The commission can only propose additions (or variations and adaptations); the conferences of bishops alone, in virtue of their legislative power, can dispose and enact them as elements of liturgical books.

[76] See Consilium, "Instruction on the Translation of Liturgical Texts," January 25, 1969, no. 43; French version, *Comme le prévoit: Notitiae* 5 (1969) 3–12; English version sent by the Apostolic See to the conferences of bishops in English-speaking countries: *DOL* 123.

[77] Order of Mass, no. 19. The overloading of the rite at this point is not adequately attended to in IGMR 49–50, 102–3. See McManus, "The Roman Order of Mass from 1964 to 1969: the Preparation of the Gifts," in *Shaping English Liturgy*, 107–39, esp. 128–9.

# The Revised Sacramentary:
# Revisiting the Eucharistic Renewal of Vatican II

*James M. Schellman*

In the fourth decade of the liturgical renewal authorized by the Second Vatican Council, English-speaking Catholics are about to receive a new edition of the words with which they celebrate the Eucharist. In preparation by the International Commission on English in the Liturgy (ICEL) since the early 1980s, this new edition, the revised *Sacramentary*, is the fruit of the experience of three decades of eucharistic renewal in the English-speaking world. It has been approved now by the Catholic leadership in countries that use English. With the review or *confirmatio* by central Church authority in Rome now pending, it is expected to be in print and in use in our communities of faith in the next several years.

This time should not be wasted. Although "several years" may seem a long while, it is little enough time to put in place renewed formation and education programs having as their focus the Eucharist as the central act of the faith community. The pending *Sacramentary* offers a concrete occasion and basis for such programs to be developed for the Catholic people and their liturgical leadership. What this new edition of the eucharistic texts offers is nothing less than a grace-filled opportunity to revisit the renewal in which the Church has been immersed now for nearly a generation. We must deepen that renewal so that our assemblies of faith will offer even more truly that active and heartfelt worship of the living God to which we rededicated ourselves during the Second Vatican Council, probably the most representative and ecumenical council the Church has achieved.

## Pastoral Introduction to the Order of Mass

In addition to the more beautiful liturgical texts and the seasonal pastoral introductions which the new *Sacramentary* will contain, it provides for the first time a Pastoral Introduction to the Order of Mass.

Meant to be studied and reflected on in conjunction with the General Instruction of the Roman Missal, this Pastoral Introduction can serve as a means to invest ourselves once again in the eucharistic renewal of the Second Vatican Council. It supplements the General Instruction with guidance provided in official documents related to Mass that have come out since the General Instruction, notably, the 1981 Introduction to the *Lectionary for Mass*. In sixty-five pages the Pastoral Introduction offers a pastoral perspective on what we as English-speaking Catholics have learned from our late twentieth-century experience of celebrating the Eucharist week by week, month by month, year by year, stretching now over more than thirty years. The Pastoral Introduction offers very little that is new. Rather, what it does in clear and unmistakable terms is clarify the persons, patterns, elements, and actions that make up the eucharistic celebration. It does this first of all by the very accessible structure and sequence of its contents, and second by its clear distinctions between what is to be done, what may be done, and, as much as it is possible to say, why this is so.

This article is intended to give an overview of the Pastoral Introduction and some impression of the value of its specific contents. This can only be a very selective taste of what the complete document contains. The document as prepared by ICEL has been adapted to greater and lesser degrees to suit the local concerns of the various regions it is meant to serve. In many instances, these changes are at the level of vocabulary and style, though some are related to local adaptations. The reflections that follow use as their basis the original ICEL edition of the Pastoral Introduction.

An outline of the overall organization of the Pastoral Introduction appears at the end of this article. As will be readily apparent, it is organized by two major divisions of material: *Part I* (The Celebration of Mass), which provides a view of the whole eucharistic celebration in terms of its principal elements, that is, people (The Assembly and Its Ministers) and things (The Eucharistic Celebration and Its Symbols); *Parts II to V*, which address the eucharistic celebration in the sequence of its component parts, that is, Introductory Rites (II), Liturgy of the Word (III), Liturgy of the Eucharist (IV), and Concluding Rite (V).

## I. The Celebration of Mass

The beginning of the Pastoral Introduction offers a brief liturgical theology of the eucharistic celebration. The experience of the resurrected Lord by the two disciples on the road to Emmaus is presented as paradigmatic of what the Lord had done in the Last Supper and of what the Church continues to do as it recognizes the Lord's presence in the same constitutive actions: "speaking, taking bread, giving thanks, breaking and sharing" (para. 2).

These opening paragraphs then briefly enunciate some of the central tenets of the liturgical reform of the Council, tenets that inform the whole of the document. The irreplaceable part which the proclaimed word occupies at the heart of the eucharistic celebration is presented in the language of the Constitution on the Liturgy and the General Instruction of the Roman Missal: the Mass is a single act of worship made up of two principal parts, the Liturgy of the Word and the Liturgy of the Eucharist (see para. 3). The great and overarching conciliar goal of the full, conscious, and active participation of all in the liturgy is then developed using the Pauline imagery of the body and its many interrelated, mutually dependent parts (see 1 Corinthians 12). It is of the very nature of the liturgy that all fulfill their own part in the same way that a body requires the sound functioning of each of its organs and limbs. So it is with Christ's body. Each of its members has a contribution to offer for the good of the whole and for God's glory (see para. 4).

## The Assembly and Its Ministers

After its several introductory paragraphs, the Pastoral Introduction turns next to the holy people who together constitute the eucharistic assembly. Basing itself on the conciliar teaching concerning the modes of Christ's real presence in the eucharistic celebration (see Constitution on the Liturgy, art. 7), this section begins with the Lord's presence "first of all in the assembly itself" (para. 5). This gathering of God's people is an exercise of their royal priesthood in Christ. Communal awareness and action are fostered particularly by the dialogues between the assembly and ministers, by singing, and by uniformity in gesture and posture (see para. 6).

Proper preparation of those who exercise liturgical ministry within the assembly is emphasized. They should receive a liturgical formation to understand the Mass as a whole, a biblical formation so as "to perceive the revealed message of the Scriptures through the light of faith" (para. 10) and to understand the liturgical cycle of Scripture readings, and a technical formation in the particular skills of their ministry. The aim is that they learn to use their personal gifts to convey Christ's person and message by reverent gesture, word, or movement. Continuing formation in liturgical ministries is also stressed. Great care for the verbal and physical elements of the liturgy is the hallmark of the liturgical ministry. This is important even when ministers are not directly engaged in their particular duties. At these times they join with the other members of the assembly in words and actions. In this way they are seen by their reverent listening, responding, and singing to contribute to the worship of the whole.

Paragraphs 13 to 23 cover the specific liturgical ministries: priest celebrant, deacon, reader, ministers of music, ministers of communion, servers, and ushers. It is not possible to treat all in this brief article. A few selected points follow. It is in this section that the overall logic of the arrangement of material in the document begins to be apparent, that is, central or numbered paragraphs of principle or theology followed by indented subparagraphs that clarify practical and rubrical matters. What is prescriptive as well as what is suggestive is indicated in the subsections.

The paragraphs on the priest celebrant return to the conciliar teaching that Christ is really present in the person of the priest, that is, the bishop or a presbyter, who presides at the celebration in the person of Christ. He "leads the people in prayer, in listening and responding to God's word, and in offering the sacrifice through Christ in the Spirit to the Father" (para. 13). In his role as presiding minister, the priest is responsible for encouraging and coordinating the participation of all. It is principally in the proclamation of the presidential prayers that he fulfills his responsibility, prayers that he addresses to God in the name of the assembly and of the entire Church.

The real presence of Christ in the word proclaimed at Mass is especially mediated by the readers: "the impact of God's message will depend significantly on their conviction, their preparation, and their delivery" (para. 16). Readers' proclamation will be more effective if they respect the variety of literary forms present in the Scriptures and develop a knowledge of the different authors' styles. This variety of forms and styles will come through more effectively if each reading has a different reader.

Paragraph 18 succinctly addresses the ministers of music. The full range of possible music ministers is referred to: psalmist, cantor, organist, other instrumentalists, choir, director of music. Their role in facilitating the full participation of the assembly is stated unequivocally. This does not mean that the choir may not sing alone on occasion, for example, in the case of more difficult music. But even in this instance it serves the worship of the assembly as its members listen in prayerful reflection. Although it will be obvious that the roles of psalmist and cantor may be and often are taken up by one person, they are briefly distinguished. The psalmist is principally responsible for "drawing the assembly into the proclamation of the word of God." This entails introducing the responsorial psalm and the alleluia or gospel acclamation to the assembly. The cantor leads and encourages the assembly's sung participation throughout Mass.

## The Eucharistic Celebration and Its Symbols

In this second half of Part I, the Pastoral Introduction moves from the people celebrating to the many elements which together form our worship. The first two paragraphs elucidate the nature of ritual as the complex interplay of actions, objects, words, and persons, which, taken together, make up the symbolism of the Eucharist. The grace and care with which the persons, actions, and objects of the liturgy are addressed, treated, and reverenced have everything to do with the spiritual effects of the celebration:

> Bread and wine, breaking and sharing, eating and drinking, standing, kneeling, bowing, and greeting should not need to be explained. It is in sharing and experiencing them in their natural integrity and consistency that their spiritual significance and effect are appropriated. (para. 25)

### 1. *Gesture and Posture*

Participation in worship must first be internal, then external, so that the bearing and gestures of the assembled worshipers are harmonious with their inner participation. It is through this interplay of internal and external elements that "the liturgy conveys the transcendence and the immanence of the living God whom the assembly worships" (para. 26). What is sought is the engagement of whole persons at worship, bodies and feelings along with minds and spirits, hands and feet, eyes and ears. Liturgical postures and gestures deserve care equal to that given to words. Not only do they lend non-verbal support to what is said, but they can also at times express what words cannot.

### 2. *Words*

Among the words of the liturgy, those from Scripture are preeminent. These include principally the biblical readings and their accompanying chants. Next are the presidential prayers. The priest, presiding in the person of Christ, proclaims these prayers in the name of the whole Church and on the assembly's behalf. It is for this reason that the assembly expresses its assent by responding *Amen*. Chief among the presidential prayers is the Eucharistic Prayer. The others are the opening prayer, prayer over the gifts, and prayer after communion. Dialogues between priest and congregation and the acclamations are particularly important as indications of the whole assembly's prayer.

### 3. *Music*

In seven paragraphs the Pastoral Introduction offers solid, general orientation to the place of music in the eucharistic celebration. The sequential introduction to the Order of Mass which follows in Parts II to V includes recommendations on elements that may or should be sung. Music is integral to worship. An art in service of corporate prayer, it draws the disparate individuals together and makes of them an assembly at worship.

While music is integral to liturgical celebration, the extent of its use varies depending on the degree of solemnity. Pride of place is, of course, given to Sundays and solemnities. In a deceptively simple paragraph (para. 46), several important guidelines are presented for the selection of music. This selection "begins with the liturgical texts themselves." The singing of the constitutive parts of Mass is given priority, and among these, priority is given to the responsorial psalm, the acclamation before the gospel and those in the Eucharistic Prayer, and the dialogues between priest and people.

### 4. *Silence*

The importance of silence in liturgical celebration can hardly be overemphasized. A form of communication in itself, silence is all the more important to the rhythms of the liturgy, where nothing less than intimate dialogue between the living God and God's people is taking place. Silence during liturgical prayer makes it possible for the members of the assembly to blend their personal prayer with God's word and the Church's public prayer.

> Liturgical silence is not merely an absence of words, a pause, or an interlude. It is a stillness, a quieting of spirits, a making of time and leisure to hear, assimilate, and respond. Any haste that hinders reflectiveness should be avoided. The dialogue between God and the community of faith taking place through the Holy Spirit requires intervals of silence, suited to the assembly, so that all can take to heart the word of God and respond to it in prayer. (para. 48)

Such silence is a corporate activity of all present by which they are sustained in profound and prayerful solidarity. And it is indispensable to the rhythms of the celebration.

### 5. *Materials and Objects*

In a series of brief paragraphs, the various materials and objects used in the Eucharist are pointed out and placed within the context of divine worship. It is noted that bishops' conferences may wish to draw up guidelines related to these and to church buildings. These materials and objects include bread and wine, vessels, particularly those for the eucharistic elements, altar, ambo, chair, cross, books, vesture, and incense.

With regard to the bread and wine, the introduction underlines the several paragraphs of the General Instruction that insist that these eucharistic elements must be recognizable in and of themselves as food and drink. An example of a suggestive element of the introduction is found here, that is, that the use of clear glass containers may be helpful so that the wine can be clearly "seen and recognized for what it is and what it signifies" (para. 50, 2nd subsection). The reflections on the vessels used in the celebration emphasize the "fundamental" symbolism of all present sharing in the one bread and cup during the Eucharist. It is suggested that this symbolism is more evident when all the bread is contained in a single vessel and the wine in one cup. For the distribution of Communion, additional vessels may be brought forward at the breaking of the bread.

The altar is the place at which the sacrifice of Christ on the cross is made sacramentally present. It is also the table of the Lord at which the Church shares in the memorial banquet, the Lord's Supper. The design of the altar is to reflect its centrality during the Liturgy of the Eucharist and its function within the assembly. In size and proportions the altar is to be suitable for the Sunday Eucharist and should accommodate the vessels for communion of the assembly. The ambo serves as the "table of God's word" and so symbolizes the surpassing dignity of that word, wherein God speaks to the assembly. Its design is to reflect its centrality during the Liturgy of the Word and its function within the assembly. The ambo is reserved for the proclamation of God's word, which includes the biblical readings, the responsorial psalm, the homily, and the general intercessions (as well as the Easter proclamation or *Exsultet*). The chair serves as a symbol of the office of the priest celebrant, who presides at the liturgy in the person of Christ. The movement of the priest and other ministers between chair, ambo, and altar helps to convey the Lord's presence in word and sacrament and to distinguish the parts of Mass more clearly. The priest leads the introductory and concluding rites and presides over the Liturgy of the Word from the chair. Here, too, the homily may be given and the prayer after communion proclaimed.

## Adapting the Celebration to Particular Circumstances

A final section of Part I offers some general observations on adaptation of the celebration for particular circumstances. It notes that the present liturgical books presuppose "that every celebration, in whatever circumstances, will fully take account of the needs, capabilities, and situation of the community which assembles for it" (para. 60). Those responsible for the liturgy are directed to various sources for helpful principles of adaptation or accommodation, for example, the *Roman Ritual, The Liturgy of the Hours,* the *Directory for Masses with Children.* Some are also found in the *General Instruction of the Roman Missal* and in the rubrics of the Order of Mass. The *General Instruction of the Liturgy of the Hours,* for example, offers the principle of "progressive solemnity." This recognizes that a liturgical celebration is made up of various parts that are not of equal importance and thus lend themselves to varying treatment. The *Directory for Masses with Children* permits some accommodation of the Mass when children make up a significant proportion of those gathered for worship. The purpose of such accommodation is gradually to lead the children to the adult celebration of Mass, on Sunday in particular.

## II. Introductory Rites

With Part II, the Pastoral Introduction begins detailed reflections and observations on the Order of Mass, proceeding sequentially through each element of the celebration. It is in this and the subsequent three parts that the editorial arrangement of the Pastoral Introduction is most obvious, that is, central paragraph(s) on principle or theology followed by subparagraphs that clarify rubrical and related matters in terms of their prescriptive or suggestive character.

Paragraph 66 provides the overarching understanding of the introductory rites. In them the assembly is "called together in Christ and established again as the Church." These rites help those who have assembled from a variety of concerns to become aware of themselves as a "gathered community, alert and ready to listen to the word and to celebrate the sacrament." These rites are led from the chair.

Briefly, succinctly, the introduction develops the several elements of the introductory rites: entrance procession, greeting, opening rite, opening prayer. Again, a few selective remarks are possible.

Formal greetings are exchanged by priest and congregation following the corporate Sign of the Cross. This act serves as an acknowledgment and evocation of Christ's presence and "as a prayer for his sustaining power" (para. 69). As such, the introduction describes this first dialogue as warm and reverent. A form of greeting that expresses merely a human exchange would be out of place. The greeting may be followed by a brief and well-prepared introductory comment on the Mass of the day. After this, special groups may be welcomed or children may be acknowledged and addressed when present in significant numbers.

What then follows under the heading "Opening Rite" is a simplification of the introductory rites as they have been celebrated until now. The combination of different elements that has been possible, for example, penitential rite (form A), Kyrie, and Gloria, would no longer occur. The simplification of the introductory rites developed by ICEL offers a choice of one ritual element between the greeting and opening prayer. This would take one of the following forms: rite of blessing and sprinkling of water, penitential rite (the present form A or form B), litany of praise (the present form C), Kyrie, or Gloria. In the United States a slight variation has been approved whereby the Gloria may, if desired, be used in combination with one of the other opening rites.

The opening prayer sets the tone of the celebration while bringing the introductory rites to a close and preparing the assembly to hear God's word. The introduction explains that the choice of opening prayer is between the (revised) text translated from the Latin and an alternative opening prayer, of which there are now three offerings, related to the (Sunday) readings of Years A, B, and C of the Lectionary for Mass.

## III. Liturgy of the Word

The proclamation of the word is an integral part of Mass, at its very heart. "The meaning of communion is proclaimed in the word; the message of Scripture is made actual once again in the communion banquet" (para. 80). In the Liturgy of the Word the faithful enter corporately into the covenant people's ever-present dialogue with God. This dialogue takes ritual form. The members of the assembly listen to the word and reflect on it in silence. They respond in song, assimilate the word, and apply it in their lives. Impelled by the word, they make their

profession of faith and take up their role as a priestly people by interceding for the needs of Church and world. The pastoral introduction
draws especially upon the introduction to the *Lectionary for Mass* for its
reflections on the elements of the Liturgy of the Word: biblical readings, responsorial psalm, gospel acclamation, gospel reading, homily,
profession of faith, general intercessions.

The significance of the gospel reading as the high point of the
Liturgy of the Word is brought out by special signs of reverence and
honor: standing, signings, the use of candles and incense, kissing of
the book. The presiding priest reads the gospel only if there is no deacon or concelebrating priest to do so. In this way the fundamental distinction of roles is evident. The presiding priest listens attentively to
the readings and responds along with the other members of the assembly. To him generally belongs the elucidation of the word in the
homily.

An integral part of the liturgy, the homily draws particularly from
the Scripture readings and the other texts of the liturgy to open up for
the assembly the mysteries of faith and the living out of these mysteries in the daily life of the believer. The one who preaches should participate in the whole celebration, that is, "experience the proclamation
of the word on which the preaching is based and the consummation of
the celebration in eucharistic communion" (para. 94, 3rd subsection).
A period of silence takes place after the homily. This rubric, buried
until now in the General Instruction, is repeated in place within the
Order of Mass rubrics in the revised *Sacramentary*. At stake here is the
overall rhythm of celebration and the restoration in the liturgical renewal of the profound place held by God's word in the Mass. Thus, the
two principal parts of the celebration have a parallel period of silence
(not a simple pause) at parallel moments, after communion in the
word and after communion in the Lord's body and blood.

The Pastoral Introduction uses the moving opening words of *the
Pastoral Constitution on the Church in the Modern World (Gaudium et
spes)*, to evoke a sense of the importance of the general intercessions:

> Enlightened and moved by God's word, the assembly exercises its
> priestly function by interceding for all humanity. Because "the joy
> and hope, the struggle and anguish of the people of this age and
> especially of the poor and those suffering in any way are the joy
> and hope, the struggle and anguish of Christ's disciples," the
> Church prays not just for its own needs but for the salvation of the
> world, for civil authorities, for those oppressed by any burden,
> and for the local community, particularly those who are sick or
> those who have died. (para. 96)

## IV. Liturgy of the Eucharist

Since apostolic times, the Church has carried out the sacrifice and paschal meal which the Lord instituted at the Last Supper and handed over to his disciples to do in his memory. The Church's Eucharist has always kept the basic shape of what the Lord did:

> the taking of the elements of bread and wine in the preparation of the gifts, the act of thanksgiving in the eucharistic prayer, the breaking of the bread, the giving and sharing of the body and blood of Christ in communion. (para. 99)

## Preparation of the Gifts

The Preparation of the Gifts is a rite which prepares the altar, the gifts placed on it, and the assembly for the eucharistic offering to follow. The faithful bring to the altar the elements for the offering along with money and other gifts for Christ's body, the poor and needy especially. The altar, as the focus of the eucharistic liturgy, becomes the major point of focus for the first time. The setting for the sacred meal is now prepared.

Following the collection of money, the gifts are brought forward in procession, an ancient and powerful expression of the assembly's participation in the Eucharist and in the Church's social mission emanating from the celebration. The bread and wine are carried in vessels that can be seen by all. The bread and wine should, if possible, each be contained in a single vessel, "so that priest and people may be seen to be sharing the same food and drink in the sacrament of unity" (para. 105, 2nd subsection). The money and other gifts are placed near the altar or in another suitable place. The vessels of bread and wine are placed by the priest on the altar. Because the presentation of the gifts is preparatory in nature, it may be more effective to have it be accompanied by either instrumental music or silence.

The preparation of the gifts concludes with the prayer over the gifts, which points also to the Eucharistic Prayer that follows. The revised *Sacramentary* provides two forms of invitation to this prayer, either the "Pray brothers and sisters . . ." or "Let us pray" followed by a silent pause, as occurs before the opening prayer and prayer after communion. A distinct pause after the prayer over the gifts and before the beginning of the preface dialogue helps make evident that the "giving thanks," the Eucharistic Prayer, is about to begin.

## Eucharistic Prayer

The Pastoral Introduction devotes fourteen extended paragraphs to the Eucharistic Prayer. Several introductory paragraphs are followed by a treatment of the elements of the Eucharistic Prayer: dialogue, preface, Sanctus acclamation, *epiclesis*, institution narrative and consecration, memorial acclamation, *anamnesis* and offering, intercessions, and doxology. It is possible here only to select and highlight some of what the introduction offers.

In a single, compact paragraph the nature of the Eucharistic Prayer is expressed:

> The eucharistic prayer is proclaimed over the people's gifts. In the rich and varied tradition of this prayer, the Church gives praise and thanks for God's holiness and justice and for all God's mighty deeds in creating and redeeming the human race, deeds which reached their climax in the incarnation, life, death, and resurrection of Jesus Christ. In the eucharistic prayer the mystery of Christ's saving death and resurrection is recalled; the Last Supper is recounted; the memorial sacrifice of his body and blood is presented to the Father; and the Holy Spirit is invoked to sanctify the gifts and transform those who partake of them into the body of Christ, uniting the assembly and the whole Church and family of God, living and dead, into one communion of love, service, and praise to the glory of the Father. (para. 112)

With the addition of the Eucharistic Prayer for Masses for Various Needs and Occasions, ten Eucharistic Prayers are included in the revised *Sacramentary*. The introduction offers some distinctive reflections on each. Concerning the three Eucharistic Prayers for children, for example, these prayers use different levels of language in anticipation of their use with children at different stages of integration into the adult community. The first prayer for children may be more appropriately used with children who have been only recently introduced to the Eucharist. The language employed in the second and third prayers would better suit children further along in the process of gaining sacramental awareness and familiarity with the Eucharist.

In order to help achieve the involvement of the assembly in the Eucharistic Prayer, the revised *Sacramentary* has taken inspiration from the positive experience with additional acclamations provided in the Eucharistic Prayers for children. This experience has led over the last twenty years to the development of settings of the other Eucharistic Prayers with further acclamations for adult assemblies. Additional, new acclamations are now provided in the *Sacramentary* with the musical settings of the other seven Eucharistic Prayers.

The invitation to the memorial acclamation is sung or said by the priest celebrant or the deacon. Each of the four memorial acclamations is now provided with a distinctive invitation that helps indicate to the assembly which acclamation follows.

The Eucharistic Prayer concludes with a solemn doxology which, by their Amen, all present endorse and ratify. According to St. Paul, the assembly's ratification is essential to the prayer of thanksgiving (see 1 Cor. 14:15-16), and other early Christian evidence lays similar stress on this confirmation by the people of what the presider has proclaimed on their behalf. It is at the doxology, the climax of the prayer, that the consecrated elements are raised high, a gesture that expresses vividly the true nature of the eucharistic sacrifice, the offering of the Church through, with, and in Christ, the High Priest.

A distinct pause at the conclusion of the Eucharistic Prayer and before beginning the communion rite will make clear that the "giving thanks" is now complete and the "breaking and sharing" about to begin.

## Communion Rite

A series of brief rites lead the assembly from the high point which is the Eucharistic Prayer to the culmination of the Eucharist in the eating and drinking together of the body and blood of the Lord. These rites are the Lord's Prayer, the sign of peace, and the breaking of the bread. The Lord's Prayer is featured in all liturgical traditions as a suitable preparation for communion. The members of the assembly, in the spirit of adoption invoked upon them in the Eucharistic Prayer, call upon God as Father. A sign of peace is an ancient element of the eucharistic liturgy. Although most liturgical traditions place it before the presentation of gifts, the Roman Rite in time placed it after the Lord's Prayer. With the revised *Sacramentary*, the bishops of the United States have approved its use at either point. Just prior to the reception of communion in particular, the exchange of peace is an acknowledgment by the assembly of "the insistent Gospel truth that communion with God in Christ is enjoyed in communion with our sisters and brothers in Christ" (para. 129). Although the invitation is optional, the sign of peace is always exchanged.

The breaking of the bread was so characteristic of Jesus' table fellowship with his disciples and so central to the Eucharist that in apostolic times it was the name given to the whole celebration. This bread, broken and shared among many, makes of them one body in the one bread which is Christ. The meaning of this action will be more evident if the bread appears clearly as food and its breaking is recognizable. Bread consecrated at a previous Mass is not ordinarily to be used for communion. At least one large bread is broken into several pieces at every Mass. The priest consumes one of these pieces and at least some of the assembly receive the rest.

Several formularies are now offered for the invitation to communion. The communion song begins immediately after the response to the invitation, while the priest celebrant is receiving the body of Christ, and continues during the communion procession. It is desirable that those who serve as communion ministers participate in the entire liturgy "and thus experience the proclamation of the word, the Eucharistic Prayer, and the consummation of the celebration in eucharistic communion" (para. 136, 2nd subsection).

A period of silence may occur once communion is completed. Alternatively, or in addition, a song of praise may take place. But the opportunity for silence may be preferable since communion has already been accompanied by singing. The prayer after communion, which asks that the assembly experience the spiritual effects of the Eucharist, concludes the communion rite.

## V. Concluding Rite

A brief concluding rite brings the Mass to a close. "Its purpose is to send the people forth to put into effect in their daily lives the paschal mystery and the unity in Christ which they have celebrated" (para. 141). Brief announcements may be made at this point. These announcements can help make members of the assembly aware of the community's faith life and pastoral activity and invite their participation in the Church's ongoing work. A final formal greeting of the assembly precedes the blessing by the celebrant. This blessing takes one of three forms: a simple blessing, solemn blessing, or prayer over the people. By means of the dismissal, the members of the congregation are sent forth "to praise and bless the Lord in the midst of their daily responsibilities" (para. 147).

### Concluding Remarks

These reflections offer a small and selective indication of the worth of the new Pastoral Introduction to the Order of Mass. Perhaps they will help to whet the appetite of those for whom the introduction may serve as a basis for renewed eucharistic formation within the community of faith. There are those who say the formation following the Council was incomplete and not given enough time and attention. The pending appearance of the revised *Sacramentary* provides the moment to revisit what we have been doing in our eucharistic worship and to address anew how we can do it even more faithfully and effectively, through, with, and in Christ, to the glory of God.

## Outline of the Pastoral Introduction to the Order of Mass

I. *The Celebration of Mass*

    The Assembly and Its Ministers
        Assembly
        Liturgical Ministers
            Priest Celebrant
            Deacon
            Reader
            Ministers of Music
            Ministers of Communion
            Servers
            Ushers
    The Eucharistic Celebration and Its Symbols
        Gesture and Posture
            Posture
            Other Postures and Gestures
        Words
            Sacred Scripture
            Presidential Prayers
            Common Prayers and Other Texts
            Sung Texts
            Invitations and Introductions
            Private Prayers
        Music
        Silence
        Materials and Objects
            Bread and Wine
            Vessels
            Altar
            Ambo
            Chair

Cross
Books
Vesture
Incense
Adapting the Celebration to Particular Circumstances


II. *Introductory Rites*

Entrance Procession
Greeting
Opening Rite
Rite of Blessing and Sprinkling of Water
Penitential Rite
Litany of Praise
Kyrie
Gloria
Other Opening Rites
Opening Prayer


III. *Liturgy of the Word*

Biblical Readings
Responsorial Psalm
Gospel Acclamation
Gospel Reading
Homily
Profession of Faith
General Intercessions


IV. *Liturgy of the Eucharist*

Preparation of the Gifts
Preparation of the Altar
Presentation of the Gifts
Placing of the Gifts on the Altar
Mixing of Wine and Water
Incense
Washing of Hands
Prayer over the Gifts
Eucharistic Prayer
Dialogue
Preface
Sanctus Acclamation

*Epiclesis*
Institution Narrative and Consecration
Memorial Acclamation
Anamnesis and Offering
Intercessions
Doxology
Communion Rite
The Lord's Prayer
Sign of Peace
Breaking of the Bread
Communion
Private Preparation of the Priest
Invitation to Communion
Distribution of Communion
Communion Song
Cleansing of Vessels
Period of Silence or Song of Praise
Prayer after Communion

V. *Concluding Rite*

Announcements
Greeting
Blessing
Dismissal

• • • • •

# From Maintenance to Mission:
# The Rite of Christian Initiation of Children and Their Families

*Jeanette Lucinio, S.P.*

## Introduction

"Our children brought us back to the faith. I left the Church and I left God. When I came back they were still there waiting for me. This parish community has had a powerful effect on my family's life."

"I've learned so much from our children going through the Rite of Christian Initiation, and having it be such a living, breathing thing. It actually changes your life."

"The rituals leave an impression on you—you remember a whole lot more. I experienced God's open arms and heard, 'Continue to carry my Word. Bring others to faith—be a disciple.'"

—Three Parents

The Catholic Church is experiencing a pastoral challenge with its children that is the result of a paradigm shift of massive proportions. During the last half of the twentieth century stable world views which have grounded culture and society for centuries have shattered in a very short period of time. Concurrently with this paradigmatic shift, the Second Vatican Council called for a discernment of "the signs of the times"[1] which mandated careful reading of our contemporary situation. A renewed liturgy was identified as a primary source for the revitalized Christian experience for which the Church had prayed. The Rite of Christian Initiation of Adults (RCIA) emerged as a jewel in the crown of this liturgical renewal. This essay focuses on one section of the ritual text, namely, "Christian Initiation of Children who have reached Catechetical Age." I will explore some general principles and practices that typically identify evangelizing parishes and then offer some first-person insights about the process of the initiation of children as articulated by children and parents in a series of interviews I conducted. It is my conviction that we will continue to refine our celebration of the rites and pastoral implementation of the process of initiation to the extent that we reflect carefully on our present experience.

It is important to grasp that the principles governing the adult rite are normative for adapting the process for other groups including children. There is one Order of Christian Initiation of which children of catechetical age[2] are included. The same ritual steps as catechumenal ministry with adults are followed but adapted to the child. The initiation of children of catechetical age is part of the inclusive vision of Christian formation of all Church members. Our task with these children is one of initiation rather than religious education or religious literacy training. Because children are never initiated in isolation, their families are often brought face to face with their own conversion. We situate the families' journeys as well, within the broader context of the Church's ministry of initiation. Because the role of parents and family is so primary in the formation of the child, the focus of all that is done in the initiation of children is family-centered and inter-generational.

Growing numbers of children in our parishes have never been baptized.[3] Many reasons account for this: inactive faith of their parents at the time of their birth, real alienation, or just drifting away that is part of the maturing process. In the past, these children were inserted into existing religious education programs in the parish without attention to their particular needs or to the needs of their parents. In many cases they were unintentionally treated as "step-children," exceptions to the norm because they were fewer in number than those who followed the "custom" of infant baptism, First Communion around age seven, followed by confirmation at a later date. Conscientious implementation of the process of the Christian initiation of children of catechetical age could profoundly alter the presuppositions we have held about what is "norm" and what is "custom."[4]

## Evangelizing Parishes:
## Some Principles and Practices

To understand the Church's catechumenal ministry, we need to identify the Church's vision of initiation. Initiation is about the *sacraments of the Church, liturgy, rituals and worship*. This is not about another program for children with curricula and lesson plans. Everything we do with these children must flow from the vision contained in the Rite

of Christian Initiation of Adults. And because of this, it is highly recommended that a parish have the adult catechumenal ministry firmly
in place before bringing children through this process. To understand
the rites and stages in the process of children's initiation, it is necessary
to grasp the principles governing the adult rite. In the RCIA there is a
progression of three major rites, each with periods of preparation and
follow-up. These four periods, which lead to and flow from the rites,
are times of Christian formation.

| First Period: | First Step: | Second Period: | Second Step: |
|---|---|---|---|
| Evangelization Precatechumenate | Rite of Acceptance | Catechumenate | Rite of Election or Enrollment of Names |

| Third Period: | Third Step: | Fourth Period: |
|---|---|---|
| Period of Purification and Enlightenment | Initiation (Easter Vigil) | Post Baptismal Catechesis or Mystagogy |

This catechumenal process does not negate the pastoral practice of
the past but rather manifests another way of initiation which involves
a paradigm shift. The following chart may illustrate this more clearly.[5]

### The Christian Initiation of Children of Catechetical Age

| Initiation as Program | Initiation as Process |
|---|---|
| Religious instruction | Spiritual formation |
| Ministerial Focus: Teaching | Ministerial Focus: Welcoming |
| Dependent upon catechist | Dependent upon community |
| Few are involved | Many are involved |
| Develop child's understanding | Supports and celebrates conversion |
| "Readiness" based on what child knows | "Readiness" based on what community does |
| Initiation occurs when child is old enough | Initiation occurs when child is ready |
| Primary tool: Textbook | Primary tool: Lectionary |
| Sequence of events: catechize, then initiate | Sequence of events: initiate, then catechize |
| Primary formational experience: classroom | Primary formational experience: liturgy |
| Content/substance: curriculum | Content/substance: relationships |
| Director's role: Administrator | Director's role: Facilitator |
| Teacher | Ritual Catechist |
| Signals an end | Signals a beginning |

My interest in this paradigm shift led me to seek out and study parishes that have experienced sweeping revitalization through serious implementation of the Rite of Christian Initiation of Adults. The theological and pastoral insight in the RCIA, along with its ecclesiological vision, its structures for enabling empowerment for ministry arising out of baptismal call, and its insistence for conversion to gospel values as the parish's primary agenda for all its members, have given great stimulus to communities which have embraced its challenge. More than simply "starting a catechumenate," these welcoming and evangelizing parishes are catechumenal in nature. They have made the vision of the Rite of Christian Initiation their own by incorporating the following principles and practices into their ministry with unbaptized and/or uncatechized children:

1. The catechumenate with adults is firmly in place and has been functioning for several years.

2. The parish has one coordinator of catechumenal ministries who oversees and facilitates this process. This wise person has gathered men and women to form a team. Someone within this team has been entrusted with the process for children and their families. The team has attended an institute offered by the North American Forum on the Catechumenate.[6]

3. The coordinator has recruited and trained sponsors and sponsoring families, sharing with them the vision of the RCIA, and has given them basic formation and insight into how the process works. Even if there are no children for initiation in a given year, the coordinator solicits sponsors in order to be ready when they do arrive.

4. The parish is prepared to accept inquirers at any time of the year. After sufficient time of evangelization, the Rite of Acceptance is celebrated and the inquirers became catechumens. If they were baptized but uncatechized, a Rite of Welcome receives them as candidates. This rite is celebrated as often as necessary during the liturgical year.

5. The parish separates sacramental initiation from religious education. Celebration of sacraments is not determined by age or grade because the purposes of initiation and religious education are different. Parishioners are informed that unbaptized and/or uncatechized children of catechetical age are now included in the catechumenal ministry of the parish. The parishioners are encouraged to create a welcoming atmosphere for the families of these children. They are given the incentive to reach out in their

neighborhoods to invite families to come and inquire about the Catholic Church or to return to the practice of their faith if they have been alienated or separated from the Church.

6. Proper attention is given to the liturgical year so that the parish can experience itself on the same journey as the catechumens, the journey toward Easter. This means a revised parish calendar centered upon the liturgical year rather than the school year.[7]

Becoming acquainted with many parishes across the United States, I chose to gather information from those communities which demonstrated fidelity to the Church's vision of initiation and which exhibited a pastoral response to the needs of families with unbaptized and/or uncatechized children of catechetical age. These parish communities offered several factors in common despite the variety of their location, ethnic make-up, and economic status: 1) Each parish had the catechumenate firmly established with adults for at least five years before admitting children into the process; 2) The success of the catechumenal ministry has been largely due to the leadership style of its pastor; 3) The liturgical worship of the parish has been given primary importance. All have liturgy teams whose formation has been given care and ongoing education; 4) Each pastor believes that within the parish, people have gifts that can be called forth. Each pastor encourages, to the limit of the parish budget, leadership formation for the laity, and nurtures this leadership once it is developed; 5) Parishioners report wonderful preaching and the pastor's ability to inspire and motivate the parish congregation; 6) These pastors continue to work at developing their own liturgical style, deepening their theological perspective through reading and study which enhance the content of the preaching; 7) Because these pastors are convinced that the Church is mission, their pastoral style is collegial and empowering; 8) The pastoral leadership in these parishes has had a dramatic influence on the vitality and involvement of the people; 9) Catechumenal ministry extends beyond the RCIA in that they refuse to do indiscriminate infant baptisms without much pastoral care and attention to the parents and families of these babies.

The success of the parishes studied relates back to the principles laid out earlier in this chapter. The commitment on the part of the pastors, their staffs, their school faculties and lay ministers clearly demonstrates their ministerial vision to be in harmony with the renewal of the sacraments coming from Vatican Council II.

Parents and other parishioners were persuaded to see the wisdom of including their unbaptized and/or uncatechized children of catechetical age in the RCIA by appealing to their own care for their children. These children are now old enough to understand what it means to be Catholic. A quick splashing of water without the formulation of relationships conveys a disinterested message. It did not take much to persuade parents that this process was best for their children.

It is true that some families, learning that the process would take two or more years, made the decision to go elsewhere. But through well constructed parent gatherings, parents began to form relationships, hear the real life faith stories of one another, realize what the Church really is, and, in the end, many stayed. They recognized that when they gathered for worship or other parish events, someone knew their name. Most of these parishes reported that all but ten per cent of the families whose children were initiated through the RCIA are still actively involved. And of the ten per cent, some have simply moved away to another parish.

## Some First Person Accounts and What They Reveal

Prior to my visit to these parishes, I requested the names of families I might interview. These were families who had children of catechetical age initiated within the last four to five years. I telephoned each family and made arrangements to meet with them either in their home or at the parish center. Some chose to gather in groups while others arranged to meet with me individually. The gatherings took place at all times of the day and evening because of the work schedules and commitments of those involved.

The adults who gathered were parents, godparents, grandparents, and even other adult family members and some neighbors. The children were interviewed separately but some chose to come with their parents, relatives, and friends.

A method of reflection was used to surface memories of the catechumenal journey. As has been emphasized, children are never initiated in isolation but in the company of family, peers, and friends. Some children were supported by sponsoring families due to parental illness or lack of involvement. These sponsoring families often had children who were also preparing for sacraments of confirmation and first Eucharist. Many times these were families of the children's peers. Conversion takes place in the midst of a believing community which is intergenerational.

The reflection process revolved around the three major rites of *Acceptance into the Order of Catechumens, The Election or Enrollment of Names* and the *Rite of Initiation through the Easter Sacraments.* An overview of the rite was given to the adults to refresh their memories. They were asked then to choose one of the major rites to reflect upon more deeply. Reading through a more detailed outline of the chosen ritual, they were asked to re-imagine the experience as they remembered it. They were invited to describe in a word or a phrase what their thoughts and feelings were while the ritual was taking place. Then they were asked to try to remember what they thought their children were feeling. Slowly the adults were invited to repeat the word or phrase they had used to describe their memories and why they had used it. Next they were asked what images of God, Christ, Church, and discipleship or mission this rite proclaimed. The final part of the reflection revolved around what their children told them after experiencing the rite. Did their children experience it as they did or differently?

The following are selected quotes from the data gathered from these interviews. Included are the interviewees' images of God, Christ, and Church; the process of conversion; the power of the cross; and discipleship or mission. These are representative of the themes gathered and do not exhaust what was shared, but reflect the principles stated above. The clustering of these quotations also illustrates some of the unique features of the contemporary practice of children's initiation according to the new rite.

1. There is one order of Christian Initiation of which children of catechetical age are included. The same ritual steps as catechumenal ministry with adults are followed but adapted to the child.[8]

> "When the congregation gathered around my wife and my two children outside the entrance to the church, it felt like everyone was saying, 'Come in. No problem.' When you see all these people surrounding you, it's a tremendous feeling of support. You see people affirming their faith."
>
> —A parent at the Rite of Acceptance

> "When we moved from outdoors to inside the church, I felt complete. I knew it was just the beginning step but I felt complete."
>
> —A mother

> "When the children were asked what they wanted from the Church, I wasn't whispering into their ears. They were speaking for themselves. I was amazed at the answers from such small children."
>
> —A mother

"Signing my children with the sign of the cross blew me away! They actually let people do this! We were blessing them for the journey. Now I encourage parents to feel free to bless their children. Sometimes I ask a blessing from them and I feel the power of God."

—A father reflecting on the signing of the senses

"The day after the signing we brought a new baby cousin into our home. Katie took the wooden cross she had been given and put it on the baby saying, 'Now you belong to us.' Then she signed the Sign of the Cross on that tiny body. She was very serious."

—A grandmother

2. This liturgical order is valuable not only for the sacramental celebration of initiation but because its movements are based on the conversion process that is lifelong.

"I drifted away from the Catholic Church over disagreement and anger after Vatican II and all the changes. I tried a lot of other denominations (secretly, because of my Hispanic relatives) but somehow I was never satisfied. When I decided to come back, I discovered the door wide open with no reservations. The Church I left was waiting for me."

—A mother

"My coming back to the Church was a miracle because I felt a lot of negativity. It used to be that I was 'Number One,' I took care of me. Now I sacrifice myself for others. The children, too, have gone from being very self-centered, constantly fighting, to just being more peaceful. They still scrap but it's not the vindictive, vicious kind of hitting they used to do. The process of the catechumenate helped all of us."

—A mother

"My favorite memory is my baptism because I pretty much had a lot of sins, if you asked me. They got washed away and I'm a nicer person than I used to be."

—A ten-year-old boy

"When Father asked me the questions on Easter night, I said I wasn't going to follow the devil's directions. Now you follow God."

—A nine-year-old child

"We were all facing each other. When I watched the children sign the book, their facial expressions were incredible. I felt a lot of power when I placed my hands on the children. This was the most wonderful thing the children could do. But it was scary, too, because this was opening the doors to life. To follow Christ isn't going to be easy for them but we'll be there to support them as they try."

—A parent at the Enrollment of Names

"Every day I grew in my understanding that God is faithful to us. The experience of the RCIA made me strong, There were situations during the year where I found myself learning to deal with hard things. I have grown a lot. And I thought I was doing this for my kids!"

—A mother

Conversion must always be understood as accommodated to the developmental level of the person of whatever age. Conversion is interpersonal and is focused on the development of a vital relationship with God. This is not a once and for all event but a process with rhythms and stages that are understood to be ongoing throughout life. Conversion is always centered in relationship with Christ as the heart of the Christian experience. The experience of conversion is not purely an interior one but must be externalized through sacramental rites. Conversion is more than religious literacy. In children as well as in adults, we look for behavioral evidence that testify to internalized values.[9]

3. Initiation is family-centered and includes immediate family, sponsor families, godparents, peers, children's companions, the parish community, and the catechumenal team.

"When the people began to pray the intercessions and I realized they were praying for us, I began to wonder, 'How can I live up to what these people expect of me?' I'm glad it was a long process because I needed to meet and get to know these people. I came back to the Church after a long time because of my children but now I realize that it was for me."

—A father

"I never realized that my responsibility in faith doesn't stop at my home. You see children of all ages in the RCIA. I feel I'm their biggest support, their biggest fan."

—A parishioner

"At Easter night the whole Church was there. I thought Father was going to stick me in the baby font but I got to go in the big one. I got water all over me from a shell. I was getting reborn, but I knew how to walk and talk. My cousins were there."

—A seven-year-old

Sponsoring relationships are key in initiation. The introduction to the ritual text[10] makes it clear that Christian initiation is a "gradual process" that takes place "within the community of the faithful." It is the responsibility of the entire community, not a specialized task done by catechists, sponsors, or priests. This stretches the community, calling it to witness in word and action to the four ingredients essential to Christian life since apostolic times: *didache* (teaching), *koinonia* (community), *leitourgia* (worship), and *diaconia* (service).[11] By joining the children on their journey, the members of the baptized community experience conversion and transformation.

4. The catechumenal process does not negate the past, rather it is another way of initiation and involves a paradigm shift. Children's initiation may extend over several years if need be. There is no set length of time. (RCIA, 253)

"My granddaughter was ready. This wasn't just what I wanted but what she wanted. When I inquired what she asked of the Church, she told me she wanted the community to help her understand about God and Jesus. This is so different from my religious education in England. The pastor would read and read at us. How wonderful to have a community not reading but living the word."

—A grandparent

"Baptism, confirmation, and First Communion was the best part of the RCIA. I used to think it was going to be a cinchy job but I figured out it was a big thing."

—A ten-year-old

"In the ceremony when we traced the Sign of the Cross on the senses of our children, I remember thinking that I hope my children know much more and learn much more than I ever did."

—A father

"The openness and warmth of the community has been wonderful. But we've got a pastor who created this atmosphere. Now belonging to the Church has new meaning: no drudgery, no more 'you have to.' Now I feel responsible for my faith and I want to witness this to my children."

—A parent

"I used to look at the cross as the death of Christ. Now I see it as the beginning, not the end. Maybe it's because of the transformation of the human Jesus to Christ the divine. What he is, we are becoming. The crucifix now is a powerful sign of beginning."

—A father

Initiation is the Christian community's basic task, the sharing with others the life-transforming, world-changing experience of encounter with God revealed in the gracious love of Jesus. One generation passes on to the next all that it has come to know about the God of Jesus Christ and the Church which mediates the divine presence in our lives. The process of initiation differs from religious education in that it is more of a mentoring experience than a course of studies. A human face is given to the Christian experience which allows the child to appropriate gospel values in a deeply personal way.[12]

5. The normative way unbaptized children of catechetical age enter the Church is through full initiation, i.e. baptism, confirmation, and Eucharist received at one ceremony.

"Our baptism, confirmation, and communion were a start of something, a long-lasting life with Jesus and a new life. We went from darkness to light; from not knowing Jesus to being his greatest friend. Our parents and grown-ups we live with became better friends of Jesus, too, by teaching us. I see people now and they wave to me."

—A child

"The oil of confirmation was slimy and gushy in my hair. My brother made me go first to see how it felt. After that we had to hold a candle our Mom decorated for us. Then we went back to read the letter our Mom wrote to us."

—A seven-year-old

"The oil smelled real good—they put cologne in it. It is very special. Father poured it all over me to say that I am more special than the expensive oil."

—A child

"We went to the bishop all by ourselves and said our name. The oil smelled like roses. It made me think of the kingdom of God. I smelled like the kingdom of God, too. It's still in me. Today people say I'm full of Jesus . . . sometimes.

—A ten-year-old girl

The Rite (304) states that in order to bring out the paschal character of the celebration of the sacraments of initiation, it is preferable that they take place at the Easter Vigil. "At this third step of their Christian initiation, the children will receive the sacrament of baptism; the bishop or priest who baptizes them will also confer confirmation, and the children will for the first time participate in the Liturgy of the Eucharist." (305)

6. Catechumenal activities are more ritual and liturgy than education and school-centered. (RCIA 75)

" I was excited. I knew what I was going to say. I was going to say 'yes' to everything good and if it wasn't something I was supposed to do, I would say 'no.'"

—A child reflecting on baptismal promises

"The church was dark, then it got brighter and brighter with all the candles and the lights turned up. We were rising—we were going from darkness to light. We were kind of shining in the light."

—A child

"When I traced the cross on the senses of my daughter, I was reflecting on what these words meant as I was signing them. It was like it was happening to me, too—like a two-way mirror."

—A mother

"I had to give testimony at the rite of election as to why I thought our daughter was ready. She was the one who came to us wanting to go to church. She really pressed for this. Our daughter is fourteen now but she wanted this since she was little. It always puzzled me because I was away from the Church for the greater part of her life. Where did she make the connection? Usually you have to pry a teenager to go to Mass on Sundays. But this is what the RCIA is supposed to do and it did it for our daughter."

—A mother

"'Elected' means you're IN. Somebody voted for you to be IN. Jesus, Mary and our Mom and Dad voted for me because they thought I was becoming a pretty good Christian. There were some people standing behind us who said 'yes' to that kind of stuff."[13]

—A child

The role of symbol is not to be explained but to be performed.[14] The liturgical rites mark the journey of those wishing to join the Christian community in faith. The parents' and children's reflective memories made present again the profound experiences of the ritual celebrations. This points out once again that liturgical actions, prayers, gestures, and symbols have the ability to break open non-verbally the sacred mysteries of Christianity. Liturgy is a catechesis in its own right. "The primary focus of such catechesis through liturgy is not on the liturgy itself but upon Christian living."[15]

7. The goal of all initiation is to lead to the Eucharist and from there to lead the children and their families into mission for the world.

"My goddaughter's anticipation for baptism after the signing of the book was incredible. At this point she began talking about being welcomed to the table. The rite of acceptance was a welcome to the community. The rite of election was a welcome to the table—you can come and eat with us very soon."

—A godmother

"Since our parish church has been renovated, the renovation opened a new understanding for me between the font and the altar just because of their prominence. And they're in a direct line of vision. I never made this connection between baptism and the Eucharist before."

—A parent

"It was my mom who brought me to the Catholic faith. She felt isolated from her Catholic community when she married a Mormon. At initiation I wasn't all that ready. I didn't think I accepted Jesus that much. But everyone told me I was. But the more I come to church now the more I really think about him. I'm happy with myself now. I'm involved with the youth ministry. I hope to pass on to the kids that God is out there for them. This past year, since my baptism, I've been on several retreats. My friends are good kids but they don't have a religious background at home. As I was in the catechumenate I saw myself change in that I began to look at people differently. My mom and dad had their marriage blessed in church. Now I wish my dad would become a catechumen."[16]

—A teenager

"My son approached me and asked if he could become a Catholic because he wanted to receive Holy Communion. That's where it all started. He was nine at the time."

—A father

"I like to look back on the whole thing when I was just a regular kid, just sitting looking at everybody going to get Communion. Now I like to remember that I can get the bread and wine and be part of the community."

—A nine-year-old boy

Much attention is given to baptism and confirmation as sacraments of initiation. But it is the Eucharist that continues our initiation into the mystery of Christ. By repeated participation in the Eucharist, children and their families share more deeply in the community's faith, understand in greater depth the community's myth, and live with a growing Christian vision of human life.[17]

## Conclusion

Welcoming children into the community of faith involves attitudinal changes in the children, their families, and in those who minister with them. Ritual celebration isn't all that takes place during the catechumenate. But it is the liturgy that unites the many phases of the journey and articulates ritually the formation occurring in the catechumens and the Christian community. The hospitality and welcome by the community, the celebrations of the Word of God, the anointings, the blessings, the prayers, the presentations of the Creed, and the Lord's Prayer form the catechetical and spiritual content of the Rite of Christian Initiation. They are of one piece and flow from one another. There are no recipes or packaged programs that will turn a parish into the kind of parishes reported about in this essay. But the principles expressed can be a guide for those who wish to venture into a new paradigm which believes that "the community into which we are initiated is not fundamentally an institution but an event, an event founded on the personal action of the triune God. We are baptized not simply into a human community but into the risen Christ and the indwelling Spirit."[18]

[1] *The Pastoral Constitution on the Church in the Modern World (Gaudium et spes),* decreed by Vatican Council II, December 7, 1965, 4.

[2] Most commentators interpret "catechetical age" to include children between 7 and 17 years of age, that is, the age when most children are engaged in their formal religious education.

[3] Paragraph 252 of the RCIA clarifies that the catechumenate for children of catechetical age is for children not baptized as infants; children who have attained the use of reason and are of catechetical age, baptized in infancy but uncatechized; children presented by their parents or guardians, or who present themselves with parental permission; children capable of receiving a personal faith and recognizing the obligation of conscience. They could be sons or daughters of catechumens or candidates, or of church members who are returning to active affiliation with the Church, or children whose parents belong to other churches or to no church.

[4] Don Neumann, "Unbaptized Children: What Can We Do?" *Today's Parish.* October, 1988.

[5] Adapted from M. Sheila Collins, *Beginnings and Beyond Participant Materials* (Arlington, Va.: North American Forum on the Catechumenate, 1992) 31.

[6] The North American Forum on the Catechumenate is an international network of pastoral ministers, liturgists, catechists and theologians united to share the vision of the Order of Christian Initiation of Adults. Forum's goals are to share the vision and experience of the RCIA, offer service at institutes, and draw out implications of the Rite for the life of the parish. The most helpful institute would be "Beginnings and Beyond" with a children's track. This is a six-day institute for parish teams that invites the participants to experience the conversion process of the Rite through presentations, private reflection, shared faith in community, and the celebration of adapted rites. The shared praxis method used for critical reflection on parish practices involving the Rite.

[7] Thomas H. Morris, *The RCIA: Transforming the Church* (New York: Paulist Press, 1989) 36–7.

[8] These principles were taken from "Unbaptized Children: A Parish Challenge," by Richelle Pearl-Koller, in *Today's Parish* (April/May, 1992) 38–9. This article addresses the pastoral concern of welcoming returning Catholics.

[9] Robert D. Duggan, "Discerning Conversion in Children," in *Issues in the Christian Initiation of Children: Catechesis and Liturgy* (Chicago: Liturgy Training Publications, 1989) 190–6.

[10] RCIA, art 4.

[11] See Maria Harris, *Fashion Me a People* (Louisville: Westminster/John Knox Press, 1989). This book outlines the necessary components for a curriculum of faith formation in the Church based on the four ingredients listed above.

[12] Duggan and Kelly, Initiation, 33.

[13] This second step is called the election or enrollment of names. It is so called because "the acceptance by the church is founded on the election by God, in whose name the church acts." (RCIA 119). Before this rite, parents and godparents give testimony on behalf of the catechumens in the presence of the community. The children then write their names in the book of the elect (213).

[14] Joseph Gelineau, "Reflection: Children and Symbols and Five Years after the Directory of Masses with Children," *The Sacred Play of Children,* ed. Diana Apostolos-Cappadona (New York: Seabury Press, 1983) 25.

[15] Gilbert Ostdiek, Catechesis for Liturgy (Washington, D.C.: The Pastoral Press, 1986) 9.

[16] This seventeen-year-old held this conversation with the author after a long day devoted to the junior high confirmation retreat. It was only when her mother came to pick her up that it was discovered this was the way she had spent her birthday.

[17] Bernard Cooke, *Sacraments and Sacramentality* (Mystic, Conn.: Twenty-Third Publications, 1985) 119–59.

[18] Ralph A. Keifer, *Made Not Born* (Notre Dame, Ind.: University of Notre Dame Press, 1980) 150.

# Musical Mystagogy:
# A Mystagogy of the Moment

*Edward Foley, Capuchin*

In this essay, I wish to explore how music in the worship event might be considered under the rubric of mystagogy.[1] This will require, first of all, a brief examination of the broader concept of mystagogy, especially as it is ordinarily considered to be a post-worship reflective exercise. Second, employing the work of George Steiner and Gordon Lathrop, I will suggest that there is a way to understand mystagogy as an active apprehension which occurs during worship, and not simply before or after the event. Finally, I will suggest how music is a most powerful form of this "mystagogy of the moment."

## Mystagogy Revisited

It is especially scholarly and pastoral work around the praxis of initiation which has reintroduced the language, concept, and practice of mystagogy (μυσταγόγια) into the contemporary Western Church. This mystagogical "recovery" was canonized for Roman Catholics and many other Christians in the west in the *Rite of Christian Initiation of Adults* (1972). This post-conciliar rite decreed that, following the initiation of adults through water, chrism, and Eucharist, the neophytes were to embark upon a "period of post-baptismal catechesis or mystagogy" [§37]. This post initiatory vision of mystagogy is enshrined in the 1986 *National Statutes for the Catechumenate* [§§22–24] and the 1988 edition of *Rite of Christian Initiation of Adults* approved for use in the United States [§§244–251].

The historical precedent which suggests this equation of mystagogy with post-baptismal instruction can be found in various ancient

Church practices highlighted in the writings of important mysta-gogues such as Cyril of Jerusalem (+386?) and Ambrose of Milan (+397). It was especially Cyril and Ambrose who insisted that appro-priate catechesis for neophytes was not possible until after the rites of initiation, in all of their fullness, had been experienced. Thus Cyril, in the opening moments of his celebrated *Mystagogical Catechesis*, com-mented:

> For some time now . . . I have desired to discourse to you on these spiritual and celestial mysteries. But I well knew that visual testi-mony is more trustworthy than mere hearsay, and therefore I awaited this chance of finding you more amenable to my words, so that out of your personal experience, I could lead you into the brighter and more fragrant meadow of Paradise on earth [1.1].[2]

Ambrose took a similar stance when, at the opening of his *Sermons on the Sacraments*, he remarked: "I shall begin now to speak of the sacra-ments which you have received. It was not proper for me to do so be-fore this, because . . . the Christian faith must come first" [1.1].[3]

It is not surprising that the contemporary Western Church should apparently rely so heavily upon the perspectives of Cyril and Am-brose for a vision of mystagogy when reshaping rites for adult initia-tion. After all, these were two of the most influential figures in the fourth century Church, presiding over important patriarchal sees at a time when the practice of adult initiation was at its apogee. It was not only the ecclesial weight of their collective vision, however, which cat-apulted this Cyrillic-Ambrosian framework into the forefront of the contemporary definition of mystagogy in the West. It was also and es-pecially the resonance between this definition and contemporary ped-agogical and philosophical developments which placed the "subjects" and their experience at the center of so-called adult models of learn-ing.

Thus we find that this post-experience reflection model of mysta-gogy acquires broad currency in the Western Church at the same time that philosophers like Hans-Georg Gadamer[4] were asserting the signifi-cance of each individual's unique historical context in contemporary hermeneutics, pedagogues like Paulo Freire[5] were stressing the impor-tant of each individual's experience in education, and even Roman Catholic sacramental theologians were taking a "turn toward the sub-ject."[6] Aidan Kavanagh, in an early commentary on post-baptismal catechesis in the *RCIA*, articulates the linkage between contemporary pedagogical thinking, the turn toward the subject and mystagogy when he comments,

> The rationale underlying post-baptismal catechesis or *mystagogia* should be seen not as having to do with some sort of *disciplina arcani* but with the pedagogical fact that it is next to impossible to discourse effectively about experiences of great moment and intensity with someone who has never really had such an experience.[7]

There are difficulties with Kavanagh's assertion, and the equation of mystagogia with post-baptismal or post-experiential reflection, however, from historical, pedagogical, and theological perspectives. From an historical perspective, for example, there is clear evidence from contemporaries of Cyril and Ambrose that the mysteries were explained before they were experienced. The golden-tongued John Chrysostom (+ 407), for example, offered some baptismal catechesis to the elect in Antioch before their full initiation. Thus, in preparation for the daily exorcisms he explained, "Since you are on the threshold of the time when you are to receive these great gifts, I must now teach you, as far as I can, the meaning of each of the rites, so that you may go from here with knowledge and a more assured faith" [2.12].[8]

And at the end of his second baptismal homily, Chrysostom reiterated,

> It is not without good reason and careful thought that I have explained all these things to you in advance, my loving people. Even before you actually enjoy them, I wanted you to feel great pleasure as you fly on the wings of hope. I wanted you to take up a disposition of soul worthy of the rite and, as the blessed Paul advised you, to "set your mind on things that are above," raising your thoughts from earth to heaven, from the visible to the invisible. We see such things more clearly with the eyes of the spirit than with the perceptions of the senses [2.28].[9]

Similarly, Theodore of Mopsuestia (+427), who also preached pre-baptismal homilies in Antioch, insisted on a form of mystagogia which at least in part preceded rather than followed the ritual experience:

> It is right and necessary that we should explain before you the power of the sacrament and of the ceremonies which are accomplished in it, and the reason for which each of them is accomplished, in order that when you have learnt what is the reason for all of them you may receive the things that take place with great love [2.2].[10]

The value of preparatory catechesis and a mystagogical method which anticipates a life-changing experience not only finds strong support in our ecclesial past but also in the present. The contemporary manner in which we prepare a wide range of ministers for the Church, for example—frequently cast in terms of theological reflection—is often reflective formation in anticipation of yet to be experienced ministerial situations. This pre-ministerial or pre-immersion approach has been especially emphasized in the preparation of missionaries. It has long been recognized that such ministers require not only data and language skills but also experience-based formation in *preparation* for their cross-cultural ministry.[11]

Returning to our example of initiation, one could make a similar point about the importance of pre-ritual formation in the RCIA itself by admitting that the contemporary catechumenate is precisely an affirmation of the value and effectiveness of pre-baptismal mystagogy. As currently conceived, the catechumenate is not an updated version of "convert instruction," but a radically different approach to initiation based upon an experience of faith, theological reflection, and *Lectionary* catechesis.[12] It is essentially mystagogical.

Such historical and contemporary examples provide an important caution to the sometimes narrow instinct to define mystagogy essentially in terms of chronology. Authentic mystagogy is less a question of when than of how. It is not so much a post-ritual or post-experience manner of formation as it is a way of entering into the mystery that respects both personal experience as well as the "event" nature of worship. According to Enrico Mazza, mystagogy is a way of bringing to light and interpreting the very core of a liturgical action, a sacrament; it is a way of "doing theology."[13] Thus Mazza suggests that mystagogy belongs less to the realm of catechesis or even spirituality than to liturgical theology itself.[14] This manner of doing theology can be achieved *before* the event, *after* the event and, we would like to suggest, even *during* the event: such is our contention about music in worship, as a particular mode of the mystagogical.

## George Steiner: an unlikely Mystagogue

In the opening pages of *Real Presences*, George Steiner sets forth a challenging yet refreshing definition of hermeneutics. Rather than the systematic method and practice of explication, "of the interpretative exposition of texts," Steiner wants to define hermeneutics as "the enactment of answerable understanding, of active apprehension."[15] This definition is most comprehensible in view of Steiner's critique of art criticism, or what he calls "the dominance of the secondary and the parasitic."[16]

According to Steiner, the direct experience of aesthetic meaning, in particular the arts, infers the necessary possibility of God's presence. He summarizes:

> This study will contend that the wager on the meaning of meaning, on the potential of insight and response when one human voice addresses another, when we come face to face with the text and work of art or music, which is to say when we encounter the *other* in the condition of freedom, is a wager on transcendence.[17]

It is in view of this hoped for transcendence that Steiner offers a critique of the "secondary," which short circuits the immediacy of the aesthetic and, by extension, diminishes the possibility of an experience of the transcendent. Employing Plato's *Republic* as a foil, Steiner imagines a counter-Platonic republic "from which the reviewer and the critique have been banished. . . . There would be an interdict on art criticism, on journalistic reviewers of painters, sculptors and architects."[18] Rather than a society of the secondary, Steiner images a "politics of the primary," which encourages the immediate experience of the text, the art work and the musical composition,[19] and thus unimpeded access to that which infers the necessity of "real presence."

The aim of Steiner's "politics of the primary" is essentially educational. He wishes to provide

> a mode of education, a definition of values devoid, to the greatest possible extent, of "meta-texts": that is to say of texts about texts (or painting or music), of academic, journalistic and academic-journalistic . . . talk about the aesthetic, a city for painters, poets, composers, choreographers, rather than one for art, literary, musical or ballet critics and reviewers, either in the market-place or in academe.[20]

Transpose Steiner's language of politics to that of theology, and one discovers what could be considered an impassioned plea for mystagogy, here recast as a "theology of the primary." His definition of hermeneutics as the "enactment of active apprehension" could as easily stand as an appropriate definition of mystagogy as a kind of "event theologizing." Steiner's contention that "the focused light of both interpretation . . . and evaluation . . . lies in the work itself"[21] is not only an insight into painting or literature, but precisely the point of contemporary liturgical theology that asserts that the worship event is *theologia prima*, and authentic catechesis is that which relies upon and makes a return to this primary source. His thesis that "the best read-

ings of art are art"[22] could be rendered liturgically as "the best introduction to, or formation for, the liturgy is the liturgy." His critique that
in the commentator "we welcome those who can domesticate . . . the
mystery"[23] could equally be said of those who comment upon rather
than engage us in worship. Finally, his challenge to the customary way
in which we experience the aesthetic in contemporary culture, which
he characterizes as an "imbalance between the secondary and its object,"[24] could similarly be posited of much of our experience in contemporary worship in which we are often disabled in our attempt to
have an encounter with the "object" (and subject) of our worship—
God in Jesus Christ—and instead diverted to a substitute encounter
with the secondary, the distracting, the amusing, or the banal.

Steiner's assertion of the primary (here explored under the rubric
of art) and the fundamental priority of the primary in revealing the
primary (art upon art) is a helpful frame for attempting to identify the
core and essence of mystagogy. It is not—as is sometimes inferred by
those who hold up the last "period" of the RCIA as the paradigm of
mystagogy—a matter of chronology. Rather, the essence of mystagogy
is in its manner of interpretation: an interpretation that 1) gives priority to the liturgical event, 2) gives parallel priority to the experience of
those who participate in the worship event: the whole of their experience (i.e., from the past, of the present, or in the future), and 3) through
some catalyst (such as the use of typology)[25] enables event and experience to interact and refract each other, providing fresh insight, appreciation, and longing for the divine encounter again. Mystagogy—as a
manner of interpretation, as a way of doing theology—might thus be
understood as an active form of juxtapositioning in order to achieve
what Steiner calls "active apprehension."

Gordon Lathrop, in his work on liturgical theology entitled *Holy
Things*, suggests that juxtaposition is a valuable tool for acquiring
meaning in and about the liturgy. He posits that the various "things" of
worship (including the assembly) "take on meaning in action as they
are used, especially as they are intentionally juxtaposed."[26] This juxtaposition in place, time, or word gives rise to interpretation and reinterpretation: traditional order is opened up to disorder; ritual is revealed
as anti-ritual; text is recontextualized; thus, order, ritual, text, and the
many other symbols of worship are required "to say a new thing."[27]

Lathrop's use of the juxtaposition of text upon text, or space upon
space to reveal meaning in and of the liturgy resonates with Steiner's
art to art, primary to primary as a way to reveal meaning in and of art.
The literal or metaphorical juxtaposition of things, texts, symbols, images and even people in worship is an effective and essential way to
achieve what Steiner calls "the enactment of answerable understand-

ing." This imaginative juxtapositioning for the purpose of enacting an answerable understanding can be achieved after an event, before an event, or—as both Steiner and Lathrop intimate—can actually be realized during the event. This is what Lathrop calls "meaning in action"; it is also thoroughly mystagogical.

One of the more accessible examples of this liturgical enactment of answerable understanding by means of juxtaposition is liturgical preaching. Liturgical preaching is not a break in the worship action but a liturgical event at its core. It is also an interpretive act: what we have defined in other places as "a liturgical event in the form of a ritual conversation between God and a liturgical assembly, which announces God's reign through the mediation of a preacher who offers a credible interpretation of the liturgical bible in the context of a particular liturgy."[28] While the juxtapositions in liturgical preaching are, on the one hand, multiform,[29] the fundamental juxtaposition which gives rise to the hoped for ritual conversation is the juxtaposition of the life stories and experiences of a particular assembly with the liturgical bible. The catalyst in this juxtaposition is the preacher, who in the preaching event attempts to facilitate "an answerable understanding" as the people encounter the Word which refracts and interprets their lives. As the preacher provides an "active apprehension" of the liturgical bible, the assembly is challenged and inspired to make a response in worship and life to the God who calls them into worship.

Authentic liturgical preaching, therefore, as a dual assertion of the primary subjects of worship (Christ and the assembly); which respects both the event nature of worship and the experiences of those who enter into the worship; which through the juxtaposition of personal experience and the liturgical bible enacts an "answerable understanding"; and which, by doing so, calls people not only to understanding but to a transformed relationship with each other and God, thus exemplifies a type of "mystagogy of the present." Maybe even more so than liturgical preaching, liturgical music is such a mystagogical moment.

## The Musical Turn

Steiner's apparent disregard for the secondary reaches new proportions when he turns the discussion to music. His concern as to whether *anything* meaningful can be said or written about music lies at the very heart of his opening essay in *Real Presences*.[30] He explains:

> This question [as to whether anything meaningful can be said or written about music] does seem to me to imply not only fundamental speculations as to the limits of language; it takes us to the

frontiers between conceptualization of a rational-logical sort and other modes of internal experience. More than any other act of intelligibility and executive form, music entails differentiation between *that which can be understood,* that is to say, paraphrased, and *that which can be thought and lived* in categories which are, rigorously considered, transcendent to such understanding.[31]

At a more radical level than any other art form, Steiner argues that the best of intelligence in music is musical; that the most exposed, engaged, and responsible act of musical interpretation is performance.[32] To understand, critique, and access the musical requires the musical. And it is music, rather than any commentary or critique on the same, which prompts Steiner's wager on the transcendent.

Steiner's passion and praise for the mystery and transcendence of music finds a parallel in the Church's official documents—and "secondary" commentaries—which assert the significance of music for worship and faith.[33] Music is heralded as the only art that is considered to be "integral" to the worship experience [CSL §112]. While there have been attempts to explain why music has this integral relationship to worship, Steiner offers what may be one of the most compelling explanations when he argues that, more than any other act of intelligibility, music entails differentiation between that which can be understood and that which can be thought and lived. This is an insightful assessment, not only of music, but of the liturgy to which the music weds itself.

Worship, as a "primary" ecclesial event, is not simply to be understood but to be believed and lived; it is "event theology"; it is our most important "enactment of answerable understanding" of what it means to be Church in the world today. Liturgy is thus to be "thought and lived": not only apprehended, but considered and embraced so that it is a transformative force in the lives of individual believers and the ecclesial body. If worship is about encountering God and living differently because of that encounter, how valuable is a medium such as music for that encounter which, like liturgy, is also about immediacy, encounter, and transformation. Music, like liturgy, is one of those ultimate "primaries" which Steiner refuses to have diminished by the secondary and parasitic; it poises us on the edge of "real presences."

Steiner's scenario for revelation within the arts (and the consequent intimation of real presences) presumes a "primary" to "primary" juxtapositioning within the same artistic category (e.g. literature to literature, or music to music). What Steiner does not explore, however, is the revelatory consequence of juxtaposing the primary across categories: literature to painting, dance to architecture, or sculpture to weaving. This is precisely what occurs, however, in the worship event when liturgy meets music, ritual event encounters melody, and text meets rhythm. Both the tradition and common practice remind us that liturgy in conversation with music—juxtaposed in respectful dialogue, rather than set against each other in inattentive monologues—is an essential way to achieve what Steiner calls "the enactment of answerable understanding." Music and liturgy refract each other *in the moment,* interpret each other in the event, and allow the worship to "say a new thing" to believers and the world. The layering of liturgy and music, therefore, is the tendering of a mystagogical moment: providing the possibility of new apprehension and motivation for Christian life *within* the worship event itself. While such mystagogy of the moment may, indeed, be enhanced by pre- or post-worship reflection, such is not necessary in order for the liturgical-musical event to have meaning or to provide new insights about and motivations for Christian life.

While examples of such musical mystagogy are innumerable, a single example will have to suffice to make the point here. In the liturgy for Holy Thursday, the Christian tradition provides a powerful juxtaposition of word and action: gospel and *mandatum.* There is a long standing tradition of singing the ninth century text "Ubi caritas" with its traditional chant melody during the *mandatum.* The juxtaposition of this rich text and haunting melody with the *mandatum* not only provides inventive commentary on the rite, but also enables the rite to "say a new thing" as music and ritual action are juxtaposed with real human stories.

In the city of Chicago, for example, Holy Thursday of 1997 occurred one week after a young black man, Lenard Clark, was allegedly attacked by three white teen-agers. Clark's head was rammed against a wall by his attackers and he was felled by repeated kicks and punches that left him unconscious. The local and national uproar which followed this beating reminded the citizens of Chicago and the rest of the U.S. that the evil of racism is yet very much alive in this country. Celebrating the *mandatum* interwoven with the text of the "Ubi caritas" on the Thursday following Clark's beating was unusually poignant. For me, washing the feet of parishioners while hearing "Ubi caritas" was a mystagogical moment. Feet had been used to kick a young black man into unconsciousness; feet that had been instruments of hatred were being baptized in the charity of the *mandatum,* as we sang:

> Therefore when we gather as one in Christ Jesus
> Let our love enfold each race, creed, every person.
> Let envy, division and strife cease among us;
> May Christ our Lord dwell among us in every heart.[34]

My "ahah" was not only that racial division needed to cease, but also that in the spirit of the *mandatum* there was no place for hatred—even of the alleged attackers. The understated melody and searing lyric, juxtaposed with cryptic ritual action was for me a mystagogical moment: meaning upon meaning, giving birth to newer meaning still.

If mystagogy is, as Mazza contends, a way of doing theology, here recognized as a "theology of the primary"; if it is the enactment of active apprehension which respects the event nature of worship and the personal experiences of those who come to worship while at the same time juxtaposing the elements of the event and human experience; then it is possible to admit that mystagogy—less a matter of chronology than method—can occur *during* the liturgical event. Liturgical preaching may be the most easily recognized form of such mystagogy of the present. Liturgical music, most assuredly, is one of its most powerful forms.

---

[1] I happily offer these reflections in honor of my colleague and friend, Gilbert Ostdiek, O.F.M., whom I salute as a twentieth-century mystagogue of unusual generosity and commitment. Throughout his teaching and writing, Gilbert Ostdiek has been concerned with issues of liturgical catechesis and mystagogy. This interest is born of his conviction that liturgy is an event in which we encounter the Holy One, and the pedagogical consequence that any preparation for worship must be a preparation for such an encounter. As Gilbert noted in *Catechesis for Liturgy*, authentic liturgical catechesis is not so much the imparting of content or information about worship, but rather a process which enables us to heighten and deepen our awareness of our individual and collective relationship to God and each other. Gilbert's work has helped to stimulate my own thinking about liturgical catechesis and, in particular, the role of music in such catechesis. See Gilbert Ostdiek, *Catechesis for Liturgy* (Washington, D.C.: Pastoral Press, 1986) 13.

[2] Translation by Edward Yarnold, *The Awe-Inspiring Rites of Initiation*, 2nd ed. (Collegeville: The Liturgical Press, 1994) 70.

[3] Ibid., 100.

[4] E.g., his *Truth and Method*, trans. Garrett Barden and John Cuming (New York: Continuum, 1975 [1960]).

[5] E.g., his *Pedagogy of the Oppressed*, trans. Myra Bergman Ramos (New York: Seabury Press, 1970).

[6] One celebrated example of such is Edward Schillebeeckx, *Christ the Sacrament of the Encounter with God* (New York: Sheed and Ward, 1963 [1960]).

[7] Aidan Kavanagh, "Christian Initiation of Adults: The Rites," *Worship* 48 (1974) 332.

[8] Translation from Yarnold, 156.

[9] Ibid., 163.

[10] Translation from Alphonse Mingana, *Commentary on Theodore of Mopsuestia*, Woodbrooke Studies 6 (Cambridge: W. Heffer & Sons, 1933) 17.

[11] Ironically, it is only quite recently that specialists in cross-cultural ministries have begun to recognize the need for theological reflection *after* an experience of mission, and not simply before one. Typical, for example, is R. Michael Paige, ed. *Education for the Intercultural Experience* (Yarmouth, Maine: Intercultural Press, 1993), in which only two of the eleven chapters focus on reentry, while the rest focus on orientation and training. I am grateful to Jo Ann McCaffrey for this reference and her insight on this topic; her own D.Min. thesis-project from Catholic Theological Union, *At Home in the Journey: A Wholistic Process of Theological Reflection for Missioners in Transition*, is designed to augment this limited but growing body of literature on the post-missionary experience.

[12] See, for example, James Dunning, *Echoing God's Word: Formation for Catechists and Homilists in a Catechumenal Church* (Arlington, Va.: North American Forum on the Catechumenate, 1993).

[13] Enrico Mazza, *Mystagogy*, trans. Matthew J. O'Connell (Collegeville: The Liturgical Press, 1989) 6.

[14] Ibid., 2–3.

[15] George Steiner, *Real Presences* (Chicago: The University of Chicago Press, 1989) 7.

[16] Ibid.

[17] Ibid., 4.

[18] Ibid., 5.

[19] Ibid., 6.

[20] Ibid., emphasis added.

[21] Ibid., 17.

[22] Ibid.

[23] Ibid., 39.

[24] Ibid., 47.

[25] Mazza suggests that typology is the proper "catalyst" or method that the fourth-century mystagogues employed in their liturgical theologies, even though each of the authors he examines employs typology differently, 166.

[26] Gordon Lathrop, *Holy Things: A Liturgical Theology* (Minneapolis: Fortress Press, 1993) 10.

[27] Ibid., 30.

[28] See my *Preaching Basics* (Chicago: Liturgy Training Publications, forthcoming).

[29] E.g., the juxtaposition of readings to readings, of readings to psalm, of readings to liturgical year, of word to sacramental action, etc.

[30] Steiner, 18.

[31] Ibid., 18–9.

[32] As an illustration of this point Steiner relates the story about Robert Schumann who, when asked to explain a difficult *étude,* sat down and played it a second time. Ibid., 20.

[33] Much of this material is rehearsed in my "Toward a Sound Theology," *Ritual Music: Studies in Liturgical Musicology* (Beltsville, Md.: The Pastoral Press, 1997) 107–26.

[34] Trans. by Richard Proulx, in *Worship,* 3rd ed. (Chicago: GIA Publications, 1986) n. 598.

# The Quest for Liturgy Both Catholic and Contemporary

*Donald W. Trautman*

The Bishops' Committee on Liturgy is presently shepherding the *Sacramentary* through the revision process of the National Conference of Catholic Bishops. There are nearly 2,000 texts in the Roman Missal that have been carefully scrutinized. Never in the history of our country have bishops taken such an active role in the examination of liturgical texts. When the revision is complete and the new *Sacramentary* has been approved by the Apostolic See, it will contain translations better suited for public proclamation, newly composed texts, and new pastoral introductions. It will offer revised translations of the prefaces and Eucharistic Prayers, and a slightly modified Order of Mass. I am happy to report that all the action items pertaining to the revision of the *Sacramentary* so far presented to the American Catholic bishops by its liturgical committee have been approved by a two-thirds vote. This is good news for all liturgists—good news for all of God's people. Scholars are also at work revising the New American Bible *Lectionary* so that it will have a balanced use of horizontal inclusive language. Certainly a new *Sacramentary* and new *Lectionary* will be formative factors for future directions in parish liturgical life. What will be the impact of these books on priest celebrants and the assembly? How will they affect liturgical ministers and the person in the pew? What other factors are operative in our Church and world that will shape future directions in parish liturgical life?

Let me first cite these additional formative factors: They are experience, culture, tradition, and Scripture. There are tensions among these factors. The quest for liturgy both Catholic and contemporary is not easy to satisfy. Witness the tension surrounding the revision of the *Sacramentary* and *Lectionary*. We must struggle to avoid one-sided simplistic approaches such as traditionalism with its emphasis on the Latin Mass, clericalism with its non-collaborative ministry, congregationalism with its forced isolation from the broader Church, radical feminism with its blurring of distinctions for sacramental ministry, biblicism, and the like. Future directions for the liturgy must be loyal to the faith, which it seeks to express, and at the same time relevant to the cultural environment, which its seeks to transform.

## Experience

I mention experience first, not because it dominates the other factors but because liturgy implies participation in a faith life, so that some experience of the life of faith precedes liturgy and may, indeed, be said to motivate it. Our experience of the life of faith is born of and nourished by our participation in a community of faith. The form of this faith experience varies widely from individual to individual, and even from one particular parish to another. The personal quality of such a faith experience ranges from that of the deeply involved and committed to that of the Christmas and Easter Catholic. The experiences themselves vary widely: some dramatic and emotional, others quiet and contemplative. We must be sensitive to the fact that people bring this varied experience of faith to the table of the Lord when they come to celebrate Eucharist. The challenge for the liturgy is to transform subjective, introspective, and individualistic experiences of faith into those which are expressive of the whole community of faith.

Good liturgy flows from life and leads us back to life. We bring our faith life, our family life, our personal life, our everyday life—with all of its experiences—to the Lord's table, so that we might be transformed and return home strengthened, renewed, more rooted in the Lord.

There is a gap, a chasm of Grand Canyon proportions, between our experience and the language with which we express it, between the reality and our descriptive word. There are parish communities which are communities in name only. There are songs which are recited, acclamations which are muttered, meals at which no one drinks, gifts of the people which they do not give, celebrations which are simply a perfunctory fulfillment of an obligation. Christopher J. Walsh has put it so well: "Reforms and revision we have had in plenty, but liturgical renewal will never be achieved until our texts, rites and affirmations are translated, not into this or that sort of English, but into reality in the lived experience of the people; and they will rarely be experienced as real until the congregations celebrating them are genuine communities of faith, witness and action."[1]

## Culture

No one can escape being conditioned by the culture in which we live. No one can remain untouched by the mentality, the intellectual climate of our contemporary culture. If our liturgy is to be intelligible, if it is to speak effectively to our age, it must speak in the language of our culture. To recognize this cultural factor is to acknowledge that there can be no final liturgical revision. Liturgical development and renewal are an unending task, for liturgical formulations themselves are culturally conditioned. As our cultural forms change, our liturgical formulations need continuing review and, at times, reformulation. This is a truth that Catholics in the United States need to hear over and over again. In my opinion and the opinion of many others, the Church in the United States today is experiencing a retreat, a falling back to an era that has passed, the era that preceded the Second Vatican Council. Are we still committed to a future built upon the vision of Vatican II? We all experience the complexity of modern life and the dominance of its secular values; some recent approaches to renewal appear to be bankrupt. Perhaps these are the reasons that prompt people to seek simpler times, simpler solutions. Those who seek a return to liturgical life, as it was prior to Vatican II, offend the teaching of that very council, which calls us to a "full, conscious and active participation in liturgical celebrations."[2]

Let us have the courage to tell it the way it is: A pre-Vatican II liturgical theology has no chance of speaking to a post-Vatican II world. The full, conscious, and active participation of all the people has been the singular goal and concern in the reform and promotion of the liturgy. Do we accept this teaching of the council fathers of Vatican II? If we do, we should not be calling for a return to a liturgy where celebrant alone, with his back to the people, in a language no one else understood, with mute spectators in pews, confected the Eucharist.

We must also be on guard against the temptation to accommodate liturgy to the mood of the time, to merge its content into contemporary cultural forms, so that it is subordinated to the culture. An example of this would be the attitudes of time management in American culture that creep into liturgy and hurt it. People view the weekend as their time and go shopping for a church with the shortest homily and Mass, where little is asked of the participants. American culture has forgotten many of its values, including those of family life, chaste sexuality, justice, and stability. By ourselves we are unable to combat and change this culture. But the Lord Jesus, present in liturgy, can transform and baptize the culture so that what is true, authentic, and uplifting in the culture will ennoble people. Our problem is one of maintaining a fine balance. On the one hand, we demand that liturgy be relevant and intelligible to the culture. On the other hand, we demand that liturgy not accommodate itself to cultural forms unworthy of the gospel. (An illustration: For some, Christian rap music reflects a proper cultural form; for others, it is not handing on the best in our tradition. We can do better.) We must emphasize a sense of the sacred, Christ's eucharistic presence, while respecting the assembly and its culture. We must maintain the fine balance between transcendence and immanence.

Permit me to suggest two basic principles that should guide liturgists in trying to maintain this balance. The first principle requires that no matter what is done, it lead to a full, conscious, and active participation in the liturgical celebrations.[3] The second principle speaks of substantial unity but not rigid uniformity.[4] For over four hundred years the Church willed that all worship in the Roman rite should everywhere show near perfect uniformity. At Vatican II there was a radical change. The council fathers realized that social and cultural conditions, and indeed the entire psychological climate, had changed drastically in our day. And so the *Constitution on the Sacred Liturgy* stated:

> Even in the liturgy, the Church has no wish to impose a rigid uniformity in matters that do not affect the faith or the good of the whole community; rather the Church respects and fosters the genius and talents of the various races and peoples. The Church considers with sympathy and, if possible, preserves intact the elements of these peoples' way of life . . . Sometimes, in fact, the Church admits such elements into the liturgy itself, providing that they are in keeping with the true and authentic spirit of the liturgy.[5]

The council fathers were even more explicit in saying: "Provision shall also be made . . . for legitimate variations and adaptations to different groups, regions and peoples, especially in mission lands."[6] And so we should not be surprised to find that in the Catholic Church in Zaire, the Liturgy of the Word comes before the Penitential Rite.

This principle coming from Vatican II gives new meaning to the word *unity* and a new vigor to the word *Catholic.*[7]

To maintain the fine balance in liturgy, we must be conscious that liturgy has two dimensions: divine and human, invisible and visible, unchanging and changeable. What is of divine institution is unchangeable. But signs and rites created by humans can grow old and outmoded, and often need to be revised and updated. We need to recall the words of Pope John XXIII: "The liturgy must not become a relic in a museum, but remain the living prayer of the Church." Let me stress that even the human part of the liturgy may often hold priceless elements that have been sanctified by age-old tradition. And these must be treated with respect and veneration. But this does not preclude us from revising the liturgy.

## Tradition and Scripture

Our Catholic faith has always had a special appreciation for the wisdom of the ages—the mystery of Christ as it has been experienced, interpreted, and transmitted throughout two thousand years. We call this tradition. The council fathers of Vatican II give us this definition of *tradition:* "the Church, in its doctrine, life and worship, perpetuates and transmits to every generation all that she herself is, all that she believes."[8] Some council fathers wanted to add the expression "all that the Church has," which would mean all of the customs and practices of the past. But the council fathers rejected that addition. As Roman Catholics we are faithful to tradition, but that does not mean slavishly copying and imposing past forms and expressions. In fact, that was rejected at Vatican II. The Church in every age is called to interpret and apply the essence of its faith, the deposit of faith, in a creative way to ever-changing needs and circumstances. Those who oppose ongoing liturgical reform and adaptation are not true traditionalists. The true traditionalist is one who applies the lived tradition of the Church in every age. Let us always remember the distinction between *tradition* and *traditional*. *Tradition* means all that the Church is, all that the Church believes. *Traditional* implies past customs and practices. Tradition comes from God. Traditional comes from men and women. That which is tradition does not change. That which is traditional must be open to change so that the Church can transmit to every generation all that it is, all that it believes.

We Catholics hold that the revelation of Christ has been transmitted to us, both in tradition and Scripture. Tradition is not a rival to Scripture but is its necessary complement. Tradition preceded the earliest Christian Scriptures and was the basis for the New Testament writings. St. Paul in First Corinthians says: "For I received from the Lord what I also handed on to you, that the Lord Jesus, on the night he was handed over, took bread, and after he had given thanks, broke it and said 'this is my body that is for you. Do this in remembrance of me'" (11:23-24). Paul also in First Corinthians says: "For I handed on to you as of first importance what I also received" (15:3). Jesus was remembered, not only in the Scriptures, but also in the sacraments of the Church, above all, in the celebration of the Eucharist.

In our consideration of the proposed revision of the *Sacramentary*, there has been much debate over changing the translation of the Creed. The doctrinal content of the Creed cannot be set aside without abandoning the faith of the Catholic community. But the language that expresses the doctrine needs continual reinterpretation. Language is historically conditioned. If it is passed on in a merely mechanical rote fashion, it becomes a lifeless tradition. Each generation must accept the tradition and make it its own. Each generation must take the ancient formula and cast it into its own categories of thought and language. In this process the liturgist is always aware of the words of St. Vincent of Lerins: "That which has been believed everywhere, always and by all" cannot be set aside without abandoning the Church itself. When people object to liturgists even attempting to recast the language of ancient formulas while preserving their doctrinal content, they do not understand what the Church itself has done at various times in its history. The Nicene Creed itself is an example of the Church's attempt to recast the language expressing the faith in the terms of the culture of the post-apostolic period.

Let me digress here for a moment to make sure that we are still focused on our topic: future directions in parish liturgical life. I have been treating the formative factors that influence liturgy, namely, experience, culture, tradition, and Scripture. But now I ask, what is the most dynamic and determining influence for liturgy today, yesterday, or tomorrow? What is the primary factor that enables the presiding minister and the assembly to experience truly a celebration of the sacred mysteries? What is the most essential element that produces a full, conscious, and active participation in the liturgy? The answer to all these questions is the gift of the Holy Spirit.

When we look at the first Pentecost in the Upper Room in Jerusalem, we see great excitement: There is the rushing wind, the flaming fire, the speaking in tongues. These elements, full of mystery, point to an extraordinary and dynamic event. Something special happened. Something unprecedented and overwhelming occurred. One fact of history is beyond question: Pentecost gave birth to the Christian Church. The result of Pentecost was the emergence of a new community that we call the "Church." A liturgist would have loved the excitement and activity manifested in the Upper Room. All in the Upper Room were intimately involved and participating. But what happened after Pentecost? It sounds almost anticlimactic. It is a liturgical letdown. What happened after the surprise and excitement had settled? St. Luke writes in the Acts of the Apostles: "They devoted themselves to the teaching of the apostles and the communal life, to the breaking of bread and prayers" (Acts 2:42). This is the routine of the Church.

This is the daily lived experience of the Church. It may not be exciting or glamorous but it is the biblical answer.

We, today and in the future, belong to the Church after Pentecost. That means we are called to the routine life of the Church. That word *routine* is not appealing to us.

Routine presents the image of boring, ordinary, painstaking work. We would much more prefer the surprise and excitement of the first Pentecost. What we need to comprehend is the fact that the first Christians "devoted themselves to the teaching of the apostles and communal life, to the breaking of bread and prayers." Christ summons us today and in the future to this same activity of the Church.

We are called to faithfulness and perseverance in handing on what the apostles taught. We do not add or subtract, but we teach the saving truths revealed by Christ, ever the same, but also ever new.

When the Church celebrates Eucharist it uses a common rite in order to forge separate individuals into the single body of Christ—a community of faith. By its very nature the Church's liturgy is communal. Christians do not pray "My Father" when they pray, but rather "Our Father." The liturgy is communal because through the saving events of Christ's life, that liturgy unites us to the risen Christ. The assembly gathered for worship is the visible body of Christ. But this is hardly the prevailing understanding in our parishes. A future direction for parish liturgical life is to rediscover the importance and meaning of the liturgical assembly. Liturgy is the work of the people. Liturgy is the action of the People of God. The worshiping assembly is not a passive audience. The council fathers of Vatican II stated: "In the liturgy full public worship is performed by the mystical body of Jesus Christ, that is, by the head and members."[9] The liturgical assembly and the body of Christ are one. The liturgical assembly is the body of Christ present at a particular time and place. The liturgical assembly is the sign and symbol of God's people—yes, a symbol of the Christian community transformed into the body of Christ. We are the priestly People of God. We belong to the community of the baptized—the community of believers who share a common faith and mission. When we are assembled around the Lord's table we recognize the Lord's presence in the gifts transformed into Christ's body and blood by the Eucharistic Prayer offered by the priest. In communion we receive the body and blood of Christ which makes us the body of Christ in the world. When the eucharistic celebration concludes, this body of Christ, the community of believers, is sent forth to continue Christ's presence and mission in the world. The words "Go in peace to love and serve the Lord" are a call to evangelization, a call to share the good news, a call to mission, a call to give witness.

The task for pastors and liturgy committees is to help those, who constitute the liturgical assembly, experience the risen Lord. Then we can speak of what we have experienced—we can witness. We will be men and women with one idea: The Lord is risen, the Lord is truly risen. By and large, we do not do this. We are more reluctant to share our faith than anything else we have.

We have much to learn from the early Christians who clearly understood the meaning of community and the sharing of their resources in a communal way.

After Pentecost the disciples "devoted themselves to the teaching of the apostles and communal life, to the breaking of bread and prayers." This is the routine of the Church since the day of Pentecost. It is not glamorous or exciting, but it is the answer of Christ and his Church to our needs. It has been the right answer for two thousand years. It must be the ultimate guide and formative factor for the future direction of parish liturgical life.

Let me conclude with a personal remembrance. From 1958–1962 I had the great privilege of studying in Innsbruck, Austria. My professor of liturgy was the renowned Jesuit, Father Josef Jungmann. He was a saintly man who loved the liturgy and loved the Church. With his classical and unsurpassed work, on *The Mass of the Roman Rite*, Josef Jungmann became one of the chief architects of liturgical reform at Vatican II. I recall especially a lecture he gave titled: "The Role of the Liturgy in the Transformation of Pagan Society." Its central message well serves our topic today.

Jungmann always approached liturgy from the standpoint of history. If you were arguing for the vernacular, he would go to history and show the early Church's use of the vernacular. If you were arguing for simplification of rites, he would go to history and show the noble simplicity of the original. In approaching the topic of this keynote—future directions in parish liturgical life—we need to go back to history, to former ages that can point us in the right direction and remind us of the consequences of taking the wrong direction. What Jungmann cites about the fourth century is truly astounding and has enormous pastoral and liturgical application for future directions in parish liturgical life.

In the fourth century, Church institutions were lacking—institutions which today we would consider essential. There was an extensive organization of charity supervised by the deacons, but there were no Christian schools; no Christian schools at either the elementary level or college level. "The Church gave no systematic catechetical instruction to the children; their religious training was left entirely to the parents. The Church made no special provision for the care of the youth; they were left to fend for themselves. There were no Christian societies or confraternities or institutions comparable to organized Catholic action. All this was lacking . . . And yet there existed a flourishing, Christian life, for there existed a living liturgy."[10] The liturgy substituted for other structures, programs, and institutions.

The Church in the fourth century was gradually transforming the pagan society of the day into a Christian society. Although Christianity was a religion of the minority, the Church played a decisive role in changing the world of the Mediterranean Basin. In the course of the fourth century, Christianity changed from being a persecuted religion to being the official religion of the empire. Jungmann asked: How did this happen with no formal Church structures or institutions as we know them today? What was the part played by the liturgy in bringing about this vast transformation?

Our American society today is secular; some might even say pagan. Are there parallels between the Church of the fourth century and the Church in this final decade of the twentieth century?

Liturgists know how the traditions and beliefs of the pagan converts influenced the liturgical life of the Church. These converts brought their Hellenistic Greek and Roman cultures into the liturgy. Just as grace builds on nature, liturgy builds on culture. Liturgical research shows a great deal of the Greco-Roman world embodied in Christian liturgy.

What about the reverse of that situation? What influence did the Christian liturgy exert on these pagan converts? Did the liturgy really exercise a formative influence upon them? Jungmann responds, "The formative power of the liturgy was both profound and vast."

Recall that the fourth and fifth centuries were the era of the great patristic fathers of the Church. Jungmann notes, "Society, political life, the lives of the people, family life, the position of woman, the appreciation of human dignity whether slave, child, or infant yet unborn—all this was transformed into a slow but sure process of fermentation: Out of a pagan society, a Christian society was born."[11] How did the liturgy accomplish this? What was the secret of this living liturgy?

The liturgy came from the forms of expression taken from the peoples' own living culture. The Church's buildings, clothing, gestures, song, and language were forms familiar to all. There was much reading of the holy Scripture at the Eucharist. In particular, the Psalms became familiar to the people. After each lesson there followed a psalm sung in common. The cantor would sing the refrain, and the congregation repeated it. (At Naples the candidates for baptism had to memorize Psalms 116 and 22, and had to recite them for baptism, confirmation and Eucharist.) The peoples' "amen," after the great thanksgiving prayer of the Eucharist, was a fervent statement of faith. St. Jerome boasts that in the Roman basilicas, the "amen" resounded like heavenly thunder. Would that describe any of our liturgies today? Body posture corresponded to the celebrant. Like him, the people stood facing the east, and with him they raised their hands in the prayer posture. When the deacon cried out *Flectamus genua* (Let us kneel), priest and people knelt for silent prayer until *Levate* (Stand up).

The Christians of the fourth century had a living liturgy. They participated. They learned not by theory but by activity. They learned by doing. A good illustration of this was their Offertory procession. It was obligatory for all to take part. The entire congregation joined in the offertory procession on Sundays and feast days. The chief characteristic of living liturgy was unity in the assembly—all prayed together, all sang together, all cried out their responses, all offered at the same time, and all or nearly all received the holy sacrament.

In the fourth and fifth centuries, we see that liturgy was a formative factor. In those days important institutions, programs, and structures were lacking which we rightly consider essential and indispensable. But there was a living liturgy. The liturgy was the Catholic school. The liturgy was the religious education program that instructed parents to teach their children. The liturgy was the impetus to social action and deeds of charity. The liturgy was the one community that united Christians. It was through the living liturgy that pagan society became a Christian society.

Liturgists, let us learn a lesson from the past. Here is the future direction for parish liturgical life. Here is your mandate for the next millennium. In the name of God's people, give us living liturgy, living liturgy, living liturgy.

---

[1] Gabe Huck, ed. *A Sourcebook About Liturgy* (Chicago: Liturgy Training Publications, 1994) 169.

[2] *Constitution on the Sacred Liturgy,* 14.

[3] Ibid.

[4] Ibid., 38.

[5] Ibid., 37.

[6] Ibid., 38.

[7] Cultural adaptations are not left to the decision of individual presiders or parish liturgical committees, but are determined by competent Church authorities: universal, national, diocesan.

[8] *Dogmatic Constitution on Divine Revelation*, 8.

[9] *Constitution on the Sacred Liturgy*, 7.

[10] *The Early Liturgy to the Time of Gregory the Great*, University of Notre Dame Press, 1980.

[11] Ibid.

# The Very Nature of the Liturgy

## Gabe Huck

As a way of assessing our present situation and tasks, I know no tool more effective than paragraph 14 of the *Constitution on the Sacred Liturgy*. There the document states its own goal most clearly. These few sentences allow us to judge our own condition, lament the lamentable, and move on with some new purpose.

> The Church earnestly desires that all the faithful be led to that full, conscious and active participation in liturgical celebrations called for by the very nature of the liturgy. Such participation by the Christian people as "a chosen race, a royal priesthood, a holy nation, God's own people" (1 Pet 2:9; see 2:4-5) is their right and duty by reason of their baptism.

"Full, conscious and active participation" became shorthand for this paragraph and, indeed, for the whole document. Thus magnificent adjectives too often overshadowed the question being asked: Why full and conscious and active participation? The answer is: That's liturgy. The answer is not: Because the Church has always taught this. The answer is not: Because we the bishops say so. The answer is not: Because in some golden age of liturgy it was this way. None of this. Rather: Such participation—the full and active and conscious kind—is what we are after because that is "the very nature of the liturgy." In other words: No such participation, no liturgy.

That means it is the nature of the liturgy to be done by the people. It is not done *to* people. It is not done *for* people. It is not done *in the presence of* people. People do it and the plural is correct because it is as a Church assembled that people do liturgy.

A liturgy has not "worked" simply because people leave uplifted, made peaceful, made cheerful, made warm, made smarter, or all of the above. When we look to liturgy to be primarily about such things, we miss this clear but hard saying that the bishops got straight: The kind of human activity liturgy is can't tolerate an audience, can't tolerate those who do and those who are done to. A liturgy then has "worked" when we have worked, when we are exhausted with doing what we are so well trained in doing and yet so passionate to do again.

The second sentence of paragraph 14 does another amazing thing. At the time of the council, baptism for most Catholics was a very private moment about original sin. Yet here is baptism rather offhandedly named the root of the liturgical reform. Here it says: Being baptized gives us a right and a duty to do our liturgy. Baptism, the plunging into Christ's death and the clothing in Christ's life that is both once-for-all and life-long, weighs on us and exalts us all at once. We have rights. We have duties. And they are the same. The council proclaimed: If we have put on Christ, we are compelled to do liturgy as our own full, conscious, and active work. And: If we have put on Christ, then doing the liturgy fully, consciously, and actively is a right that cannot be taken from us.

That is the measure of our efforts and our present condition. Do we think of the Sunday assembly in this way? Do we act as if on the Lord's Day the baptized are both obliged and delighted to assemble and do what is in their hearts, minds, bones, and muscles to do (for liturgy is not liturgy if you have to learn it new each time, if you have to make it up as you go along, if you have to read it out of a book, if you aren't utterly freed by its gracious and yet terrible repetition)?

It is this Christ-clothed Church that fills all sorts of rooms and there speaks and sings and moves through the deep and familiar vocabulary: the opening and reading of the book that we cling to and hand on from one generation to another, the incessant intercession that seems to believe that what a church is here for is to clamor to God on behalf of mostly non-church people, the coming around a table set with simple sorts of bread and wine and there to sing praise and thanks that flow from a long and churning memory, the quiet and indiscriminate embrace before the bread is broken and then the sharing of bread and cup in a severe and joyous equality that would undermine most everything the lopsided world outside has taught us. But that world, that world God loves, that world that has death written all over it, is exactly why the Church rehearses what it rehearses on its Lord's Day. Being here is not about being saved, not about being lifted a bit, not even about some experience of community. Being here is about the life of the world.

The second part of paragraph 14 reads:

> In the reform and promotion of the liturgy, this full and active par-
> ticipation by all the people is the aim to be considered before all
> else. For it is the primary and indispensable source from which the
> faithful are to derive the true Christian spirit and therefore pastors
> must zealously strive in all their pastoral work to achieve such
> participation by means of the necessary instruction.

If it had only been so simple! The "it" in the second sentence is not the
liturgy but "full and active participation." So we have: Full and active
participation by all the people is "the primary and indispensable
source from which the faithful are to derive the true Christian spirit."
In doing the liturgy the baptized become the baptized, the Church becomes the Church, the body of Christ becomes the body of Christ. In
doing the liturgy—over many Sundays, many seasons and festivals,
many weddings and initiations and anointings and funerals—whatever is the "true Christian spirit," Christ's own spirit, seeps and creeps
into us, into the person, into the people. That is the way it works.

And that is the measure of our situation. Does the liturgy belong to
the assembly? Or do the rights of the baptized go unrecognized, our
duties undone? Are we being done to? Sometimes this "being done to"
is with great preparation and care, sometimes it is totally thoughtless.
Sometimes it is with huge amounts of feeling and good will, sometimes with no sensitivity at all. Too often those thought to have
"strong" liturgy have a reputation for putting effort and care into a few
areas—music, homilies, hospitality—but the liturgy may yet belong
less to the people than did the old devotions. So well trained are we by
television and all the ways of consuming, that few have grasped that
liturgy is cut off at the pass when those in leadership come to their
tasks with notions of entertainment, of inspiration, of healing, of education.

We must come at our task with this one central notion: It is the right
and the duty of this assembly of baptized Catholics to assemble, to
proclaim, and to hear the places marked in the Bible for that Sunday,
to attend to a homily that is as worthy as possible of the Scriptures and
the Church, to clamor before God on behalf of the world, to bless God,
and remember, and make present in eucharistic action the paschal
working of God in this world, then to share and share alike (exactly
alike as we can humanly get) the bread and cup become for us the
body and blood of Christ, saying Amen to what we are.

How to make this happen: Build and renovate buildings in which
assemblies can do these sorts of things (when the room, its furniture,
and its public address system say "audience," we are going to act like
an audience). Open up even the present rubrics so that all those who

take on some ministry, presiders especially, understand themselves as members of the assembly exercising some service to the assembly—to the Church, that is, which in turn is in service to its Lord for the life of the world. Sing the liturgy (you can't "speak" a liturgy any more than you can speak "Happy Birthday" or the Star-Spangled Banner) with words and with melodies that can bear the weight of repetition, of being by heart, of being about things deep and ambiguous. Seek the primary objects before the secondary: a worthy book, worthy vessels, bread that is bread to every one of the senses and wine that is wine for all.

In great and small ways, Sunday by Sunday, the liturgy is taken from the people by those who mean well and by those who do not mean at all. When presiders and homilists believe that their job is to carry it all, to provide weary people with some relief or indifferent people with some affirmation, they will fail at their real task. Thus do they take the liturgy from the people, engaging in performance (good or not) rather than ministering at a ritual that the Church knows in its heart and does out of both love and need.

The work of those who take some responsibility for a parish liturgy is to fashion for the Lord's Day a ritual so strong that its repetition and its seasonal variations make, little by little, full and conscious and active participation. This can only be when people know their liturgy by heart. When we know how to sing it, walk it, feel it, keep its silences, bear its gestures of kissing and embracing and lifting open hands, gaze at its simple objects and at one another, smell and taste the differences that come with a Lent or an Advent—then the liturgy is ours or, better, then we are the liturgy's, we are the sacrifice, we are the praise.

The things that keep this from being are often so small, so unconscious. We enter the room without a word from or to anyone. We cling to the end space in the row. (Ask: Is this a public transportation vehicle or is it something like the union hall or the town plaza? But here is a hall or a plaza where those who are closer than blood relations meet.) We are provided with printed material (often unworthy of the occasion) so that we can read the readings and prayers. (Ask: Is this about one human being opening our book and reading what is there to other human beings, to the Church?) The presider offers a warm "good morning." (Ask: Why is this person shying away from the phrases that proclaim this a gathering of the Church, phrases that offer the assembly a strong response?)

If there are a hundred of these little things that keep the people from doing their liturgy, then ninety-five of them are self-imposed, are not part of the rite of Mass as we have it now. They are in our power to correct—it is not that hard to have a Sunday ritual that would belong to this local Church. What it takes is understanding and follow-through and a honing of the skills to be a minister at the assembly's ritual.

A favorite example. For a generation the instructions in the book have been clear: People at Mass should share in the bread and wine of that Mass. Why is this so seldom observed (the big ciborium comes regularly from the tabernacle and is divided out into the dishes)? Is it simply that it would take some effort to do otherwise? Is it that we do not see why it is worth the effort? Does no one believe that it makes any difference? What we believe, to judge from what we do, is that the people should "receive" consecrated bread and it makes no difference when or where it was consecrated, just so it was on some altar during the Eucharistic Prayer. What then do we believe this assembly in this hall on this Lord's Day just did in the Eucharistic Prayer? Watched it? Listened to it? Gave some sort of abstract affirmation to what was being said by the presider? Why are we there at all then?

How could we come to a strong sense of what a eucharistic deed would look like, what its implications would be? Why does our tradition join Eucharist (a verb) to the Lord's Day as the central work of this assembly of baptized people? In our current ritual practice for the Eucharistic Prayer, little of what we sing, how we stand, how we gesture, how we conduct ourselves, would make it clear that over this table with this bread and this wine, the baptized people are gathering up what their life is all about, doing it in words and gestures and melodies of thanksgiving, doing it in dialogue with a presider who embodies their bond to a larger Church, and—when done—are ready to take that bread and wine and proclaim to and about themselves: The body of Christ, the blood of Christ. It matters: flesh and blood and bread and wine and words sung and gestures made. If we could just do Sunday by Sunday what baptized people are to do around their table, around their bread and wine, we would know why it is this bread we are to eat, this cup we are to drink. And with that we would be shaping ourselves and our Church as eucharistic—day in, day out, everywhere.

In such things as this, and there are many, is the measure of how worthwhile and how hard it is for any of us to grasp the person- and tribe-making power of our ritual.

Paragraph 14 has this much more to say:

> Yet it would be futile to entertain any hopes of realizing this unless, in the first place, the pastors themselves become thoroughly imbued with the spirit and power of the liturgy and make themselves its teachers. A prime need, therefore, is that attention be directed, first of all, to the liturgical formation of the clergy.

The wisdom is amazing! "Futile" is a serious word and should be so heard. The authors of the *Constitution*, having stated why the reform of the liturgy was vital (nothing less than the "true Christian spirit" is at stake), say that it will not happen "unless." What then is this "imbued" and has it happened? It is not the same as "knowledgeable." It is "informed by," perhaps. It is people—for more than pastors are responsible for this today—who have been shaped to live by the rituals of the Church, people whose liturgy has revealed how to be in and toward the world. They have understood (or, better, absorbed) justice and gotten it into their bones not first from articles and lectures, but from the Scriptures proclaimed and the eucharistic deeds celebrated. (And here they have understood that the ritual as we know it is not justice but striving for justice: this poor Church cannot itself get it straight about the dignity of baptized women and men.) They have understood/absorbed that thanksgiving is our stance and so they stand in thanksgiving in the morning and at night. They have understood/absorbed that the baptized have their eyes constantly on the troubles and needs of the world, that the world in fact absorbs the baptized who love it as God does (so they know: liturgy isn't about getting saved, getting grace, getting ahead, getting peace, but it is about this weak Church trying to act for the life of the world).

Much has been done, but the task is hardly started, the difficulties in this culture hardly faced. They were right to say it would not happen unless and until the "imbuing" happened, and that has not happened to any great extent—yet.

Where are we to look? Little that is worthwhile happens at official levels. The scholarly and pastoral prophets long ago gave way to the bureaucrats. That is to be expected. We can live for several generations on the work begun in the decade after the council. Still, some fine work gets done today for English speakers by the International Commission on English in the Liturgy.

In the United States, leadership has come from outside the official places. The liturgy degree programs, at Notre Dame and The Catholic University especially, have continued to bring varied and important perspectives. A few other theology schools (Chicago's Catholic Theological Union, for example) have created serious departments where liturgy is taught well and with thoroughness, and where liturgy is constantly associated with a multicultural world and with the study of Scripture, ethics, and other disciplines. Though the bishops never followed up their own plans to have centers of experimentation, the Notre Dame Center for Pastoral Liturgy has continued on its own to do important work, depending on grants and on income generated by their programs.

The Liturgical Conference (mainly in the last twenty years through its publications) and the North American Academy of Liturgy, each with its own constituency, have maintained an ecumenical conversation about the liturgy that is crucial.

The National Association of Pastoral Musicians has, in its meetings and publications, quite often raised the right issues. It is difficult to be effective though when so much about the way parishes are run makes stability impossible for parish musicians. An ever shifting membership means little is possible for those furthest along.

A series of Form/Reform conferences has addressed issues of architecture and the visual arts. Here is a conversation continuing from decades ago, but we have far to go in establishing some bonds and some respect among those who should be participants: artists in various media, architects, critics, art historians, authorities in liturgical history and practice, pastors, diocesan officials. So much needs to come together if the worship spaces that are built and renovated in the next generation are to serve the people who assemble there.

Important leadership has also come from the North American Forum on the Catechumenate whose many training sessions involve the participants in recognizing how integral is the celebration of the liturgy to Christian Initiation.

Add to these organizations and events the several diocesan offices that have been directed over the long run with imagination and authority (examples only: Chicago, Houston, Los Angeles, Milwaukee, Seattle). And add some of the publishers of periodicals, books, and music.

Is it too much to look at any of these institutions and businesses and expect to see Church people "imbued" with the spirit of the liturgy? Too much to expect here people who understand that liturgy is going to count for nothing in the end, so we had best stay humble while we chomp at the bit to see assemblies formed by their Catholic liturgy to lead gospel lives? Those of us with some little leadership roles are as much creatures of our culture and our egos as the rest of the world. We got here for all sorts of reasons. But here we are, the enterprise in near ruins compared to where we hoped it would be this many years after the council, but with a few exemplary assemblies to sustain us. As with anything, the little piece we do—publish magazines, do research, compose music, organize conferences—can become an end in itself, cranking out year after year of material, doing well by the movement's very stagnation.

What should happen? Let me propose just three possibilities of different orders.

First. The liturgical movement grew and took strong roots because there were a few places where people could go and be part of the day-by-day and Sunday-by-Sunday and season-by-season liturgy celebrated with fidelity and humility and care (that is, not at all the liturgy of extravaganzas, all of which we would do better without). These were not, I think, regarded so much as "shrines" whose liturgy would always be different from that of the local parish, whose rites would always be different from those of our own households. They were, rather, hope for what that local liturgy would be.

Are there such places today? Yes, but not by design, and perhaps that is where we should work. Should not every diocese have a parish or two where—in these years when the "imbuing" is still rare—extra care has been taken with leadership, and extra commitment to the long term presence of that leadership? This is not to say: Over here let us have a parish where the leadership knows how to do liturgy, and over there one that is good at justice issues, and then over there . . . nothing of this. The definition of the parish's liturgy is going to mean constant challenge to set priorities and do all else that a Catholic parish should be and do. But for now, it seems this will not happen until the diocesan liturgy office says (with support from personnel and finance offices): "We are going to stop a lot of other things, and instead, use our time and budget to help St. Mary's. And after five years or more, we will help somebody else. We must learn by doing and we have not done. We have talked. And we have let people off the hook—in their buildings and renovations, in their ministries, in the basic expectations for what an assembly deserves."

That is a top-down approach perhaps. Probably it will happen the other way around: A parish that has been striving to live by its liturgy, demanding that the diocese not ignore such efforts but rejoice in them.

Second. Take it home. In this culture, the things we do together on Sundays do not get practiced Monday through Saturday. In the absence of a ritual that permeates daily life, many have looked to a variety of spiritualities to hold their reality together. These cover an immense spectrum. But if the *Constitution* was correct in its bold but very traditional statement that it is full and conscious participation in the Church's liturgy that imparts the authentic Christian spirit, then how is that liturgy, that participation, to be our spirituality? How is there to be a practice that would give to all our days the shape of the fundamental work we do together on Sunday? That is: If on the Lord's Day we are to be a people who know how to open and listen to the Scriptures, where do we train for that work? If on Sundays we are to be a people who bring fervor, breadth, and eloquence to our charge to lift up to God all the grief, fear, and harshness of this exile place that is also joy for us, where do we get used to being such interceding people? If on Sundays we are to have in our hearts and muscles and bones how a people gives thanks (does Eucharist), where does this get rehearsed day by day? If on Sundays we can join ourselves through baptism and Eucharist to the proclamation that, despite all appearances to the contrary, death has been destroyed by a death, where are the words and gestures that allow us each morning and each night to make our own the vocabulary of passover, of sacrifice, that would gradually define the way we are to walk here? If on Sundays we are a people who come hungry and thirsty, where do we practice hunger and thirst?

We will not be without rituals. Lacking any that reflect and rehearse the ritual of Sunday, we will have those that the culture offers in abundance. And they will rehearse us in another sort of life. It is hard to seek out the rituals that can support individuals and households through their mornings and meals and evenings, through the cycle of the week, the cycle of the year, and the cycle of each life. It is hard to make those deeds the Church does on Sunday the source and summit of a daily practice. That is as difficult for the pastor of a parish as it is for any parishioner.

We know little of the ways that allow such things as the wordless Sign of the Cross as first and last gesture of the day, or the ways we do or do not eat (and what we eat and when), or the clearing of life at so many levels that Lent brings. Ritual, to be sure, is a dangerous thing; but we are going to have it in any case. The task is a very long one: to seek out ourselves and to share with others not simply something from a menu of spiritualities, but something of daily practice that is derived from and leads to the defining Sunday deeds of the Church.

Third. We can imagine what is possible and let that vision of this church's Sunday work give us the strength and the patience for what is a long task. Long, but possible. Imagine a room, a hall, maybe very old, where people of all ages and conditions are gathering. They don't all know each other, but here who you know or who you like does not carry so much weight. Instead, you pass by the waters where all here became one body and that bond—at least in this Sunday work of imagining God's reign—is all. Gradually these few hundred people begin to sing/chant, then to sign themselves with the cross and to say their Amen to a prayer whose words are spoken with a direct eloquence by the one who will preside, one who is also a member of this assembly, one whose "order" in the Church is a bond to the other Churches that are now also assembled.

Then this assembly sits itself down while the book that has been carried into their midst is opened. There is a sense of hungry people

gathering at a table. Here are people who know that the text proclaimed is proclaimed to the Church. It is the Church that reads and
listens and ponders. That is not the same as everybody doing their
own listening simultaneously. The book has been carried by the ancestors, entrusted to this generation for a while, and will be handed on. It
is read through and begun again. It is met each week, each year, from
the new place. With psalms and alleluias, with kisses and crosses, book
and its proclaimed texts are held dear by these people. The people
have this rhythm of listening and singing, sitting and standing, being
silent and shouting. The liturgy is theirs. It climaxes, for now, in a long
and diverse litany: people who have kept their eyes open now would
remind their God of all they have seen. Most of it is not sweetness. Not
yet.

That done, the assembly moves around a table that is kissed. Some
place bread and wine on that table. Some move around, gathering
money for the poor and the Church. It is an informal moment between
the intensity before and the intensity to come. Then the presider,
standing with all at the table, invites them to lift up their hearts and to
give thanks and praise. These are words the people understand. The
presider can then continue to give words to this thanks and praise, to
voice how this Church remembers where it has been with its God and,
at the heart of that, the love of God poured out in Jesus, all that manifest here in doing what Jesus did, giving thanks over bread and cup.
There is the sense: This is why we have come, this is what we want to
do until we are grasped by it. That is what baptized people do. The assembly many times interrupts the presider to acclaim what has been
said in well-known chants whose words and melody are their best
theology. And when they have said Amen to this strong prayer, these
people chant the Lord's Prayer, embrace or clasp hands in an image of
peace, begin chanting again as the large bread is broken into many
pieces.

Then some come forward so that all can be given this bread to eat
and this cup to drink. Here is hunger satisfied and intensified, thirst
quenched and yet become almost unbearable. Here is the Church at its
holy meal, in few words and in ample gestures practicing what a baptized life is to do and be, day-in, day-out.

All that remains is a few moments of silence, some simple prayer,
and a long time of sharing all the activities that this group has en-
countered; then to make that cross on the body again and adjourn.

That is possible. Nothing is needed from Rome or Washington.
We need a room, leadership itself imbued with the liturgy, time. We
need leadership dedicated not to the occasional or even weekly ex-
travaganza (something "moving" or "healing"), but dedicated to

fashioning for this parish the ritual structure that will belong to the assembly, theirs to do week in and week out as they are served by ministers who come from their midst and who know the skills and rhythms of service. And we need that vision itself—and the courage to live by it.

*This essay appeared in a slightly different form in* Church *magazine, Spring 1993.*

*Photo by John Hue Tran, S.V.D.*

# Gilbert W. Ostdiek, O.F.M.:
# Franciscan, Scholar, Educator, Liturgist

*Zachary Hayes, O.F.M.*

Father Gilbert Ostdiek, O.F.M., was born in Lawrence, Nebraska on March 20, 1933. He is one of ten children born to Henry Stephen Ostdiek and Dora Rita (nee Rempe) Ostdiek. After completing primary school, he attended the minor seminary of the Franciscan Province of the Sacred Heart at Mayslake, near Westmont, Illinois, from 1947 to 1953. In the summer of 1953 he entered the novitiate of the same province, situated at that time in Teutopolis, Illinois. Following simple profession of vows as a Franciscan at the end of the novitiate year in 1954, he pursued the study of philosophy at Our Lady of Angels Friary in Cleveland, Ohio, in a program accredited through Quincy College (now Quincy University) in Quincy, Illinois. He completed the program in 1957 and then made solemn vows as a friar and received a Bachelor of Arts degree conferred by Quincy College. The degree included a major in philosophy and a minor in psychology.

From 1957 until 1961, Fr. Gilbert studied theology at St. Joseph Seminary, the Franciscan House of Studies in Teutopolis. In accordance with the common practice of the time, he was ordained as presbyter after his third year of theology and spent one more year in the seminary to complete the course of theological studies prescribed for ordination.

In 1961 he began further studies at the Franciscan Pontifical Athenaeum Antonianum where his concentration was in doctrinal and sacramental theology. Since his earlier Franciscan formation had taken place at a time when great emphasis was given to the importance of liturgy properly celebrated, and at which the early fruits of the liturgical movement in North America were already beginning to be felt, it is not surprising that Fr. Gilbert would have approached these studies with a distinct concern for the area of liturgy and sacraments. It had been his hope to do special work in the area of contemporary sacramental theology. This interest was reflected in his 1962 Master's thesis entitled *De Nexu Sacramentorum cum Ecclesia in Theologia Sacramentali Hodierna*. In recognition of the quality of this work, he received the License in Sacred Theology (S.T.L.) in 1962. The same interest was reflected when he presented his magistral lecture to the faculty of the Antonianum in 1964. It was entitled "Christ's Saving Work in the Sacraments according to Polycarp Wegenaer" (an exposition and critique of P. Wegenaer, *Heilsgegenwart. Das Heilswerk Christi und die Virtus divina in den Sakramenten unter besonderer Berücksichitgung von Eucharistie und Taufe* [Aschendorf, 1958]). Fr. Gilbert's doctoral thesis, done under the direction of Eligius Buytaert, O.F.M., was entitled "Disquisitio Comparativa in Prologos Lecturae Oxoniensis et Ordinationis I.D. Scoti." The thesis was approved *summa cum laude,* and the doctoral degree in theology (S.T.D.) was conferred in 1967.

Meanwhile, in 1965, Fr. Gilbert had begun teaching doctrinal and sacramental theology as Assistant Professor at St. Joseph Seminary in Teutopolis, and continued in this capacity until 1968 when the Franciscan Province of the Sacred Heart moved its theologate to Chicago as one of the founding communities of the Catholic Theological Union (CTU). Fr. Gilbert was a major participant in the discussions and planning that led to the opening of this new school for ministerial education. In the ensuing years CTU was to become the largest Roman Catholic school of studies for ministry in the United States. There, from 1968 until 1977, he worked as Associate Professor of Liturgy; in 1977 he was promoted to the rank of Professor of Liturgy. He has continued in that capacity until the present.

Other teaching experiences have included a summer course in philosophy in the undergraduate summer program at Quincy College (1961), and a course in theology in the undergraduate program of Briar Cliff College, Sioux City (1968, 1969). The summers of 1971 to 1987 found him an active participant in the summer M.A. program in theology at St. Bonaventure University, New York. In 1986 he was Lecturer in Theology in the M.A. program at the Seminary of the Immaculate Conception, Huntington, New York. In the summer of 1993, he lectured on liturgy in the M.A. program at the University of Notre Dame in Indiana. In 1994, he taught ritual studies in the doctoral program at Notre Dame.

Over the years, Fr. Gilbert's primary teaching areas have been: fundamentals of liturgy; ritual and symbol; history, theology, and celebration of the various sacraments; presidential style; worship and pastoral care; liturgical spirituality; liturgical catechesis; liturgical environment; and ritual studies. Secondary areas have been: fundamental theology;

christology; and ecclesiology. He spent 1970–1971 doing post-doctoral study in hermeneutics at Harvard Divinity School, Cambridge, Massachussetts. In 1978, he did a year-long study of ritual in anthropology and social psychology at the University of California/ Graduate Theological Union, in Berkeley.

Heavy as this schedule may seem, teaching has not been the whole of Fr. Gilbert's contribution to the world of theological education. He has also carried a heavy load of administrative work over the years. From 1968 until 1974, he was a member of the Board of Education of the Franciscan Province of the Sacred Heart and chairperson of the Board's Committee on Five-Year Planning for the educational ministry of the Province. Beginning in 1971, he assumed the office of Academic Dean and Vice President at CTU, holding this position until 1977. From 1979 until 1984, he served as chairperson of the Board of Education of his Franciscan Province. During the same years, he was Director of the Word and Worship Program at CTU. The summer of 1984 found him working as Acting Director of the summer M.A. program at St. Bonaventure University. From 1985 until 1988 he served as chairperson and program director of the Word and Worship Department at CTU, and most recently, from 1993 until 1996, he has filled the office of director of the Master of Divinity Program at the school. From 1990 to the present, he has served as a member of the Board of Trustees at Quincy University, Quincy, Illinois. Fr. Gilbert is a member of the Catholic Theological Society of America, the North American Academy of Liturgy, and the *Societas Liturgica.*

Outside the directly educational context, Fr. Gilbert's contribution to the development of liturgical awareness and liturgical texts has been immense over the years. Since 1986 he has been a member of the Advisory Committee of the International Commission on English in the Liturgy (ICEL), and has served as vice-chairperson of that committee since 1992. He has been a member of the ICEL General Editorial Committee for the Revision of the *Sacramentary* since 1991, and chairperson of the Subcommittee on the Translation and Revision of Texts since 1987. He has also served as a consultant to the American Franciscan Liturgical Commission for the revision of the *Roman-Seraphic Sacramentary*. From 1978 until 1991, he coordinated a study group on ritual for the North American Academy of Liturgy, and in 1992, he served as president of the same Academy. In Chicago, he has served as a member of the Advisory Board of the Liturgical Institute of the Archdiocese. From 1989 to the present, he has worked as co-designer and director of the *Institute for Liturgical Consultants: Church Architecture and Design,* which has been co-sponsored by the Office for Divine Worship of the Archdiocese of Chicago and the Catholic Theological Union. He has worked as consultant for the renovation of liturgical space on numerous occasions, and has himself designed and crafted a variety of liturgical furnishings. Beyond that, he is well known throughout the English-speaking world for his numerous lectures, study days, and workshops dealing with liturgy and the sacraments, as well as for continuing adult education programs for clergy, religious, and laity.

Fr. Gilbert's work over the years has manifested a deep sense of Christian tradition and liturgical reality, grounded even more deeply in a Franciscan sense of the sacredness and beauty of the incarnational universe in which God has placed human beings, and which—in the Franciscan tradition—is seen as the primal revelation of the divine. Together with this, he has shown a keen pastoral sense which recognizes, at the practical level, the need for appropriate, functional space and beautiful surroundings as the context for meaningful liturgical celebrations. Over these many years, his work and study has made a remarkable contribution to the enrichment of the life of the Church in the English-speaking world.

# Major Works of Gilbert W. Ostdiek, O.F.M.

1967    *Duns Scotus and Fundamental Theology* (Teutopolis, Ill., 1967) (Dissertation extract).

1972    "Faith, Language, and Theological Discourse about God in Duns Scotus," in *Studia Scholastico-Scotistica*, vol. 5, *Deus et Homo ad Mentem I. Duns Scoti* (Acts of the Third International Scotistic Congress, Vienna, 1970) (Rome, 1972) 573–608.

1975    "Marriage in Catholic Tradition," Alba Cassettes, 1975.

1978    "The Ordination of Women and the Force of Tradition," in C. Stuhlmueller, ed. *Women and Priesthood: Future Directions* (Collegeville: The Liturgical Press, 1978) 85–102.

1981    "The Role of Sunday," in *The Assembly: A People Gathered in Your Name* (Washington: FDLC, 1981) 6–11.

1983    "A Sacramental World," in *Franciscan Herald* 62 (1983) 34–8.

        Audio/visual reviews, in *The Bible Today* 21/5 (1983) 350–2.

        Cover photos, *Franciscan Herald* 62 (1983) 12 issues.

1984    "Liturgical Essay: A Communal Celebration of the Sacrament of Reconciliation during Advent," in *Scripture in Church* 14/56 (1984) 476–82.

        "Bridging our Divisions: Sacramental Reconciliation," in *Franciscan Herald* 63 (1984) 34–7.

        Audio/visual reviews in *The Bible Today* 22/4 (1984) 269–71; 22/6 (1984) 406.

        Cover photo, *Franciscan Herald* 63 (1984) Feb. issue.

1985    "The Threefold Fruits of the Mass: Notes and Reflections on Scotus' Quodlibetal Questions, q. 20," in Frank, W. and Etzkorn, G. (ed.) *Essays Honoring Allan B. Wolter* (St. Bonaventure, N.Y.: The Franciscan Institute, 1985) 203–19.

1986    *Catechesis for Liturgy: A Program for Parish Involvement* (Washington: The Pastoral Press, 1986).

"The Liturgy is Ours: Twenty Years after Vatican II," in *Franciscan Herald* 65 (1986) 166–8.

1987    "Body of Christ, Blood of Christ," in Komonchak, J., Collins, M., Lane, D. (ed). *The New Dictionary of Theology* (Wilmington: Michael Glazier, 1987) 141–4.

"Opening Up Our Symbols," in *Assembly* 13/5 (June, 1987) 370–1.

1988    "How Do Initiatory Symbols Come Alive for Adults?" in Wilde, J. (ed.), *Before and After Baptism: The Work of Teachers and Catechists* (Chicago: Liturgy Training Publications, 1988) 97–113.

"What We Have Seen and Heard and Touched," in *Sent Forth by God's Blessing. The 1987 Institute of Liturgical Studies (Institute of Liturgical Studies Occasional Papers No. 3)* (Valparaiso: The Liturgical Institute, 1988) 87–103 (on liturgical catechesis).

Contributor to Ramshaw, G. (ed.), *Intercessions for the Christian People* (New York: Pueblo, 1988).

Reviews: D. Power, *The Sacrifice We Offer: The Tridentine Dogma and its Reinterpretation*, in *New Theology Review* 1/2 (May, 1988) 113–5.

M. Lawler, *Symbol and Sacrament: A Contemporary Sacramental Theology*, and L. Mick, *Understanding the Sacraments Today*, in *New Theology Review* 1/4 (Nov. 1988) 93–4.

1990    "Catechesis, Liturgical," in Fink, P. (ed.), *The New Dictionary of Sacramental Worship* (Collegeville: The Liturgical Press/ Michael Glazier book, 1990) 163–72.

"Concelebration Revisited," in Finn, P., Schellman, J. (eds.), *Shaping English Liturgy: Studies in Honor of Archbishop Denis Hurley* (Washington: The Pastoral Press, 1990) 139–71.

"Human Situations in Need of Ritualization," in *New Theology Review* 3/2 (May, 1990) 36–50.

1991    "Examining Liturgical Catechesis," in *Modern Liturgy* 18/9 (Nov. 1991) 10–12.

"Liturgical Catechesis and Justice," in Hughes, K., Francis, M. (eds.). *Living No Longer for Ourselves: Liturgy and Justice in the Nineties* (Collegeville: The Liturgical Press, 1991) 170–84.

*Religious Priesthood within the Franciscan Tradition: An Initial Statement and Theological Outline*, editor and contributor (Chicago: Croatian Franciscan Press, for the Franciscan O.F.M. English Speaking Conference, 1991).

Review: Michael O'Carroll, *Corpus Christi: An Encyclopedia of the Eucharist*, in *New Theology Review*, 3/2 (May, 1991) 111–3.

1992 "Getting Down to Cases," in *New Theology Review* 5/2 (May 1992) 92–5.

"Ritual and Symbol in Secular Society," in *Horizon, Journal of the National Religious Vocation Conference* 17/3 (Spring, 1992) 29–33.

"Unfinished Conversations: Vice-Presidential Address," in *Proceedings of the North American Academy of Liturgy* (Valparaiso, Ind.: North American Academy of Liturgy, 1992) 3–14.

1993 "Here's a Catechetical Resource Waiting To Be Used," in *Pastoral Music* 17/5 (June/July, 1993) 28–30.

"Presiding: Preparing to Celebrate," in *Liturgy* 90 24/8 (Nov.–Dec., 1993) 9.

"Ritual and Transformation: Reflections on Liturgy and the Social Sciences," in *Liturgical Ministry* 2 (Spring, 1993) 38–48.

"Ritual Process and the Human Journey," in Bernstein, E. (ed.) *Disciples at the Crossroads: Perspectives on Worship and Church Leadership* (Collegeville: The Liturgical Press, 1993) 123–40.

1994 "Instruction on the Translation of Liturgical Texts: A Commentary," in: *FDLC Newsletter* 21/2 (Mar.–Apr., 1994) 9–14, 15, 16.

"The Preparatory Rites: A Case Study in Liturgical Ecology," with Edward Foley and Kathleen Hughes, in Fragomeni, R. and Pawlikowski, J. (eds)., *The Ecological Challenge: Ethical, Liturgical, and Spiritual Responses* (Collegeville: The Liturgical Press, 1994) 83–101 (reprinted from *Worship* 67 [1993] 17–38).

"Translations and Revisions," in *FDLC Newsletter* 21/1 (Jan.–Feb., 1994) 1–5.

1996 "Crafting English Prayer Texts: The ICEL Revision of the Sacramentary," in *Studia Liturgica* 26/1 (1996) 128–39.

Brief entries under: "Kneeling," "Mercy," "Reconciliation," "Repentance," and "Weeping," in Stuhlmueller, C., (ed.), *The Collegeville Pastoral Dictionary of Biblical Theology* (Collegeville: The Liturgical Press, 1996).

1997 "Who's Invited?" in: *Word and World* 27/1 (Winter, 1997) 67–72.

"Zachary Hayes: Franciscan Educator and Scholar," in *That Others May Know and Love: Essays in Honor of Zachary Hayes, O.F.M.*, ed. M. Cusato, O.F.M., and E. Coughlin, O.F.M. (Franciscan Institute: St. Bonaventure, N.Y., 1997) 1–21.

1998 "Liturgy-Based Catechesis: Pastoral Perspectives," *Liturgical Ministry*, Spring 1998.

**Unpublished**

1986    "The New Rite of Penance Ten Years Later" (Washington, D.C.: FDLC, 1986). (Reflection paper prepared for the national meeting of the Federation of Diocesan Liturgical Commissions, October 13-16, 1986, Portland, Maine).

1987    "Laity in the Mission of the Church: A Sacramental Paradigm" (theological brief prepared for the NCCB Committee on the Laity, 1987).

# Contributors

Herbert Anderson is Professor of Pastoral Theology at the Catholic Theological Union at Chicago and the author of a series of books on worship and pastoral care.

John F. Baldovin, S.J., is Professor of Historical and Liturgical Theology at the Jesuit School of Theology and Graduate Theological Union, Berkeley, California, and a member of the Advisory Committee of the International Commission on English in the Liturgy.

Anscar J. Chupuncgo, O.S.B., former president of the Liturgical Institue of Sant' Anselmo, Rome, is currently Director of the Paul VI Liturgical Institute in Malaybalay, Bukidnon, Philippines, and a member of the Advisory Committee of the International Commission on English in the Liturgy.

Margaret Daly-Denton, a liturgical musician and biblical scholar, holds the Elrington fellowship at the School of Hebrew, Biblical and Theological Studies, Trinity College, Dublin. She also teaches Scripture at the Milltown Institute and the Kimmage Mission Institute and serves on the Advisory Committee of the International Commission on English in the Liturgy.

James Devereux, S.J., pastor of St. Peter's Catholic Church in Charlotte, North Carolina, and an expert in Cranmerian English, is a member of the Roman Missal Editorial Committee of the International Commission on English in the Liturgy.

Edward B. Foley, Capuchin, is Professor of Liturgy and Music at the Catholic Theological Union at Chicago and President of the North American Academy of Liturgy.

Richard N. Fragomeni, a priest of the Diocese of Albany, New York, is Associate Professor of Liturgy and Preaching at the Catholic Theological Union at Chicago.

319

Mark R. Francis, C.S.V., is Associate Professor of Liturgy at the Catholic Theological Union at Chicago and co-author with Arturo Perez of *Primero Dios:* Hispanic Liturgical Resource.

Virgil C. Funk, a priest of the Diocese of Richmond, is founder and president of the National Association of Pastoral Musicians, a membership organization of musicians and clergy dedicated to fostering the art of musical liturgy.

Anthony J. Gittins, C.S.Sp., is Professor of Theological Anthropology at the Catholic Theological Union at Chicago.

Zachary Hayes, O.F.M., is Professor of Doctrinal Theology at the Catholic Theological Union at Chicago and an expert in Bonaventure.

Lawrence A. Hoffman is Professor of Liturgy at the Hebrew Union College—Jewish Institute of Religion in New York.

Gabe Huck is Director of Liturgy Training Publications in Chicago, Illinois.

Kathleen Hughes, R.S.C.J., is Professor of Liturgy at the Catholic Theological Union at Chicago and has been associated with the International Commission on English in the Liturgy for nineteen years.

Jeanette Lucinio, S.P., is Associate Professor of Religious Education at the Catholic Theological Union at Chicago and a frequent collaborator with the North American Forum on the Catechumenate.

Marchita B. Mauck is Professor of Art History at Louisiana State University.

Patrick McGoldrick is Professor of Liturgy at St. Patrick's College, Maynooth, Ireland, where he was Dean of the Faculty of Theology from 1985 to 1996. He has been involved in the work of the International Commission on English in the Liturgy for many years.

Frederick R. McManus, a priest of the Archdiocese of Boston, is Professor Emeritus of Canon Law at The Catholic University of America and a founding member of the Advisory Committee of the International Commission on English in the Liturgy.

Thomas A. Nairn, O.F.M., is Associate Professor of Moral Theology at the Catholic Theological Union and a specialist in medical ethics.

Frank C. Quinn, O.P., is Professor of Liturgical Theology at Aquinas School of Theology, St. Louis, Missouri, and has served on the Advisory Committee and the Music Subcommittee of the International Commission on English in the Liturgy.

Gail Ramshaw, Professor of Religion at La Salle University, is a scholar of liturgical language.

James M. Schellman has served since 1986 as associate executive secretary of the International Commission on English in the Liturgy. He completed liturgical studies at the University of Notre Dame in 1975.

Donald W. Trautman is bishop of the Diocese of Erie. As Chairperson of the Bishops' Committee on the Liturgy (1994–1997), he shepherded the eight segments of the revised *Sacramentary* through the voting procedures of the National Conference of Catholic Bishops.

Richard S. Vosko, a priest of the Diocese of Albany, has been working as a designer and consultant for worship environments throughout North America since 1970.

James F. White is Professor of Liturgical Studies at the University of Notre Dame and author of numerous books.